P9-DOF-953

DISTAFF DIPLOMACY

The Empress Eugénie and the Foreign Policy
of the Second Empire

Bettmann Archive

The Empress Eugénie

DISTAFF DIPLOMACY

The Empress Eugénie and the Foreign Policy
of the Second Empire

BY NANCY NICHOLS BARKER

University of Texas Press, Austin & London

Library of Congress Catalogue Card No. 67–30910
Copyright © 1967 by Nancy Nichols Barker
All Rights Reserved

Printed in the United States of America
by the Printing Division of The University of Texas, Austin
Bound by Universal Bookbindery, Inc., San Antonio

In grateful tribute to
my father and my mother
who believed in education for
a daughter

PREFACE

This study examines the development of the views of the Empress Eugénie on foreign affairs and attempts to ascertain the extent of their influence in the formulation of the foreign policy of the Second Empire. It covers only those areas of imperial diplomacy in which the Empress was actively concerned. Some questions, such as China, Cochin-China, and Algeria, seem not to have attracted her attention or, if they did, have not so far produced a record of her views which the historian can describe. The study passes rapidly over the years before the Italian War, when the Empress took little part in affairs of state, and focuses on the questions of Italian and German unification and French relations with Austria and Spain.

Although many excellent biographies of the Empress exist, none has attempted any systematic examination of her influence in foreign affairs. Serious students of the diplomacy of the Second Empire have usually shied at the theme of *cherchez la femme,* fearing to sink in an undocumented mire of sensational literature. The result is that the Empress' role, although usually conceded to have been important, has gone largely unexplored and unevaluated.

With the passage of time much new evidence has become available for the study of the Empress which provides some planks across the formerly impenetrable mires. I have used unpublished documentary material from the Foreign Ministries in London, Madrid, Paris, and Vienna, and have supplemented this material with the many volumes of published documents from archives of Germany, Italy, France, and Austria. Descendants of friends and relatives of the Empress have permitted examination of their collections, either in institutions where they have been deposited or in the privacy of their own homes. Recently published diaries and memoirs have greatly enriched the knowledge of the period. The work of other scholars on the diplomacy of the Empire has provided an essential scaffolding. Although recognizing the impossibility of using all published works on imperial foreign policy, I hope that my coverage has been sufficiently comprehensive to present the image of the Empress against the backdrop of official policy. In some instances research in unpublished documents has shown the need for revision of previous interpretations. Perhaps this study may yield a clearer understanding of the endemic problems of the Second Empire in its foreign policy and of the reasons for the many deviations in the Emperor's course.

During many years of collecting and preparing the material for this study I have incurred numerous debts of gratitude to individuals and institutions, both in this country and in Europe. The Duke of Alba gave unhindered access to the Empress' papers at the Palacio de Liria in Madrid. The Duke of Mouchy permitted me to examine in his Paris library the hundreds of letters in his possession from the Empress to Anna Murat. The Earl of Clarendon gave permission to use the family papers deposited in the Bodleian Library at Oxford. The staffs of the following archives and libraries generously cooperated to further my research: in Paris the Archives Nationales, Bibliothèque Nationale, the Archives du Ministère des Affaires Etrangères, and the University of Paris; in London the Public Record Office; in Oxford the Bodleian Library; in Vienna the Haus-, Hof-, und Staatsarchiv; in Madrid the Archivo del Ministerio de Asuntos Exteriores; in the United States the Library of Congress and the libraries of the University of Pennsylvania and The University of Texas. Special thanks are due Ramón Paz and A. Blanco for assistance in using the Empress' papers at the Palacio de Liria; to Marvin L. Brown and Dorothy Quynn for aid in tracking down private papers; to Anna Benna for aid in research in Vienna; to Georges Dethan for permission to examine private collections in the French Foreign Ministry; to Suzanne Desternes for friendly and scholarly advice and (with Henriette Chandet) for excellent biographies of the Empress; to Joe B. Frantz, Helen Taft Manning, Ramón Martínez-López, and R. John Rath for, among other things, introductions to scholars abroad; to Noel Blakiston for information on British private papers; and to Margaret Ritchie for her skillful typing of the manuscript.

I also wish to thank *The Historian* for permission to use parts of my article "Napoleon III and the Hohenzollern Candidacy for the Spanish Throne," published in May, 1967. Translations of Crown copyright records in the Public Record Office appear by permission of the Controller of Her Majesty's Stationery Office.

The accumulated debt to Lynn M. Case, professor of history at the University of Pennsylvania, may not be exaggerated. In his seminars years ago he first stimulated my interest in the Empress; since then he has never been too busy to help in the various stages of preparation of this study. He consented to read the manuscript, and has offered valuable suggestions for its improvement. I owe to him whatever skills in research I may possess. May he not be held responsible for my shortcomings. Finally, the inexhaustible support of my husband, Steve Barker, has been the *sine qua non* to make possible completion of this work.

Nancy Nichols Barker
Austin, Texas

CONTENTS

MAPS

ABBREVIATIONS USED IN THE FOOTNOTES

AA	Alba Archives (Montijo) in the Palacio de Liria, Madrid
AMAE (Madrid)	Archivo del Ministerio de Asuntos Exteriores, Madrid
AMAE (Paris)	Archives du Ministère des Affaires Etrangères, Paris
APP	Reichsinstitut für Geschichte des neuen Deutschlands, *Die auswärtige Politik Preussens*
DDI	*I Documenti diplomatici italiana*
HHSA	Haus-, Hof-, und Staatsarchiv, Vienna
HKM	Hausarchiv Kaiser Maximilians von Mexico, MSS in the Haus-, Hof-, und Staatsarchiv, photostatic copies in the Library of Congress, Washington, D.C.
OD	[France, Ministère des Affaires Etrangères], *Les Origines diplomatiques de la guerre de 1870–1871*
PRO	Public Record Office, London

DISTAFF DIPLOMACY

*The Empress Eugénie and the Foreign Policy
of the Second Empire*

CHAPTER 1

FROM COUNTESS TO EMPRESS
"La Montijo Triomphe"

A MÉSALLIANCE?

In January, 1853, the announcement that Napoleon III, Emperor of the French, intended to share his recently created throne with the Spanish Mademoiselle de Montijo, Countess of Teba, summoned forth wails of protest and indignation in the Emperor's family, court, and government. His uncle, ex-King Jérôme, at first refused to credit such folly. Princess Matilda, Napoleon's cousin, who had in her youth missed a chance to marry the future ruler, fell on her knees to implore him to reconsider. Edouard Drouyn de Lhuys, Foreign Minister, threatened to resign if the marriage took place. Legitimists and Orleanists were reported to be jubilant, confident that the imprudent match would weaken the Empire. Gossip, gleefully recorded in diplomatic pouches, had it that the Emperor, unable to marry into royalty, was marrying into the demimonde and had fallen prey to an intriguer who would scheme against her adopted country.

Typical of the observations made in the diplomatic world is a letter from Lord John Russell, British Foreign Secretary: "I have not written to you upon the marriage. It is a very false step. A marriage with a well-behaved young Frenchwoman would, I think, have been very politick, but to put this *intrigante* on the throne is a lowering of the Imperial dignity with a vengeance!"[1] The Austrian ambassador at Paris, Count Hübner, noted

---

[1] Russell to Cowley, January 21, 1853, private, PRO FO 519/197. For the comments of Lord Cowley, British ambassador at Paris, on the marriage see Cowley to Howden, Paris, February 10, 1853, copy, PRO FO 519/210; Cowley to Russell, January, 26, 1853, copy, *ibid*. Excerpts from these letters are published by Frederick Arthur Wellesley (ed.), *Secrets of the Second Empire: Private Letters from the Paris Embassy; Selections from the Papers of Henry Richard Charles Wellesley, 1st Earl Cowley*, pp. 17–18. For other accounts of opposition to the marriage see especially Françoise Chalamon de Bernardy, "Un Fils de Napoléon: Le Comte Walewski, 1810–1868," MS, pp.

that the betrothal was ill received by the French people in general. No matter how democratic they might profess themselves, he wrote, the French "would have preferred a princess."[2] When the religious ceremony was celebrated at Notre Dame on January 30 amid all the pageantry that could be hastily contrived, no one could deny the exquisite beauty of the bride. "A more lovely *coup d'œil* could not be conceived," admitted an English spectator.[3] But the crowds stood coldly silent as the cortege swept through the streets. Embarrassingly infrequent were the cries of "Vive l'Impératrice!"

Why were the French, by reputation willing to overlook almost any defect where a pretty woman is concerned, so hostile to the Emperor's choice? It is interesting to note that almost none of the accusations hurled at the Empress at the time of her marriage proved justified by subsequent events. Of course, there was no gainsaying her lack of royal lineage. Yet, compared with the family tree of the Emperor, Eugénie's was incontestably, even incomparably, the more aristocratic of the two. She was the daughter of Don Cipriano Guzmán y Porto Carrero, Count of Teba, a grandee of Spain who could establish kinship with the great ducal families of Olivares and Medina Sidonia. On the death of his older brother, Eugenio, Eugénie's father became Count of Montijo and possessor of a fair fortune. The Empress' mother, Manuela Kirkpatrick, was also very proud of her ancestors. On the maternal side she was a Grévigné of old Walloon nobility. The Kirkpatricks were a good Scottish family, of which a branch had been barons of Closeburn. True, the family had come down in the world after having backed Bonnie Prince Charlie, and William, father of Manuela, had become a wine merchant in Málaga. But Manuela, enamoured of genealogies and blueblooded forebears, ignored the offending odor of the sherry trade and traced her descent back to Finn MacCaul, the leader of the Fenians, who lived in the early Christian era. " 'I am very much afraid,' the Count said sometimes, 'that Manuela may have contracted a misalliance in marrying me; for the Montijos barely go back to

---

192–197; Marguerite Castillon du Perron, *La Princesse Mathilde, un règne féminin sous le Second Empire*, pp. 121–126; Robert Sencourt, *The Life of the Empress Eugénie*, pp. 71–73, 96. Drouyn de Lhuys apparently played a double game. While threatening to resign his portfolio he privately wrote to Eugénie's mother, whom he had long known: "Your mother's heart must be filled with happiness over the letter inserted in the *Moniteur* [announcing the betrothal]. For myself, your old friend, I congratulate you with all my soul, and am very proud of it" (Paris, January 29, 1853, AA, c. 8–3).

[2] Joseph Alexander Hübner, *Neuf ans de souvenirs d'un ambassadeur d'Autriche à Paris sous le Second Empire, 1851–1859*, I, 102.

[3] Lady Augusta Bruce to the Duchess of Kent, Rue de Varennes, January 31, 1853, Arthur Christopher Benson and Viscount Esher (eds.), *The Letters of Queen Victoria from Her Majesty's Correspondence between the Years 1837 and 1861*, II, 435.

the fourteenth century, under Alfonso XI'."[4] Although Eugénie disagreed with her mother on many things, she shared her enthusiasm for illustrious ancestors and never forgot that among them was the great St. Dominic (Domingo de Guzmán), founder of the order of preachers. According to Matilda, she looked down on her husband as a parvenu and reacted angrily to his teasing over her patrician vanity. Spiteful, jealous Matilda may have exaggerated.[5] Yet by birth, by training, by the example of those she daily saw as a child, the Empress was an aristocrat, acquainted with the nobility of several countries and always close to the Spanish court. Her only sister married their childhood friend, the Duke of Alba, whose title was regarded by some as better than royalty itself. As Empress, Eugénie treasured, more than did the Emperor, the marks of acceptance by Europe's ruling families. Far from demeaning or vulgarizing the Empire, as her critics had feared, she strove to create a court of distinction, which would compare favorably in moral tone and elegance with those of Vienna or London.

At first, she did not always succeed. Conscious of the many hostile eyes ready to note the slightest lapse, the nervous bride struggled with her unfamiliar roles of wife and Empress and inevitably committed *faux pas*. For the most part they were sins arising from impetuosity or a loss of temper resulting in a regretted speech. Yet much of the criticism was picayune carping. When she visited Queen Victoria in the spring of 1855, although she won the wholehearted approval of the Queen and Prince, many were still bewailing her free and easy manners. Benjamin Disraeli found her without a charm, with "Chinese eyes," and a detestable simper. "I understand she is very natural—too natural for a sovereign. . . . She was always playing with the royal children, who doted on her, and was sometimes found sitting on the edge of a table! What do you think of that? The courtiers were horrified."[6] Poor Eugénie! Even a romp with little Princess Louise or Prince Arthur was forbidden her.

The Austrians also at first regarded her with lifted eyebrows. To Hübner, accustomed to the formality of the court of the Habsburgs, the lively Empress was always "Doña Eugenia." The Archduke Ferdinand Maximilian, brother of Emperor Franz Joseph, visiting Paris in 1856, thought her court "irresistibly comic" and described its society as "distinguished for

---

[4] Octave Aubry, *Eugénie: Empress of the French*, trans. by F. M. Atkinson, p. 19.

[5] Castillon du Perron, *La Princesse Mathilde*, pp. 132–133, 135. But from a friendly source, the late Duke of Alba, grandson of Eugénie's sister, we learn that the Empress "never forgot" her kinship with St. Dominic (Duke of Alba, *L'Impératrice Eugénie, conférence prononcée à l'Institut français de Madrid*, p. 11).

[6] Disraeli to Mrs. Brydges Willyams, May Day, 1855, William Flavelle Monypenny and George Earle Buckle, *The Life of Benjamin Disraeli, Earl of Beaconsfield*, IV, 5.

its disgusting dress and tactless behaviour."[7] Not many years were to pass, however, before the Archduke and his wife, having accepted the Mexican throne from France, were to extoll to the skies the graces, virtues, and exalted qualities of the patroness of their new empire. Moreover, Hübner's successor as ambassador at Paris, Prince Metternich, found in the Empress his most valuable ally in his long efforts to effect an Austro-French alliance.

The malicious gossip assailing the Empress' personal virtue was, of course, totally false. She was neither a Miss Howard nor a Madame Gordon, two former well-known *maîtresses en titre* of Napoleon. The accounts of how the Prince-President strove to win Eugénie without first passing through the chapel are too well known to require repetition. During the years of their marriage, while the Emperor wounded her repeatedly by his infidelities, she never succumbed to the temptation to retaliate in kind. Ironically, her very chastity eventually became the target for reproach. She acquired a reputation for coldness which supposedly drove the Emperor from her comfortless bed to those of a succession of mistresses. Matilda, who for years maintained an open liaison with Count Nieuwerkerke, saw something of the *sainte nitouche* in Eugénie's refusal to accept the amorous advances made to her. The Empress herself attributed her moral code to the requirements of her religion and once confided to Prince Napoleon: "If I were not a believer, I would have had too many lovers. To love, that is the only thing worthwhile."[8] Whatever may have been the reasons, like Caesar's wife, she lived above reproach.

Nor was the Empress an intriguer. Although a foreigner, she came to the throne of France with an honest desire to serve her adopted country. While she was often homesick for Spain, more than once worked to promote Spanish interests, and at times experienced real difficulty in her role as wife of a Bonaparte, she was never consciously disloyal to France or to the Empire. A letter written to her sister on the eve of her marriage reveals the sense of responsibility and idealism with which she approached her reign.

On the eve of mounting one of the greatest thrones of Europe, I cannot help feeling a certain terror. . . . Good and evil will be attributed to me. . . . Two things protect me, I hope: the faith I have in God, and the immense desire I have to help the classes who are deprived of everything, even the chance to work. . . . So I have accepted this great position as a Divine mission.[9]

---

[7] Report of Ferdinand Maximilian to Franz Joseph, Paris, 1856, Egon Caesar Corti, *Maximilian and Charlotte of Mexico*, trans. by C. A. Phillips, I, 56.

[8] January 22, 1867, Emile Ollivier, *Journal, 1846–1869*, ed. by Theodore Zeldin, II, 279.

[9] Eugénie to Duchess of Alba, undated, Sencourt, *Eugénie*, p. 78.

The marriage, nevertheless, had not come about purely by chance. The Countess of Montijo, "the most famous matchmaker of the century," had been drawn to Paris with her marriageable daughter as to the lodestone when the French Republic elected a bachelor as its President. She guided Eugénie carefully through the period of courtship, and undeniably played her cards well. Eugénie, then in her mid-twenties and unlucky in love, favored the match. She was in love, if not with the man, with the Emperor, and felt herself marked by providence for a high position in the world. But she stooped to no unworthy schemes to bring her suitor to declare himself. Her mother's experienced hand was hardly necessary. Napoleon saw her and fell in love. When his prospects of marriage into one of the royal houses of Europe dwindled, he braved the opposition and followed his heart.

According to the late Duke of Alba, who should have known perhaps better than anyone else, Eugénie at the last minute flinched and sought an avenue of escape from the marriage. Hoping to strike a response in the Marquis of Alcañisez, Duke of Sexto, a Spanish nobleman with whom she had long been in love, she wired him the news of the Emperor's proposal of marriage. Only when Alcañisez returned laconically, "Accept my most cordial felicitations," did she consent definitively to be Empress of the French.[10] Alba recalled that in later years, when Eugénie and Sexto were very old and reminiscing on their past life, Sexto would exclaim: "No, Eugénie, not even today would I want to marry you"; to which she would reply with a burst of laughter. The biographers of the Empress do not always agree on the details of Eugénie's romances as a girl and on her marriage to the Emperor. But whatever the version, none yields material either to her discredit or to her dishonor.

What of the preparation of the Empress for her new position? Neither her family background nor her education was in any way the ordinary thing, and together they go far to explain the contradictions in and confusion of her political ideas in the early years of her reign.

Eugénie's formal education was sketchy at best. A year spent at the Convent of the Sacred Heart in Paris, a school in vogue for the daughters of the nobility, was about the extent of it. For short periods she and her sister also attended a progressive *gymnase normal* and a boarding school at Clifton, in England. A succession of governesses—the most enduring and well known of them, the very proper Miss Flowers—filled in

---

[10] According to Alba the telegram was intercepted by the police and shown to Napoleon by those who opposed his marriage to Eugénie. He replied that he was well acquainted with the facts of the case (Alba, *L'Impératrice Eugénie*, p. 19). As a child and young man Alba knew the Empress well and customarily spent several months with her in England each year until her death.

the gaps. The girls' mother was frequently too busy with her own affairs to worry over their lack of book learning. In any case, she had little faith in it. "Life is the best teacher," she was fond of saying. The ubiquitous Countess dragged her children from country to country, from fashionable spa to a season in London, from political salon in Paris to a *tertulia* at Carabanchel, her estate on the outskirts of Madrid. With her frenetic pace and catholic tastes in people she gave Eugénie an unusual opportunity not only to meet but to know many of the outstanding men of the day. The little girl perched on the distinguished knees of Stendhal, the novelist, drinking in his stories of the first Empire is one of the most charming vignettes of her childhood. Her friendship with Prosper Mérimée, savant and man of letters, began before she reached her teens and continued uninterruptedly until Mérimée's death in 1870. In her mother's circle she could meet statesmen of the caliber of Lord Clarendon, gilded youth like Pepe Alcañisez, Europe's bluebloods such as Antoine de Noailles, the Duke of Mouchy, the Duke of Alba, or the Duke of Aumale. To Carabanchel and to Plaza del Angel, the Countess' homes in and near Madrid, flocked the rich, the famous, the clever, and the amusing of mid-nineteenth-century Europe. After her husband's death, the Countess aimed at becoming a factor in politics in Madrid and, with the help of Ramón María Narváez, then in a dominant position in the Spanish court, she became *camerera mayor* of Queen Isabella's household. During her mother's brief tenure of office Eugénie served as maid of honor to Isabella.[11]

From this background Eugénie acquired the ease of manner and polished way of a woman of highest society. Her experience at court was invaluable in later ceremonial duties. The excitement of her mother's life and the variety of people she met almost certainly broadened Eugénie's interests beyond the usual ones of childhood. Letters published by the Duke of Alba reveal her precocious penchant for politics. This urbane, cosmopolitan society, moreover, was an excellent school for language. Eugénie was equally at ease in French and Spanish, although she never mastered the technicalities of grammar of either, she acquitted herself very creditably in English, and later she acquired a smattering of Italian—excellent assets for a future empress.

On the other hand, her education gave her no systematic knowledge of the institutions or customs of France or of any other European country.

[11] Many biographies give accounts of the Empress' background and girlhood. Among older works are those by Sencourt, Daudet, Aubry, Filon, Dame Ethel Smyth, and Maxime du Camp (the last very hostile). Recently Harold Kurtz has published a lengthy study designed to rehabilitate the Empress (*The Empress Eugénie, 1826–1920*). Suzanne Desternes and Henriette Chandet have done a remarkable job of assimilating most of the published French works on Eugénie into a beautifully written and objective verbal portrait (*L'Impératrice Eugénie intime*).

Her acquaintance with history and economics was slight—a serious deficiency that revealed itself later in the naïveté of some of her projects for French foreign policy. Worse yet, her ideas on the principles of government were ill formed and included a jumble of Bonapartism and Legitimism, whose incompatibility she seemed not even to recognize.

Unusual in the aristocracy of Spain, Eugénie's father had been an *afrancesado*, who had served the cause of Napoleon I as an artillery officer. In 1814 he was one of the last defenders of the heights of Montmartre against the attacks of the Allies shortly before the fall of the first Empire. On his return to Spain under the Bourbon restoration he escaped severe punishment only through the intercession of his older brother, who had remained loyal to the monarchy. From the letters published by the Duke of Alba, we know that Eugénie adored her father and regarded him in the light of a hero. Stendhal kept alive in her imagination the glories of the reign for which Cipriano had fought. Later, shortly before the advent of the Second Republic, Eugénie met Madame Gordon, a famous singer who had helped Louis Napoleon in his abortive coup at Strasbourg in 1836, and she proposed a visit to the prisoner at Ham. The trip was never made, but the encounter and Madame Gordon's faithful devotion had again stimulated Eugénie's interest in the Bonaparte tradition. In 1849 Eugénie and her mother had not been in Paris more than a fortnight before they began attending the President's *soirées*. By the time of the *coup d'état*, Eugénie, in admiration of Napoleon's daring, wrote to his cousin and social secretary, M. Bacciochi, that all her worldly goods were at the Prince-President's disposal should they be necessary for his success.

With this admiration for Bonapartism, Eugénie combined an instinctive devotion to the principles of legitimate monarchy. In February, 1849, Prince Napoleon, the Emperor's cousin, met the future Empress when he served briefly at Madrid as French ambassador of the Second Republic. He may have been her suitor. In any case, he enjoyed talking politics with her and boasting of his republicanism. Eugénie riposted: "Republicans, . . . but that's nothing but a word. A Republic cannot last in France. For my part I would be delighted to see the President exalted to the Empire, if the Bourbons are not to come back. For at bottom I am a legitimist myself."[12]

The statement was not the result of a passing fancy. During her years on the throne of France and later in exile she made no secret of her reverence for hereditary monarchy and evidenced it in both sentimental and realistic ways. The violets of Parma, for example, were always her favorite flower.

[12] Aubry, *Eugénie*, pp. 45–46. See also Desternes and Chandet, *L'Impératrice Eugénie* (p. 60) and Kurtz, *Empress Eugénie* (p. 23) for the Empress' acquaintance with Prince Napoleon.

Her well-advertised cult of Marie Antoinette, for whom she felt a powerful affinity, was based on half superstition, half political reasoning. She took more interest in the tragic Queen than in either of the wives of Napoleon I and was persuaded that one day she would share her fate. In a more practical vein, during her reign she made repeated attempts to aid beleaguered members of royalty, such as the Queen of Naples or the Duchess of Parma, who lost their thrones as a result of revolution. One of her last moves as Empress was her strong support of Bourbon restoration in Spain. She even went so far as to hope that her own son could cross over the unbridgeable chasm between Bonapartism and Legitimism and bear on his own emblem the white lilies of France. In 1875, after the death of the Emperor, through the intermediacy of ex-Queen Isabella, she approached the Count of Chambord, childless Bourbon pretender to the French throne. She proposed that he adopt her son, the Prince Imperial, and thus unite a large segment of the royalists with the Bonapartists against the Republic. Through his emissary, Chambord explained that the principle which he represented made it impossible for him to *choose* his successor.[13]

Whence came this wellspring of Legitimism? The dichotomy of political views in the Empress' family may afford a partial explanation. While Eugénie's father went over to Napoleon, her uncle and godfather, Don Eugenio, fought against "the French dogs" and remained loyal to the Bourbon, Ferdinand VII. In the royal favor after the restoration, he was able to intercede successfully for his younger brother and repatriate him in southern Spain.[14] A haughty aristocrat, he had approved only reluctantly Cipriano's marriage to Manuela Kirkpatrick, despite a certificate attesting to the family's affiliation with the barons of Closeborn. His attitude toward legitimate monarchy is epitomized in the family motto: "My king before my blood" ("Mon roi plutôt que mon sang").

Eugénie's mother was fundamentally conservative, even reactionary, in her political views. To her, Philip II represented monarchy at its greatest. An ultraroyalist, she found the Carlists[15] in Spain the best practitioners of her political philosophy and formed ties with them that later proved a serious embarrassment to the Empress of the French. While the Empress was still a child Manuela received Carlists in her Paris salon, much to the dis-

[13] Count René de Monti de Rezé, *Souvenirs sur le Comte de Chambord*, pp. 86–88. The author was Chambord's emissary who talked with Isabella.

[14] To my knowledge the fullest account of Eugenio and Cipriano during and after the first Empire is in Desternes and Chandet, *L'Impératrice Eugénie*, pp. 10–19.

[15] Ferdinand VII, King of Spain, abolished the Salic law in Spain by a pragmatic sanction in 1830 in order to permit his daughter, Isabella, to inherit the throne. Don Carlos, younger brother of Ferdinand, refused to renounce his rights and revolted; hence "Carlism" and "Carlist," pretenders to the throne. The party was known for its conservative political outlook and its rigid religious orthodoxy.

tress of Cipriano, and acquired a reputation as their patroness. The salon came to the attention of the Spanish ambassador at Paris who reproached Cipriano: "The house of your wife is the center of Carlist reunions."[16] Only her friendship with M. Gabriel Delessert, prefect of the police in Paris, saved her from expulsion from the country.

But the Countess was adept at mending her fences. Not long after this incident she re-established good relations with the Spanish Regent, Christine, and her daughter, Isabella, and became an intimate of the court. Moreover, she never permitted her political principles to interfere with her life in the world. She maintained ties in every direction and could count among her close friends Legitimists, Orleanists, Bonapartists, and even republicans. Witness the ease with which she managed her daughter's entry at the Elysée in 1849.

Biographers of the Empress frequently note that as a child and young girl she often quarrelled violently with her mother over her ultraconservative ideas. At one time Eugénie apparently passed through a socialist phase and briefly counted herself a disciple of Fourier and his phalanxes. Certainly she was never a Carlist, although she was to intercede actively to save the lives of her Carlist relatives implicated in the revolt against Isabella in 1860. Her letters preserved in the archives of the Duke of Alba that were written just before her marriage give little insight on her political philosophy at the time she mounted the throne. Apparently no conscious conflict of principle was warring within her. "The iron hand in the velvet glove" was one of her favorite mottos.[17] Strength, boldness, and daring she always admired. These qualities, which seemed to sum up her political credo in 1853, she believed she had found in Napoleon III. Her reckless, chivalric outlook as well as the germ of future friction between the Emperor and his spirited wife can be detected in her letter to her sister before her marriage.

He [the Emperor] is a man with an irresistible will power without being obstinate, capable of great and small sacrifices: he would go in the woods on a winter night to find a flower, tearing himself from the fire into the wet in order to satisfy the caprice of a woman he loved. The next day he risked his crown

---

[16] Desternes and Chandet, *L'Impératrice Eugénie*, p. 26. For the Countess' political views and her association with Carlism see also Theodor von Bernhardi, *Aus dem Leben Theodor von Bernhardis*, Vol. IX: *In Spanien und Portugal, Tagebuchblätter aus den Jahren 1869–1871*, pp. 169, 199; and a letter from Barrot to Thouvenel, Madrid, April 10, 1860, private and confidential, AMAE (Paris), Papiers Thouvenel, III.

[17] See Desternes and Chandet, *L'Impératrice Eugénie*, p. 74, for excerpts from Eugénie's papers before her marriage. See also Eugénie to Charlotte, July 30, 1864, Corti, *Maximilian and Charlotte*, II, 844.

rather than forego sharing it with me; he does not count the cost; he always stakes his future on one card, that is why he always wins.[18]

It was going to be difficult for her middle-aged and mild-tempered husband to live up to the heroics expected of him.

Her religious views were no more clearly formulated. From earliest childhood to the day of her death Eugénie was always a practicing Roman Catholic and willingly subjected herself to the disciplines of the Church. Yet she had a decided taste for the occult and felt herself surrounded by mysterious spirits and forces beyond her control. Her ignorance of physical science made her the victim of freakish superstitions. She was a believer in table turning, in spirit rapping, in the mutterings of an old gypsy woman, in palmistry, and in the gift of second sight of mediums. Of course, she was not alone in her gullibility. The Emperor, far more intellectual than she, was powerfully affected by omens. Occultism was a weakness of the times in which, unfortunately, she shared in full measure. Her worship of Marie Antoinette was nearly an obsession. She collected her portraits and trinkets, lived in her suite at Saint-Cloud, had constructed a small model of the Petit Trianon in the park, and frequently engaged Hübner in lugubrious conversation on the fate of the martyred queen. She likewise had a morbid fascination for the dead and apparently sensed a spiritual presence around or near the body of the deceased. Her distraught prayers at the sarcophagus of her sister in 1860 were so unnaturally protracted that the Emperor, fearing for her physical and mental health, hastened the removal of the body to Spain.

Traces of her superstitions were always with her. She confessed to one of her most sympathetic biographers, Lucien Daudet, that she was convinced that the golden rose given to her by the Pope on the occasion of the baptism of the Prince Imperial brought her bad luck. After 1872, for forty years, she never dared to remove it from its case.[19] But as she matured, the grip of the supernatural on her gradually relaxed. In the late years of the Empire one hears no more of the veil of Marie Antoinette or of the Scottish medium Douglas Hume, who had once introduced the Empress to the shade of her father. A generous fund of common sense as well as the knowledge accumulated while on the throne came to her rescue.

The young Empress brought many assets to the Empire. Unquestionably a good woman, motivated by honorable instincts, she was valorous as well. In moments of physical danger she performed superbly. The mistakes

---

[18] Eugénie to Duchess of Alba, January, 1853, Empress Eugénie, *Lettres familières de l'Impératrice Eugénie conservées dans les archives du Palais de Liria et publiées par les soins du Duc d'Albe avec le concours de F. de Llanos y Torriglia et Pierre Josserand,* I, 53.

[19] Lucien Daudet, *Dans l'ombre de l'Impératrice Eugénie,* p. 224.

she made never arose from deceit or cowardice. Finally, her great beauty, her charm, and her youthful vitality lent color and distinction to the court and government. Much of the aura of glamour surrounding France under the Empire was of her creation. Without her ability to organize spectacular entertainments and her endurance to sustain them, without her enthusiasm for large palaces filled with gay courtiers and pretty women, without her love of travel and movement, always surrounded by a brilliant cortege, without even her undoubted flair for fashion, Paris could not again have been the cynosure of Europe. Undeniably her taste was not always good. The garishness of the decor, the overdone lavishness of dress, the low level of the arts were certainly in large measure a reflection of her preferences and interests. Nonetheless, the Empress gave to the Empire a style and an individuality which had been lacking in the reigns of Louis Philippe and of the Bourbons after the restoration.

THE EASTERN QUESTION

Until the Italian War of 1859 Eugénie's role in foreign affairs was negligible. Excepting a few isolated occasions and a few issues of personal interest to her, she evinced neither a serious nor a consistent concern for the great questions of state. Her letters to her sister in the early years of her reign speak only of people, clothes, and babies. Even after two years of marriage, during their visit at the Court of St. James, Eugénie was excluded from the deliberations of Napoleon with Prince Albert on the conduct of the war. When the discussions ran overtime, Eugénie begged Victoria to intervene: "I dare not go in, but your Majesty can; that is your concern."[20] As late as April, 1858, in a letter to Lord Cowley, British ambassador at Paris, protesting the acquittal in a British court of a conspirator against the life of the Emperor, she declared that she left politics alone and apologized for interfering with matters outside her province.[21] Until 1859 diplomats assigned to the French court generally regarded her views as of little importance and rarely bothered to recount their conversations with her. Her contacts with them were confined to ceremonial or social occasions. She had not begun her later practice of receiving ambassadors and ministers in private audience.

Yet the early years of her reign as Empress-Consort are not totally devoid of political interest. During the fifties, even before she was truly conscious of the political and ideological issues of the day, she made some important enemies among the liberals, the advocates of "the revolution,"

[20] Thomas A. B. Corley, *Democratic Despot: A Life of Napoleon III*, p. 163.
[21] April 18, 1858, Wellesley, *Secrets of the Second Empire*, p. 163.

and identified herself with the clericals and the conservatives. Especially in questions concerning Austria, Spain, and the Papacy, her reactions and conduct frequently anticipated the shape of things to come.

Soon after Eugénie's marriage the Eastern question dominated the political scene. In the ensuing Crimean War, Napoleon, allied with the traditional enemy of his house, Great Britain, fought with Sardinia and Turkey against Russia. Ostensibly, the aim of France was the protection of Christians in the Holy Land. Yet the war could not be seen in terms of a religious crusade. With Protestant England, revolutionary Sardinia (aiming at annexation of papal territory), and Moslem Turkey phalanxed against Christian, Greek Orthodox Russia, the welfare of the Christians was distinctly secondary to the real aim of the Allies—the military and naval withdrawal of Russia from Moldavia and Wallachia, and from the Black Sea. The French people never thoroughly undertood the remote and complex issues and gave the war only tepid support.[22] Within the Emperor's own family the Eastern question became a cause of great friction.

Violent objections to Napoleon's Eastern policies came from Matilda and her salon on the Rue de Courcelles. Her story was that Eugénie, prompted by her fanatical Catholicism, had nagged and pushed the Emperor into a chivalric but ruinous undertaking in behalf of the Christians in the Holy Land. She laid a large share of the responsibility for the outbreak of the war at the Empress' door. In 1855, when Napoleon announced his intention of going in person to Sebastopol to take command of the military forces, Matilda, mistakenly believing that Eugénie was to be named Regent, predicted the downfall of the Empire.[23] Matilda was strongly sympathetic to the Tsar, who had befriended her when she had lived in Russia with her husband, Demidoff. She detested England as heartily as she admired Russia, and she found particularly odious Eugénie's cordial acceptance of the British alliance and her efforts to make herself agreeable to Victoria and Albert.[24] The bitter exchange between the court and the Rue de Courcelles resulted in a permanent estrangement. Although Ma-

---

[22] Lynn M. Case, *French Opinion on War and Diplomacy during the Second Empire*, pp. 15–43.

[23] Castillon du Perron, *La Princesse Mathilde*, pp. 139–140. Castillon du Perron used the private papers of Matilda formerly in the possession of Count Joseph Primoli and now housed in the palace of Countess Gugliemina Campello in Spoleto.

[24] The private letters of Cowley during the Crimean War attest to the increase in cordiality between the Empress and the Court of St. James. Cowley himself soon realized the erroneousness of his first impressions of Eugénie. By the fall of 1856, when Anglo-French relations were strained over the enforcement of the terms of the peace, he wrote Clarendon: "That for which I am most sorry in it all is that the attacks upon the Empress [in the British press] have made a deep impression upon her, and as she was *sincerely* attached to the English alliance, I regret everything that can loosen that feeling" (Compiègne, October 25, 1856, copy, PRO FO 519/220).

tilda tried to make amends after the war and behaved with admirable enthusiasm when the Prince Imperial was born in March, 1856, she was unable to re-establish her former solid footing at court.

The Crimean War contributed its share to the mounting animosity with which the Empress and Prince Napoleon regarded each other. Pleading bad health although to all appearances sound of limb, the Prince returned from the military operations in the Crimea and opened himself to the charge of cowardice. In Paris he vigorously opposed the Emperor's plan to go himself to Sebastopol, attributing the idea to the Empress, and refused to accompany him. Entering the fray, the Empress threw her support to a project to declare the Duke of Morny, Napoleon's illegitimate half brother, as the heir to the throne. According to Cowley, who witnessed some of the scenes, the result was a "precious blow up" between Emperor and Prince in which the Prince was told he would be under the surveillance of the police during the ruler's absence.[25] Henceforward Eugénie and the Prince were declared enemies.

The accusation of Matilda that the Empress pushed France into a war of religion may be quickly dismissed. When war broke out in the spring of 1854 Eugénie had evidently heard far more about the Christians, the Holy Places, and the Black Sea than she cared to. She wailed to her sister:

I am boring you, my good sister . . . but such is the egoism of our heart: we wish all those who love us to share in the boredom one feels always being surrounded by *serious people.* Talking only of *serious things,* I have become *serious* also: people give me so many counsels that I pass them on to you indirectly, and you can be very glad indeed that I do not speak to you of the *Eastern* question!![26]

In January, 1854, Cowley reported that she dwelt for some time on the horrors of war in talking with him, and that he saw from her manner how desirous the Emperor was to keep the peace.[27] The British ambassador was later one of the most relentless critics of Eugénie's clericalism. Yet his private letters before and during the Crimean War contain not the slightest allusion to religious enthusiasm on her part. Moreover, it was the clerical Ultramontanes who were among the most alarmed in France over the war and who thoroughly disliked the alliance with Britain and Sardinia. Like

[25] Cowley to Clarendon, Paris, February 22, 1855, copy, PRO FO 519/215. See also Cowley to Clarendon, January 31, 1855, *ibid.*

[26] Eugénie to Duchess of Alba, spring, 1854, *Lettres familières,* I, 106.

[27] Cowley to Clarendon, Paris, January 24, 1854, PRO FO 519/212, reproduced in Victor Wellesley and Robert Sencourt, *Conversations with Napoleon III,* p. 53. About the same time he worried at the marked favoritism that the Empress had shown to the Russian ambassador at a ball—a "little coquetterie," which might indicate Napoleon's hope of negotiating himself out of his quarrel with Russia (Cowley to Clarendon, January 12, 1854, *ibid.*).

the Carlists in Spain they sided with Russia on the Eastern question as the government of Louis XVIII had done earlier.[28] If ideology was in the war, it was the contraposition of liberal, revolutionary governments of Western Europe against autocratic, orthodox Russia.[29] Matilda seems to have completely misunderstood the issues at play.

Certainly Eugénie favored Napoleon's plan to take command himself in the Crimea. After receiving the imperial couple at Windsor, Queen Victoria noted that the Empress was "all for the Emperor's going," and saw no greater danger for him in Sebastopol than in Paris.[30] Eugénie herself told Cowley that she had not been won over to the voyage until Marshal Vaillant, an experienced soldier, had convinced her that the military campaign simply could not miss.[31] But she had no intention of remaining in Paris, even as Regent, while the Emperor had all the excitement for himself. She fully counted on going with him as far as Constantinople. No warnings about the dangers to their persons that were lurking in the narrow streets deterred her. Plans were made for a glittering reception straight from *A Thousand and One Nights*. The Sultan himself would lend his arm to the Empress to escort her to his palace and to a dinner of state. The fairy scene never materialized, since the Emperor, dissuaded by the objections of the British and of his own Ministers, reluctantly abandoned the project. The Empress' attitude was typical of her later reactions to situations in which personal risk and honor were involved. The premature return of Prince Napoleon from the Crimea had made him an object of ridicule in Paris. Eugénie believed an act of courage on the part of the Emperor necessary to rehabilitate the name of Bonaparte. Characteristically, she ignored the risks and, when confronted with a choice, came down on the side of action.[32]

During the course of the war Hübner had several extended conversations

---

[28] Hübner, *Neuf ans*, I, 198, 203; Case, *French Opinion on War*, pp. 20, 22. For the Carlists see Turgot to Walewski, Madrid, August 3, 1855, and September 17, 1855, AMAE (Paris), Espagne, Vol. 847, Nos. 10 and 15.

[29] The lines were far from clearly defined. The presence of Turkey in the alliance was an embarrassment. Moreover, although France and Sardinia were "revolutionary" they were not liberal. Alan John Percivale Taylor has pointed out that one of Napoleon's chief difficulties in the war was his attempt to follow simultaneously a conservative and a revolutionary foreign policy (*The Struggle for Mastery in Europe, 1848–1918*, p. 67).

[30] Theodore Martin, *The Life of H. R. H., the Prince Consort*, III, 202.

[31] Cowley to Clarendon, Paris, March 8, 1855, copy, PRO FO 519/215, reproduced in part by Wellesley and Sencourt, *Conversations with Napoleon III*, p. 74 .

[32] Curious details of the reception planned are given by Louis Thouvenel, son of Edouard Thouvenel, French ambassador at Constantinople (*Revue de Paris*, June 15, 1876, summarized by Imbert de Saint-Amand, *Napoleon III and His Court*, trans. by E. G. Martin, pp. 257–258). For Eugénie's desire to go to the Crimea see Eugénie to Duchess of Alba, March 22, 1855, *Lettres familières*, I, 121–122; Cowley to Clarendon, Paris, February 17, 1855, copy, PRO FO 519/215; Corley, *Democratic Despot*, p. 164.

with the Empress and found her fully conversant with the negotiations pertaining to Austria's entrance into the alliance. Evidently she argued strongly for an Austro-French *rapprochement*. It was to be the remedy that she prescribed frequently for most of the following fifteen years. Hübner found that elevation to a throne had agreeably metamorphosed a capricious young thing into a "serious and amiable" empress. Yet he kept the exchange on a half-joking level and did not trouble to report her words systematically. Did she promote Napoleon's plan for Austria to give up her Italian possessions in exchange for Moldavia and Wallachia? Hübner does not say. She was certainly thinking of a reward for Austria somewhere in Europe, perhaps in return for the cession of Lombardy and Venetia, perhaps in return for Austrian cooperation in the Crimean War. During a ball in January, 1854, the Empress predicted to the ambassador that Queen Isabella would soon be overthrown and added: "He will have Spain who gets there first." Hübner replied discreetly that he had heard much good spoken of the King of Portugal.

"*Comment*," she exclaimed with a smile, "and the Archduke Maximilian, brother of the Emperor?"
"Oh, Madame, you are making diplomacy."
"Not at all, I just tell you the truth."

Hübner, noting that this was not the first time she had spoken thus, concluded that France evidently badly needed Austria in the Eastern question.[33] The conversation was a significant straw in the wind. Already the Empress, and probably the Emperor, was casting about for a plum for the brother of Franz Joseph which would induce Austria to cooperate in French plans for Europe.

EYES ACROSS THE PYRENEES

The turbulent internal conditions of Spain were one of the first as well as one of the last concerns of the Second Empire. The capriciousness of temper and the immorality of young Queen Isabella and the rapacity of Christine, Queen-Mother, had alienated large groups within Spain in addition to the already rebellious Carlists. Conflicts between progressive and reactionary elements in the court, the rapid succession of ministries and constitutions, and the despotic inclinations of Isabella seriously demoralized the monarchy in the early 1850's. In the summer of 1854 Christine took refuge in France. The following fall Paris was full of talk of the impending fall of Isabella.

[33] January 23, 1854, Hübner, *Neuf ans*, I, 203–204. See Hübner's conversations with Eugénie on November 17, 1853, December 11, 1854, February 8, 1855, April 27, 1855, December 18, 1855, January 26, 1856, *ibid.*, pp. 175, 286, 310, 323, 372–373, 386.

Napoleon and Eugénie were more than casually interested in Spain's troubles. French governments traditionally sought to maintain and sometimes even to create friendly governments across the Pyrenees. More than once their direct and nepotic acts had provoked international repercussions. Louis XIV and Napoleon I, the one in placing his grandson, the other his brother, on the throne of Spain, had triggered major wars. In 1848 Louis Philippe had managed the affair of the Spanish marriages whereby Isabella was constrained to marry Don Francisco de Asís de Borbón on the same day her sister married the French King's son, Antoine, Duke of Montpensier. The King's interference in Spain had broken the entente with England and contributed to the fall of the July monarchy. Military and strategic reasons in part lay behind these interventions. If France was to be involved in a war elsewhere in Europe she needed the assurance of tranquility in and neutrality from Spain. The Iberian campaign of the first Empire had demonstrated the truth of that lesson.

When revolutionary tremors threatened to undermine Isabella's throne in the 1850's, the British government anxiously enquired the Emperor's intentions. Cowley noted: "France has immense power for evil or for good in that unfortunate country [Spain], and it may be doubted whether any combination to which she is not a party w[oul]d succeed."[34] If the Bourbon dynasty were supplanted, what combination would Napoleon favor? He sounded the Empress first. Knowing her special interest in the subject and hoping to turn her influence with the Emperor to good account, he determined to "give her a turn" in September, 1853. It was his first political conversation with her.

The ambassador reported that Eugénie expressed herself most reasonably. Although she admitted to anticipating a convulsion in the near future, she declared that France would not oppose whatever Spain wanted in the way of government. To Cowley's relief, Napoleon too denied any intention of intervention. Should the Queen fall, the Emperor indicated that he would not object either to Iberian union or to the election of a Sardinian prince. But both Emperor and Empress agreed that the best hope for France lay in the maintenance of Isabella on the throne.[35] Eugénie had suggested the Archduke Ferdinand Maximilian to Hübner as a possible successor to the Queen, but she hoped that his opportunity would not knock. Prompted by Napoleon, she wrote to her brother-in-law, Alba, a letter obviously designed to be shown to the Spanish ministers. "It is easy to say: the dynasty must be changed, but where to get a new one? The present queen is better."[36]

---

[34] Cowley to Clarendon, Paris, January 9, 1854, copy, PRO FO 519/212.
[35] Cowley to Clarendon, Dieppe, September 2, 1853, PRO FO 519/211.
[36] Eugénie to Duke of Alba, July 18, 1854, *Lettres familières*, I, 107–108.

Support of Isabella became the officially stated policy of the French government and continued as such until the Queen's overthrow in 1868. In a note to the French representative at Madrid, Foreign Minister Drouyn de Lhuys described in the name of the Emperor the many disadvantages for France which would result from any other government in Madrid, be it republican, Orleanist, or Carlist, and instructed the representative to discourage and reject any project hostile to the Queen.[37] In the summer of 1856 Napoleon was on the verge of sending armed forces across the Pyrenees to suppress the dissidents, especially the Carlists. Although the British government was willing to recognize the special interest of France in Spain, it objected to military intervention and threatened to terminate the entente. Eugénie also opposed a military occupation, seemingly out of the realization that she, as a Spaniard, would be blamed for the measure. Sulkily, the Emperor desisted—his arms proved unnecessary in any case—but asserted his right to aid the Queen if the interests of France required it and if she should apply to him for aid.[38]

The Empress hoped to turn the Crimean War to the advantage of her native land and worked personally in December of 1854 to bring Spain into the French alliance with Great Britain. Learning from the Emperor that the British were looking to Sardinia and perhaps even to Switzerland for military re-enforcements, Eugénie suggested that they turn to Spain instead and recruit a brigade for use in the Crimea. According to her own account, which sounds rather too naïve to be the whole truth, the Emperor was pleased with her sudden inspiration and instructed her to sound the terrain with Alba, president of the municipal council of Madrid. He should take the matter unofficially to the Queen's Ministers, with whom he maintained a close connection. Eugénie warmed to her subject with Alba: "You know that the Spanish are poor but very proud: let them enter in the alliance treaty that the great powers will sign, that will flatter them and will be advantageous for all." If Spain signed the treaty, she continued, she could count on the help of the Allies to defend Cuba and would benefit from her recognition by the other countries as a power. "She [Spain] will gain more than she risks, and her influence and her credit will grow."[39]

Unfortunately, Alba misunderstood her intention and immediately had the question brought before the Spanish Council of Ministers. Out of fear of French intervention in the internal affairs of Spain, the Ministers re-

<hr />

[37] Espagne, question dynastique, note pour le Ministre (Turgot), May 18, 1855, AMAE (Paris), Mémoires et documents, Espagne, Vol. 366.

[38] Napoleon's plan to intervene in Spain and the objections of the British are recounted by Cowley in his private letters to Clarendon, Paris, July 25, 1856, July 27, 1856, August 10, 1856, and October 13, 1856, PRO FO 519/219.

[39] Eugénie to Duke of Alba, December 2, 1854, *Lettres familières*, I, 115.

jected the proposal out of hand. In high dudgeon Eugénie scolded her brother-in-law:

I do not know if I am mistaken but there is in the destinies of Spain a fatality which makes her reject what could be useful to her and throw herself head-long into the arms of those who can ruin her, when I trusted you to sound the ground . . . I was far from believing that they would make it an affair of the council and that they would think themselves obliged to refuse *what had not even been proposed* to them up to now.

Her initiative, she continued, had arisen from her shame in seeing Spain ignored while tiny Sardinia and Switzerland were approached for help and from her desire to see Spain elevated to the ranks of the great powers. She concluded: "You fear an intervention: fear rather the profound oblivion in which you are left, you no longer have any voice, you are no longer in the second rank, you drop to the third."[40]

A document in the Spanish Foreign Ministry reveals that the proposal to Spain was not altogether a sudden inspiration on the part of the Empress. During the opening weeks of the war in 1854 Napoleon and Drouyn de Lhuys had both explored with the Spanish representative in Paris, the Marquis of Viluma, the eventuality of a Spanish war against the United States in which the Crimean alliance would share the defense of Cuba. It was generally feared in London and Paris that Russia, disregarding principles, would ally with the United States and that she was actually inciting that country to aggression against Spain. Viluma reported that on April 27, 1854, the Emperor had proffered *"the entire moral influence of France and up to a squadron for the defense of the Isle of Cuba."* Drouyn de Lhuys had said nearly the same thing although in less emphatic words.[41] But their remarks had failed to culminate in a concrete offer and fell to the ground. Viluma thought it likely that Britain had balked at the idea of placing her Empire in opposition to the United States. And the Spanish government itself preferred neutrality as long as Cuba was not directly threatened.

When the Empress revived the negotiation late in 1854 it moved eventually into regular diplomatic channels and hung fire until the very close of the war. While the outcome of the fighting remained in doubt, the Spanish government temporized, reluctant to make a definite offer of troops. During August, 1855, while Napoleon was at Biarritz, Spain declared its willingness to join the alliance and to place 25,000 to 30,000 men in the field. But the government stopped short of an official proposal. The

---

[40] Eugénie to Duke of Alba, December 12, 1854, AA, c. 146–5. The editors of *Lettres familières* reproduced the letter of December 2 to Alba but not this second one of December 12.

[41] Viluma to the first secretary of state, Paris, May 16, 1854, reserved, AMAE (Madrid), Correspondencia, Francia, XB, 1506, No. 298.

fall of Sebastopol ended Spanish hesitations. Then it was the turn of France to quench Spanish eagerness to become a belated belligerent and a member of the peace conference. Britain showed little enthusiasm for Spain as an ally and raised "some rather serious practical objections" to her proffered help.[42]

It is hardly possible that Napoleon's proposal of a Spanish alliance had no more serious purpose than that given by the Empress. Nor is it likely that he took up the negotiation merely to humor his wife. Yet the fragmentary record of the negotiation in the archives of the French and Spanish Foreign Ministries fails to illuminate his motives. Perhaps the attraction to the alliance of Catholic, Legitimist Spain was part of his gambit to entice Austria into the war. Perhaps he saw a Spanish alliance simply as a means of enlarging the forces in the Crimea. Whatever may have been his reasons for the negotiation, its frustrating course was typical of the many difficulties he and the Empress would encounter in their repeated efforts to prop up and at the same time live with the Bourbon regime in Madrid.

THE BEGINNING OF TROUBLE WITH ROME

Napoleon's Empire and marriage in their early years were blessedly free from friction over relations with the Papacy and the clergy. French bishops and priests had responded with unmeasured enthusiasm to the establishment of the Empire and had hailed their ruler as a Constantine, a Charlemagne, even a new Saint Louis who would inaugurate a blessed era in relations between Church and state. The Emperor, whose troops were in Rome protecting the temporal power of the Pope, had replied with the most courteous and reassuring expressions of his devotion to Catholic interests.[43] His betrothal to a practicing Catholic, acceptable to the Church party, had created no problem.

A few off-pitch notes, nevertheless, jangled in the harmonious chorus. Napoleon wished to follow the precedent of his uncle and inaugurate his reign with a papal coronation. But Pius IX would agree to the ceremony only if Napoleon would "open the door for him"—by which he meant that

[42] Walewski to Turgot, Paris, September 25, 1855, AMAE (Paris), Correspondance politique, Espagne, Vol. 847, No. 26. For the course of the negotiation see Turgot to Napoleon, Madrid, July 27, 1855, AMAE (Paris), Mémoires et documents, Espagne, Vol. 366; Turgot to Walewski, Madrid, August 3, 1855, *ibid.*, Correspondance politique, Espagne, Vol. 847, No. 10; Turgot to Walewski, September 17, 1855, *ibid.*, No. 15; Turgot to Walewski, telegram, September 21, 1855, *ibid.*; Walewski to Turgot, Paris, August 10, 1855, *ibid.*, No. 24; Walewski to Turgot, December 10, 1855, *ibid.* The correspondence preserved in the Foreign Ministry in Madrid unfortunately gives no counterpart for this negotiation. I examined Bundles 1506, 1507, and 1508 for the years 1854–1856, Correspondencia, Embajadas y Legaciones, Francia, XB.

[43] Pierre de La Gorce, *Histoire du Second Empire*, II, 138–139.

the French government should abolish the organic articles which defined and restricted the concordat and should consider the abolition of civil marriage as a prerequisite for the religious rite.[44] Then, in 1853, the Empress wanted to be married by the Pope. Pius declined, pleading his "great age and infirmities," although twenty-five years were to elapse before either overpowered him.[45]

Serious difficulty with the Papacy commenced during the Crimean War when the Emperor undertook his tutelage of revolution in Italy. In the fall of 1855 Victor Emmanuel, King of Sardinia, arrived in Paris preceded by his Minister, Count Cavour. The King and his government were engaged in an acrid debate with the Papacy on the question of lay laws. Cavour was planning to extend the controversy to the question of the Pope's temporal power as a means of obtaining his reward for the troops sent to the Crimea. At the peace conference to be held in Paris he hoped to claim, with the support of Britain and France, the evacuation of the Austrians from the papal territory of Romagna, the autonomy of that province, and eventually its independence.[46]

The affair was in this stage when Eugénie, expecting the birth of her child in the spring of 1856, voiced her hope that the Pope would serve as the baby's godfather. Very likely she was innocently unaware of the negotiation then being carried on between Napoleon and the Sardinians and uncomprehending of the complication she was interjecting into it. Her behavior even as late as the spring of 1859 indicates that she had not yet formulated any griefs against Victor Emmanuel. Yet her project, taken up by Napoleon, effectively quashed Cavour's scheme. He complained to his friend, Count Francesco Arese: "The devil has arranged that the empress wanted the pope as godfather to the child to be born. That has spoiled much of my original plan. I have conceived of another, but I don't know how well it will succeed."[47]

The result of the negotiation was one of those compromises, so characteristic of later phases of the Roman question, which left everyone dissatisfied. The Pope accepted the role of godfather but remained in Rome. He designated Cardinal Patrizi as his representative and presented the Empress with the gold rose, which he blessed each year during Lent. Again he held out for the abolition of the organic articles and abolition of civil

[44] *Ibid.*, pp. 147–152. See also Cowley to Russell, Paris, February 4, 1853, copy, and February 9, 1853, PRO FO 519/210; Cowley to Clarendon, March 4, 1853, and April 6, 1853, *ibid.*

[45] Aubry, *Eugénie*, p. 80; Sencourt, *Eugénie*, p. 81.

[46] Jean Maurain, *La Politique ecclésiastique du Second Empire de 1852 à 1869*, p. 112.

[47] Cavour to Arese, Paris, February 22, 1856, Count Joseph Grabinski, *Un Ami de Napoléon III: Le Comte Arese et la politique italienne sous le Second Empire*, p. 139.

marriage as the price of his appearance at the altar of Notre Dame in Paris.[48] On the other hand, Cavour obtained neither the evacuation nor the autonomy of the Romagna. At the Congress of Paris in 1856 the French Foreign Minister, Count Walewski, who had replaced Drouyn de Lhuys, expressed the view of the French government that the occupation of the Roman states was an anomaly which would soon disappear. The British plenipotentiary criticized papal administration in strong terms. Pius IX received a copy of the proceedings of the session along with French suggestions for reform. The Pope was offended, Cavour and Victor Emmanuel dissatisfied. While the baptism in Paris passed off in splendid pageantry, the Emperor had again failed to deliver the living proof of papal sanction of his house.

At the same time, although we have no evidence that the Empress at any time during the affair acted in opposition to the Emperor, Eugénie's reputation as a papist was established. In June, 1856, the government presented a *senatus-consultum* that, in the event the Emperor should die before his son was of age, conferred the regency on the Empress. In the Senate the Marquis of La Valette proposed that the Regent should not only swear to observe the constitution but should take a special oath to respect the laws of the concordat and freedom of worship. The amendment was designed as a safeguard against Eugénie's reputed Ultramontanism and had great success with the Gallicans as well as those, like La Valette, who were anticlericals. The amendment failed, but only by 8 votes out of 120. The closeness of the vote as well as the divisions of opinion which had appeared during the negotiation about the baptism heralded the rise of a strong anticlerical movement in the government and the resulting Roman question.[49] Just faintly could be perceived the outline of that unhappy triangle of the early sixties in which the Empress, siding with the Pope, opposed the plans of the Emperor to aid the revolution in Italy.

Eugénie all but disappeared from the world of diplomacy for nearly two years after the birth and baptism of the Prince Imperial. Her conversations with the ambassadors were widely scattered and of small importance. Aside from the internal problems of Spain, about which she continued to talk with Cowley, no other question long attracted her attention. The relative calmness of the European scene from 1856 to 1858 and the secure position of the Emperor were undoubtedly major reasons for her indifference. Poor health was another. The delivery of the Prince, on March 16, while the Congress of Paris was in session, was difficult and

[48] Sampayo, first secretary at Rome, to Thouvenel, Rome, April 9, 1856, AMAE (Paris), Correspondance politique, Papiers Thouvenel, XVII, 7072.

[49] Maurain, *La Politique ecclésiastique*, p. 176; Jean Maurain, *Baroche, ministre de Napoléon III*, p. 155.

rendered her *hors de combat* for months. Even after her recovery she endured periods of severe depression. Her letters to her sister in 1857 and 1858 were dispirited and restless. She coughed incessantly and could scarcely find energy to organize and attend the lavish court entertainments expected of her. She moaned to her sister "[Whether I am] Pale or rosy, what difference? The winter season must be gay, and that is all that is necessary."⁵⁰ Never one to understate matters, she claimed that her courage failed her, that she could not go on, and that she would be better off in the grave. Quarrels with the Emperor may have lain behind this melancholy. During those years Napoleon stepped frequently and flagrantly outside the marital bonds. She thus remained outside of political affairs until 1858. Only then, when the question of revolution in Italy dominated the diplomatic scene and aroused both her intellect and her emotions, did she seriously attempt to influence foreign policy.

⁵⁰ Eugénie to Duchess of Alba, January 2, 1858, *Lettres familières,* II, 135.

CHAPTER 2

THE ITALIAN WAR
An Apprentice in Revolt

ORSINI AND THE EMPRESS' ITALIAN PHASE

The Empress' introduction to the Italian question was dramatic and very nearly fatal. On the evening of January 14, 1858, Napoleon and Eugénie, drawing up in front of the opera house to attend a benefit performance, narrowly escaped death from the bombs of an Italian revolutionary, Felice Orsini, and his accomplices. A triple explosion shattered the imperial coach, mangled the horses, and wounded or killed nearly two hundred on-lookers. Shaken but luckily unhurt, they were able to make their way to their box in the theater, where they saluted the wildly cheering crowd. Both behaved with admirable *sang-froid* and the next day drove un-attended along the boulevards to visit the surviving victims in the hospital.

The Empress was at first horrified by the terrible slaughter. But as the first shock passed, she began very naturally to enjoy her role of heroine and basked in the praise of her undeniable bravery. The Empress Elizabeth of Austria wrote personally to congratulate her on her "courageous firmness" and to render thanks to heaven for her and the Emperor's miraculous es-cape.[1] The *Moniteur*, official organ of the French government, compared Eugénie to the great Habsburg Empress Maria Theresa in her hour of peril. Eugénie enjoyed reliving the terror of the moment and would tear-fully repeat to her ladies the awful details of the conspiracy.[2]

---

[1] Elizabeth to Eugénie, Vienna, January 17, 1858, AA, 33–12.

[2] *Moniteur*, January 16, 1858. See also Joseph Alexander Hübner, *Neuf ans de souvenirs d'un ambassadeur d'Autriche à Paris sous le Second Empire*, II, 89, 93, and 97. For Eugénie's description of the Orsini attempt see Eugénie to Countess of Montijo, January 15, 1858, Empress Eugénie, *Lettres familières de l'Impératrice Eu-génie conservées dans les archives du Palais de Liria et publiées par les soins du Duc d'Albe avec le concours de F. de Llanos y Torriglia et Pierre Josserand*, I, 147. For her reactions see Eugénie to Countess of Montijo, January 20, 1858, *ibid.*, 148–149; Eugénie to Duchess of Alba, January 21, 1858, *ibid.*, pp. 150–152. See also Villamarina to Cavour, Paris, February 6, 1858, *Il Carteggio Cavour-Nigra*, I, 61.

The trial of the handsome Italian, who had courage and a flair for the dramatic, touched off still a third reaction in the Empress. Orsini's impassioned letters to the Emperor pleading the cause of Italian independence and his defiant posturing aroused her admiration. Suddenly she saw the prisoner in the dock as a hero and martyr, and she set the pace among the fashionable ladies in Paris in pleading his cause.

"He is no vulgar assassin," she told the Emperor. "Rather, he is a bold, proud man who has my esteem."

He who had been the main target of the bombs replied dryly: "Be careful, my dear, to whom you grant your esteem."[3]

From the day of Orsini's condemnation to death late in February until the execution of the sentence on March 13 Eugénie's entreaties mounted in volume and intensity. To the despair of the Ministers, the Emperor showed signs of yielding. At the last minute only their threat to resign in a body if the sentence were not carried out made Napoleon hold out. Count Walewski, Foreign Minister, took a strong stand on the question in a letter to his master. "It would take volumes to tell Your Majesty the reasons for my deep conviction," he wrote. "I will add only one: the empress. It has become so widely known that she exerts all her influence to decide Your Majesty to pardon him [Orsini] that, if it were to be thus, . . . all the blame in France and abroad would unanimously fall on the empress."[4]

That Napoleon, to gratify the wishes of his wife, came near to flying in the face of his Privy Council and his Council of Ministers would appear to be an impressive demonstration of her power over him even in these early years of the Empire when he was still in health and she without partisans in the government. Yet such a conclusion fails to consider the Emperor's own desires. With his Buonaparte heritage and *Carbonari* beginnings, he was secretly sympathetic to Orsini's cause. Lord Cowley thought he was "regularly bitten by this miscreant."[5] Very likely the Empress was merely giving voice to the arguments he most wished to hear.

Unwittingly, the Empress was laying up future trouble for herself. Her well-known support of Orsini helped to publicize the Italian cause and to

[3] Georges Lacour-Gayet, *L'Impératrice Eugénie: Documents et souvenirs,* p. 36.

[4] Walewski to Napoleon, March 11, 1858, Françoise Chalamon de Bernardy, "Un Fils de Napoléon: Le Comte Walewski, 1810–1868," MS, p. 532. See also Hübner, *Neuf ans,* I, 119–120; Victor Wellesley and Robert Sencourt, *Conversations with Napoleon III,* p. 160; George Maurice Paléologue, *The Tragic Empress: A Record of Intimate Talks with the Empress Eugénie, 1901–1919,* trans. by Hamish Miles, pp. 156–157; Dr. Thomas W. Evans, *The Memoirs of Dr. Thomas Evans: Recollections of the Second Empire,* ed. by E. A. Crane, M.D., II, 548; Baron Napoléon Beyens, *Le Second Empire vu par un diplomate belge,* I, 137–138.

[5] Cowley to Malmesbury, Paris, March 4, 1858, Wellesley and Sencourt, *Conversations with Napoleon III,* p. 134.

create the climate of opinion in which the war against Austria became possible. She later bitterly regretted her unthinking and rash behavior.[6] But in January, 1858, Austria had not yet engaged her sympathies. Hübner, lacking both a great name and wealth, had failed to establish a strong place in her court. Nor had she yet formulated any views on Italian nationalism and apparently foresaw none of the complications which were to arise from the aggrandizement of Sardinia. Although she had never travelled in Italy, she felt attracted to the country for sentimental reasons and from both Bonapartist and Legitimist predilections. Prosper Mérimée had in the past spoken to her of Italy's great beauty, of its artists and poets. Stendhal had regaled her with the glorious campaigns of Napoleon I.[7] More recently she had come to admire the Duchess of Parma, sister of the Bourbon pretender to the throne of France.[8] The Duchess had lost both her father and her husband through attacks by assassins and was carrying on as Regent in Parma for her small son. Moreover, her opinions of King Victor Emmanuel II of Sardinia, widower of a Habsburg, were still cast in a gracious mold. Soon after the birth of the Prince Imperial she remarked that the King's house of Savoy was the only one in Europe into which she would desire her son to marry.[9]

"OUR CAUSE IS GOOD . . ."

The Empress later believed that the Orsini affair provided the Emperor with the decisive impulse to go to war against Austria.[10] But for many years he had been obsessed with the Italian question and had long cherished what he called "his dream"—that Austria should exchange her Italian provinces for the Danubian principalities. Turkey, who held the provinces, should be indemnified in Asia Minor. During the Crimean War the Emperor had spoken to Cowley of this arrangement, which would free north Italy from foreign rule and allow the Habsburg empire to expand where, according to him, its true interests lay.[11] As the French Emperor later saw it, the brief Austro-French alliance during the Crimean War had foundered in effect on Austria's unwillingness to give up Lombardy and

---

[6] Hübner to Buol, January 14, 1859, reserved, Hübner, *Neuf ans,* II, 256.

[7] Carlo Pagani, "Felice Orsini, Eugenia de Montijo et Napoleone III," *Nuova antologia,* CCXXXIX (1925), 53.

[8] Cowley to Clarendon, Paris, July 21, 1856, copy, PRO FO 519/219.

[9] Dr. Henri Conneau to Count Arese, Tuileries, May 18, 1856, Count Joseph Grabinski, *Un Ami de Napoléon III: Le Comte Arese et la politique italienne sous le Second Empire,* p. 141.

[10] Paléologue, *Tragic Empress,* p. 157.

[11] Cowley to Stratford, Paris, July 23, 1854, copy, PRO FO 519/213; Cowley to Clarendon, Paris, November 30, 1854, copy, *ibid.,* 519/214; Cowley to Clarendon, December 10, 1855, *ibid.,* 519/218.

Venetia and had rendered the Italian War inevitable.[12] He told Cowley
that the marriage of Prince Napoleon with the daughter of Victor Emmanuel, celebrated in January, 1859, and generally seen as a portent of a
Franco-Sardinian alliance against Austria, had been arranged as early as
January, 1857.[13]

The Emperor kept his wife in ignorance of the important events in 1858
and 1859 which laid the basis for the war in 1859—the confidential agreements between Cavour and Napoleon at Plombières in the summer of
1858, the revolutionary agitation in central Italy of Sardinian agents, and
the secret treaty between France and Sardinia of January, 1859. With
Prince Napoleon as his chief adviser, he formulated his own foreign policy
and did not even take his Foreign Minister into his confidence. He later
admitted: "I carefully avoided the topic [the Italian question] in my conversations with the Empress and Count Walewski."[14]

The fact that Napoleon felt concealment from the Empress necessary
perhaps indicates that had she known of his policy she would not have approved. According to the memoirs of Count Fleury, son of Napoleon's
aide-de-camp and close friend, she now began to regard Cavour's ideas as
dangerous to the temporal power of the Pope.[15] By January, 1859, the
Empress clearly had reason to experience some doubts over her earlier enthusiastic "Italian phase." Prince Napoleon was a ringleader of the "Italianissimes," those persons promoting the aggrandizement of Sardinia and
the unity of Italy. This fact in itself was almost enough to disenchant the
Empress. Prince Napoleon's hatred of her had intensified when she gave
birth to the Prince Imperial, thus reducing his hopes of succeeding the Emperor on the throne, and manifested itself in open scorn when she was designated as eventual Regent for her son. Moreover, the Countess of Castiglione, an agent of Cavour, had established herself in Paris in 1856 and had
successfully captivated the Emperor. The affair endured at least until 1860

---

[12] Hübner to Rechberg, Paris, May 28, 1863, HHSA, IX/76. Drouyn de Lhuys said
essentially the same thing to Count Mülinen, Austrian chargé d'affaires at Paris
(Mülinen to Rechberg, October 25, 1863, *ibid.*).

[13] Cowley to Malmesbury, Paris, January 20, 1859, copy, PRO FO 519/224.

[14] Count Maurice Fleury, *Memoirs of the Empress Eugénie. Compiled from Statements, Private Documents, and Personal Letters,* II, 100. Walewski admitted to Cowley
that Prince Napoleon's marriage had been arranged without his knowledge (Cowley
to Malmesbury, Paris, January 10, 1859, copy, PRO FO 519/224). He had not been
permitted to see the secret correspondence exchanged between Napoleon and Cavour
after their meeting at Plombières in 1858 (Cowley to Malmesbury, Paris, March 20,
1859, PRO FO 519/225), and he was invited to only one of the conferences with
Cavour when he came to Paris in March, 1859 (Hübner to Buol, telegram, Paris, March
31, 1859, HHSA, IX/62, No. 38). See also Chalamon de Bernardy, "Le Comte Walewski," p. 535.

[15] Fleury, *Memoirs,* II, 90.

and while it probably had no influence on the Emperor's political views it was the source of gossip keenly humiliating to the Empress.[16]

At the same time many of Eugénie's closest associates in the court were determined opponents of the Italianissimes. Chief among them were the Walewskis, man and wife. In 1853, anxious for the Emperor to marry into royalty, Walewski had opposed the match with Eugénie, but he soon after became her loyal friend. Later his disapproval of her championship of Orsini and of her weakness for table turning—especially when the table talked politics and told her that the Emperor should deliver the Italians from the yoke of the Austrians—caused only momentary hard feeling.[17] The position of Walewski and his wife in the court was unusual to say the least. Because he was the natural son of Napoleon I he was *famille en ligne courbe,* but family all the same and treated as such. Marie Walewska managed another and more intimate kind of connection with the Emperor. Strangely enough, the Empress was ignorant of her liaison, or at least pretended to be, and lavished favors on the pretty Florentine. She had her portrait painted on one of the doors of the blue salon of the Tuileries, constantly invited her to the court, and lent her clothes and jewels.[18]

Another good friend and relative of her husband who echoed the anti-Sardinian views of the Walewskis was the Duchess of Hamilton, née Maria, Princess of Baden, a zealous Legitimist and Ultramontane. She was the special champion of the Bourbon Princess Louise Marie Thérèse, whose Duchy of Parma was coveted by Cavour. The Baden Princess was a daughter of Stéphanie de Beauharnais, a niece of the Empress Josephine. The family of her father, the Grand Duke, was a stronghold of Legitimism, and in the 1850's its daughters had married into the major ruling houses of

[16] Many accounts exist of the Castiglione affair. See Cowley to Malmesbury, Paris, November 13, 1860, Frederick Arthur Wellesley (ed.), *Secrets of the Second Empire: Private Letters from the Paris Embassy; Selections from the Papers of Henry Richard Charles Wellesley, 1st Earl Cowley,* p. 211; Robert Sencourt, *The Life of the Empress Eugénie,* pp. 138–140; Albert Guérard, *Napoleon III: An Interpretation,* p. 154; Edward Legge, *The Comedy and Tragedy of the Second Empire: Paris Society in the Sixties, Including Letters of Napoleon III, M. Pietri, and Comte de La Chapelle and Portraits of the Period,* p. 137.

[17] Chalamon de Bernardy, "Le Comte Walewski," pp. 654–655.

[18] For the Walewska liaison see Cowley to Malmesbury, Paris, July 26, 1858, PRO FO 519/224; Horace de Viel-Castel, *Mémoires sur le règne de Napoléon III, 1851–1864, publiés d'après le manuscrit original,* IV, 145, and V, 27. It has been suggested that Eugénie, more sovereign than wife, encouraged the affair, believing this connection better than others such as that with the pro-Italian Countess of Castiglione (Chalamon de Bernardy, "Le Comte Walewski," pp. 503–504). A letter from the Empress to the Duchess of Mouchy reveals that later, at least, she detested Marie Walewska. Just after Walewski's death she wrote: "I am sincerely sorry for his wife for she must be very unhappy to see the scaffolding of her ambition fall [but] I don't pity her heart, *I don't believe she has one*" (Biarritz, October 20, 1868, Mouchy Papers, No. 84).

Europe. The Baden Princesses were known for their great piety and their Carlist sympathies.[19] For several years before the outbreak of war in 1859 Eugénie had infuriated Prince Napoleon and Matilda by her preferential treatment of Maria, especially by her habit, in matters of protocol, of seating her with the imperial family although her connection with it was very distant. At the very banquet in honor of the marriage of Prince Napoleon and Clotilda, Eugénie placed the Ultramontane Duchess, who epitomized politically everything the Prince detested, in a seat of honor on the left of the Emperor.[20]

The Empress probably did not become aware of the seriousness of Napoleon's plans in regard to Italy until New Year's Day, 1859. At the annual reception of the diplomatic corps the Emperor greeted Hübner: "I regret that our relations with your government are not as happy as I would wish." Uttered with apparent deliberation on this most formal of occasions, the words sent a tremor of alarm through Europe. Hübner reported that the Empress was visibly upset and soon began to regret her former imprudent flirtations with the Italianissimes. Together with the Walewskis she tried to regain lost ground with the Emperor and to prevail upon him to keep the peace. Late in January, taking advantage of the absence of Prince Napoleon, who went to claim his bride, they managed, at least in the opinion of the Foreign Minister, to make some impression.[21]

But despite this belated flurry of anxiety, the record shows that Eugénie did not work consistently to avoid an outbreak of war in the spring of 1859. She was fundamentally a fighter with a strong and touchy sense of pride. She felt there was something shameful, even cowardly, in a too eager pursuit of peace. In February when Napoleon told the Legislative Body that France was not to be intimidated and would refuse to adopt a pusillanimous policy the Empress approved his attitude. "Don't you think it [his speech] was firm and dignified?" she wrote to her sister. "Some people here would have liked him to say that *he would never make war,* in short, *the peace at any price* of King Louis Philippe. As for me, I'm not warlike, but I can not approve of this shameful headlong rout."[22]

Hübner was unable to convince her of the correctness of the Austrian

---

[19] In 1870 Bismarck was much annoyed when the Baden Princesses supported the Carlist claimant to the Spanish throne instead of the candidate of their own family, Leopold of Hohenzollern-Sigmaringen (Bismarck to Rudolph Delbrück, May 13, 1870, Otto Eduard Leopold von Bismarck-Schönhausen, *Die gesammelten Werke,* XIV, 776). See also Constance Wright, *Daughter to Napoleon: A Biography of Hortense, Queen of Holland,* p. 271, for information on the Baden Princesses.

[20] Cowley to Malmesbury, Paris, February 6, 1859, copy, PRO FO 519/225; Viel-Castel, *Mémoires,* III, 163, 166, 206; IV, 27.

[21] Hübner to Buol, Paris, January 14, 1859, reserved, HHSA, IX/62, Nos. 8 A-C and 8 B; Hübner, *Neuf ans,* II, 252, 253, 256, 263.

[22] Eugénie to Duchess of Alba, February 8, 1859, *Lettres familières,* I, 161.

position as his successor was later able to do. As the spring came on she often spoke curtly to him or avoided him altogether. Shortly after Napoleon's speech in February the ambassador told her that although the Emperor's words had seemed reassuring no one would believe in peace until France had ceased to arm. "Well, then," retorted Eugénie, "you will have to stop sending troops into Lombardy."[23] Moreover, she emphatically endorsed the double election of Prince Couza in Moldavia and Wallachia even though the Austrians, predicting the union of the principalities, loudly denounced it. To Hübner's protests she replied: "It is the national will; they wish union there."[24] Incongruous words from the woman who later believed that support of the principle of nationality was the undoing of the Second Empire.

If war should break out in Italy the Emperor planned to go to the front himself and establish a regency in Paris. The prospect of playing the role of Madame la Régente offered the Empress an opportunity to strengthen her position in the government and her popularity in France at the expense of Prince Napoleon, who would have to accompany the army to Italy. The Prince had been openly contemptuous of the *senatus-consultum* which designated the Empress as the eventual Regent for her son and he had declared in the hearing of Matilda: "I . . . believe my position good, . . . if something should happen to the emperor certainly no one would look to this simpleton of an empress or to this brat of a prince imperial."[25] While no evidence exists that Eugénie grasped at the regency in 1859, she was plainly not loath to accept it. In June she wrote her sister: ". . . I even think it is fortunate for the Emperor for people to accustom themselves to the regency, for assassins will have less reason to make attempts when they are convinced that, even if their infamous projects succeeded they would not have the upper hand."[26]

If the Empress had had any reservations about the coming war they were removed by the Austrian ultimatum in April demanding that Sar-

[23] Hübner to Buol, February 10, 1859, reserved, HHSA, IX/62, No. 18c; Hübner, *Neuf ans*, II, 284.

[24] Hübner to Buol, Paris, February 10, 1859, private, HHSA, IX/62; Hübner, *Neuf ans*, II, 287.

[25] Marguerite Castillon du Perron, *La Princesse Mathilde, un règne féminin sous le Second Empire*, p. 156. See also Mme Jules Baroche, *Second Empire: Notes et souvenirs*, p. 39. The influence of Prince Napoleon had seemed to prevail with the Emperor in the spring of 1859 despite a temporary victory of Eugénie and Walewski in March which forced his resignation as minister of Algeria and the colonies (Hübner to Buol, telegram March 12, 1859, HHSA, IX/62, No. 25; Ernest d'Hauterive, *The Second Empire and Its Downfall: The Correspondence of the Emperor Napoleon III and His Cousin Prince Napoleon*, trans. by H. Wilson, p. 120). See also Baron d'Ambès, *Intimate Memoirs of Napoleon III: Personal Reminiscences of the Man and the Emperor*, trans. by A. R. Allinson, II, 126–129.

[26] Eugénie to Duchess of Alba, June 15, 1859, *Lettres familières*, I, 165.

dinia reduce its army and the Austrian invasion of Sardinian territory. At one of her earliest appearances at the meetings of the Council of Ministers, she opposed acceptance of a British offer of mediation and lined up with Prince Napoleon and Jérôme to pronounce war inevitable.[27] To her sister she confided: "You will know that we are about to have war, Austria has *wished* it."[28] As the French troops began moving southward toward the front, followed by sympathetic and excited crowds, the Empress declared that she was happier than she had been in months. "Our cause is good, our army is excellent, and *he* is full of confidence and energy."[29]

MADAME LA RÉGENTE

Unfortunately, the glad unanimity with which the Emperor's entourage greeted the declaration of war rapidly disintegrated when he set about establishing a government of the Regency. Because of the opposition of Prince Napoleon and Jérôme, he was unable to designate definitively the Empress as sole Regent until late in April. "What stupidity," sneered the Prince, ". . . to entrust the government to a fashion plate, for the empress is nothing else."[30] Even so, Jérôme, who had wanted at least a co-regency with the Empress, won a partial victory in being appointed President of the Council of Ministers and being named special counselor to the Regent. A dualism was thus created in the government which, if internal difficulties had arisen, might have proved dangerous.[31]

The Emperor found no less difficulty in deciding on the Ministers. He strove to give his Council a complexion that would soothe clerical fears over the future of the temporal power and at the same time would leave him unhampered in his relations with Cavour and Victor Emmanuel. For the benefit of the clericals he named the Duke of Padua, reputed to be devoted to the interests of the Papacy, as Minister of the Interior, although he permitted his predecessor, Claude Delangle, to remain on the Council as Minister of Justice. On the other hand, to balance the clericals in the government such as the Empress and Marshal Randon, Minister of War, he wished to replace Walewski in the Foreign Ministry with the pro-

---

[27] Jean Maurain, *Baroche, ministre de Napoléon III*, p. 175. Maurain used the notes taken by Baroche during the meeting of the Council.

[28] Eugénie to Duchess of Alba, April 22, 1859, *Lettres familières*, I, 163.

[29] Blanchard Jerrold, *The Life of Napoleon III. Derived from State Records, from Unpublished Family Correspondence, and from Personal Testimony*, IV, 198.

[30] Alfred Darimon, *Notes pour servir à l'histoire de la guerre de 1870*, p. 236. On April 15 Eugénie wrote that she could not say what her position would be during the war (Eugénie to Duchess of Alba, *Lettres familières*, I, 162). By April 22 the question had been settled, she thought (*ibid.*, p. 163); yet on April 24 Cowley still believed the question of the Regency had not been settled (Cowley to Malmesbury, Paris, April 24, 1859, copy, PRO FO 519/225).

[31] Emile Ollivier, *L'Empire libéral: Etudes, récits, souvenirs*, IV, 124.

Sardinian Duke of Persigny. But this plan ran afoul of both his wife and his mistress. The one because of her enmity for Prince Napoleon, close friend of Persigny, and the other because of her ambitions for her husband, went on their knees to the Emperor and persuaded him to keep Walewski in the Quai d'Orsay.[32] Persigny was packed off to London as ambassador. Thus arose the anomaly: Napoleon went to fight against Austria leaving behind him a Foreign Minister who feared his Sardinian, revolutionary ally almost as much as the enemy, and who dreaded the Emperor's success no less than his defeat.

Despite the jeers of Prince Napoleon, the Empress had developed a taste for politics and took her duties as Regent very seriously. After Napoleon left Paris for the front on May 10 she settled down with the Prince Imperial at Saint-Cloud and conscientiously devoted herself to a study of affairs of state. Emile Ollivier, often a bitter critic of the Empress in his *L'Empire libéral*, agreed that she exercised the functions of Regent intelligently and carefully. Jules Baroche, President of the Council of State, wrote that she presided over the Privy and Ministerial Councils "with assiduity, with a religious attention, and without flattery [to her], with great distinction."[33] Nervous and uncertain at first, she approached her duties with sober humility. Before addressing the Legislative Body she prepared her own speech and telegraphed the draft to the Emperor for his approval. Within two hours back came his encouraging answer: "It is very good except this sentence: '*Your support will help me in the accomplishment of a task too heavy for hands as unskilled as mine.*' One never says such things when they are not true."[34]

She quickly used her position to form closer relationships with the Ministers, especially Baroche, and Marshal Randon, newly appointed Minister of War. In the latent rivalry with Jérôme, the Empress found herself in an advantageous position. The Ministers were generally antagonistic to the truculent old man and usually sided with her. Jérôme, furious at his isolation, complained to the Emperor of the Regent's habit of conferring privately with the Ministers and of circumventing the Privy Council. His protest availed him nothing. The Emperor relayed Jérôme's letter of complaint to Eugénie, who maliciously showed it to the Ministers and continued her separate parleys with them.[35]

The relations between the Regent and her "special counselor" became openly rancorous when Prince Napoleon, at the head of an army, entered

[32] Chalamon de Bernardy, "Le Comte Walewski," p. 595; Ollivier, *L'Empire libéral*, IV, 124; Maurain, *Baroche*, p. 177; Cowley to Malmesbury, Paris, May 12, 1859, copy, PRO FO 519/225.

[33] Maurain, *Baroche*, p. 179; Ollivier, *L'Empire libéral*, IV, 258.

[34] Baroche, *Second Empire*, p. 125.

[35] Maurain, *Baroche,* pp. 179–180.

Tuscany, where the ducal throne then lay vacant. When Walewski, in the Council of Ministers, raised the question of the intention of the Prince, the Empress announced that she had already written to the Emperor of the bad effect produced on Europe by the Prince's apparent attempt to conquer a throne for himself. Jérôme jumped to the defense of his son. How could anyone believe, he queried, that the Prince would be willing to exchange his rights to the throne of France for the title of a grand duke? The mother of the Prince Imperial quickly reminded him: "Rights, rights which are remote at best!"[36] As was so often the case, Jérôme found himself alone in his opinion. Cavour and the British government added their protests to those of the Regent and made imperative a disavowal of French ambitions for the Prince. Sardinian fears subsided when the Emperor subordinated his cousin to the orders of Victor Emmanuel.[37]

Despite Eugénie's evident enjoyment of her new role, she hoped the war would be quickly over. While the Emperor was absent her closest companions were the Walewskis, who came nearly every evening to her residence at Saint-Cloud. Gradually she assimilated Walewski's antirevolutionary views and opposed the aggrandizement of Sardinia.[38] Even before Napoleon left for the front she tasted the uncertainties of armed conflict and had a "mauvais moment" as she saw that Austria, in possession of the valley of the Po, was in a position to cross into Sardinia, take Turin, and push into the sea the newly disembarked French troops bottled up in Genoa.[39] Although Austria let slip the first moment and retreated into Lombardy, the Empress had been badly shaken. Before a major engagement had taken place she wrote to Victoria of her fears of a general war and asked the Queen's help in forestalling such "an incalculable evil." Victoria's reply could not have been reassuring. If the Emperor wished to localize the war, she wrote, he had only to refrain from invasion of Austrian territory. If, on the other hand, he entered Lombardy, it would be only natural that Germany, alarmed at this attack on a member of the Confederation, should go to the aid of Austria and threaten the framework of the treaties of 1815.[40]

As rumbles from across the Rhine became alarmingly loud the Empress' desire for an armistice became acute. After the Battle of Magenta early in

---

[36] *Ibid.*, p. 179.

[37] Ollivier, *L'Empire libéral,* IV, 142–143; Pierre de La Gorce, *Histoire du Second Empire,* III, 62; Cowley to Sir James Hudson, Paris, May 21, 1859, copy, PRO FO 519/225.

[38] Chalamon de Bernardy, "Le Comte Walewski," p. 650.

[39] She confided her fears to Prince Metternich, Austrian ambassador at Paris after the war (Metternich to Rechberg, Paris, August 13, 1859, HHSA, IX/63, No. 2).

[40] Victoria to Eugénie, May 25, 1859, AA. The contests of Eugénie's letter to the Queen may be inferred from Victoria's answer which quotes some of the Empress' words.

June and the French entry into Milan she began, by letter and telegram, to call to Napoleon's attention the danger of an invasion across France's unprotected eastern frontier. She later credited her influence to have been decisive in causing the Emperor to stop short of the conquest of Venetia and to sign the armistice of Villafranca of July 12. In speaking of the reasons for the Emperor's decisions to end the war, she later told Emile Ollivier: "I wrote to the emperor, and the peace of Villafranca was signed."[41]

A good deal of evidence, both direct and indirect, bears out the Empress' claim to have strongly urged a quick end to the war.[42] On the eve of the decisive Battle of Solferino on June 24, Victor Emmanuel's chief of staff tells us that he was present when the Emperor read aloud to the King a letter from the Empress which warned of war on the Rhine if the French passed the Mincio into Venetia. "The king, having listened in silence, made no reply. He understood . . . that everything was over."[43] Shortly after the battle she sent another urgent warning in which, although recognizing the embarrassment which the quarrels for the supreme command between Austria and Prussia might cause their war effort, she emphasized the unsettled state of Europe, the obvious desire of Russia to see the cessation of hostilities, and the state of extreme excitement in Germany. She wrote that she had been informed by a diplomat whom she trusted that "The old feeling of 1813 is rekindled, and no patriotic assurances on your [France's] part will satisfy Prussia."[44]

The danger of a German invasion was anxiously debated in the meetings of the Ministers at Saint-Cloud. Randon dwelt on the inadequacy of

---

[41] Ollivier, *L'Empire libéral,* IX, 202. See also Paléologue, *Tragic Empress,* pp. 64–65.

[42] The correspondence between Napoleon and Eugénie during the war either by letter or telegram is scattered and exists in fragmentary form. At least one telegram from the Empress is in the Archives Nationales, Paris, F 90 365 980ᴮ. Several are in the French Foreign Ministry among the Papiers Charles Robert. Robert was attached to the headquarters of the Emperor and left his papers in the keeping of his daughter who gave them to the Ministry in 1934. Fleury (*Memoirs,* II, 30–32) has published several extracts from Eugénie's letters to Napoleon taken from her private papers. *Lettres familières* (June 28, 1859, I, 166) reproduces a letter from Eugénie to her sister on the subject of her hope for a quick end to the war. Indirect evidence that she corresponded with Napoleon and urged an armistice is supplied by Carlo Pagani, "Napoleone III, Eugenia de Montijo e Francesco Arese in un carteggio inedito," *Nuova antologia,* CCX (1921), 16–33, and by Luigi Chiala (ed.), *Lettere edite ed inedite di Camillo Cavour,* "Extracts from an Unedited Diary," VI, 406. See also Darimon, *La guerre de 1870,* p. 236; Ollivier, *L'Empire libéral,* IV, 195.

[43] Count Enrico Morozzo della Rocca, *Autobiografia di un veterano: Ricordi Storici e aneddotici del Generale Enrico della Rocca,* II, 461; Ollivier, *L'Empire libéral,* IV, 196; William Roscoe Thayer, *The Life and Times of Cavour,* II, 90.

[44] Fleury, *Memoirs,* II, 30–32. Fleury gives no date for the letter, but its context suggests it must have been written in late June or early July, soon after the Battle of Solferino.

French manpower and suggested calling up the National Guard. The discussion sparked another fracas between Jérôme, who seconded Randon, and the Empress, who saw the measure as a confession to the world of French desperation. Accused by Jérôme of betraying France in her hour of peril, Eugénie, stung by his implied allusion to the second wife of Napoleon I, also a foreigner, retorted that he need never fear her becoming another Marie Louise.[45] The Empress won her point as Randon's motion failed to carry.

It is clear that the Empress urged the localization and swift termination of the war. But whether or not it was her personal influence which drew the Emperor up short after Solferino and caused the armistice to be signed is another and more difficult question. When she advocated an armistice she was in an almost unique position of knowing with absolute certainty that she was expressing the wishes of the French people in general. Beginning with the period of May 8 to May 15, she received each week through July 10 an extensive report prepared by the inspector general of the police on the state of public opinion in the departments. Very likely the information she derived from them carried more weight with the Emperor than her personal wishes.

These reports, each headed with the words "For the Empress," were digests of the detailed bulletins prepared on the local level—either by the *procureurs généraux* or by agents of the police—and were obviously earnest efforts to supply the Regent with the unvarnished truth on the state of opinion.[46] They are remarkable for their frank admission of opposition to imperial policy and for their absence of hollow, stereotyped flattery. The reports usually opened with a description of opinion in general, which was always more satisfactory than in the nests of opposition later signalled. But even these introductory paragraphs, referring to the mass of the people loyal to the Empire, noted a widespread desire that the war be rapid and limited. Each called attention to the alarm and disaffection within the clergy. At least four out of the nine in the series spoke of concern over the attitude of Prussia, especially on the part of the border populations.

Any hint from official quarters of an approaching armistice was greeted with joy. On May 26 the Empress concluded her address to the Legislative Body with the words: "I count on your enlightened patriotism to maintain

[45] Archduchess of Austria, second wife of Napoleon I, who went over to Austria late in the Napoleonic Wars. Lacour-Gayet, *L'Impératrice Eugénie*, pp. 60–61; Octave Aubry, *The Second Empire*, trans. by A. Livingston, p. 226; Ollivier, *L'Empire libéral*, IX, 202.

[46] Bulletin politique hebdomadaire sur les départements, service confidentiel, AA, c. 48–10. There are nine reports in the series, covering the period of the Regency. Of them, No. 5, for the period June 5 to June 12, is missing. Each is signed by l'Inspecteur Général Permanent de la Gendarmerie, Président de Comité. Signature is illegible.

the faith that we must have in the energy of the army and, when the day arrives, in the moderation of the emperor." The sentence was widely interpreted to mean that the Emperor would stop after the first victory and make a peace requiring few sacrifices from Austria. The political bulletin for that week remarked: "The popularity of the empress is growing; the last speeches given by Her Majesty have been much applauded; the words which ended the one addressed to the legislative body produced a particularly happy sensation."[47] On June 4 the Battle of Magenta enabled the Franco-Sardinian forces to cross the Tessin River and enter Lombardy. The report for that week asserted: "Everywhere one hopes, one even believes that the war will be limited and of short duration."[48] The great victory at Solferino on June 24 caused general rejoicing but did not touch off warlike enthusiasm for escalation of the conflict to a larger European war. The digest for the week of June 26 to July 3 contained this prudent comment: "People worry over the attitude of Germany but they are not afraid; they think that if Prussia had intended to back up Austria with arms, she would not have waited until that power had endured such considerable losses."[49] The cessation of hostilities was hailed with satisfaction. "In the eyes of everyone, this armistice, whatever may be the results of it, appears to be wise policy; it should satisfy England at the same time that it restrains and embarrasses Germany."[50]

Other voices urged the advisability of a limited war as loudly and insistently as did that of the Empress and public opinion. Marshal Randon, unwilling to strip completely bare France's eastern frontier, sent inadequate numbers of replacements to Lombardy and only too plainly desired an armistice before the German states should become involved.[51] Count Shuvalov, aide-de-camp of Emperor Alexander, was sent by Prince Gorchakov, Russian Chancellor, to Paris and thence to imperial headquarters in Italy with the warning: "Make peace quickly or Prussia will attack France across the Rhine."[52] The Russian government made it clear that it would stand aside should France become involved in a war on two fronts. The report of a special emissary sent to sound the views of the German courts and the opinion of the people was so unsettling that

---

[47] Bulletin politique No. 3, *ibid.*
[48] Bulletin politique No. 4, *ibid.*
[49] Bulletin politique No. 8, *ibid.*
[50] Bulletin politique No. 9, *ibid.*
[51] Thayer, *Cavour,* II, 87–88; D'Ambès, *Intimate Memoirs,* II, 177; Jacques Louis César Alexandre Randon, *Mémoires,* II, 36; Cavour to La Marmora, Turin, July 16, 1859, Chiala *Lettere,* III, 111.
[52] Robert Henrey (ed.), *Letters from Paris, 1870–1875,* p. 10; Abel Hermant, *Eugénie, Impératrice des Français, 1826–1920,* pp. 111–112; Ollivier, *L'Empire libéral,* IV, 215–216.

it was rushed by special train and steamboat to Genoa and thence to the Emperor.[53]

Walewski had been one of the most regular in his direful predictions of involvement with Prussia. "The news from Germany is always alarming," he wrote the Emperor on May 16.[54] Three days later he added: "The agitation [in Germany] grows, and the hostility fomented . . . against us by the partisans of Austria serves to perfection the designs of demagogy which uses it as a powerful means of destroying order."[55] A month later he reported: "Prussia has just mobilized ten army corps. This resolution produces quite a sensation here and in Germany."[56]

It seems likely, all things considered, that the Empress gave herself too much credit in determining the Emperor to call a halt to the war. Her opinion undoubtedly carried special weight because of her access to the reports on public opinion. But her voice was only one of the swelling chorus. Even Jérôme and Prince Napoleon, among the most eager to evict the Austrians from Italy, contributed to the refrain. As for the middle-aged, war-weary Emperor, mindful of the mighty Quadrilateral looming before him—the four Austrian forts commanding the passage into Venetia at Verona, Peschiera, Mantua, and Legnano—and of the gaps in the ranks of his typhus-stricken army, he was only too willing to listen to the arguments for peace. The circumstances themselves rather than the personal wishes of the Empress brought about the armistice at Villafranca. The Empress was merely one of those who brought them urgently to the Emperor's attention.

IN DEFENSE OF ALTAR—

In controversial issues arising during the war in which her voice was not supported either by most of the Emperor's family and government or by a clear expression of public opinion, the Empress was much less successful in seeing her views prevail. In the case of the Pope's northernmost province, the Romagna, she was unable to thwart the revolutionary, anticlerical forces of the Sardinians and their sympathizers, eager to detach it from papal sovereignty, even though she could call upon Walewski and clerical opinion in France to sustain her.

---

[53] Gustave Rothan, *Les Origines de la guerre de 1870: La Politique française en 1866,* p. 22 n.

[54] Walewski to Napoleon, Paris, May 16, 1859, G. Raindre, "Les Papiers inédits du Cte Walewski," *Revue de France,* XL (1925), 83.

[55] Walewski to Napoleon, May 19, 1859, AMAE (Paris), Mémoires et documents, Vol. 2119, No. 5.

[56] Walewski to Napoleon, June 16, 1859, Raindre, "Les Papiers," *Revue de France* XL (1925), 90.

Before the beginning of the war, the Austrians had occupied the Romagna to enable the Pope to maintain his authority there. But after the Battle of Magenta early in June they retreated eastward along the valley of the Po. The evacuation triggered a series of revolts, or at least demonstrations, not only in the Romagna, but in the Duchies of Parma, Modena, and Tuscany. Sardinian commissioners moved into the vacuum of power and took over the governments as temporary executives.

The presence of the Sardinian officials in the Duchies and in the Romagna awakened Eugénie to the threat implied in an Italian national movement to the temporal power of the Pope and to the holdings of the legitimate rulers in the peninsula. Count Fleury, son of Napoleon's aide-de-camp and emissary to Franz Joseph during the war, wrote: "All these facts [concerning the uprisings in the Romagna and the Duchies] reached the Empress in Paris some time before they reached the Emperor in Italy, and she always made haste to send him her impressions of the event."[57] Those impressions, especially where the Romagna was concerned, were uniformly bad. " 'But will you be able to check the unity movement?' she asked, 'which seems destined to prevail, if we may judge by the attitude adopted by the Piedmontese [Sardinian] Government in the different principalities and in the Romagna'."[58] The burning question was whether Victor Emmanuel would be proclaimed dictator in the Romagna as he was in the Duchies. Eugénie wired: "The Legations [the Romagna] cause concern. Mr. Wki [Walewski] must have already written by mail. I have too. Please simply [say] whether the king [Victor Emmanuel] has accepted the dictatorship and whether this fact does not violate recognized neutrality."[59] From several reliable authorities we know that this was merely one of many urgent despatches she sent calling attention to the dismay of clerical opinion over Sardinian inroads.[60]

What motivated the Empress to protest so vigorously against the threat to the temporal power? Foes like Prince Napoleon or Jérôme put her action down simply as her blind partisanship for a detestable institution and her religious bigotry. Word of her strong stand evidently circulated in Paris and increased her already established reputation as a clerical. Two weeks after the revolt in the Romagna, Cowley reported: "There are many people who think his [Napoleon's] fears of the Clergy exaggerated—his uncle and

---

[57] Fleury, *Memoirs*, II, 29.

[58] *Ibid.*

[59] Eugénie to Napoleon, Saint-Cloud, June 16, 1859, 1:35 P.M., Archives Nationales, F 90 365 980B, No. 5169. This telegram was copied for me by a colleague. It is also cited by Lynn M. Case, *French Opinion on War and Diplomacy during the Second Empire*, p. 87, and Harold Kurtz, *The Empress Eugénie, 1826–1920*, p. 136.

[60] See Antonin Debidour, *Histoire diplomatique de l'Europe*, II, 197; Case, *French Opinion on War*, p. 87; Fleury, *Memoirs*, II, 29.

Cousin among the number—but in the Empress the Pope has a very warm partisan."[61]

Instinctive loyalty to papal interests may well have been partly responsible for her reaction. But she had plenty of hard facts to substantiate her warnings. Professor Lynn M. Case in his *French Opinion on War and Diplomacy during the Second Empire* has proven the existence of widespread alarm among French Catholics and the clergy after the revolt in the Romagna and the intrusion of the Sardinian commissioners. His extensive study of the reports of the procureurs general, pouring in each week to the Ministry of Justice from each of the twenty-seven legal districts of France, leaves no doubt of clerical hostility to the war. But "The big question," according to Case, was "whether the government paid any attention to these reports."[62] Case thinks the government was mindful of them, and he uses much indirect evidence to show that concern for clerical opinion was a factor in the Emperor's decision to agree to an armistice. Yet the very volume of the reports of the procureurs general would have made it impossible for the Regent and the Foreign Minister to have personally examined more than a few samples each week. No one could determine in what form the information on public opinion actually reached the Empress' desk. The digests of public opinion preserved in the Empress' papers in the archives of the Duke of Alba provide the missing link, or at least one of several. The Empress may also have read at random among the reports of the prefects, or may even have had other summaries of opinion prepared for her from other sources. But from these reports at least we know positively that she did keep in weekly touch with public opinion and that one of her sources of information, the political bulletins prepared by the inspector general of the police, warned her of serious opposition developing among large sections of the clergy.

The bulletins show clearly that from the outset of the war the clergy had scented dire prospects for the Papacy. Their dissatisfaction burgeoned after the revolt in the Romagna. A few excerpts suffice to demonstrate their tenor. The report for the week of June 12 to June 19 cited some twenty departments where the parish priests or even the mayors of towns had failed to illuminate the public buildings for the celebration after the Battle of Magenta.[63] The report for the week ending July 3 listed seventeen departments in which the clergy was making common cause with the Legitimists. Priests in nine departments had either refused to sing the *Te Deum* after the Battle of Solferino or had used language hostile to the government in the pulpit. Irritation of the clerical party was reported to be so extreme that great vigi-

61 Cowley to Russell, Paris, June 27, 1859, copy, PRO FO 519/225.
62 Case, *French Opinion on War*, p. 85.
63 Bulletin politique No. 6, AA, c. 48–10.

lance was necessary to guard against violent action by a fanatic.[64] Dissent reached its height in the second week of July. The report submitted on July 10 read: "The clergy is reassured with the difficulty; its opposition to the war may be seen in *approximately half* of our departments." Two pages of citations followed listing parishes where the clergy were either actively or passively hostile.[65] The warnings that the Empress directed to the front may not be dismissed merely as the bigoted and groundless outpourings of a religious fanatic.

Walewski was as aroused as the Empress over the revolts in Italy and correctly prophesied Sardinian annexation of north and central Italy. In a voluminous correspondence he implored the Emperor to understand that the real aim of Cavour was Italian unity and to forestall him before it was too late. He insisted that the creation of a kingdom of Italy would be incompatible with the interests of France and would be unworkable in the peninsula. He warned: "I know the appetite grows in eating, but when the appetite is so great indigestion is sure to follow."[66] Of a like mind were Randon, keen on the protection of the temporal power, the Duke of Gramont, French ambassador at Rome, who passed on to the Emperor the remonstrances of Pius IX, and the Duke of Padua, Minister of the Interior.

A tug of war by telegraph began between the Regent and Walewski in Paris, on the one hand, both appalled by the aggressive revolutionary movement in Italy, and the Emperor at the front, influenced by the arguments of the Sardinians and his pro-Italian cousin, on the other. Irritated at the barrage of protests he was receiving from Paris, Napoleon pettishly wired his wife: "I am thoroughly pained, in the midst of my labors, to have to reply to all the stupid suppositions of diplomacy. I am maintaining the pope in Rome with my army. . . . Everything they say about Piedmont [Sardinia] is false."[67] Probably as a concession to clerical opinion in France, he refused to permit Victor Emmanuel to accept the dictatorship of the Romagna. A soothing note appeared in the *Moniteur* of June 23 denying Sardinian annexation of papal territory.

Yet the revolutionary trend seemed inexorable. The official newspaper at Bologna reported that Sardinia *had* accepted jurisdiction over the Romagna,[68] and a Sardinian general, Massimo d'Azeglio, moved in, apparently as commissioner.[69] Walewski begged the Emperor to allow papal troops to enter Bologna to restore the authority of the Pope. When the Em-

---

[64] Bulletin politique No. 8, *ibid.*

[65] Bulletin politique No. 9, *ibid.* Italics are mine.

[66] Walewski to Napoleon, Paris, June 17, 1859, AMAE (Paris), Mémoires et documents, France, Vol. 2119, No. 33.

[67] Napoleon to Eugénie, telegram, Brescia, June 19, 1859, 10:10 A.M., *ibid.*, No. 30.

[68] Gramont to Walewski, Rome, June 28, 1859, *ibid.*, No. 21.

[69] Walewski to Napoleon, Paris, June 1, 1859, *ibid.*, No. 46.

peror not only rejected this plea but added that he would oppose the Pope's troops should they set foot across the border, the Foreign Minister refused to give the Emperor's message to Rome without a second, explicit order to do so.[70]

His patience exhausted, the Emperor made clear to Walewski and the Empress who was master. To his wife he explained that although he had invited the King to prevent the spread of insurrection, the "massacres" committed by the papal troops in Perugia made its containment difficult.[71] To Walewski he snapped that the King had promised to counteract the revolutionary trend; now it was the turn of the Pope to do something.[72] If the Pope would promise not to try to restore his rule by force, he, Napoleon, would agree that no attempt would be made to incite revolt in the states still remaining under papal authority. "But if he [the Pope] wishes to treat the Romagna like Perugia," threatened the Emperor, "a bloody civil war will take place and the revolution will go to the doors of Rome." D'Azeglio, he added, was in Bologna not as a Sardinian commissioner but simply as a general to organize volunteers. With a rare show of lordliness he concluded: "He who wishes to change the present *status quo* [rule of provisional government in the Romagna] will have me for an adversary. Write that to Rome."[73]

The protests of Regent and Foreign Minister over the Romagna subsided for the duration of the war. It was plain to Cavour, who had been allowed to see many of Napoleon's despatches to Walewski, that the Emperor intended to deprive the Pope of the Romagna but to leave him the Marches.[74] The importunities of Eugénie, even supported by the Foreign Minister and the force of clerical opinion, had achieved only minor concessions and had been insufficient to induce Napoleon to return the Romagna to the Pope. True, the terms of the armistice of Villafranca stipulated papal sovereignty there with a civil government in control. But three days after the Preliminaries of Villafranca were signed, D'Azeglio took over with full powers.[75] The Romagna was irretrievably lost.

[70] Walewski to Napoleon, July 4, 1859, *ibid.,* No. 49.

[71] Napoleon to Eugénie, telegram, Valeggio, July 3, 1859, in Napoleon's hand, AMAE (Paris), Papiers Charles Robert, No. 4a.

[73] Napoleon to Walewski, telegram, July 4, 1859, 8:04 A.M., *ibid.,* No. 38. moires et documents. France, Vol. 2119, No. 37.

[73] Napoleon to Walewski, telegram, July 4, 1859, 8:04 A.M., *ibid.,* No. 38.

[74] Cavour to Prince Napoleon, July 1, 1859, Alfredo Comandini, *Il Principe Napoleone nel risorgimento italiano,* p. 175.

[75] For a good recent account of how Sardinia extended its control into the Duchies and the Romagna see Raymond Grew, "How Success Spoiled the Risorgimento," *The Journal of Modern History,* XXXIV (September, 1962), 239–253.

—AND THRONE

Of the other states affected by the revolts in June, Eugénie took special interest in only one—the Duchy of Parma. Grand Duke Leopold II of Tuscany had abandoned his duchy at the first hint of trouble and had fled precipitately to Vienna. Duke Francis V of Modena, in the past unpleasantly haughty in his dealings with the parvenu Emperor in Paris, had likewise run to the Austrians in 1859. By their haste both forfeited Eugénie's sympathy for their exile.

But the case of Louise, Regent in Parma for her small son, was different, and to her the Empress' heart went out. Sister of the Count of Chambord, Bourbon pretender to the throne of France, she was a gallant representative of the Legitimist cause and of the family which the Empress admired. Forced out of Parma as early as May 1, she had resolutely returned a few days later in an act of courage loudly acclaimed by the monarchist press. But misfortune was only briefly stayed. With the retreat of the Austrians in June the Sardinians moved in. Louise proclaimed her neutrality and in vain sought protection from France. On June 9 she once more packed her trunks and fled to Switzerland. A Sardinian commissioner took control eight days later.

Eugénie stood very nearly alone in her championship of the Duchess Louise. Napoleon well knew that an issue of this kind, the fate of a single Bourbon princess, would not greatly arouse public opinion in France. True, the weekly political bulletins received by the Empress during the war cited many instances of Legitimist excitement over the revolts in Italy and of Legitimist subversive activity, even including a purported plot to assassinate the Emperor, and the sale of medals bearing the image of Chambord as Henry V.[76] But the Emperor could always expect hostility from the Legitimists. He may have figured that since no other political party could be expected to be greatly interested in Louise, he could safely use Parma as a pawn in his game of diplomacy with little fear of serious opposition at home.[77] Louise was expendable. The duchy became a sort of consolation prize for Sardinia—a partial compensation for the Emperor's nonperformance in Venetia. As for the Duchess herself, Napoleon thought she might be compensated either by a sum of money or by a substitute throne in Modena at the expense of Duke Francis.[78] The matter could the more easily be ar-

[76] Bulletin politique hebdomadaire, AA, c. 48–10, Nos. 3, 4, 6, 8, 9.

[77] If such were his calculation, he was correct. In the fall of 1859 the reports of the procureurs general indicated a general lack of interest of the French public in the fate of the duchies (Case, *French Opinion on War*, p. 103).

[78] Napoleon to Walewski, telegram, Valeggio, July 12, 8:03 A.M., AMAE (Paris), Papiers Charles Robert No. 14; Napoleon to Franz Joseph, Saint-Sauveur, August 26,

ranged as Franz Joseph himself was ready to concede Parma to Sardinia. Poor Louise had lost the right to his protection by her declaration of neutrality and her plea to France for help during the war. In Franz Joseph's opinion she had played "a very double game," and he personally did not care what happened to her.[79] The Austrian Emperor was primarily interested in the restoration of his Habsburg relative in Tuscany and secondarily in the fate of Francis of Modena, of the house of D'Este-Lorraine but closely linked to Austria. Although on general principles he upheld the right of the Duchess to hold the throne for her son, he was not inclined to make difficulties for the sake of a Bourbon princess. During the negotiations at Villafranca he demurred only at Napoleon's scheme to transplant the Duchess to Modena.[80]

In Walewski the Empress had slight support. At the last minute, after learning that Parma was to go to Sardinia, he wired the Emperor: "I beg Your Majesty to arrange it so that Parma remains to the duchess, without that the effect will be very bad."[81] But the Foreign Minister realistically saw the hopelessness of saving the duchy. Geographically, it lay within the eager, cradling arm of Sardinia and was in fact governed at that moment by a Sardinian commissioner. Thus, when the Duchess' emissary had come to him on June 3 he had only replied that while he was certain that the Emperor had "the most friendly" intentions regarding the Regent, he regarded the position of her duchy as "bien difficile."[82] Moreover, if Sardinia were to annex any territory, he preferred that it be the small state of Parma rather than the richer prize of Lombardy. For Walewski the thought of any territorial reward for Sardinia was almost intolerable. Two things only had reconciled him to the Italian War in the spring: the hope of French acquisition of Nice and Savoy and the thought of the creation of a Lombardo-Venetian kingdom to be given to an Austrian archduke, probably Ferdinand Maximilian, former viceroy in those provinces.[83] Now both of these

1859, copy, AMAE (Paris), Mémoires et documents, France, Vol. 2119. See also Fleury, *Memoirs,* II, 52–53.

[79] This was the account as given by Prince Napoleon to Cowley. The Prince arranged the final terms about Parma with Franz Joseph at Villafranca. See Cowley to Russell, Compiègne, November 17, 1859, PRO FO 519/226.

[80] For the account of the negotiations regarding Parma between Prince Napoleon and Franz Joseph see Prince Napoleon, "Les Préliminaries de la paix, 11 Juillet 1859: Journal de ma mission à Vérone auprès de l'Empereur d'Autriche," *Revue des deux mondes,* LII (1909), 495. See also La Gorce, *Second Empire,* III, 109–112.

[81] Walewski to Napoleon, telegram, Paris, July 12, 3:30 P.M., AMAE (Paris), Papiers Charles Robert, No. 17.

[82] Walewski to Napoleon, Paris, June 3, 1859, AMAE (Paris), Mémoires et documents, France, Vol. 2119, No. 27.

[83] Cowley to Malmesbury, Paris, May 12, 1859 and June 3, 1859, copy, PRO FO 519/225; Walewski to Napoleon, telegram, Paris, July 10, 1859, 2:39 P.M., AMAE (Paris), Mémoires et documents, France, Vol. 2119, No. 69; Walewski to Napoleon,

plans were frustrated by the premature armistice which left Venetia in the possession of Franz Joseph. When he learned that Napoleon would forbear to ask for Nice and Savoy since he had not fulfilled his bargain on Venetia but would permit Sardinian annexation of Lombardy, Walewski placed Parma on the sacrificial altar as an offering to satisfy the Sardinians. "Permit me at this moment to suggest . . . another very acceptable combination," he wired urgently to Napoleon. "Lombardy to the Duchess of Parma; Parma and Piacenza to Piedmont [Sardinia]; Modena and Venice to an archduke."[84]

Eugénie apparently appreciated none of these diplomatic difficulties and saw only that her protégée was being plundered of her land. On the morning of July 12 Napoleon wired that he and Franz Joseph had agreed to permit Sardinia to annex both Lombardy and Parma with only a monetary indemnity for Louise. The furious reception that the Empress gave this information can be readily imagined from her blistering answer:

It is impossible for Parma to be joined to Piedmont; everybody will see in it an act of spoliation and will believe you are persecuting a woman of a race enemy to yours. I implore you in the name of your honor do not do such a thing.[85]

Napoleon excused himself lamely but made no change in his arrangements. "The telegraph is very dangerous as nothing can be explained," he offered by way of placation to Walewski.[86] In reply to his wife's outburst he sent: *"It is not I but the powers who will decide for Parma."*[87]

A few days earlier the Empress had made known her determination to go herself to Milan to meet the Emperor. Perhaps to forestall such a confrontation, Napoleon explained on July 7 that everything would soon be arranged, then he would be free to leave. "I fly to you," he sent over the wires in the familiar form of address.[88] If such were its intent his gallantry availed him little. The Empress was determined to fly to him, and quite evidently not on the wings of love. Three days later Walewski in effect asked the Emperor to forbid her departure because of the bad impression it would produce in Paris.[89]

---

telegram, Paris, July 12, 1859, 3:30 P.M., AMAE (Paris), Papiers Charles Robert, No. 17.

[84] Walewski to Napoleon, Paris, July 10, 1859, 8:00 P.M., AMAE (Paris), Papiers Charles Robert, No. 8.

[85] Eugénie to Napoleon, telegram, Saint-Cloud, July 12, 1859, 8:00 P.M., *ibid.*, No. 19.

[86] Napoleon to Walewski, telegram, Desenzano, July 13, 1859, draft in Napoleon's hand, *ibid.*, No. 20.

[87] Napoleon to Eugénie, July 13, 1859, draft in Napoleon's hand and underscored by him, *ibid.*, no number.

[88] "Je vole vers toi!" Valeggio, July 7, 1859, AMAE (Paris), Mémoires et documents, France, Vol. 2119, No. 45.

[89] Walewski to Napoleon, telegram, Paris, July 10, 1859, 2:39 P.M., *ibid.*, No. 69.

Emile Ollivier in his *L'Empire libéral* has explicitly denied the existence of any friction between Napoleon and Eugénie over her proposed trip. According to him she readily and docilely deferred to her husband's wish that she remain in Paris. Stories that the Empress wished to express her indignation over the Emperor's treatment of the Pope, he declared, were completely false.[90] Yet Ollivier could offer no feasible reason for the voyage. A pleasure trip must be entirely ruled out. Departure of the Regent from the capital for frivolous reasons when France was at war would have been a very serious matter—virtually a betrayal of trust. Walewski had pointed out this fact in his telegram to the Emperor: "She [the Empress] is Regent, and she ought not to leave the territory except for very exceptional reasons." Her absence would have rendered the whole idea of the Regency meaningless. All the evidence shows unmistakably that Eugénie had been neither light-minded nor casual about the war and her position as head of the government. Her messages to the front manifested her intense, not to say inordinate, interest in the problems arising from the invasion of Austrian territory. How completely unlikely that she would have wished, by a giddy junket, to demonstrate to Prince Napoleon and his friends that she was not a fit regent for her son. The trip must have had a serious even if injudicious purpose. Ollivier may have been right in one respect: the trip may have had little or no connection with the Pope. Napoleon had effectively quashed the protests of Regent and Foreign Minister over the presence of a Sardinian general in the Romagna earlier in July, and, by giving at least lip service to papal sovereignty there during his negotiations at Villafranca, he had put the issue on ice for a time. Yet Ollivier's version can not have been the whole truth. The telegrams preserved in the French Foreign Ministry attest to the sharp disagreement between Napoleon and Eugénie over the Duchy of Parma. We also know from another source that the Empress heaped recriminations on her husband upon his return to Paris.[91] Thus, since other motive for her voyage is wanting, it seems a reasonable assumption that her purpose was a forceful and face-to-face presentation of her arguments. How else explain her urge to throw over the Regency and expose herself to criticism? The censure which she was willing to risk is the measure of the intensity of her feeling for the cause of legitimate monarchy in Italy.

The fragmentary evidence does not tell us precisely when and why Eugénie relinquished her trip. Perhaps the objections of Walewski elicited

[90] Ollivier, *L'Empire libéral,* IV, 258. The Empress' proposed trip seems to have been one of the best-kept secrets of the reign. So far as I know, Ollivier's brief allusion to it is unique among published works. Not even the comprehensive recent biographies of the Empress of Kurtz and Desternes and Chandet mention it.

[91] Castillon du Perron, *La Princesse Mathilde,* p. 133.

a direct command from Napoleon. Perhaps the swiftness of the negotiations simply rendered the proposed trip useless. Possibly two, more likely three, days would have been required for passage from Paris to Milan. We know that on July 10 she was still determined to leave. But late in the evening of July 11 the Emperor wired that he had signed the peace and two days later tentatively fixed his departure from Italy for July 14.[92] By July 17 he was back in Paris.

The Empress had been utterly powerless to effect the restoration of Louise in Parma. True, the published terms of the Preliminaries of Villafranca did not award Parma outright to Sardinia and made no provision whatever for its future. But this minor victory was a concession to the scruples of Franz Joseph and not to the wishes of Eugénie and availed the Duchess nothing. As a matter of principle the Austrian Emperor was unwilling to put his name to a document which reserved the rights of the Dukes of Modena and Tuscany but signed away those of Louise. But he would concede privately what he would refuse to acknowledge openly, and, as Napoleon had wired, he agreed to raise no objection to the annexation of Parma to Sardinia. Abandoned by both Austria and France, the unfortunate Duchess remained in exile in Switzerland with her children until her death in 1864.

The terms agreed upon indicated the unfinished and indecisive character of the war. Austria gave up Lombardy, but, secure behind her Quadrilateral, retained Venetia. The Pope kept the Romagna but was to serve as honorary president of an Italian confederation and was to initiate a broad program of reforms in his states. Austria, as holder of Venetia, would be a member of the projected confederation. The rulers of Modena and Tuscany could return if they came without armed support and granted a general amnesty. France received nothing for her pains except the honor of bestowing Lombardy on Sardinia. Finally, a congress of the powers should convene to ratify a definitive settlement for the Italian question.

Napoleon later remarked that the occupation of Rome in 1849 was the only mistake of which he ever repented.[93] Yet surely the Italian War with its flaccid ending was another. He had managed to sow enough dissatisfaction in all quarters to render his way brambly indeed when his crop sprouted. His erstwhile allies, the Sardinians, were made sore by his concessions to Austria in central Italy and by his premature armis-

---

[92] Napoleon to Walewski, telegram, Valeggio, July 11, 1859, evening, AMAE (Paris), Mémoires et documents, France, Vol. 2119, No. 53; Napoleon to Eugénie, telegram, Desenzano, July 13, 1859, draft in his own hand, AMAE (Paris), Papiers Charles Robert, no number.

[93] Nigra to Cavour, July 13, 1860, *Il Carteggio Cavour-Nigra*, IV, No. 966.

tice, which left Venetia outside of their grasp. At the same time he had created what came to be called the "Venetian question," the bane of his diplomatic life until 1866. His belated and compulsive efforts to detach Venetia from Austria to fulfill his broken promise of 1858 to Sardinia at Plombières were to be the perfect foil for his simultaneous and equally strenuous exertions toward an Austro-French *rapprochement*. Consider also that he had raised his sails to the revolutionary winds in Italy, taken on board Cavour and Victor Emmanuel, apparently jettisoned clerical opinion in France, yet had been unable to detach his anchor from Rome. Finally, he abandoned ship with nothing tangible to show France except the lists of casualties and the moneys expended. Perhaps he had no alternative to these disserviceable terms unless he were prepared to fight a war on the Rhine. But the question of localizing the war should have been thoroughly plumbed in Berlin and Moscow with frankness and thorough understanding before the first French soldier had disembarked at Genoa.

It seems almost as if the French people sensed instinctively the trouble in store for the Empire. Napoleon's return was a sad contrast to his triumphant departure. No cheering crowds, no parades, no illuminated buildings greeted the victorious ruler as he slipped silently and inconspicuously into his capital. And at home he found an irate wife who created a public scene at their first meeting with the vehemence of her reproaches.[94] He had intended the Regency as an educational apprenticeship for the Empress in the craft which she might some day be required to practice in earnest, and as a demonstration to the French people of the solidarity of his dynasty. But in rebellion over his lessons on tolerance of attacks against legitimate monarchy in Italy, his student had advanced rapidly from docile neophyte to self-willed, argumentative mistress. In his own household no less than abroad he had opened up rifts which were in time to undermine the effectiveness of his foreign policy.

[94] Castillon du Perron, *La Princesse Mathilde*, p. 133.

CHAPTER 3

THE COLD WAR OF 1859–1861
The Triumph of the "Italianissimes"

THE ARGUMENT OVER THE PRELIMINARIES OF VILLAFRANCA

Scarcely had the preliminary peace terms been signed at Villafranca than the swift movement of events in the Italian peninsula seemed to render them obsolete. Within a few weeks after the armistice the army, the police, and the administration of all of north-central Italy were in the hands of the friends of Sardinia. In August and September the revolutionary, provisional governments in the Duchies and the Romagna elected representatives to assemblies which quickly, in defiance of the provisions of Villafranca, voted dethronement of their former rulers. By direct action they wiped out the major concessions made to Franz Joseph in July.

Napoleon had signed the peace preliminaries in apparent good faith, but he could not, or at least would not, contain the revolutionary trend. For weeks after Villafranca he irritated both former ally and enemy by his impenetrable irresolution. To the protests of the Austrians and his own Foreign Minister, who wanted to hold to the letter of the armistice terms, he proclaimed his embarrassment and helplessness; to the Sardinians he addressed Delphic statements which, while not dashing all hope of their annexation of the revolted provinces, restrained them from accepting them outright as their own.

In reality the Emperor was not drifting quite as purposelessly as he appeared to be. He well perceived that of all the terms of the peace preliminaries, the one the most dear to Franz Joseph, the one which was a point of honor to him, was the restoration of his house in Tuscany. On the other hand, Napoleon's own honor had been engaged, and, he felt, tarnished, in the Venetian question. When he had pulled up short in front of the Austrian Quadrilateral early in July he had broken his promise to Sardinia to free Italy from the Alps to the Adriatic. But what he had not accomplished by war, he might effect by diplomacy. By August he was scheming craftily to make use of the revolutionary government in Tuscany to disengage Venetia from Austria. Although he had once conceded the restoration of the Grand Duke, he now raised the price and made the Grand Duke's return contingent on fresh Austrian concessions in Venetia—concessions which would make that province a quasi-independent state with an Italian administration and army. As a sop to the Legitimist sympathizers in France, especially his wife, who was still harassing him about the Duchess of Parma, he would, if Franz Joseph would consent, give Modena to Louise and marry her son to the daughter of the sacrificed Duke of Modena.[1]

The request in August of the provisional government in Tuscany for annexation to Sardinia afforded Napoleon a strong lever to pry Venetia from Austria. If Franz Joseph held fast to Venetia the French Emperor, with a pious invocation of the principle of national self-determination, could calmly permit Victor Emmanuel to extend his rule over land rightfully belonging to a Habsburg. Quite expectedly, the Austrian government was outraged at this threat of a flagrant violation of the Preliminaries, signed so recently at Villafranca. The resentment was the greater since in Franz Joseph's opinion the revolution in Tuscany was the trumped-up concoction of the Sardinians that would rapidly disappear if left without outside support. The Austrian ambassador at Paris thus pronounced the French demands regarding Venetia totally unacceptable and threatened to break off negotiations.[2] The cold war began as diplomacy took over the Tuscan and Venetian questions left unfinished by the French Emperor's arms.

Napoleon's relations with his wife and his Foreign Minister were nearly as uncomfortable as those with the Austrians. Although no longer Regent, Eugénie had not relinquished her seat at the Council of Ministers and, deeply suspicious of Sardinian maneuvers, she sided resolutely with the

---

[1] At Villafranca it had been agreed that the position of Venetia in the Italian confederation would be like that of Luxemburg *vis-à-vis* the Germanic Confederation. This was Napoleon's justification for his new demands (Napoleon to Franz Joseph, August 1, 1859, copy, AMAE [Paris], Correspondance politique, Autriche, Vol. 474; Napoleon to Franz Joseph, Saint-Sauveur, August 26, 1859, copy, *ibid.*, Mémoires et documents, France, Vol. 2119). The first of these two letters proposed the settlement of the Grand Duke of Tuscany in Modena. Franz Joseph refused (Franz Joseph to Napoleon, August 2, 1859, copy, *ibid.*, Correspondance politique, Autriche, Vol. 474). For the Emperor's maneuvers see also Eugénie to Arese, Saint-Cloud, September, 1859, Carlo Pagani, "Napoleone III, Eugénie de Montijo e Francesco Arese in un carteggio inedito," *Nuova antologia*, CCX (1921), 25; Count Maurice Fleury, *Memoirs of the Empress Eugénie. Compiled from Statements, Private Documents, and Personal Letters* II, 52–53, 64–65.

[2] Metternich to Rechberg, telegrams, Paris, August 30, 1859, cypher, HHSA, IX/63, Nos. 15 and 16.

Austrophil Walewski.[3] She intervened directly when the Foreign Minister, in protest against Napoleon's intended violation of the Preliminaries of Villafranca, tendered his resignation. From Biarritz, Napoleon telegraphed his Minister: "I was going to write you a long letter, [but] the empress is opposed to it saying that a few minutes of conversation at Biarritz will better put us in agreement than all the correspondence in the world. Until then, a truce."[4] A second and more insistent invitation to Biarritz followed the next day. Relieved that he still had a chance to keep his portfolio, Walewski returned: "I am very, but very grateful to the empress; . . . We keenly hope to go to Biarritz at the first opportunity."[5] Late in September the Foreign Minister presented himself to his master and made temporary peace. The Emperor continued his pressure on Venetia but agreed for the moment that Sardinia should not be permitted to annex Tuscany. Retention of the pro-Austrian Walewski in office served merely to thicken the fog surrounding the Emperor's policy in the Italian peninsula. The Empress added a postscriptum to the episode in a word of warning to Walewski: "I advise you to stop this game; one of these days you may well be taken at your word."[6]

But the conversion of the Empress to the Austrophil position was not yet complete. Although she supported Walewski, she was not entirely convinced of the necessity of following the letter of the peace preliminaries. Like Napoleon, she hoped that Austria could be induced to detach herself from Venetia, and she understood and appreciated Napoleon's plan to make the restoration of the Grand Duke in Tuscany contingent on Austrian concessions. But whereas the Emperor blamed Austrian resistance, the Empress scolded the Sardinians for opposing the return of the Archduke and thus rendering Franz Joseph obdurate on Venetia. Early in September she wrote Francesco Arese, special emissary from the Sardinian court:

The motive of the emperor, at Villafranca and since, has been to obtain from Austria, without prolongation of the war, the complete independence of Italy. In other words, the emperor tried to make Venetia independent with the bait of the restoration of the archdukes. No one else in Italy has wanted to understand the profundity of this policy and instead of trusting in the

---

[3] In October the Sardinian minister at Paris wrote: ". . . you know that for some time the empress has been hostile to the policy of Cavour and that she applies herself a great deal to politics" (Des Ambrois to Dabormida, Paris, circa October 17, 1859, Luigi Chiala [ed.], *Lettere edite ed inedite di Camillo Cavour,* III, 297).

[4] Napoleon to Walewski, telegram, September 3, 1859, 12:10 p.m., Françoise Chalamon de Bernardy, "Un Fils de Napoléon: Le Comte Walewski, 1810–1868," MS, p. 622.

[5] Walewski to Napoleon, telegram, September 5, 1859, *ibid.,* pp. 627–628.

[6] Chalamon de Bernardy, "Le Comte Walewski," p. 627; Mme Jules Baroche, *Second Empire: Notes et souvenirs,* p. 133.

ITALY

Savoy

Tyrol

1859
Lombardy
Milan
Peschiera
Mantua

1866
Venetia
Verona
Legnago
Venice

Turin

Piedmont

Genoa

PARMA
1860

MODENA
1860

1860
Romagna

PAPAL

Nice

KINGDOM OF SARDINIA

Elba

TUSCANY
1860

Marches
1860

ADRIATIC

SEA

Umbria
1860

Corsica
(Fr.)

STATES

Rome
1870

Gaeta

KINGDOM

Naples

1860

Sardinia

OF THE

TYRRHENIAN SEA

TWO

SICILIES
1860

N

Territory ceded by Austria, 1859

Territory ceded by Austria, 1866

Territory ceded to France, 1860

■ Fortresses of the Quadrilateral

The dates are those of
annexation, first to Sardinia,
and after 1861, to Italy.

0   100   200

Scale in Miles   VMB

powerful hands which saved them from Austrian invasion, the Piedmontese [Sardinians] have preferred a policy of encroachment which has had the triple evil of placing France in a false position, of prolonging the hostility of Austria, Rome, and Naples, and of making the great powers of Europe uneasy.[7]

She was thus still trying to see both sides of the question but felt her temper rise at the despoilment of the Pope and the Archdukes and at the frustration of French plans for Venetia. Yet the arguments of Arese, an old friend of Napoleon's who exerted himself to please the Empress, had the power to move if not to convince. "I try *as hard as I can* to become Italian," she wrote to him in August after his visit at court; "[but] aren't you afraid of proving to Europe that the trade of saviours is a trade *of fools?*"[8]

It remained for Prince Richard von Metternich, special ambassador from Franz Joseph, to bring the Empress all the way around to the Austrian position. The choice of this personable son of the distinguished Austrian statesman for the post at Paris flattered Napoleon and Eugénie and was a clever move on the part of the Austrian government.[9] Having served as attaché to the Austrian embassy from 1850 to 1856, he was already well acquainted with the Emperor and the Empress and had attained an established position in French society. With his great name and wealth, his youth and good looks, he possessed the qualities which Hübner had lacked. His gifts for social repartee and for music—he was a facile composer of light waltzes and a better-than-average pianist—enabled him to shine in the drawing room. Possessed of a cool, analytical head and a steady set of nerves, he could tolerate the mercurial temperature of the French court and weather the worst upheavals. His aristocratic wife, Pauline, a granddaughter of old Metternich by his first marriage, with Eleanor, Princess von Kaunitz, contributed not a little to the success of her husband's mission.[10] Talented, witty, and irrepressible, she added sparkle to court society and quickly became one of the Empress' friends.

[7] Eugénie to Arese, Saint-Cloud, September, 1859, Pagani, "Napoleon III, Eugenia de Montijo e Francesco Arese," *Nuova antologia,* CCX (1921), 23.

[8] Eugénie to Arese, Saint-Sauveur, August 26, 1859, *ibid.,* p. 22; Count Joseph Grabinski, *Un Ami de Napoléon III: Le Comte Arese et la politique italienne sous le Second Empire,* p. 160.

[9] After the Preliminaries of Villafranca, Napoleon had requested that Metternich be sent to Paris (Fleury, *Memoirs,* II, 71). But Metternich had obviously been groomed for the post, having served as ablatus to Franz Joseph during the Italian War. He became the regular ambassador in December, 1859.

[10] Metternich reported that his wife wanted to have specific instructions as ambassadress. "She would like to be received with special amiability by the empress and has already sung for the emperor her repertoire of French . . . songs which he particularly likes" (Metternich to Rechberg, Paris, October 23, 1859, private, HHSA, IX/64).

Between them, the Metternichs staked out a privileged position in the imperial household that endured throughout the Empire and was the envy and sometimes the despair of other ambassadors.

Metternich perceived, long before any other diplomat assigned to the French court, how greatly the loquacious Empress could aid him in his task of interpreting the imperial mind and implanting in it views favorable to Austria. By treating the Empress as a personage of importance and by discussing foreign affairs with her he could often pick up valuable clues on future actions of the Emperor. She was, as he said, an excellent barometer of Napoleon's intentions. Moreover, he realized, and at first exaggerated, the influence which she could exert over her husband. No sooner did he arrive in Paris than he reviewed the situation in Italy with her and set to work to convert her to the Austrophil viewpoint.

His first political conversation with Eugénie must have severely taxed his *savoir faire* and acquainted him with the size of the task ahead. First he had to endure a play-by-play review of the recent war and join in a discussion of the strategy of the campaigns which had brought the armies of his own country to defeat. Next he had to listen to an account of the many obstacles in the path of the restoration of the Archdukes. On the other hand, he found it very significant that the Empress did not seem to oppose their use of force to win back their lost thrones. "If I were the young grand duke," she told him, "I would already be in Florence, sword in hand." He extracted this sentence from their conversation to wire ahead of his written report to Vienna.[11] In the Romagna as well the Empress foresaw great difficulty in the restoration of papal sovereignty, although she agreed with the ambassador that the resistance to papal authority was the result of well-organized intrigues emanating from Cavour. She closed with some complaints about the attitude of the German confederation during the war and with a jab at Prince Napoleon, whose agile footwork had kept him out of the shooting during the war. Metternich was amazed at the "thousand contradictions" which he had heard— "the mash of good intentions and impracticable notions, of sound reasoning and utopian phantasies"—and which he feared characterized imperial policy generally.[12]

Despite this discouraging beginning Metternich soon believed that he was making good progress. Two days after this conversation the young hereditary prince of Tuscany, Grand Duke Ferdinand, successor to the throne recently abdicated by his father, Leopold, appeared at the court in Paris to plead his cause. Metternich reported that the visit was having

[11] Metternich to Rechberg, telegram, Paris, August 12, 1859, cypher, HHSA, IX/63, No. 3.
[12] Metternich to Rechberg, Paris, August 13, 1859, HHSA, IX/63, No. 2.

a very "salutary effect" and that the Grand Duke was "much under the charm of the Emperor and especially *the Empress*."[13] The attraction must have been mutual, for Ferdinand went away much encouraged by the cordiality of his reception and the cheering words he had heard. Like Metternich, he perceived the value of the Empress' good will. After his departure he wrote to her of his eternal gratitude for her special kindness: "I beg Your Majesty to maintain these friendly intentions which are so precious to me in the misfortunes of my house, and I hope that she will be pleased to intercede with the Emperor whose protection seems providentially reserved to just causes and noble adversities."[14] Within a few weeks of this visit Metternich completed the conversion of the Empress. The ambassador believed that he had even succeeded in opening up a new and far more pleasant era in Austro-French relations.

The scene of his early triumph was Biarritz, the Empress' favorite seaside resort, close to the Spanish border. Metternich and his wife paid the court a long visit and worked hard at making themselves agreeable. The young ambassador did not hesitate to employ the distaff side to plead his cause with the Emperor on Italian affairs. He boasted: "Walewski works well, his wife and the empress help with all their force. . . . We are the whole day and half the night with the imperial couple and are overwhelmed with favors."[15]

But he found the Emperor almost obsessed with the Venetian question and had to listen to all manner of schemes whereby Austria could render Venetia independent and compensate herself elsewhere—perhaps in the Balkans, perhaps even in Egypt, the latter suggestion being the contribution of the Empress. The tactic employed on him was the pretense that Franz Joseph had made promises respecting the status of Venetia on which he was now reneging. Napoleon thus declared himself freed from any obligation toward the Archdukes.[16] With such pressure being exerted on him, Metternich was overjoyed to get at last the Emperor's signature on a confidential memorandum stipulating the return of Ferdinand to Tuscany without the outright cession of Venetia to an Italian confederation. By the terms of this memorandum, accepted by both countries, Austria was to give Venetia provincial assemblies and federal forces manned by Italian regiments. Franz Joseph agreed also to permit Francis of Modena to name the son of Louise of Parma as his successor. But these con-

[13] Metternich to Rechberg, Paris, August 16, 1859, HHSA, IX/63, No. 4 B; Metternich to Rechberg, August 17, private letter, HHSA, IX/64.

[14] Ferdinand to Eugénie, Munich, November 12, 1859, AA, c. 33–91.

[15] Metternich to Rechberg, Biarritz, September 23, 1859, private, HHSA, IX/64.

[16] Metternich to Rechberg, Biarritz, September 27, 1859, HHSA, IX/63, No. 11. For the various compensations suggested for Venetia see Metternich to Rechberg, September 27, 1859, private letter, HHSA, IX/64, and October 23, 1859, IX/63, No. 12 B.

cessions were made contingent on the restoration in Tuscany, for which Napoleon now promised to work. In addition, the French Emperor agreed to obtain the concurrence of Victor Emmanuel to the pacification of Italy on these terms.[17]

The ambassador regarded his signed memorandum as a veritable triumph for Austria. His elation was the greater as he thought, with youthful optimism, that the Emperor had now broken with the Italianissimes. "In seeking to pacify Italy, I have positively succeeded in pacifying the Emperor and in accustoming him to more correct and loyal ideas."[18] As for the Empress, he was certain that she had learned her lessons. After only a few days of exposure to his coaching she spoke an entirely different language, and, he exulted, she was visibly impressed when informed of Franz Joseph's gratitude for her good offices in securing right and justice in Italy. Upon Metternich's departure from Biarritz she questioned him significantly: "Are you more satisfied now?"[19]

The Prince had not yet learned his Napoleon, but he was not far off in his estimate of the Empress. The argument over Villafranca advanced her far along the road—away from the Italianissimes—which she had been travelling since the beginning of the Italian War. Her Austrophilism was now the antipode of her earlier infatuation with Orsini. In the space of approximately eighteen months she had passed from positive encouragement of revolution in Italy to declared hostility to Sardinian intervention in the Romagna and Parma. Now she was not only anti-Sardinian but also pro-Austrian and extended her hand in friendship to the recent enemy of France. As she had picked up the cudgels for Louise of Parma she now commenced battle for the restoration of a Habsburg grand duke. As the scene of the dispute moved from Biarritz to Compiègne with the French court in November, the Empress was a loyal and effective ally of the Austrian ambassador.

"THE BATTLE OF COMPIÈGNE"

The Prince's victory made possible the conclusion of the negotiations on the final peace treaty then in progress at Zurich. Signed on November 10, the treaty was the embodiment of the agreements hammered out at Villafranca and Biarritz. But Metternich soon found out that his was a fool's paradise. The first hint of trouble came even before the conclusion of the

---

[17] Metternich to Rechberg, telegram, September 26, HHSA, IX/63, No. 30. The terms are summarized by Charles W. Hallberg, *Franz Joseph and Napoleon III, 1852–1864: A Study of Austro-French Relations,* pp. 208–209.

[18] Metternich to Rechberg, Biarritz, September 27, 1859, private letter, HHSA, IX/64.

[19] Metternich to Rechberg, Paris, October 23, 1859, HHSA, IX/63, No. 12 B.

treaty. A letter from Napoleon to Victor Emmanuel on November 1 in the *Constitutionnel,* organ of the French Foreign Ministry, defended the Italian cause. Although the French Emperor dismissed it as of no importance—merely a gesture to quiet the Sardinians—Metternich was uneasy. Could the Emperor be playing a double or even a triple game?

Napoleon was preparing to change his tack. The Biarritz memorandum had been as disagreeable to the Emperor as it had been satisfying to Metternich. Especially galling was the meagerness of Austrian concessions on Venetia. Having failed to wrench Venetia from Franz Joseph by his diplomacy, he lost all interest in the restoration of Grand Duke Ferdinand. He perceived that he might permit Sardinia to annex the Duchies and the Romagna, and exact something for France in the bargain. Sardinia with Tuscany should be Sardinia without Nice and Savoy. A reward for France would increase his popularity at home and perhaps go a long way toward reconciling the clericals to the Pope's loss of the Romagna.[20]

The moment for putting over the helm for the new course came in November. The Duchies and the Romagna had combined under Prince Carignano, brother of Victor Emmanuel, and were requesting the King to accept the Prince as his regent. If Napoleon condoned the regency, as he seemed inclined to do, he would have agreed in effect to the Sardinian annexation of central Italy and have abandoned the terms of his memorandum and of the Treaty of Zurich.

The question was in this critical stage when Metternich descended on Compiègne prepared to do battle with the Emperor. As at Biarritz he did not hesitate to employ the Empress in his behalf, and to his joy he found that she had prepared the ground for him. Like Walewski, Eugénie looked longingly at Savoy; but she felt honor-bound by the terms of the memorandum. She informed Metternich that his arguments at Biarritz had greatly impressed her and that she had at the time taken as her motto: "I do what I must, come what may!" ("Fais ce que dois, advienne que pourra!") She resolutely averted her eyes from Nice and Savoy and insisted on the terms of the signed memorandum. Forbidden to talk politics with Metternich at Compiègne by orders "from higher up," she managed to let him know through Walewski that the Emperor, despite his vacillation, would "remain true." The ambassador should not hesitate to "speak right up" to the Emperor.[21]

[20] Lynn M. Case, *French Opinion on War and Diplomacy during the Second Empire,* pp. 118–123.

[21] The account of the Empress' intercession and of Metternich's subsequent interview with Napoleon is taken from a private letter from Metternich to Rechberg (Paris, November 15, 1859, HHSA, IX/64) and a report of Metternich to Rechberg (Paris, November 16, 1859, HHSA, IX/63, No. 16 A–B).

Encouraged by the tip, Metternich acted on it with a boldness approximating rashness and created one of the most perilous moments of the cold war. "I owe it to my iron constitution that I was not struck down by apoplexy," wrote Metternich of the scene in the Emperor's study. He voiced the Austrian position in plain terms. If France should permit Victor Emmanuel to accept Carignano's regency, and if the King moved to intervene in central Italy, Austria would not confine herself to protests but would *act* to save the terms of Villafranca. With menacing intent, Napoleon countered that any such action would cause French retaliation and resumption of war.

Metternich then pushed to the brink. "Better to begin the war again," he asserted, *"war even with France,"* than for Austria to accept *faits accomplis* provoked by enemy influence.

One can readily imagine the excruciating anxiety of the inexperienced ambassador in the silence that followed. Had he overstepped, by listening to the Empress' advice, and exposed Austria again to French gunpowder?

But the Empress had been right after all. Napoleon let lie the gage thrown down and tried diversionary tactics. Had the ambassador seen the map of Europe "invented by *je ne sais qui*" which placed Egypt under Austrian sovereignty? The idea struck him as a rather good one. But Metternich refused to be drawn into a discussion of what was obviously intended as a renewed attempt to strike a bargain on Venetia. He tenaciously came back to central Italy and Carignano's regency. In vain the Emperor tried to shake him off and dismiss him. Finally, since all alternatives except war had apparently been exhausted, Napoleon yielded. "All right," he conceded, "I will write to the king to refuse [the regency]," and closed with a quotation from his wife's favorite motto: "advienne que pourra." Evidently Eugénie's arguments had produced their effect.

Metternich emerged from the study in an exhilarated daze. "My excitement was shared by the entire court and . . . every eye was directed at me and I heard from right and left the words 'did he succeed? Yes, no, et cetera,' really a melodramatic scene." The very next day before Metternich left Compiègne, Napoleon showed him the despatch he had sent Victor Emmanuel in which he had threatened to abandon him if he accepted his brother's regency. Count Walewski meanwhile drew up a note for the *Moniteur* and a diplomatic circular to confirm this statement of policy.

The jubilation of Metternich, Walewski, and Eugénie was cut short by the farcical manner by which Victor Emmanuel complied with the Emperor's wish. Instead of Carignano as his regent, the King accepted Carlo Boncompagni, a patriot well known to favor annexation of central

Italy to Sardinia. He was to act as a sort of deputy for a deputy. Once again the Austrians had been fooled.

In haste Metternich returned to the fray at Compiègne to marshal his forces. But he found Walewski in despair. The Foreign Minister regarded the Biarritz memorandum as hopelessly compromised and a congress of the powers to ratify the Zurich treaty a vanishing dream.[22] Napoleon was thinking only of Nice and Savoy. The Emperor told Metternich that he saw only two alternatives: either restore the Archdukes by force, or detach Venetia from Austria, make an independent kingdom in central Italy, and find compensation for Austria elsewhere. But since he was pledged not to do the first, and Austria refused to consider the second, he could see no way out of the impasse. Metternich comprehended that the Emperor was humoring Sardinia on the regency in central Italy in order to extract compensation for France.[23]

Despondent at the apparent hopelessness of the situation he turned again to the Empress and to her gave full credit for his rescue. True, the form of rescue was not all that he could have desired. Worn down by Eugénie's insistence on the sanctity of signed agreements, the Emperor reluctantly signed a postscriptum to the now famous memorandum in which he pledged himself to uphold the terms to which he had earlier put his signature. It was a pledge to honor a former pledge, and as such seemed rather absurd. Metternich was not entirely satisfied with the result, but he relied on it at least to paralyze the effect of the Boncompagni regency. It had been obtained, he reported, only by the greatest effort and through the persistence with which the Empress had held to her arguments. He concluded: "The empress decidedly is completely converted to our viewpoint. It is she who determined the emperor to cede on the question of the Post Scriptum, and her language *at the council* [of ministers] is perfectly correct."[24] As he took his leave, he thanked her profusely for her intercession in his behalf.

"THE POPE AND THE CONGRESS"

If the Austrian ambassador believed Eugénie capable of effecting a sincere conversion of her husband to a more conservative, pro-Austrian outlook, he was quickly disappointed. No sooner did he arrive in Paris than the roller-coaster on which he had been riding during the fall took its steepest plunge

---

[22] Metternich to Rechberg, telegram, Paris, November 25, 1859, HHSA, IX/63, No. 72.

[23] Metternich to Rechberg, Paris, November 26, 1859, *very secret*, HHSA, IX/63, No. 18 A–B.

[24] Metternich to Rechberg, Paris, November 26, 1859, private, HHSA, IX/64.

yet. The *Moniteur* ceased its backing and filling, suddenly resumed its "ultra Italian tone," and announced that Victor Emmanuel had accepted Carignano's regency.[25] On the heels of this "utter defeat" followed another blow—the publication on December 22 of *Le Pape et le congrès*. The brochure was detestable from the Austrian point of view for its advocacy of the reduction of the temporal power of the Pope and by its implied sanction of the revolutionary forces in central Italy. The Emperor had not himself written the pamphlet; but no one in diplomatic circles had the slightest doubt of its official origin and its real significance.[26]

Napoleon had decided to end the futile bargaining *à trois* and was openly turning into the wind for this new tack. He was now ready to concede the Duchies and even the Romagna to Sardinia at the price of Nice and Savoy for France.[27] A change in personnel underlined the change in policy. On January 4 the Emperor at last accepted the resignation of Walewski and replaced him in the Foreign Ministry with Edouard Thouvenel, known to be one of the Italianissimes.[28] A new French ambassador, the Marquis of Moustier, arrived in Vienna almost simultaneously with the news of *Le Pape et le congrès*. An opponent of Austrian influence in Italy and unencumbered by the pledges of his predecessor, he serenely explained the

[25] Metternich to Rechberg, Paris, November 26, 1859, HHSA, IX/63, No. 18 B.

[26] The author was A. de La Guéronnière, a well-known ghost writer for the Emperor. Napoleon admitted that the ideas in the pamphlet were his own, and refused to disavow them. Metternich noted that it had appeared without stamps and without previous deposition with the government—a sure sign of its official status. Millions of copies circulated simultaneously across Europe, indicating careful previous preparation (Metternich to Rechberg, Paris, December 28, 1859, private, HHSA, IX/64; Metternich to Rechberg, December 27, 1859, reserved, HHSA, IX/63, No. 24; telegram, December 30, 1859, HHSA, IX/63, No. 90; and telegram, December 31, 1859, *ibid.*). See also Memorandum of a conversation with the Emperor, January 1, 1860, communicated to Lord John Russell by Cowley, January 6, 1860, PRO 519/226; Case, *French Opinion on War*, pp. 110–112; and Hallberg, *Franz Joseph and Napoleon III*, p. 215.

[27] Although apparently many tergiversations on imperial policy took place in the early months of 1860 (see Hallberg, *Franz Joseph and Napoleon III*, pp. 216–229), including a plan which evidently offered again to restore the Grand Duke to Tuscany, the French determination to trade central Italy for Nice and Savoy remained generally unshaken. In Vienna the new French ambassador told Rechberg that plebiscites should determine the future of the Duchies and Romagna. France asked Austria not to interfere in Italy and in return promised not to support a Sardinian attack on Venetia. See Moustier to Thouvenel, Vienna, February 4, 1860, AMAE (Paris), Correspondance politique, Autriche, Vol. 476, No. 12. See also Thouvenel to Moustier, February 9, 1860, *ibid.*, No. 18; Moustier to Thouvenel, February 11, 1860, *ibid.*, No. 13; and Rechberg to Metternich, Vienna, February 17, 1860, copy, *ibid.*

[28] Thouvenel believed Italy should "be allowed to go her own way," and was opposed to the convocation of a European congress, earlier agreed upon between Austria and France (Cowley to Lord John Russell, Paris, January 25, 1860, copy, PRO FO 519/226).

new line of policy to an unsmiling Count Rechberg, Austrian Foreign Minister. Austro-French relations chilled appreciably.

The imperial ghost writer of the brochure argued that for the good of the Papacy, for the very welfare of the Pope, the size of the temporal holdings should be reduced. "The smaller is his territory, the greater will be the sovereign." The Romagna, awarded to the Pope by the treaties of 1815, should be independent. Rome, of course, should stay under the Pope, but with its own municipal government, protected by an army of the Italian federation, and subsidized by contributions of the Catholic powers. The pamphlet was vague on the future of Umbria and the Marches; but a strict application of its logic implied further accretion of power to the Holy Father should he lose those territories as well. Furthermore, the pamphlet gave the *coup de grâce* to the hopes of Ferdinand and company. In stating that France herself would not intervene in Italy or permit Austria or Naples to do so, it ruled out the employment of force to restore the Archduke and let stand the Sardinian-controlled provisional governments. The new ambassador at Vienna neatly summarized the implications in the change in policy: "[It amounts to] nothing less than your giving us [France] *carte blanche* in Italy in return for the salvation of Venetia."[29]

The Emperor had concealed his intentions not only from the Austrians but from his wife as well until the publication of the pamphlet. Her first reaction was one of disbelief. She proclaimed to any who would listen that the Emperor had no connection with this "impious" work which negated the sermons she had apparently preached so successfully at Compiègne.[30] Aware of the Pope's resistance to any reforms in his government and keenly sensitive to the indignant clerical protest aroused by the brochure, she feared an open break with Rome and the alienation of the clericals from the Empire. But helpless to combat the new trend, she could neither persuade the Emperor to disavow the pamphlet nor save Walewski in the Foreign Ministry.[31] On December 31 the Emperor wrote a letter to the Pope in which he advised him to relinquish the disaffected province.[32] On his part, Pius IX denounced the "ignoble tissue of contradictions" of the pamphlet and declared in an encyclical on January 19 that he would suffer torture and death rather than acquiesce to the loss of even part of his temporal power. The conflict between Empire and Papacy was squarely joined. The

[29] Moustier to Thouvenel, Vienna, February 4, 1860, AMAE (Paris), Correspondance politique, Autriche, Vol. 476, No. 12.

[30] Metternich to Rechberg, Paris, December 28, 1859, private, HHSA, IX/64; Metternich to Rechberg, telegram, Fontainebleau, December 30, 1859, *ibid.*, No. 90.

[31] Fleury, *Memoirs*, II, 78–80; Chalamon de Bernardy, "Le Comte Walewski," pp. 645–646.

[32] Napoleon to Pius IX, Paris, December 31, 1859, *Moniteur*, January 11, 1860.

projected European congress which was to have settled the affairs of Italy was indefinitely postponed.

Grieved at this rupture, Eugénie was yet blind to the far-reaching implications in the pamphlet—the insinuation that the Pope should give up *all* of his territory except Rome and subsist on the charity of the Catholic powers. To her sister, who had apparently written her in anguished protest against the pamphlet, she replied: ". . . I see by your letter that you have not *read* it [the pamphlet]." Neither had the Empress, if one may judge by her letter; or perhaps she read *into* it a soothing but false interpretation arising from her own wishes or from suggestions made by those anxious to abate her wrath. She wrote:

The point made is not to take away the temporal power from the Holy Father but rather, since he can retain the Legations [Romagna] only by force, would it not be better to indemnify the pope and leave this part of his territory which he has held *only since the treaties of 1815* outside of the rest, which would make him stronger in his remaining state [Marches, Umbria, and Rome]?

On the other hand, her comprehension of the obstacles in the path of restoration in central Italy was good. She complained:

Here is the congress postponed to I don't know when, and yet the more time passes the more difficult a solution becomes, for to return a province to obedience there are only two means: one, that of wise concessions *made at the right time,* which is past; the other, the use of force, and that seems difficult to me, for *who* would use it? The Austrians can not according to the treaty of Zurich, we can't without being inconsistent, the Holy Father has no army, Spain can't fly in the face of the whole world.

But exposition did not carry with it her endorsement of the proposed solution. "I merely explain the pamphlet to you; as for myself, I pray that the whole world may be imbued with the spirit of the Gospel." Her heart was breaking, she continued, over the complications forthcoming over the states of the Church. ". . . What will come of it all? God only knows, but I only ask with all my heart that the Emperor may not have the responsibility for it."[33]

COMPLICATIONS AT HOME

The change in direction of imperial policy meant a temporary eclipse of the influence of the Empress on foreign policy. Her voice and that of the few remaining Austrophils in the government went almost unheard and

[33] Eugénie to Duchess of Alba, January 14, 1860, Empress Eugénie, *Lettres familières de l'Impératrice Eugénie conservées dans les archives du Palais de Liria et publiées par les soins du Duc d'Albe avec le concours de F. de Llanos y Torriglia et Pierre Josserand,* I, 166–167.

always unheeded for many months. Walewski's resignation had been a heavy blow. Thouvenel, former ambassador at Constantinople, was virtually a stranger to her. Closer acquaintance brought no meeting of minds. Her *tête-à-têtes* with Metternich, too, were abruptly cut off. Having observed the effectiveness of the Prince's arguments in molding his wife's views, the Emperor forbade her to talk politics with him. Aware of this interdict, Metternich was careful not to give offense to the Emperor. Moreover, the inexperienced ambassador felt that he had blundered badly in having placed too much faith in the influence of the Empress and thus having failed to read correctly the Emperor's mind. The optimistic predictions of his earlier reports came back to mock him now that they had proved unjustified. Either his government would believe him "unpardonably ignorant," he apologized, or would conclude that the Emperor had acted in deliberate bad faith.[34] For some time he was only too willing to confine his conversations with Eugénie to social chitchat.

Personal concerns also tended to divert the Empress' attention away from affairs of state in the spring of 1860. Her sister, the Duchess of Alba, suffering from a mysterious ailment of the spine, took an alarming turn for the worse. Yielding to Eugénie's wishes, she left Madrid to install herself in her luxurious residence on the Champs Elysées. Nearly every day during the spring the two sisters drove through the Bois de Boulogne in a carriage especially designed to accommodate the invalid. The Empress' own health was affected by her anxiety. By August, *très souffrante,* she was obliged to spend several weeks at Eaux-Bonnes for rest and a course of the thermal waters.[35]

Another cause for her temporary retirement from the political scene was the Carlist revolt in Spain. Early in April, Don Jaime Ortega, captain general of the Balearic Islands, landed at San Carlos with a handful of troops, composed of many of the bluebloods of Spain, in a vain attempt to overthrow Isabella and establish the Count of Montemolín as Carlos VI on the throne. The insurrection would have amounted to little, as it was easily

[34] Metternich to Rechberg, Paris, January 3, 1860, HHSA, IX/65, No. 1 A–D. The Empress did not resume political conversations with Metternich until January 25, 1861, and then only with the express permission of the Emperor. On that occasion Metternich wrote:

"You know, sir, that I have known the Empress since and even before her marriage and that H[er] M[ajesty] . . . has always shown me a sincere and genuine friendship which she has shared with my wife since my arrival in Paris in 1859.

"The closeness of our relations has been in fact an obstacle to my political interests, as the Emperor, after the scenes I had with the Empress at St. Sauveur when she flew at me because of our Italian policy, forbade her to talk of diplomatic subjects with me" (Metternich to Rechberg, Paris, January 25, 1861, secret, *ibid.*, Nachlass Rechberg).

[35] Baroche, *Second Empire,* p. 159.

and instantly quelled, except for the fact that a number of Eugénie's cousins, descendants of her father's sisters, were among the insurgents taken prisoner. The French representative in Madrid wrote to Thouvenel:

Public opinion is keenly aroused over the presumed complicity almost proved and over the arrests of several members of the family of H. M. the Empress— up to the present there are M. de la Romana, his two brothers, General Elío, and D. F. Cabero, all five relatives of some degree of Her Majesty. It is said that other members of the same family are also compromised, and they cite, among others, the M[arquis] of Villafranca and his son, the Duke of Fernandina, but for these last two, may a merciful God grant that it is only the fertile *imagination Madrilène* in play.[36]

Two sisters of the captives were among the Empress' ladies in Paris.[37] With their wails resounding in her ears she begged the Queen by telegraph for mercy. Leaving no stone unturned she applied to Cowley and to all the ambassadors of the major powers for the influence of their governments in behalf of the prisoners. She urgently advised her sister, who had not yet departed for Paris, that she should band together the other relatives of the prisoners and that they should then present themselves en masse to the Queen. "What may be refused to an individual will not be denied to the first twenty families of the country," she wrote.[38]

The Empress' many efforts had their desired effect. Although Isabella condemned Ortega and many of the other insurgents to death, she released the venturous relatives of her sister sovereign. Yet the episode was an embarrassment to Eugénie, and even to Napoleon, in a number of ways. Carlists were known for their rigid religious orthodoxy and their firm belief in the divine right of kings. They were more Catholic than the Pope and more Legitimist than the reigning Bourbons. Inevitably, many people now supposed that the Empress too was a Carlist. The prominence of the Spaniards in the French court, the Empress' championship of the Duchess of Parma, a close relative of the Count of Montemolín, her friendship with

[36] Barrot to Thouvenel, Madrid, April 10, 1860, private and very confidential, AMAE (Paris), Papiers Thouvenel, III. Villafranca was the husband of Eugénie's aunt, María Tomasa, on her father's side. Don Francisco Cabero y Álvarez de Toledo was the grandson of María Tomasa. He was aide-de-camp of Ortega. Don Joaquin Elío y Ezpeleta, Cabero's brother, was the Secretary of State of the Count of Montemolín.
[37] The Countess of Fuentes, sister of Cabero, and the sister of Elío.
[38] Eugénie to Duchess of Alba, April 8, 1860, *Lettres familières*, I, 168–169; Cowley to Lord John Russell, Paris, April 9, 1860, copy, PRO FO 519/227. The ministers from Russia, Prussia, England, and Austria asked the Queen to spare the lives of the Empress' relatives, but to the disappointment of the French minister in Madrid, made it clear they had acted on Eugénie's request and not on instructions from their respective governments (Barrot to Thouvenel, Madrid, April 15, 1860, private. AMAE [Paris], Papiers Thouvenel, III). See also F. de Llanos y Torriglia, *María Manuela Kirkpatrick, Condesa del Montijo, la gran dama*, pp. 183–185.

the Duchess of Hamilton, a declared Carlist, her concern for clerical opinion in France, and her support of Legitimist principles—all seemed to point to this conclusion. It was a case of guilt by association.

Nor was the supposition without its grain of truth. Unquestionably Eugénie had not conspired against Isabella's throne and had no connection with Ortega's revolt; but she felt genuine sympathy and affection for individuals among the insurgents. If she considered them misguided and impractical, she did not class them as traitors or criminals. Her most censorious term reserved for them was "those unfortunate madcaps" ("ces malheureux fous").[39] She admired their courage in captivity and was indignant at the "furia constitutionelle" of the Queen's advisers which prompted the sovereign to pronounce the death sentence on the leaders of the revolt.[40] There was a warm spot in her heart for these proud, reckless aristocrats, members of Spain's finest families, who would risk their lives in the spirit of *noblesse oblige*. Soon they were to figure in the Empress' hopes and plans for the establishment of monarchy in Mexico.

Matters were not helped by the indiscreet actions of the Countess of Montijo in Madrid. The meddling old lady was known to have flirted with Carlism for years in cities across Europe. Now it was found that she had opened her home to Ortega and had received him even when he was in disgrace at court because of his Carlist associations. She was one of the loudest in pleading his cause with Isabella after his capture. Rumors were flying about Madrid that she had actually been in collusion with the Carlist captain and that she had lent her hand to his plot. The French minister at Madrid found himself in a very delicate position. He dared not bring the behavior of the mother to the attention of the august daughter, yet he worried over the effect of the town talk on Franco-Spanish relations.[41]

The minister's alarm was well justified. Ever since the Italian War and especially after the publication of *Le Pape et le congrès*, Isabella had strongly opposed French policy in Italy. She had protested the overthrow of Louise of Parma and wanted to send troops to the aid of the Pope. Only the preceding February the Emperor had been obliged to let her know that he would regard such action as intolerable to France.[42] Now it was being said, perhaps even by the Queen herself, that the Emperor had engineered the Carlist plot either to prevent Spanish action in Rome, or, still more

[39] Eugénie to Duchess of Alba, April 8, 1860, *Lettres familières*, I, 168; Eugénie to Duchess of Alba, April 18, 1860, *ibid.*, pp. 169–170.

[40] Metternich to Rechberg, Paris, April 23, 1860, private, HHSA, IX/68, *varia*.

[41] Barrot to Thouvenel, Madrid, April 10, 1860, private and very confidential, AMAE (Paris), Papiers Thouvenel, III. On the eve of the execution of his sentence Ortega wrote the Countess a letter in which he expressed his gratitude for her efforts (Llanos y Torriglia, *María Manuela Kirkpatrick*, pp. 184–185).

[42] Cowley to Lord John Russell, Paris, February 10, 1860, copy PRO FO 519/227.

startling, as a preparatory move to seize the Balearic Islands in the Mediterranean for France.[43]

If these accusations were irritating to Napoleon, they were doubly so to Eugénie. Her cherished hope was for an alliance between France and Spain, which would raise the prestige of Spain and would tie France to a more conservative policy in Italy. To mend the fences between the two countries damaged by the recriminations over the Ortega revolt, she again asked Napoleon to raise Spain to a power of the first rank by demanding her presence in the councils of Europe.[44]

Inexplicably, the Emperor acquiesced and took the initiative in broaching the question with the other powers after Spain expressed her willingness to assume the duties and responsibilities of such a position. Austria, of course, welcomed the addition of anti-Sardinian, propapal, Catholic Spain in the councils of Europe. Russia and Prussia apparently raised no obstacle. But the Emperor must certainly have expected England's veto and the annoying political repercussions the *démarche* would bring. The Spanish, galled by Britain's attitude, blamed Napoleon for their exposure to this humiliation. The British ambassador thought he detected "the cloven hoof" in Catholic Austria's cooperation. Napoleon seemed to be working at cross purposes in his simultaneous sponsorship of both conservative Spain and revolutionary Sardinia.[45]

The Ortega revolt and its diplomatic aftermath amounted merely to a dismal little tempest in a teapot and an insignificant zigzag in Napoleon's wake; but it was politically disastrous for Eugénie. Her "papistical," Legitimist proclivities were underlined and exaggerated. Her influence at low ebb, she quarrelled bitterly with the Emperor and watched in impotent rage the beginning of Garibaldi's expedition to Sicily to attack still another of the legitimate thrones of the Italian peninsula.

ANNEXATION OF NICE AND SAVOY: AN IDYLLIC INTERLUDE

On only one question did Eugénie find herself in complete harmony with the imperial policy in the spring of 1860—French annexation of Nice and Savoy. Since Sardinia was to have the Duchies and the Romagna, she was as eager as anyone to extract a *quid pro quo* for France. The memorandum,

[43] Cowley to Buchanan, Paris, April 12, 1860, copy, PRO FO 519/227; Lord John Russell to Cowley, October 26, 1860, *ibid.*, 519/198; Barrot to Thouvenel, Madrid, April 10, 1860, private and very confidential, AMAE (Paris), Papiers Thouvenel, III; *Lettres familières*, I, 259 n.

[44] Eugénie to Duchess of Alba, Tuileries, May 16, 1860. *Lettres familières*, I, 171.

[45] Cowley to Lord John Russell, Paris, May 21, 1860, copy, PRO FO 519/227. See also Barrot to Thouvenel, Madrid, June 17, 1860, private, AMAE (Paris), Papiers Thouvenel, III; Barrot to Thouvenel, LaGranaja, August 20, 1860, *ibid.*

which she had earlier felt obliged to honor, was a discarded scrap of paper. The Treaty of Turin of March 24, stipulating cession of Nice and Savoy to France with plebiscites to determine the wishes of the population, afforded her real pleasure. For a short time she viewed even Cavour with gracious benignancy and told the delighted young Sardinian chargé d'affaires, Count Nigra: "I was wrong to bear a grudge against Count Cavour. I have altogether changed my mind about him."[46]

But the annexation of Nice and Savoy was not the only reason for the Empress' forgiving mood. The preceding February, Cavour had hand-picked Nigra for the post in Paris with instruction to make himself charming to the Empress and counter the only-too-effective persuasions of Metternich. The winsome, gallant Italian, with his graceful manners, had proved a happy choice. Delighted with the progress report he received from Paris, Cavour added a few words of advice on the conduct of the courtship.

Evidently she wants to seduce you. Let her do it. Don't play the *Joseph* too much. In the long run her influence could be harmful to us. You must neglect nothing to make her favorable to us. Tell her over and over again that we other Italians find her charming. As for the rest, it seems to me you have no need of instruction.[47]

The official transfer of the areas took place on June 14, 1860, and was followed by a splendid imperial tour of the newly-French provinces. "It was not a journey; it was a triumphal progress," which the Empress later recalled as one of the most brilliant and moving events of her reign.[48] As they travelled southward from Paris a tumultuous and enthusiastic crowd met them at every turn. Despite the fatigue occasioned by the incessant travel and the inevitable banquet and ball at each town, she beamed with pleasure during the continuous choruses of "Vive l'Empereur" and "Vive l'Impératrice."[49] Savoy especially enchanted her with its rugged mountains and beautiful lakes. The benefits of imperial administration, she predicted, would soon restore the economic health of this magnificent land which asked only to join itself completely to the French Empire.[50]

If the Empress had only realized what was taking place under her nose

[46] Nigra to Cavour, Paris, May 2, 1860, *Il Carteggio Cavour-Nigra*, III, 279.

[47] Cavour to Nigra, Turin, May 9, 1860, *ibid.*, III, 290.

[48] George Maurice Paléologue, *The Tragic Empress: A Record of Intimate Talks with the Empress Eugénie, 1901–1919*, p. 15.

[49] The emotions of the Empress are clearly reflected in the many letters she wrote to her sister during the course of this trip. Although tender and solicitous of the health of the invalid, they record her great satisfaction and joy over the acclamation of the people (August 23, August 25, August 30, September 4, September 6, September 9, 1860, *Lettres familières*, I, 175–184).

[50] Eugénie to Duchess of Alba, Annecy, August 30, 1860, *ibid.*, p. 177.

while she was innocently delighting in the splendid scenery, she would have been less radiant over the voyage. One stop of the imperial cortege in Savoy was at the town of Chambéry. There Napoleon and Eugénie found Luigi Farini and General Cialdini, emissaries from Cavour, waiting to greet them. Ostensibly their mission was one of simple courtesy; in reality they were come to seek the Emperor's permission for Sardinian occupation of the Marches and Umbria, states of the Pope, and for a Sardinian march toward Naples. In a private interview with Napoleon they succeeded beyond even their own hopes, which were not modest. "The Emperor was perfect," as Cavour later wrote, and with few reservations readily acquiesced to the entire bold scheme.[51]

But the Empress was mercifully unaware that her husband that day had paved the way for the enormous Sardinian annexations which were to bring into existence a unified Italian state in 1861. Still aglow over the friendly spontaneity of the people, she gaily sat through the festive banquet in the evening, Farini on her left, Cialdini on her right.[52] Cavour was later told that the impressionable and mercurial sovereign, charmed with her beautiful Savoy, had entirely recovered from her former prejudices against him.[53] The imperial tour must have convinced Napoleon that he had been correct in thinking that an aggrandizement of territory would overcome the dissatisfaction of the French public over the Italian War. Now it appeared that aggrandizement had had equally as salutary a result in his own ménage.

FRUSTRATION AND FLIGHT

The glorious tour had an abrupt and tragic ending for the Empress. From Savoy the cortege had travelled to Marseilles and embarked for Algiers and a week of galas. While the Empress was reviewing the troops, riding sidesaddle à la Queen Victoria in a vastly becoming uniform of the Imperial Guard tailored especially for the occasion, and dancing at the great balls in her honor, the Duchess of Alba died in Paris. Napoleon received word of her death a day later, on September 17, but, wishing to spare his wife during the unavoidable ceremonies, concealed the knowledge from her. When their ship put in at Marseilles on September 22 she at last learned the truth and fell into a wild and despondent grief.

She had not even the sad consolation of arranging and attending the funeral of her sister. Before her arrival in Paris the Minister of State, Achille Fould, had supervised a modest ceremony totally unbefitting—at

[51] Cavour to Nigra, August 29, 1860, Chiala, *Lettere,* VI, 582.
[52] Harold Kurtz, *The Empress Eugénie, 1826–1920,* p. 151.
[53] Cavour to Nigra, Turin, September 5, 1860, *Carteggio Cavour-Nigra,* IV, 194.

least in the Empress' view—the august rank of the deceased. For days Eugénie exhausted herself in prayers and tears at the side of the Duchess' coffin at its temporary resting place in the little church at Rueil, where lay Josephine and her daughter, Hortense. The Empress' morbidity was such that Napoleon, alarmed for her physical and mental health, overrode her pleas for delay, and urged the Duke of Alba to hasten the transportation of the body to its final burial place in Spain. It was the beginning of an anguishing autumn.[54]

The death of the Duchess coincided with the high noon of Napoleon's support of revolution in Italy. After the Emperor had given the Sardinians a green light at Chambéry they had moved swiftly. In mid September they routed the papal troops, led by the Legitimist General Lamoricière, and moved to occupy the Marches and Umbria. The Pope, now in possession of only the Patrimony of St. Peter, proclaimed himself abandoned and loudly threatened to dramatize his martyrdom by flight from the city. Farther to the south "the thousand" of the great Italian patriot Garibaldi had evicted the Bourbon Francis II from his Neapolitan capital. In October the King was bottled up at Gaeta, a coastal town close to the border of the Patrimony of St. Peter, besieged by the Sardinians. Faithful to his word given at Chambéry, the Emperor stood by permissively. His withdrawal of his minister from Turin as a token of his official disapproval and his maintenance of his garrison at Rome did not at all perturb Cavour. The Sardinian Foreign Minister comprehended that Napoleon could not appear as the overt accomplice of Sardinia. He would be obliged to bark a little for form's sake, but he would not bite.

In truth, the Emperor was thoroughly out of patience with the Pope. Many of the diplomats assigned to the French court during the autumn believed that should Pius IX be so rash as to carry out his threat to flee, Napoleon would be willing—and perhaps wanted—to let Sardinia take the Patrimony itself and settle the Roman question for all time.[55] The Pope had done himself no good in Napoleon's book by his alliance with the Legitimists, the sworn enemies of the Emperor's house. Scions of the old French and Spanish nobility had flocked to join the papal army commanded by the Legitimist Lamoricière.

The Pope's connection with the Bourbon royalists had brought the Emperor many problems. After the catastrophe at Castelfidardo, where some of the bluest blood of France had flowed, the clerical and Legitimist

---

[54] See *Lettres familières*, I, 170–185; Napoleon to Duke of Alba, *ibid.*, I, 264 n.

[55] See, for example, Mülinen to Rechberg, Paris, September 25, 1860, secret, HHSA, IX/66, No. 69C; Mülinen to Rechberg, telegram, September 26, *ibid.*, No. 113; Metternich to Rechberg, Paris, November 15, 1860, HHSA, IX/67, No. 86C; Cowley to Palmerston, Paris, October 12, 1860, copy, PRO FO 519/228.

clamor in France had achieved great volume. In tone it was less propapal than it was anti-imperial.[56] The union of French clericals with the Legitimists was a bogey not to be dismissed lightly. The Emperor feared that the Pope in exile, surrounded by the great Legitimist families of France, could seriously affect his popularity at home.[57] This reflection probably restrained him from yielding entirely to the Italianissimes.

The despair of the conservative, Austrophil element in the French court was commensurate with the enormity of their defeat. Walewski, out of office, utilized a letter of condolence to the Emperor on the death of the Duchess of Alba to sputter his impotent wrath against the "insane and culpable ambition" of Cavour.[58] Even Thouvenel, rightly considered one of the Italianissimes, was appalled at the extent of the Emperor's concessions and seriously considered tendering his resignation. When asked of his master's intentions in Italy he shook his head helplessly. "To the whole world the Emperor is impenetrable; to me he is incomprehensible."[59]

The reaction of the overwrought Empress was extreme. These blows fell upon her when she was already in a state of emotional instability and brought her closer to nervous collapse than at any other time of her life. The passage of years brought her an unmatched ability to endure misfortune and tragedy with dignified fortitude, but in the fall of 1860 she passed her time in tears and ceaseless reproaches. The catastrophe at Castelfidardo affected her deeply, and she wept at the words of Monseigneur Dupanloup, bishop of Orléans, extolling "the martyrs fallen in defense of the faith."[60] She could neither eat nor sleep, and she fell prey to morbid and superstitious notions. She became convinced that the death of her sister had been a divine punishment for the Emperor's anticlerical policies and she feared lest a similar "justice" be meted out to her son or even to her husband. Cavour was told that if the Prince Imperial had but the colic she predicted the child's death to the Emperor. The Sardinian diplomats were alarmed lest her tantrums and accusations unnerve him and shake his decision to abet the Sardinian annexations.[61]

[56] Thouvenel to Gramont, Paris, October 20, 1860, Louis Thouvenel (ed.), *Le Secret de l'Empereur: Correspondance confidentielle et inédite échangée entre M. Thouvenel, le Duc de Gramont, et le général Comte de Flahault, 1860–1863*, I, 254; see also Pierre de La Gorce, *Histoire du Second Empire*, III, 434–435.

[57] Cowley to Lord John Russell, Paris, January 11, 1861, copy, PRO FO 519/228.

[58] Walewski to Napoleon, September 23, 1860, Chalamon de Bernardy, "Le Comte Walewski," p. 665.

[59] Metternich to Rechberg, Paris, November 21, 1860, HHSA, IX/67, No. 87B. See also Mülinen to Rechberg, Paris, September 28, 1860, secret, HHSA, IX/66, No. 91E.

[60] Octave Aubry, *Eugénie: Empress of the French*, p. 155.

[61] Bixio to Cavour, Paris, October 24, 1860, *Carteggio Cavour-Nigra*, IV, 264. The unanimity in the diplomatic world in expressing the existence of a bitter quarrel be-

But the most the Empress could produce in the fall and winter of 1860 were a few minor counterirritants, exasperating to the Italianissimes, but in the long run ineffective. One irritation was her protection of an intrigue with Legitimist ramifications to keep the propapal, anti-Sardinian General Goyon in Rome as commander of the French forces. For months the General had worked in a direction diametrically opposed to that of the French ambassador at Rome, the Duke of Gramont. Exceeding and distorting his instructions, the General had intruded into the realm of politics, had shown an open and imprudent sympathy for Lamoricière, and had several times called down upon himself sharp reprimands from Thouvenel on orders from the Emperor himself.[62] Gramont continuously pushed for Goyon's dismissal and succeeded in having him recalled to Paris in the summer of 1860. But curiously enough, while deploring Goyon's conduct, Napoleon sent him back to his post. In the fall, contrary to his orders, he risked armed encounter with the Sardinian troops on the southern border

---

tween husband and wife over French policy in Italy is impressive. The reports are not mere idle gossip by malicious tongues; they are rather the expression of opinion of ambassadors and other diplomats whose duty it was to inform themselves on anything that might influence Napoleon's policies. See, for example, Cowley to Lord John Russell, Frederick Arthur Wellesley (ed.), *Secrets of the Second Empire: Private Letters from the Paris Embassy; Selections from the Papers of Henry Richard Charles Wellesley, 1st Earl Cowley*, p. 212. Cowley obtained information on the court from his own close association with the Emperor and with Fould, a favorite of the ruler. See also Victoria to King of the Belgians, Windsor Castle, December 4, 1860, Arthur Christopher Benson and Viscount Esher (eds.), *The Letters of Queen Victoria from Her Majesty's Correspondence between the Years 1837–1861*, III, 418; King of the Belgians to Victoria, Laeken, November 22, 1860, *ibid.*, p. 415; Gropello to Cavour, Paris, November 17, 1860, *Carteggio Cavour-Nigra*, IV, 275; Bixio to Cavour, Paris, October 24, 1860, *ibid.*, 264. Mme Baroche, among many others, attributed the Empress' flight to Scotland in November to a dispute over the treatment of the Pope (Baroche, *Second Empire*, p. 167). Because Mme Baroche was generally sympathetic to the Empress, her comment has special significance. See also Baron Napoléon Beyens, *Le Second Empire vu par un diplomate belge*, I, 188, on the Empress' devotion to the Pope. Beyens had been assigned to Madrid before the time of Eugénie's marriage and, with his wife, was an old friend of the Empress.

Harold Kurtz' assertion that the Empress' opposition to the Emperor's Italian policy was the deliberate invention of Mme Walewska (*Empress Eugénie*, pp. 145–146), resentful at her fall from favor, is implausible for many reasons. It is difficult to see why she would have been so universally believed had there been no substance to the story. Moreover, she was by no means out of favor in the fall of 1860, when these stories were circulating; rather, she was seeing the Emperor "a great deal," and was protected by the Empress "with all her might" (Metternich to Rechberg, Paris, November 12, 1860, private, HHSA, IX/68). Finally, she was doing her best to have her husband reinstated in the Council of Ministers and was fully as clerical and anti-Sardinian as the Empress.

[62] Napoleon to Randon, August 26, Jacques Louis César Alexandre Randon, *Mémoires*, II, 55; September 23, 1861, *ibid.*, p. 55; Napoleon to Randon, September 14, 1859, Alfred Rastoul, *Le Maréchal Randon, 1795–1871, d'après ses mémoires et des documents inédits: Etude militaire et politique*, p. 245.

of the Patrimony and drew down another verbal thunderbolt from the Emperor.[63] Moreover, he supplied information to the clerical Minister of War in Paris, Randon, that contradicted the pro-Sardinian reports emanating from the French embassy in Rome. While Goyon remained at Rome, Napoleon appeared to be following simultaneously a propapal and a pro-Sardinian line. Yet the Emperor was strangely reluctant to part with his disobedient subordinate.

Goyon, however, was serving the interests of Lamoricière and M. de Mérode, Pius' Minister of War, whose main objective was to keep the French General at Rome. They, in turn, had the ardent support of a number of Ultramontane ladies in Eugénie's court, ladies chosen insofar as it was possible from the ranks of the old nobility. Prominent clericals among them were Mesdames Malaret, née Segur, de Viry, de Lourmet, and de Montebello.[64] Also involved were the Ultramontane Duchess of Hamilton and the ladies of the Spanish party, then much in favor with the Empress.[65] In collusion with this group frustrating the official foreign policy was Marshal Randon, Minister of War. He plied the Emperor with profuse evidence of Sardinian clandestine incitement of revolution to justify Goyon's energetic measures and his calls for an increase in the occupying forces. That this conspiracy—for such it amounted to—was no invention of the cloak-and-dagger school of historians is shown by a letter from Gramont to Thouvenel when the matter of Goyon's dismissal was in question.

Please, I beg of you, keep for yourself alone what I write you. . . . I have seen the proofs of what I am going to write, namely: that the minister of war [Randon] is working beyond you and in a sense diametrically opposed to the ministry of foreign affairs on the subject of the affairs of Rome. General Goyon is the instrument of this intrigue and some *ladies* whom you may guess without my naming them, are the heart of it. . . . Someone has written to Goyon that you had caused him to be recalled, but it would not be difficult to undo what you had done and that the best means was to procure information contrary to ours. . . . The emperor is ignorant of all this . . . and the proof of it is that the plan of intrigue is tending to win his confidence and to persuade him that Goyon should return and stay.

It is not a question of the personality of the general; it is a question much more serious. It is a question of party, it is the work of a party that you know about and to which . . . the general has been devoted, or serves unknowingly as a blind instrument . . . a party fatal to the emperor whom it detests, fatal to France which it sacrifices to its mystical exaggerations. You have been warned,

[63] Napoleon to Randon, October 22, 1860, Randon, *Mémoires*, II, 35.

[64] Jean Maurain, *La Politique ecclésiastique du Second Empire de 1852 à 1869*, p. 414.

[65] Gropello to Cavour, Paris, November 28, 1860, *Carteggio Cavour-Nigra*, IV, 279.

and I guarantee you that you can believe what I tell you, as I assure you that it has cost me much to write you this and that, knowing all the power and all the resources of the secret organization of which I alert you, it is not without uneasiness that I write these lines. But I have given you my entire confidence.

P.S. I would be happy to learn that you have burned this little note and I will do the same for your answer.[66]

The letter survived because Thouvenel thought it too valuable as evidence to be destroyed. But he was apparently unable to use it effectively to score against Goyon. Later in the summer he learned indirectly from the papal nuncio at Paris that "the ladies" had successfully intervened with the Emperor to save their protégé.[67] Thouvenel in fact had to endure Goyon's presence in Rome for many months to come. The victory of the Empress' clerical friends, nevertheless, was a minor one and marked no real *détente* in the swift march of revolution in Italy.

While Goyon was thus embroiling French policy at Rome, a few miles to the south on the Tyrrhenian coast the Bourbon Francis II and his eighteen-year-old bride, Maria Sophia Amalia, were making their last stand at Gaeta. The imminence of the fall of still another royal throne to the Sardinian bandits, as the Empress now regarded them, enraged her fully as much as the plight of the Pope. Their case was the more appealing because of the spirit and pluck of the young Queen. A Wittelsbach, younger sister of Elizabeth of Austria, she was, like the Austrian Empress, of exquisite loveliness. During the siege she would ride up to the batteries, indifferent to the shells falling about her, to encourage the gunners and to comfort the wounded.[68] The thought of so much beauty in distress— for her conduct was well broadcast in the Legitimist press throughout Europe—had the power to exact sympathy from the most hardened anti-royalist. To the Empress it was emotional dynamite. Eugénie herself had been known to say that if France were in danger she would be the first to mount her horse and rally the troops. Maria Sophia's heroism exactly suited Eugénie's romantic conceptions of queenly conduct. As in the case of Louise of Parma, the Empress took the young Queen's cause as her own and began begging the Emperor to send the French fleet to the aid of the besieged royal couple.

[66] Gramont to Thouvenel, Rome, July 21, 1860, Thouvenel, *Le Secret de l'Empereur*, I, 157–159. Cavour also complained of the existence of a secret organization working against him. He said: "The government of Rome conspires and acts against us as well as an immense and profound secret association whose powers and means of action we can not measure" (Conversation with Signora L. Colet, Turin, April 2, 1860, Chiala, *Lettere*, III, 403).

[67] Gramont to Thouvenel, Rome, August 11, 1860, Thouvenel, *Le Secret de l'Empereur*, I, 168–171.

[68] Harold Mario Mitchell Acton, *The Last Bourbons of Naples, 1825–1861,* pp. 508–509.

Napoleon himself as early as September 26, on his return from Algeria, had already conceived of the idea of sending a naval force to Gaeta as part of his formal, public opposition to the invasion of southern Italy. Perhaps he had in mind the reports of Legitimist agitation and believed the presence of his fleet would be a fitting gesture to placate clerical opinion. On October 13 the French government announced that Rear Admiral de Tinan would proceed to Gaeta to forestall a Sardinian attack by sea.[69]

How much the Empress had to do with this decision is conjectural. Whatever the truth of the matter, the British and Italian diplomats attributed this "politique de sentiment" to her "inspiration" and blamed her for the creation of a maddening situation.[70] The French fleet did not interfere with the siege operations on land but it did hold at bay the Sardinian fleet on the sea and made possible the revictualling of the beleaguered town. The move, inconsistent with the rest of French policy, seemingly irrational, was infuriating to Cavour.

Yet after all, even if the Empress had brought to pass this demonstration of sympathy for Francis and his wife, she had not accomplished much. Admiral Tinan was told that the policy of the French government had not changed. He was to station his fleet offshore only to assure the Bourbon King a dignified means of escape, and he should try to persuade him to capitulate. The outcome of the siege was never in doubt. As Gramont remarked, the French gesture had been rather like dangling a rope always out of reach in front of a drowning man.[71]

Thus by early November, 1860, the Empress could look back on a depressing list of failures. No less than seven territories or monarchies had succumbed to the revolution and Sardinian aggression in the months since the Italian War. And the Kingdom of the Two Sicilies was as good as gone. A plebiscite on October 21 apparently indicated an overwhelming desire on the part of the citizens of south Italy to join Sardinia. On November 7 Victor Emmanuel entered Naples and named Farini as his lieutenant general for his southern provinces. The Emperor seemed more than ever under the thumb of the Italianissimes. Early in November the Empress and the Walewskis, together with the Emperor's aide-de-camp, Fleury, had failed utterly in an attempt to force the resignation of Thouvenel.[72] At the same time Napoleon was exasperated beyond endurance

[69] Lynn M. Case, *Franco-Italian Relations, 1860–1865*, p. 26.

[70] D'Azeglio to Cavour, telegram, London, November 1, 1860, 4:20 p.m., Chiala, *Lettere*, VI, 633.

[71] Gramont to Thouvenel, La Gorce, *Second Empire*, III, 450.

[72] Metternich to Rechberg, Paris, November 12, 1860, private, HHSA, IX/68; Chalamon de Bernardy, "Le Comte Walewski," pp. 666–668. While the Empress was

with the Pope. He interpreted Pius' threats of flight as a shabby trick to lever him into evicting the Sardinians from Umbria and the Marches. When the Empress defended the Pope's claims to his lost territories, news of the terrible scene at the palace ran like wildfire across Paris and, in diplomatic pouches, abroad to Turin. After the quarrel the Emperor was reported to have threatened: "The Pope thought he could better his own affairs by upsetting my household, but he has made a mistake."[73]

Suddenly the accumulation of griefs and resentments—old and recent, personal and political—welled to a frightful climax. Physically and mentally exhausted, panic-stricken and rebellious at the invisible but hateful fetters of her position, the Empress thought of escape. ". . . But where to go? I would like to flee, and I don't know *where*."[74] Indeed, the question was not easy to answer. Eugénie's health was delicate, and it was November. But the sunny climate of Italy, of course, was beyond consideration. Spain, too, must be rejected. French relations with Isabella were strained over the Queen's indignant protests of the treatment afforded her Bourbon relative in Naples. Also the Carlist revolt in which the Empress' cousins had participated was an embarrassing and fresh memory. A state visit to any of the major powers, be they Catholic or Protestant, would produce undesired political significance. "The ladies" provided the solution. The sympathetic Marie of Baden, Duchess of Hamilton, offered the Empress hospitality. On November 14, travelling incognito as the Countess of Pierrefonds and with Mesdames de Montebello and de Soulcy as companions, Eugénie left abruptly for Scotland to stay quietly at the ancestral home of Marie's husband.

The noise of scandal was everywhere. Few accepted as the whole truth the official explanation—that the Empress' poor health and grief for her sister required a change of scene. The voyage was variously set down to quarrels with the Emperor over the Pope, over Mme de Castiglione, over another, new mistress. Resentment toward the Emperor for withholding the news of the Duchess' death was mentioned. Some asserted that the Empress was dying of the same disease which killed her sister and that she went abroad to seek medical help.[75]

---

in Scotland, Napoleon accepted Walewski as his Minister of State in place of Fould, but retained Thouvenel in the Foreign Ministry. Despite Walewski's hopes, the appointment did not portend any change in the Emperor's Italian policy.

[73] Gropello to Cavour, Paris, November 17, 1860, *Carteggio Cavour-Nigra*, IV, 275.

[74] Eugénie to Duke of Alba, October 21, 1860, *Lettres familières*, I, 195.

[75] See, for example, Gropello to Nigra, Paris, November 10, *Carteggio Cavour-Nigra*, IV, 272; Cowley to Lord John Russell, Paris, November 13, 1860, copy, PRO FO 519/228; Wellesley, *Secrets of the Second Empire*, p. 214; Victoria to King of the Belgians, Windsor Castle, December 4, 1860, Benson and Esher, *Letters of Queen Victoria*, III, 418; Baroche, *Second Empire*, pp. 167, 184.

The Empress was absent from Paris slightly over a month. Her trip had a beneficial effect upon her health but did little to raise her spirits. A week before her return she called on Victoria, who found her composed, looking very pretty, much better, but very sad. "She never mentioned the Emperor but once when she offered his compliments, and there was not the slightest allusion to politics. It is altogether very strange."[76] Back in Paris, Eugénie faced the new year with a cheerless outlook. At the annual reception of the diplomatic corps on New Year's Day she stood mute by the Emperor's side, still dressed in deep mourning. "Excuse the empress if she does not speak to you; she is heartbroken," apologized the Emperor to the bowing diplomats.[77]

The winter saw a resumption of her futile efforts to save Francis II and the commencement of a long correspondence with Maria Sophia. The Queen initiated the exchange on January 4 in order to express her gratitude to the Empress for the "generous interest" that she had taken in her plight. "In the situation where I find myself there is nothing more consoling than the sympathy of friends as highly placed as you; your approbation is the sweetest encouragement possible to strengthen the convictions of my heart,"[78] wrote the wife of a Bourbon to the wife of a Bonaparte.

Despite the fact that on January 19 the Emperor suddenly withdrew his fleet and permitted Sardinian operations on both sea and land, the Empress resolved to reassure Maria Sophia of her unaltered good will. Her letter, apparently shown to many ladies in the court, made a sensation. The Sardinian chargé d'affaires reported to Cavour that everyone was quoting one sentence in particular: "I like to proclaim it, Madam; you can be assured of all my admiration, of all my sympathy, and furthermore, you have right and justice on your side."[79]

Brave words, but they availed nothing. Within less than a month after

[76] Victoria to King of the Belgians, December 4, 1860, Benson and Esher, *Letters of Queen Victoria,* III, 418.

[77] Baroche, *Second Empire,* p. 172.

[78] Maria Sophia to Eugénie, Gaeta, January 4, 1861, AA, c. 33–89. The Alba Archives contain seven letters from the Queen to Eugénie, dating from January, 1861, to July, 1899.

[79] Gropello to Cavour, Paris, January 28, 1861, *Carteggio Cavour-Nigra,* IV, 322. The delivery of this letter was accomplished with no little difficulty and considerable attendant embarrassment. Gramont, ambassador at Rome, entrusted the letter to a secretary at the embassy for delivery to Gaeta. Received by the King, the messenger was charged to carry back to Gramont a blunt message enquiring, from one gentleman to another, if there was any hope of French aid. Gramont relayed the request to Thouvenel and the Emperor. They were spared the necessity of a reply. By the time Gramont's letter arrived in Paris, Francis II had fled to Rome. For an account of this episode see Gramont to Thouvenel, Rome, January 29, February 2, and February 12, 1861, AMAE (Paris), Papiers Thouvenel, X; La Gorce, *Second Empire,* III, 451–452.

the withdrawal of Tinan's squadron came the capitulation. Francis and Maria Sophia escaped on a French ship kept in readiness for this purpose in Naples and fled to Rome and to the protection of the Pope. But for years the Empress clung tenaciously to the hope of a Bourbon restoration in Naples. In October, 1861, she told the papal nuncio: ". . . you can not doubt all the sympathy I felt for that great and noble misfortune. Well, I hope, I ardently desire that Her Majesty [Maria Sophia] will recover the crown of Naples."[80] In 1863 the resurrection of an independent Bourbon kingdom was to become an integral part of her master plan for French reorganization of the map of Europe, to be accomplished with the help of Austria.

REVOLUTION PREVAILS

The onward march of revolution in Italy appeared as inexorable as the limits of Napoleon's tolerance were inexhaustible. After annexing the Kingdom of Two Sicilies and all of the Pope's territories except the Patrimony of St. Peter, Sardinia proclaimed itself the Kingdom of Italy in March, 1861. Only Venetia and Rome lay "unredeemed" outside the union. Worse yet, from Eugénie's point of view, Cavour immediately sought diplomatic recognition of the newly formed state from France and began secret negotiations with Napoleon for evacuation of French troops from Rome. Although the Empress packed her court with clericals and Legitimist supporters of Francis II so that the Italian diplomats fancied themselves at the Trianon in the Ancien Régime, she could not change Napoleon's very obvious desire to strike a bargain. Count Vimercati, military attaché, wrote Cavour: "Only a small coterie of the empress will be invited [to Fontainebleau]. . . . On my word of honor, one would think himself at the Trianon! Fortunately, Napoleon III is not Louis XVI."[81] A pact stipulating French military evacuation of Rome in return for an Italian guarantee of the Pope's remaining territory in all probability would have accompanied the recognition of Italy had it not been for two startling and unforeseeable events—the sudden death of Cavour on June 6 and the severe epileptic seizures suffered by Pius IX. Without the great Minister's responsible influence in the Turin government, Napoleon felt unable to rely on Italian promises to respect the Pope in the Patrimony. And the apparently imminent demise of the Pope made it desirable for the Emperor

---

[80] Mülinen to Rechberg, October 29, 1861, secret, Henry Salomon, "Le Prince Richard de Metternich et sa correspondance pendant son ambassade à Paris, 1859–1871," *Revue de Paris,* XXXI (1924), 515.

[81] Vimercati to Cavour, June 1, 1861, *DDI,* First series 1861–1870, I, No. 118, p. 153.

to keep his troops in Rome in order to influence the election of the new pontiff.[82]

If the death of Cavour spared the Empress the military evacuation of Rome, it acted as a spur to hasten French diplomatic recognition of the Italian kingdom. To Eugénie renewal of normal diplomatic relations with Turin meant endorsement of highway robbery, and she worked feverishly to prevent it. With her were Walewski, Randon, and Baroche. But Prince Napoleon and the majority of the Council of Ministers, including Thouvenel, Persigny, and Rouher, were Italianissimes. Moreover, the reports of the procureurs general for the spring of 1861 showed the public in general to be either favorable to the new Italian state or apathetic. The nests of clerical and Legitimist hostility were small.[83]

The struggle between the two factions at court began a few days after Cavour's death and continued for nearly a week. The Emperor was at Fontainebleau, surrounded by the Empress' favored few—the Walewskis, Metternich, and the Spaniards. Thouvenel waited anxiously in Paris for Napoleon's signal to convene the Council of Ministers and to read his prepared memorandum proposing recognition. Whatever prompted the Emperor to declare himself and brave the recriminations of his wife is not known; but on June 14 he convened the renowned meeting of the Council that decided for recognition. The Empress was present. When Thouvenel, at the request of the Emperor, began reading his memorandum, Eugénie realized her defeat. With tears starting from her eyes, she rose abruptly and fled the room. Apparently she returned, as she did not confine her expression of resentment to tears. Thouvenel later told Cowley: ". . . nothing could surpass the bitter language of the Empress or the violence of Baroche. Walewski was much more moderate."[84] Eugénie never forgave Thouvenel for his part in this "act of folly," and henceforth treated him with marked coldness.

From 1859 through the early part of 1861 the Empress found herself swimming against the strong revolutionary current set in motion by the Italian War. It proved to be too strong for her. Her small successes in that period provided only slight zigzags in imperial policy or temporary *temps*

[82] Lynn M. Case, "Anticipating the Death of Pope Pius IX in 1861," *Catholic Historical Review*, XLIII (1957), 309–323.

[83] Case, *French Opinion on War*, pp. 140–143; Maurain, *Politique ecclésiastique*, p. 506.

[84] Cowley to Lord John Russell, Paris, June 28, 1861, copy, PRO FO 519/229. Metternich wrote of the event: "The empress wept all one day at this new concession of the emperor. She flew into a passion at the council but unfortunately her voice is a voice in the wilderness" (Metternich to Rechberg, Paris, June 17, 1861, HHSA, Nachlass Rechberg, No. 1). For a description of the Council meeting see Thouvenel, *Le Secret de l'Empereur*, II, 138–139 n. 1. See also Maurain, *Politique ecclésiastique*, pp. 507–508.

d'arrêt in the sweep of the Italianissimes. If it had not been for the Emperor's fear of clerical opinion the Sardinians probably would have had Rome along with all of the other of the Pope's states. The counterirritants of the Empress served merely to make the Emperor appear hesitant and to antagonize the very people he was helping.

She was facing very formidable odds. The Emperor's innate sympathy for the Italian cause and the mistake of the recalcitrant Pope in taking the Legitimists into his fold lent enchantment to the birdcalls of Prince Napoleon. Except for Rome itself the French public was in general either favorable to the revolutionary policy or quietly indifferent. The loss of the Romagna, the Marches, and Umbria evoked thunder from the pulpit and the clerical press but failed to arouse the masses. The causes of the Bourbon and Habsburg Princes were championed ardently only by the Legitimists, already enemies of the Empire. Out of step with the country and its master, the Empress, a Spaniard and tarred by her connection with Carlism, seemed to represent principles antipodal to those of Bonapartism. Small wonder that near the time of the recognition of Italy the Emperor is reported to have fumed: "Really, Eugénie, you forget two things—that you are French and that you have married a Bonaparte!"[85]

[85] Horace de Viel-Castel, *Mémoires sur le règne de Napoléon III, 1851–1864, publiés d'après le manuscrit original,* VI, 111–112. The Emperor was reported to have made this remark at a dinner where Matilda and his physician, Dr. Conneau, were present.

CHAPTER 4

THE GRAND DESIGN
Italy, Mexico, and Poland, 1861–1863

REVERSING THE REVOLUTIONARY TREND

French diplomatic recognition of the Kingdom of Italy apparently crowned the revolutionary edifice of Cavour and Garibaldi with an official symbol of imperial benediction. Many interpreted it as an announcement to Europe that the Pope, the King of the Two Sicilies, and the Archdukes could expect no encouragement from the Emperor of the French in their efforts to win back their lost territory. Yet the course of Napoleon's foreign policy rarely ran true. Even while he seemed to glide effortlessly with the revolution, he was secretly beginning to respond to the tug of the conservatives in his court and government and to look to Austria as the sheet anchor of his diplomacy. It is an ironic fact but one entirely in harmony with the character of the Emperor that he made war against Austria with the Austrophil Walewski as his Foreign Minister and a few years later sought an alliance with his erstwhile enemy with the pro-Italian Thouvenel in the Quai d'Orsay.

A hint of the presence of the *double courant*, invariably present in his government and so deplored by his Ministers, could be detected in the form of the act of recognition. It included two significant reservations: that recognition did not imply sanction of the incorporation of the Pope's territories in the new kingdom and that French troops should remain in Rome pending either a reconciliation with the Papacy or Italian guarantees of the temporal power. If one read the small print one learned that the act was not in fact an official endorsement of the unity of the Italian peninsula.

During the spring of 1861 Metternich had been aware of much talk in diplomatic circles of a plan to divide the Italian peninsula into three parts. Francis should have back his Neapolitan kingdom, Pius IX should be restored to the Marches and Umbria, and in the north Victor Emmanuel should reign over an Italian kingdom comprised not only of Lombardy and the Duchies, but Venetia as well. This schema was spawned outside of the Foreign Ministry in the minds of such conservatives as Walewski and Drouyn de Lhuys, who were hoping for a *rapprochement* with Austria. In return for the cession of Venetia, France would promise to help Austria find compensation elsewhere—perhaps in Bosnia, perhaps in Moldavia and Wallachia. But Austria had already vehemently rejected proposals that she exchange Venetia for a reward in the Balkans. The fresh bait served up in this plan was the promise of destruction of Italian unity and in the conversion of France to conservative policies in Rome and Naples.[1] Although Metternich was then unaware of it, this combination, with a multitude of variations, was to be the leitmotif of Austro-French negotiations until 1863.

For many weeks Napoleon gave no indication that he knew of this plan; and his renewal of diplomatic relations with Turin much discomfited the Austrians. But the subtle mind of the Emperor discerned a pregnant difference between the independence of Italy and the unity of Italy. At the very moment that he recognized the independence, he was scheming to destroy the unity. Thus, late in June, only a fortnight after Thouvenel had read his memorandum in the Council of Ministers, Napoleon proposed a bargain with Austria. If Franz Joseph would cede Venetia to Victor Emmanuel he would not only promise to help Austria take what she wanted "in the east" but would reinstate Pius IX and Francis II by force of his arms. In true conspiratorial fashion he told Metternich: "Oh, if you would come and say to me . . . that as of today you were ready to arrange with me in this sense, it would be quickly done. You would make your conditions, you would impose on me what you wished. . . . well, I would promise all, and we would make a fine secret alliance."[2]

The Austrians were not to be drawn into such adventures. Count Rechberg, Austrian Foreign Minister, doubted the sincerity of Napoleon's profession of conservative principles and refused to entertain any proposition entailing the cession of Venetia. In his opinion such a sacrifice was entirely unnecessary to shatter the superficial unity of the peninsula. The so-called Kingdom of Italy was a temporary and disgusting excrescence of revolutionary intrigue which needed only time to work its own destruction. Only

---

[1] Metternich to Rechberg, Paris, January 2, 1861, HHSA, IX/69, No. 1 C; Metternich to Rechberg, May 14, 1861, *ibid.,* No. 36 C. For a discussion of the effects of this proposal to divide Italy into three parts see Nancy Nichols Barker, "Austria, France, and the Venetian Question, 1861–66," *The Journal of Modern History,* XXXVI (1964), 145–154. Thouvenel favored Austrian cession of Venetia for compensation in the Balkans but did not include the destruction of Italian unity in his package (Metternich to Rechberg, Paris, March 12, 1861, HHSA, IX/69, No. 21 D; Metternich to Rechberg, May 8, 1861, *ibid.,* No. 35 C).

[2] Metternich to Rechberg, Paris, June 30, 1861, private, HHSA, IX/71.

after its inevitable disappearance would he be willing to discuss the future shape of the peninsular map.[3]

Yet this rebuff did not return the Emperor to the camp of the Italianissimes. During the summer he replaced Moustier at Vienna with the Duke of Gramont—credited with Austrophil sympathies—and continuously put out feelers for cooperation with Austria. Before taking up his new post Gramont visited the Emperor at Vichy. Napoleon expounded his plans to divide Italy into three kingdoms and astounded the diplomat with the vehemence of his criticisms of the Italians. Gramont wrote to Thouvenel:

I never heard him [the Emperor] say a single sympathetic word for Italy or for Victor Emmanuel; he had nothing but unfeigned reproaches and irritable predictions. Three or four times he declared that in his opinion Italian unity was an impossible myth and that the ambition of Piedmont [Sardinia] was endangering the independence of the peninsula.[4]

The Emperor was in fact entering a "nouvelle phase"—one which drew him closer to the policies of the Empress, Walewski, and Drouyn de Lhuys and estranged him from his Foreign Minister. Thouvenel, vacationing in the country, replied to Gramont that he had long known of the existence of the plans for destroying Italian unity, but he regarded them as decidedly unpracticable at the present time. Since he had little faith in the success of the reaction in Naples, he believed Austrian cession of Venetia hinged entirely on finding compensation for her in the Balkans.[5] But Thouvenel was far out of touch with his master. He was not invited to join the parleys at Vichy nor to follow the court to Biarritz in September. In office little more than a year and a half, he was already beginning to experience the same fate suffered by Walewski during the Italian War. By the fall of 1861 those in diplomatic circles in Paris were well aware that the views expressed by the Minister were very often not those of the Emperor.[6]

How much did Eugénie contribute to the changed frame of the Em-

[3] Rechberg to Metternich, Vienna, July 28, 1861, secret, HHSA, No. 9.

[4] Gramont to Thouvenel, Vichy, July 21, 1861, AMAE (Paris), Papiers Thouvenel, X. The Emperor repeated these ideas to Gramont in the fall at Biarritz (Gramont to Thouvenel, Biarritz, September 2, 1861, *ibid.*). See also Cowley to Russell, Paris, August 20, 1861, copy, PRO FO 519/229; Cowley to Russell, October 25, 1861, *ibid.* On his return from Vichy to Paris, Napoleon delayed so long in receiving Nigra, sent to him as extraordinary envoy from Victor Emmanuel, that even the Empress felt sorry for him and told Mme Walewska: "The emperor's hesitations make me so impatient that I'll end by becoming *Italianissime*" (Metternich to Rechberg, Paris, August 12, 1861, confidential, HHSA, IX/70, No. 49 D).

[5] Thouvenel to Gramont, Paris, July 30, 1861, Louis Thouvenel (ed.), *Le Secret de l'Empereur: Correspondance confidentielle et inédite échangée entre M. Thouvenel, le Duc de Gramont, et le général Comte de Flahault, 1860–1863*, II, 157–158.

[6] Metternich to Rechberg, Paris, December 22, 1861, HHSA, IX/70, No. 72 B; Cowley to Hudson, Foreign Office, December 24, 1861, copy, PRO FO 519/229.

peror's mind and to his expressed willingness to destroy Italian unity? The evidence shows clearly that she endorsed the plan of the three kingdoms even if she did not originate it. True, as late as December, 1860, she had still been hoping for the restoration of the Grand Duke of Tuscany and, indefatigable matchmaker that she was, had tried to arrange a match between the Grand Duke and her protégée, Princess Anna Murat, granddaughter of Joachim Murat, former king at Naples.[7] But the Habsburg Prince proved unresponsive and the time proved inauspicious for a restoration. Nor did any prospect of hope appear for the small son of the Duchess of Parma, still in exile in Switzerland. The Empress had had to reconcile herself to the incorporation of the northern peninsula into an Italian state. With the rest of the plan, as the champion of the temporal power and of Bourbon restoration in Naples, she was in full agreement. She was quite ready to ask Austria to award Venetia to a north Italian kingdom and soon after the Italian War had annoyed Metternich with her plans to arrange an Austrian exchange of her Italian province for Egypt.[8] Quite unusual harmony, in fact, reigned in the French court on the subject of Venetia. People who could agree on little else, such as Prince Napoleon and the Empress, Drouyn de Lhuys, and Thouvenel, Persigny and Walewski, agreed on the necessity of the Austrian sacrifice. The Italianissimes regarded Venetia in Italian hands as yet another step toward complete unification; the Austrophils saw Venetia as requisite to an alliance with Austria and the restorations in southern Italy. The Empress once told Metternich:

The emperor is pledged by the blood which has flowed in Italy—as long as he lives he will not be able to come to an agreement with you if you maintain your influence there [Venetia]. . . . Right or wrong, the emperor went into Italy to make you leave—he will no longer be able to let you return, and I, who detest the Italians and who am known in the peninsula to be *autrichienne*—which honors me, I understand and am obliged to share the sentiment of the emperor. After our death, the deluge, but before we will be *against* you if you want to annul the effects of that unfortunate war which has cost me so many tears—we will be your most faithful allies if you would leave Venice or make it as independent a place as possible.[9]

The Empress and the clericals, moreover, saw the Venetian question as a counterirritant, a convenient means of diverting the Italians from Rome. "Why do not the Italians, instead of taking Rome, seize upon Venetia,

    [7] Metternich to Rechberg, Paris, December 13, 1860, private, HHSA, IX/68, *varia*. The Grand Duke had recently been widowed.
    [8] Metternich to Rechberg, Biarritz, September 27, 1859, private, HHSA, IX/64.
    [9] Metternich to Rechberg, Paris, September 1, 1862, secret, HHSA, IX/72, No. 50 A–C.

which has much more to put up with than the Romans?" she asked
Mérimée.[10]

Some circumstantial evidence exists which suggests that Eugénie may
have been instrumental in the Emperor's deciding to adopt the new plan.
In June, even though her influence had been insufficient to thwart recognition of Italy, it was still a force to be reckoned with. When Baron Ricasoli, the new Foreign Minister at Turin, needed a representative to receive the French recognition and to reopen negotiations regarding Rome,
he was careful to select Count Arese, known to be *persona grata* with the
Empress. Dr. Conneau wrote to him from Paris:

Your trip to Paris is not only useful but necessary. No one save you can make
the recognition of the Kingdom of Italy acceptable to a person [the Empress]
whom I shall not name, but who is not the emperor. I don't tell you all I have
in my heart because that would be to say too much; but I assure you that only
you can do some good. . . . You are loved by one who detests us.[11]

A few weeks later Count Vimercati, Italian military attaché in Paris,
warned Ricasoli to walk softly on the question of Rome because of the
strength of the clericals and Legitimists at court protected by the Empress.
Too rash or too sustained pressure on the Emperor would serve only to
throw him in the arms of these enemies of Italy.[12]

At the same time the personal influence of Eugénie was increased by the
disgrace and absence of Prince Napoleon. During the spring the Prince,
in an insolent attack on the Papacy in the Senate, had rashly alluded to
many members of the old French nobility in unflattering terms. One of
their number, the Duke of Aumale, son of Louis Philippe, was a man of
great energy and reputed to be a first-rate shot and swordsman. In his
defense of his Bourbon and Orleanist relatives he wielded his pen as deftly
as he had his sword and replied so devastatingly, so scathingly, in a brochure of April 13 that he all but issued an invitation to a duel. But no
challenge to the field of honor was forthcoming from Prince Napoleon.
All of Paris jeered at this fresh demonstration of his reputed physical cowardice. The Empress declared publicly that if her son had been the age
of the Prince she would herself have placed the pistol in his hands.[13] It
was the opinion of Cowley and Metternich, who gauged closely possible
repercussions of the affair on foreign policy, that the Prince's disgrace

[10] Mérimée to Panizzi, Paris, October 11, 1862, Prosper Mérimée, *Letters to Panizzi*,
ed. Louis Fagan, I, 286–287.
[11] Conneau to Arese, June 24, 1861, Count Joseph Grabinski, *Un Ami de Napoléon
III: Le Comte Arese et la politique italienne sous le Second Empire,* p. 192.
[12] Vimercati to Ricasoli, Paris, July 24, 1861, *DDI,* I, No. 239, pp. 279–280.
[13] Metternich to Rechberg, Paris, April 20, 1861, private, HHSA, IX/70.

could adversely affect the cause of revolution in Italy.[14] As if this imbroglio were not enough, Prince Napoleon then gave further offense to the Emperor in May by planning to have himself elected as grand master of the Freemasons. When the Emperor vetoed his official association with an organization that was the epitome of anticlericalism, the Prince, his reputation in tatters, left for distant parts. The itinerary of his cruise, which took him to Algeria, Portugal, and the United States, was planned by the Emperor to keep him at a safe distance from Italian intrigues. During the five months of his absence, imperial foreign policy underwent its change of course. Later in June, Metternich reported that the influence of Walewski and Eugénie appeared strong. On June 25 Thouvenel had "another fight" with them over Italian policy and got the worst of it.[15] A few days later the Emperor made his offer to the Austrian ambassador to destroy Italian unity in return for the cession of Venetia.

But we have no real proof that the Empress played more than a supporting role. Caesar's interdict on political conversations between the Empress and Metternich was still in force.[16] She did not, as she was soon to do, intervene directly in the negotiations. Walewski seems to have been far more prominent than she. While the Empress remained at Paris during the summer, Walewski followed the Emperor to Vichy and exuded smug satisfaction while Napoleon lectured to Gramont on the dangerous ambitions of Victor Emmanuel.[17]

The Emperor himself seemed convinced of the impermanence of Italian unity and probably needed little persuasion to accept the plan of the three kingdoms. He believed and frequently said that the centrifugal forces of Italian sectionalism would forever thwart complete unification. When Naples, Florence, and other historic cities found themselves reduced to the status of provincial towns, "the old leaven would break out." Thus, he favored a confederation, although he had no "abstract senti-

---

[14] *Ibid.*; Cowley to Russell, Paris, April 19, copy, PRO FO 519/228. Cowley said that public opinion was "*unanimous*, man, woman and child look upon him as completely dishonored." For accounts of the incident see Ernest d'Hauterive, *The Second Empire and Its Downfall: The Correspondence of the Emperor Napoleon III and His Cousin Prince Napoleon*, pp. 169–177; Pierre de La Gorce, *Histoire du Second Empire*, III, 453–457; Frederick Arthur Wellesley (ed.), *Secrets of the Second Empire: Private Letters from the Paris Embassy; Selections from the Papers of Henry Richard Charles Wellesley, 1st Earl Cowley*, pp. 216–219.

[15] Metternich to Rechberg, telegram, Paris, June 25, 1861, HHSA, IX/69.

[16] The one exception to the Emperor's rule was Eugénie's conversation with Metternich—clearly with her husband's permission—in January, 1861, in which she expressed her concern over Austrian friendship with Prussia (Metternich to Rechberg, Paris, January 25, 1861, secret, HHSA, Nachlass Rechberg).

[17] Gramont to Thouvenel, Vichy, July 21, 1861, AMAE (Paris), Papiers Thouvenel, X.

ment" against unity.[18] He worried over the effect on public opinion should Rome fall to Italy. The public had been either indifferent or favorable to an Italy including the Duchies, the Kingdom of Two Sicilies, and part of the Papal States. But Rome was something else again. It might be a different story should the Pope flee and the Garibaldians enter the Holy City.[19] In the spring of 1861 the debates in the Legislative Body had been impressively unfavorable toward the unity movement.[20] Then had occurred the nearly simultaneous death of Cavour and illness of the Pope, wrecking for the foreseeable future an arrangement with Italy to evacuate French troops from Rome. The Emperor had come to an impasse with Turin. Perhaps, if he turned to Austria, he might solve his Venetian problem. By June the Emperor thus had many reasons for wishing to rein in the revolutionary Italians.

The force of these circumstances worked powerfully to the advantage of the Empress and the conservative Ministers even though they were unable to prevent the formal diplomatic recognition of Italy. Perhaps, as in 1859 when the Emperor decided to make peace after the Battle of Solferino, he needed little urging. On the other hand, these same circumstances had merely persuaded Thouvenel of the need for a hiatus in the negotiations concerning Rome, not for the restoration of Naples, the Marches, and Umbria to their former rulers. Evidence is too scanty to permit precise knowledge of why and how the Emperor decided to bargain with Austria on the basis of the destruction of Italian unity. The initiation of these negotiations, however, marked an important turning point in the foreign policy of the Empire, and, even though the Austrian government steadfastly refused to relinquish Venetia, it constituted a major victory for Eugénie and the other Austrophils. The Austrophils were to exploit the turn of events to the fullest.

The Origin of the Mexican Venture

The immediate effects of the Emperor's changed outlook were nil. Since Austria continued to deny the necessity of ceding Venetia in order to de-

---

[18] Cowley to Russell, Paris, January 11, 1861, copy, PRO FO 519/228. See also Cowley to Russell, Paris, October 25, 1861, *ibid.*, 519/229. Prince Napoleon told Cowley that he knew the Emperor's thoughts well—"that there was no hostility to the Unity of Italy, tho a deep conviction that it never can be accomplished" (Cowley to Russell, April 11, 1862, *ibid.*).

[19] Cowley to Russell, January 11, 1861, copy, PRO FO 519/228.

[20] Cowley reported that the impact of these debates "entirely changed" Thouvenel's language. Before the debates he favored Italian unity and "bringing the Pope to terms. He now says that it will be impossible to attempt it, and that he sees nothing for Cavour to do but to consolidate what he has got" (Cowley to Russell, March 25, 1861, *ibid.*).

tach central and southern Italy from Victor Emmanuel, Napoleon found himself stalemated. He had been unable to take Venetia away from Austria either by war or diplomacy, and he was unwilling to let Italy seize Rome. Unless he were willing to recommence the war with Austria to conquer the one or to alienate the clericals in France to satisfy the other, he could not come to terms. Affairs were in these doldrums when the Emperor was persuaded of the feasibility of tacking far around his European problems by the establishment of a monarchy in Mexico. With this bold diversion, he could not only fulfill a long cherished dream, but also, by offering the newly created throne to the younger brother of the Austrian Emperor, further his suit in Vienna.

Friends and foes of the Empress have generally agreed in assigning to her an important role in the Mexican venture. Denial of her influence would be difficult inasmuch as the Empress herself admitted her responsibility.[21] Undoubtedly no other project during the course of the Empire so fired her enthusiasm and imagination. Her Spanish birth, her scorn for the American republics, her missionary point of view, her restless and quixotic temperament let her imagine herself a latter-day Isabella I or a participant in the adventures which centuries before had brought Cortés and his men to the land of the Aztecs. One of the Mexican *émigrés*, Gutiérrez de Estrada, stated the case in his usual florid style: "A Spanish woman discovered America, another woman, also Spanish, will so to speak, make the spiritual discovery of one of the most beautiful parts of this continent."[22]

[21] It is impossible to give anything like a complete bibliography for the subject. Two accounts very sympathetic to the Empress which admit her responsibility in this affair are Count Maurice Fleury, *Memoirs of the Empress Eugénie. Compiled from Statements, Private Documents, and Personal Letters,* II, 105, and Harold Kurtz, *The Empress Eugénie, 1826–1920,* pp. 168–175. Kurtz, without offering proof for his statement, alleges that the Emperor's interest in Mexico was originally financial, and that Eugénie became involved in the venture only after it had begun. For accounts, ranging from hostile to friendly, that see the Empress as a prime mover of the enterprise see Octave Aubry, *Eugénie: Empress of the French,* p. 159; Baron Napoléon Beyens, *Le Second Empire vu par un diplomate belge,* I, 227–228; Viscount E. de Beaumont-Vassy, *Histoire intime du Second Empire,* p. 307; John Bigelow, *Retrospections of an Active Life,* II, 281; Frédéric Loliée, *The Life of an Empress,* pp. 229–233; Henry Salomon, "Le Prince Richard de Metternich et sa correspondance pendant son ambassade à Paris, 1859–1871," *Revue de Paris,* XXXI (1924), 521; George Maurice Paléologue, *The Tragic Empress: A Record of Intimate Talks with the Empress Eugénie, 1901–1919,* trans. Hamish Miles, p. 90; Baron d'Ambès, *Intimate Memoirs of Napoleon III: Personal Reminiscences of the Man and the Emperor,* trans. A. R. Allinson, II, 353; General François Charles Du Barail, *Mes souvenirs,* II, 292; Nancy Nichols Barker, "Empress Eugénie and the Origin of the Mexican Venture," *The Historian,* XXII, No. 1, 9–23; Egon Caesar Corti, *Maximilian and Charlotte of Mexico,* trans. C. A. Phillips, I, 98–101.

[22] Mülinen to Rechberg, Paris, October 15, 1861, secret, HHSA, IX/70, No. 63 C.

Eugénie had long been interested in the condition of Mexico. According to Cowley, people said that even before her marriage she had made the Emperor promise "to do something" for the revolt-torn land.[23] Her curiosity through the years had been fed by the moving narratives of the Mexican *émigrés*—those who had fled their country either to escape the consequences of their political attachments, or to seek aid for Mexico in one or the other of the European courts. As far as the Empress was concerned, the most important *émigré* was Don José Manuel Hidalgo y Esnaurrizar. Although born in Mexico, he was actually more Spanish than Mexican and had lived a large part of his adult life in London and Madrid. Descended of a noble Andalusian family, he had connections with the Carlist party. In Madrid he had been a frequent guest in the salon of the Countess of Montijo and was already accepted as a friend of the family when Eugénie ascended the throne of France. Her marriage to the Emperor was a magnificent stroke of luck for the *émigré*. Transferring to Paris, he battened on her favor in the inner circle of her court and followed her seasonal peregrinations from Saint-Cloud to Fontainebleau, from Biarritz to Compiègne. In 1860 the Empress so relied upon him that she awarded him the sacrosanct honor of accompanying the mortal remains of the Duchess of Alba to Madrid.[24] Never a sure judge of character, she allowed herself to be hoodwinked by the façade—the slender and elegant appearance, the exquisite manners and courtly flattery. She never made a more serious mistake in her life. Hidalgo was a fair-weather friend—self-seeking, vain, untruthful, disloyal, and even cowardly. Could she have taken his true measure she would have despised him.

Through Hidalgo, in 1857, the Empress came to support a scheme to establish Don Juan de Borbón, brother of the Carlist claimant to the Spanish throne, as ruler in Mexico. The purpose of the plan was to revive Spanish influence in Latin America and to appease the Carlists in Spain. Queen Isabella and a few of her Ministers saw Mexico as a convenient instrument for solving their Carlist problems. But realization of the plan depended on France. Unless Don Juan received material aid from France he could never hope to mount the Mexican throne. The Emperor was interested, but, despite Eugénie's enthusiasm, did not permit himself to

---

[23] Cowley to Russell, December 9, 1861, Victor Wellesley and Robert Sencourt, *Conversations with Napoleon III. A Collection of Documents Mostly Unpublished and Almost Entirely Diplomatic. Selected and Arranged with Introductions*, p. 200.

[24] Emmanuel Henri Dieudonné Domenech, *Histoire du Mexique, Juarez et Maximilien*, I, 366.

be drawn in. Projects in the Italian peninsula, then fermenting in the imperial mind, took precedence.[25]

The Empress' next essay took place in 1861 when events both in Europe and overseas were more auspicious for active intervention. The outbreak of civil war in the United States eliminated the prospect of effective opposition from Washington for the time being. In Mexico, Benito Juárez, leader of the liberal republicans, had taken over the government, but was unable to restore order or to meet payments on European loans. In Europe, the unsuccessful Carlist revolt and the Italian War had left many noblemen superfluous and unemployed. In May the Empress proposed to Hidalgo that General Elío, her Carlist relative, released from a Spanish prison on her intercession, be given command of an army to be composed of Mexican monarchists. She suggested the Duke of Modena, throneless since 1859, as a possible ruler.[26] But the Duke had the good sense to reject the idea out of hand. Since even the Empress (probably on orders from the Emperor) refused French military support, the enterprise collapsed.

Archduke Ferdinand Maximilian, eventually designated as candidate for the Mexican throne, had much in common with these others suggested for the honor. Viceroy of Lombardy-Venetia before the Italian War, he was yet another prince who had joined the ranks of the unemployed because of the revolution in Italy. Little depth of penetration was required to visualize Mexico as compensation for Austria's recent loss of Lombardy and prospective relinquishment of Venetia. Those in diplomatic circles easily grasped the Emperor's *arrière pensée*.[27]

Although the documents do not make clear which half of the imperial couple first seized on Ferdinand Maximilian as their chosen candidate for

[25] The incident is related by Hidalgo in his "Notes secrètes de M. Hidalgo à développer le jour où il conviendra d'écrire l'histoire de la fondation de l'Empire Mexicain," preserved in HKM, Carton 19 (1865), No. 46. These notes have been used with reservation in the knowledge that Hidalgo always exaggerated his own role and belittled that of his compatriots. They reveal starkly the man's unbearable vanity and utter disloyalty. Corti related this incident but was not aware of, or at least did not mention, the Carlist ramification of this intrigue (*Maximilian and Charlotte*, I, 35, 78–80).

[26] Hidalgo, "Notes secrètes," HKM, Carton 19 (1865), No. 46. Hidalgo did not explain why the Empress singled out the Duke of Modena. However, since the Duke of Parma was still a child, and the Grand Duke of Tuscany and the King of Two Sicilies were still hoping to be restored to their thrones, he was, except for Ferdinand Maximilian, the only possible choice among the rulers overthrown by the Italian War. Corti (*Maximilian and Charlotte*, I, 96–97) described the incident but mistakenly placed it in 1860.

[27] Copious documentary proof exists of the connection between the origin of the Mexican expedition and the Venetian question. See Barker, "France, Austria, and the Mexican Venture, 1861–1864," *French Historical Studies*, III (1963), 224–228.

the throne, they plainly reveal the Empress' active support of the idea. According to Hidalgo, the Archduke was mentioned for the first time in September, 1861, at Biarritz and was offered the throne as a result of Eugénie's intuitive premonition that he would accept.[28] But Hidalgo either did not know or, in order to inflate his own part in the affair, did not admit that Ferdinand Maximilian had been sounded through regular diplomatic channels at least as early as the preceding July. Rechberg had returned a noncommittal answer in the Archduke's name leaving the door open to further overtures.[29]

But Hidalgo was correct at least in attributing to the Empress the key role in reopening the negotiation with the Archduke in the fall and obtaining from him the commitment requisite to the commencement of an expedition to Mexico. In the archives of Ferdinand Maximilian is an extract of a letter of September 16 from Walewski to Metternich that shows she supplied the needed impetus. When it was written the decision to intervene had all but been made and hinged only upon Ferdinand Maximilian's acceptance.

The empress is again concerned with the Mexican affair which she spoke to you about at Etiolles [Walewski's country estate], and a solution seems to her more than ever desirable. . . .

Here [at Biarritz] they are disposed to uphold, morally, of course, the candidacy of the Archduke Maximilian if that is agreeable to Vienna. In this case, they would be ready, I even believe, to *take the initiative at the opportune time with England, Spain, and others.*

Write me a word so that I can, in a measure, enlighten the empress, whose interest in the result . . . to this affair never flags.[30]

As a result Rechberg, with the permission of Franz Joseph, again sounded Ferdinand Maximilian. On October 7 the Foreign Minister wrote to Paris that, in view of the Archduke's favorable reaction, the Austrian government would consent to his elevation to the throne in Mexico if certain condi-

---

[28] Hidalgo, "Notes secrètes," HKM, Carton 19 (1865), No. 46; Corti, *Maximilian and Charlotte*, I, 101.

[29] Rechberg to Metternich, July 28, 1861, HKM, Carton 1 (1861), No. 2.

[30] Extract of a letter from Walewski to Metternich, September 16, 1861, *ibid.*, No. 3. Corti mentions this letter but probably owing to a mistake on the part of a copying clerk, incorrectly dates it as of November 16 (Corti, *Maximilian and Charlotte*, I, 106 n. 14). Metternich sent the extract on to Baron Oldenburg on September 25, 1861 (HKM, No. 4).

For some examples of the Empress' enthusiasm over the choice of Ferdinand Maximilian see Mülinen to Rechberg, telegram, Paris, October 12, 1861, HHSA, IX/70, No. 67; Mülinen to Rechberg, October 15, 1861, secret, *ibid.*, No. 63 C; Metternich to Rechberg, Paris, December 22, 1861, HKM, Carton 1 (1861), 91–B.

tions were fulfilled.[31] Thus assured, the Emperor wrote an official letter to his ambassador in London, Count Flahault, which set the joint expedition in motion.

Perhaps the Empress' satisfaction over the conditional acceptance of the Austrian Archduke[32] was increased by her hope that room remained for the Spanish Carlists in the project. Ferdinand Maximilian and his wife, Archduchess Charlotte, were childless after four years of marriage, and— if the rumors were true—likely to remain so. The Empress saw an opportunity for the children of Don Juan de Borbón, who had succeeded to the role of Carlist pretender, and suggested them as heirs to the Mexican throne. "I am completely flabbergasted," wrote Metternich when he heard of the plan.[33]

Although nothing came of her proposal the Empress persisted in seeing the new world as a sort of convenient repository for throneless royalty or for princes unable, for political reasons, to live in their own country. Their transposition overseas not only would extend the system of monarchy but would solve vexatious European problems as well. Such had been the obvious intent with the Carlists, the Duke of Modena, and Ferdinand Maximilian. Even as late as 1863, when the French expeditionary force was stalled in the interior, she suggested that certain German princes, to be dispossessed by some audacious French plans to remake the map of Europe, should compensate themselves in Latin America for what they had lost in Europe.[34] To the Empress, the "greatest idea of the century" was not merely an isolated undertaking for the glory of France and the regeneration of Mexico but an integral part of her grand design for Europe.

How much responsibility should devolve on the Empress for her husband's decision to order the intervention? Emile Ollivier wrote that the Emperor was not talked into the expedition by the exhortations of his wife but that rather he had strong reasons of his own for his action.[35] Certainly Napoleon's interest in Central America dated back to the days of his reveries as prisoner at Ham. The upheavals in the Mexican government; the news, which arrived in France early in September, 1861, that Juárez had abruptly ordered the suspension of all payments due on foreign loans;

---

[31] Rechberg to Mülinen, Vienna, October 7, 1861, secret, HHSA, IX/71, No. 4. See also Paul Gaulot, *L'Expédition du Mexique, 1861–1867, d'après les documents et souvenirs de Ernest Louet,* I, 3–4.

[32] Mülinen to Rechberg, telegram, Paris, October 22, 1861, HKM, Carton 1 (1861), No. 16.

[33] Extract of a letter from Metternich to Oldenburg, October 6, 1861, *ibid.,* No. 9–C.

[34] Metternich to Rechberg, Paris, February 22, 1863, HHSA, reproduced by Hermann Oncken, *Die Rheinpolitik Kaiser Napoleons III. von 1863 bis 1870 und der Ursprung des Krieges von 1870/71,* I, No. 1, p. 5.

[35] Emile Ollivier, *L'Empire libéral: Etudes, récits, souvenirs,* V, 258.

the urgent reports of Count Alphonse Dubois de Saligny, French minister in Mexico, pressing for intervention; and the civil war in the United States provided auspicious circumstances for an already bruited project. In July, 1861, the Emperor listened to the arguments of the ambitious Spanish general, Juan Prim, eager to command an invading army.[36] Not to be discounted is the Emperor's desire for alliance with Austria and for a solution to the Venetian question. He had never seriously contemplated action in Mexico until he had commenced his suit in Vienna and had foreseen the possibility of the acceptance of the Austrian Archduke.[37] Austria, of course, saw the danger in a connection between Mexico and Venetia and sidestepped briskly. Count Mülinen, Austrian chargé d'affaires, and Metternich succeeded in extracting statements from Napoleon and Thouvenel that exonerated Austria from the onus of "gratitude" toward France for the creation of the new crown.[38] Notwithstanding the fancy footwork of the Austrians, there was no evading the fact that the elevation of an Austrian archduke to a throne in Mexico would lend "new distinction" to the Habsburgs.[39] One day in the future Napoleon intended to place Mexico in the scales against Venetia.[40]

But the final decision to commence action, should the Archduke respond favorably, was made in conclaves at Biarritz. The participants were only the Emperor and the Empress, Walewski, and the sycophantic Hidalgo. Of these, Walewski, although a thorough monarchist, an advocate of the Austrian alliance, was far from sharing the Empress' enthusiasm. He followed instead of leading and acted as her amanuensis rather than as her

[36] Conversations with Arrangoiz, May 24, 1863, HKM, Carton 3 (1863), No. 505; H. Leonardon, "L'Espagne et la question du Mexique," *Annales des sciences politiques,* XVI (1901), 62.

[37] Cowley learned that Napoleon had toyed with the idea of appeasing the Orleanists by supporting the candidacy of the Duke of Aumale, son of Louis Philippe (Cowley to Russell, Paris, October 16, 1861, copy, PRO FO 519/229). But the ambassador did not think the Emperor's intent was serious. See also Hidalgo, "Notes secrètes," HKM, Carton 19 (1865), No. 46.

[38] Rechberg was concerned over Italian concentration on acquiring Venetia at this time, especially since Napoleon had recently refused to evacuate Rome (Rechberg to Metternich, Vienna, November 13, 1861, HHSA, IX/71, No. 1). Metternich elicited reassurance from the Emperor that no connection should be made between the Venetian and Mexican questions and wired: "Satisfactory declarations from the emperor about Italy; the Mexican question on a safe track" (Metternich to Rechberg, November 13, 1861, HHSA, IX/70, No. 80). See also Mülinen to Rechberg, October 15, 1861, HHSA, Nos. 63 B, 63 C; October 15, 1861, HKM, Carton 1 (1861), No. 11 A; Paris, October 21, 1861, secret, HHSA, IX/70, No. 64 B; Cowley to Russell, Paris, February 11, 1862, copy, PRO FO 519/229.

[39] Rechberg to Mülinen, Vienna, October 7, 1861, secret, HHSA, IX/71, No. 4.

[40] Cowley to Russell, Paris, March 5, 1862, copy PRO FO 519/229; Paris, February 17, 1863, *ibid.,* 519/230.

mentor.[41] Hidalgo was little more than the Empress' shadow, present at the court only by her invitation and permitted to speak with the Emperor only through her intercession.

Who else or what else may have influenced the Emperor in making his decision? Thouvenel was nowhere in the affair. Although he approved of the venture insofar as it might lead to a solution of the Venetian question, he feared that the Emperor underestimated the difficulties of establishing a monarchy in Mexico. But he was not invited to the parleys at Biarritz and, from the Quai d'Orsay, simply executed the Emperor's orders. Napoleon did not even keep him very well informed. Some days passed before the Foreign Ministers learned that the Emperor had set the project in motion with his letter to Flahault.[42]

Prince Napoleon, at times able to exert a strange fascination over his cousin, was still in distant parts on his tour of punishment. He returned only to find the enterprise under way. Randon regretted the use of French soldiers and French money in a vain attempt to capture a utopia.[43] With the possible exceptions of the Duke of Morny, half brother of the Emperor, who scented interesting financial possibilities in Mexico, and Dubois, interested in promoting his career, no one in the French government could approach Eugénie's impassioned patronage of the project. Neither Morny nor Dubois was present at Biarritz. Nor could public opinion exert influence. The French people were unaware of the great adventure being planned in high places. Later apprised, they were almost to a man hostile to it.[44]

No other feature of imperial foreign policy can be identified so exclusively with the Empress. Left in the field at the moment of decision were only the husband and the wife. Perhaps at Biarritz the Empress, rather than overbearing the objections of a hesitant ruler, found herself preaching to one already converted. If so, nevertheless, to her must go much credit for the process of conversion. For several years she had taken the initiative in the concoction of combinations of rulers and armies for Mexico. She had set the stage by her invitations to the *émigrés*, by her eloquent arguments for the Austrian alliance, and by her championship of the candidacy of Ferdi-

[41] Corti, *Maximilian and Charlotte*, I, 106; Mülinen to Rechberg, Paris, October 21, 1861, secret, HHSA, IX/70, No. 64 C; Mülinen to Rechberg, November 3, *ibid.*, No. 65 E.

[42] Cowley to Russell, Paris, October 16, 1861, copy, PRO FO 519/229. See also Thouvenel to Flahault, Paris, September 19, 1861, Thouvenel, *Le Secret de l'Empereur*, II, 167–169; September 26, *ibid.*, pp. 174–176; October 12, 1861, *ibid.*, p. 179.

[43] Jacques Louis César Alexandre Randon, *Mémoires*, II, 75, 91.

[44] The reports of the procureurs general from early in 1862 to the conclusion of the expedition were almost uniformly hostile to it (Lynn M. Case, *French Opinion on the United States and Mexico, 1860–1867: Extracts from the Reports of the Procureurs Généraux*, pp. 311–340).

nand Maximilian. The Empress later held herself accountable for the fate of the expeditionary forces and the ultimate catastrophe. Metternich often commented on the feverish anxiety with which she followed events in Mexico and the crushing sense of responsibility which oppressed her.[45] Even in 1867, after the death of Ferdinand Maximilian at Querétaro, the fundamental honesty of her character would prompt her to confess: "For me the most painful thing in the world would be to find myself face to face with a brother and a mother [Franz Joseph and Archduchess Sophia] to whose grief I have contributed by the instigation of the Mexican expedition."[46]

THE ROMAN QUESTION: A TRIAL OF STRENGTH

With the Mexican expedition temporarily clear of diplomatic channels and launched on the high seas, the Emperor was obliged to return his attention to the vexatious Roman question. The controversy over whether or not to evacuate French troops from Rome became the major issue of French diplomacy in 1862 and caused the dismissal of Thouvenel from the Foreign Ministry.

The Emperor very naturally wanted to escape the embarrassments and expense of the occupation. The Pope was unappreciative and was angry at his loss of the Romagna, the Marches, and Umbria. The presence of the garrison in Rome was galling to Italy and might serve to throw her in the arms of her British suitors and to isolate France. But the difficulties involved in evacuation were enormous. The Italians tended to regard French withdrawal from Rome as a first step toward its acquisition and increased the Emperor's difficulties by their claims to the Holy City as their rightful capital. The Emperor, mindful of Catholic opinion in France and with the honor of the French flag engaged, could never appear to hand over Rome to Victor Emmanuel. Only the most extreme of Italianissimes, such as Prince Napoleon, who regarded the Papacy as an "antiquated idol," advocated such a drastic solution. On the other hand, the Emperor disliked posing as the champion of the notoriously reactionary government of the Papacy. Pius IX always refused to consider reforms until all of his "stolen" land had been returned to him. Since Italy would not agree to the restoration of the lands separated from papal authority since the Italian War, an arrangement agreeable to all three parties seemed an extremely remote possibility.

[45] Metternich to Rechberg, Paris, March 14, 1864, private, HHSA, IX/79. See also Beyens, *Le Second Empire,* II, 265; Bigelow to Seward, Paris, February 15, 1866, Bigelow, *Retrospections,* III, 357.

[46] Metternich to Beust, July 11, 1867, HHSA, Oncken, *Rheinpolitik,* II, No. 499, p. 437.

A matter of principle was involved. If France made an arrangement with Italy to evacuate her troops, even though an agreement might stipulate Italian respect for the Pope's remaining temporal possessions, she would be turning away from conservative, legitimate ideas and lending further endorsement to the Italian union that had been formed by revolution. It would rule out the possibility of restoration in central and southern Italy. Austrian diplomats saw the Empire approaching a crossroad. If, as they feared, the soul of Cavour should descend upon Bismarck, Napoleon might ally with the revolutionary forces in Germany and, in return for a Nice and Savoy on the Rhine, work to exclude Austria from the confederation. The Emperor's decision on Rome would denote whether he intended to continue or retrace the halting steps made in the summer and fall of 1861 toward an alliance with Austria.

As Napoleon hesitated in the spring of 1862 over his course, the cross action of the "double courant" in the Tuileries and the Ministry churned up some angry waters. The Foreign Minister appeared to be losing out to the Empress, Walewski, and Randon. Thouvenel was never *bien en cour*. A plain man and a very independent one, he neither would nor could play the courtier, and he refused to submit to the Empress' intrusion into his field. Perhaps because of the poor health of his wife he took little part in the social life of the court. In any case he was rarely to be seen in the imperial residences except on official business. He was further embarrassed by the support of Prince Napoleon, now returned from abroad. The intemperate policy advocated by the Prince would have brought about a complete break with the head of Catholicism and in no way resembled the Foreign Minister's plan of a measured, legal exodus from the Holy City with guarantees for the Pope's remaining temporal possessions. In February, 1862, in the Senate the Prince described the Papacy as a power condemned by history and called for immediate withdrawal of all French troops. The Emperor was obliged to disassociate himself from these politically ruinous ideas and had them repudiated in the Legislative Body by Auguste Billault, Minister of Interior. Since Billault's speech endorsed for all time the principle of French occupation, it was a slap not only at the Prince but at the Foreign Minister as well. "The Empress and the Clerical Party are very triumphant as well they may be," wrote Cowley. "They [the clerical party] have got hold of 'the gentle sex' and thro the latter have turned the tables."[47] The Empress indulged in some ironic humor at the Prince's ex-

---

[47] Cowley to Odo Russell, Paris, March 4, 1862, copy, PRO FO 519/229; Cowley to John Russell, February 28, 1862, *ibid*. See also Cowley to Hudson, March 4, *ibid*.; Metternich to Rechberg, telegram, Paris, February 24, 1862, HHSA, IX/72; Metternich to Rechberg, February 26, *ibid*.

pense. "He has a really brilliant mind [*infiniment d'esprit*]," she told Hübner, "and he makes detestable use of it. But what to do? . . . We are not in the Middle Ages, and the time is past when inconvenient cousins can be disposed of."[48]

The Emperor let fall hints that he might be about to don a conservative face. He was heard to remark that he would not be sorry if Garibaldi came down with cholera. To Metternich he observed: "I wish the king of Naples were a *man of action* and would place himself at the head of a military reaction."[49] Both the Empress and the ambassador believed that a *volte face* was in the making.[50]

Eugénie threw herself into the contest unrestrainedly. Cowley, whose usual informants were Thouvenel, Morny, Fould, and Prince Napoleon, saw with growing dismay her increasing influence over her husband. "The way in which the Empress now meddles in foreign politics and the influence she is evidently acquiring is very sad."[51] "You think the Emperor is not afraid of the priests. Of them perhaps not. . . . The Empress' temper . . . has done more for the Pope than all his Clergy together."[52]

As the British ambassador grumbled, the Austrian diplomats rejoiced. Their information came from their own observations at the court and from Walewski. The interdict on political conversations between the Empress and the Austrians was at last lifted late in April, 1862. Hübner passed through Paris in April; he was careful to sound the Empress, "who, as you know is very much concerned now with politics," and sent home a voluminous report on her views which had ranged from the halls of Montezuma, across Italy to the Balkan peninsula.[53] At the same time Metternich became the recipient once more of her confidential hopes for an Austro-French alliance. He encouraged her with alacrity. Everyone in Vienna, he declared, well knew that the *temps d'arrêt* in the Emperor's revolutionary policy was her handiwork. "I told her that we had a secret hope of seeing her efforts in the interest of religion and a conservative policy prevail and that nothing would make us happier than to owe peace and security to her."[54]

The Roman question became a trial of strength between Empress and Foreign Minister. Although Thouvenel was far more moderate than Prince Napoleon and the Empress was not the bigoted, Protestant-burning papalina pictured by Lord John Russell, the differences between their views

[48] Hübner to Rechberg, Paris, April 18, 1862, HHSA, IX/72, No. 2.
[49] Metternich to Rechberg, March 14, 1862, HHSA, IX/74.
[50] Metternich to Rechberg, April 1, 1862, private, *ibid.*
[51] Cowley to Russell, Paris, April 22, 1862, copy, PRO FO 519/229.
[52] Cowley to Russell, Paris, April 1, 1862, *ibid.*
[53] Hübner to Rechberg, Paris, April 18, 1862, HHSA, IX/72, No. 2.
[54] Metternich to Rechberg, Paris, April 28, 1862, HHSA, IX/72, No. 29 A–C.

were real and important. The Foreign Minister insisted upon the necessity of making some arrangement to evacuate Rome and eventually made it a question of his portfolio. He advocated an agreement essentially like that proposed in 1861 and which later formed the basis of the September Convention of 1864. After Italy had promised to respect the integrity of the Pope's remaining territory and after the Pope had been given time to organize his own army, French troops would retire. But even with these safeguards, Thouvenel could not expect the Pope's voluntary acquiescence to such a plan. It implied faith in Italy's pledge not to invade Rome and meant exposure of the Pope to revolution should he be unable to maintain himself alone. The Foreign Minister was prepared to risk the papal displeasure sure to follow. Although he was not entirely persuaded of the permanence of Italian union, he favored this additional endorsement of the new political entity. The Kingdom of Italy had been formed under his auspices; he would do nothing to destroy it. Retirement of French troops would spell an end to the possibility of French military cooperation with Francis II, living in Rome, to effect a restoration in Naples. According to Thouvenel, Napoleon III should not behave like Henry V.[55]

The Empress, who now had learned a few hard lessons in European diplomacy, had ready some practical objections to Thouvenel's policy. The unity of Italy was disadvantageous to France, she argued. The temporal power was a necessity, not just to placate the Pope, but to separate the northern part of the peninsula from the southern. The presence of Francis II was an encouragement to reaction in Naples. If revolution destroyed the temporal power, both Pope and King would be obliged to flee and render restoration in the south more difficult. She conceded the Romagna to be irretrievable, but hoped for the Pope's recovery of the Marches and Umbria. Toward this end, she thought that the Pope should make a few concessions. "No one could be more '*papaline*' than I," she told Hübner in April; "but I regret that the Pope confines himself to an absolute refusal." Should France pull out of Rome, moreover, the British influence might predominate, or even worse, that of the "Reds," revolutionaries like Garibaldi or Mazzini. Finally, she maintained that since the

---

[55] The Count of Chambord, Bourbon pretender to the French throne, styled himself Henry V. Thouvenel to Flahault, Paris, September 1, 1862, Thouvenel, *Secret*, II, 381. This summary of Thouvenel's policies is taken from a number of sources and authorities. Cowley's correspondence with Lord John Russell and Metternich's correspondence with Rechberg in the spring and summer of 1862 gave the Foreign Minister's official statements to England and Austria. See also the letters of Thouvenel in *Secret*, II, and Louis Thouvenel (ed.), *Pages d'histoire du Second Empire d'après les papiers de M. Thouvenel, ancien ministre des affaires étrangères*, for the same period. The best authorities are Lynn M. Case, *Franco-Italian Relations, 1860–1865*, pp. 105–214, and Jean Maurain, *La Politique ecclésiastique du Second Empire*, pp. 607–623.

French flag had been raised in Rome, it would be dishonored if lowered unless effective provisions for the Pope's temporal power had been made. Here was the pith of the matter. Unlike Thouvenel, she had no faith in an Italian pledge to respect the Pope's land and she was equally distrustful of the Emperor's verbal promise to restrain the Italians should they violate their promise. Always she dreaded a repetition of the Italians' success at Chambéry.[56]

The curtain riser in the struggle was a clash between the Marquis de La Valette, recently appointed French ambassador at Rome, and General Goyon, still commander of the occupying French troops. The General's blatant clericalism and support of Francis II undermined the policies and statements of the ambassador, which were in accord with the Foreign Ministry. Exasperated beyond endurance, La Valette descended on Paris late in April and declared that the Emperor must choose between him and his general. Goyon's wife arrived at nearly the same time to plead her husband's case. Thouvenel stood solidly behind La Valette and made it a question of his portfolio. Goyon, of course, had the support of the Empress, Randon, and Walewski. "The Goyon-La Valette affair *passionne les esprits*," reported Metternich. Descriptions of the rapid fluctuations of the affair filled the diplomatic pouches of the Austrian ambassador and of Cowley for weeks. "Frenchmen lie so," wrote Cowley in superior disdain, "there is no saying who is telling the truth. Lavalette and his side have one story, Walewski and Co. another. My belief is that the Emperor is regularly henpecked, and that it is fear of the Empress w[hic]h now guides his whole conduct in the Roman Question."[57]

But the first round seemed to go to Thouvenel and La Valette. Late in April the Emperor decided to recall Goyon and permitted his Ministers to

[56] Much of this summary has been compiled from the Empress' conversations in 1862 and 1864 with Hübner, Prosper Mérimée, Lord Malmesbury, and Count Goltz (Hübner to Rechberg, Paris, April 18, 1862, HHSA, IX/72, No. 2; Mérimée to Panizzi, Biarritz, September 29, 1862, Mérimée, *Letters to Panizzi*, I, 279–281; Georges Lacour-Gayet, *L'Impératrice Eugénie: Documents et Souvenirs,* fall, 1862, p. 62; Goltz to Bismarck, Paris, July 11, 1864, very confidential, *APP*, Herausgegeben von der Historischen Reichs Kommission, V, No. 201, p. 298). For her views on the restoration in Naples see Metternich to Rechberg, May 11, 1862, private, HHSA, cited in Henry Salomon, *L'Ambassade de Richard de Metternich à Paris,* pp. 60–63; Mülinen to Rechberg, Paris, October 28, 1862, telegram, HHSA, IX/73, No. 75. For her fear of Napoleon's appeasement of Italy see Metternich to Rechberg, Paris, May 12, 1862, private, HHSA, IX/74.

[57] Cowley to Hudson, copy, Paris, April 11, 1862, PRO FO 519/229. For accounts of the La Valette-Goyon affair see also Cowley to Hudson, April 1, 1862, *ibid.*; Cowley to Russell, April 11, 28, 29, *ibid.*; Metternich to Rechberg, Paris, April 10, 1862, HHSA, IX/72; Hübner to Rechberg, Paris, April 18, 1862, *ibid.*, No. 2; Thouvenel to Gramont, Paris, April 8, 1862, Thouvenel, *Secret*, II, 272; Alfred Rastoul, *Le Maréchal Randon, 1795–1871, d'après ses mémoires et des documents inédits: Etude militaire et politique,* pp. 252–253; Randon, *Mémoires,* II, 56.

discuss various plans to break the *status quo* in Rome. Learning of her defeat, the Empress rounded on her husband and refused to appear at a ball scheduled that evening in honor of the Queen of Holland.[58] Perhaps it would have been better if she had remained in her room a few more evenings; her subsequent displays of temper exceeded all becoming limits. The luckless Portuguese ambassador in Paris first drew her fire because of the reported betrothal of his King to a daughter of Victor Emmanuel.[59] But Nigra received her main salvo, discharged thunderously in the salon after a dinner early in May within the hearing of a highly amused Metternich.

What do you want, M. Nigra?
The latter answered that he wished to present her a petition.
Her Majesty: The moment is badly chosen, but speak.
Nigra: I would wish Your Majesty to desist a little from her hostility to us, and that she would use her influence to decide the emperor to retire his troops from Rome.
Her Majesty: I would drown myself sooner than lend a hand to your highway robberies. Oh! You want us to give in always and everywhere; you are insatiable; you call the subjects who have remained faithful to the king of Naples thieves; but what do you call yourselves?
Nigra stammered.
Her Majesty: You are the ones who pillage, you who rob others and who want to make us your accomplices. But just wait; the day of vengeance will come, you will see your Mazzinis and Garibaldis grow up under you, and, the day when you are hanged, I declare to you, it will not be I who will come to your rescue.
Nigra: Your Majesty is really too unfair, and to defend myself I will ask her if the King of Italy today is not doing at Naples what the emperor did in France yesterday.
Her Majesty (furious): Oh, don't say that to me, don't compare the emperor with your highway robber. The emperor did not take anything away from anybody; he found France abandoned, the throne empty, and he saved France by *crushing people of your kind.*
Nigra picks up his hat, leaps to his feet and leaves.[60]

[58] Cowley to Russell, Paris, April 30, 1862, copy, PRO FO 519/229; Metternich to Rechberg, Paris, May 12, 1862, private, HHSA, IX/74.
[59] Cowley to Russell, Paris, May 15, 1862, copy, PRO FO 519/229.
[60] Metternich to Rechberg, May 11, 1862, private, HHSA, reproduced in Salomon, *L'Ambassade,* pp. 62–63. Although this dialogue has already been published, it is given in full here because it so well illustrates the Empress' views on Italian unity, especially her ardent support of Francis II, and because it is rarely available to English-speaking readers. The most recent biographer of Eugénie, Harold Kurtz, makes only a short, oblique reference to it (*Empress Eugénie,* p. 165). Aubry (*Eugénie,* p. 156) reproduces only a single paragraph. An exception is George Peabody Gooch (*The Second Empire,* pp. 46–47), who quotes it in its entirety.

The Fall of Thouvenel

The victory of the Foreign Minister was a Pyrrhic one. Goyon's successor, appointed by the Emperor late in May, was none other than General Montebello, whose wife had accompanied the Empress to Scotland in 1860. The General himself was unobjectionable; but his nomination cancelled all joy at the vanquishment of Goyon. According to Cowley, Mme de Montebello was "a dreadful bigot like all the women here." It was generally conceded that the wife held "the whip hand" and would supplant the influence of La Valette at Rome.[61] Cowley was prejudiced, of course, but his misogynic prognostications were at least partially fulfilled. During the summer of 1862 the Empress corresponded directly with the Pope through Mme de Montebello. The French ambassador at Rome found his policies checkmated by the "high feminine influence" emanating from France.[62]

As Cowley feared, the Emperor had been influenced by the tantrums of his wife. On the very evening of the ill-fated ball for the Queen of Holland the Empress extracted from him two promises: that he would never "abandon the pope to his enemies," and that he would not again conceal from her his intentions in regard to Italy and the Pope.[63] Prince Napoleon was despatched to Turin with a letter announcing the first of these pledges; with his departure Eugénie was able to exert "a more direct influence on Italian policy." By the end of May the Emperor enunciated his formal decision to regard the territory then held by the Pope as inviolable. He was ready to enter into an agreement with the other Catholic powers to *guarantee* the temporal power and he would evacuate Rome only if he were convinced that the Pope was beyond any danger. Beaming with happiness and confident that she had won the day, Eugénie announced the glad tidings to the papal nuncio and the Austrian ambassador and hastened to inform the Pope himself in a letter ostensibly addressed to Mme de Montebello.[64] The Emperor himself soon verified these decisions and opened negotiations with Rome early in June. The long-awaited *tournure définitive* had come.

A wide chasm had opened up between the views of Foreign Minister and

---

[61] Cowley to Hudson, Paris, June 2, 1862, copy, PRO FO 519/229. See also Case, *Franco-Italian Relations*, p. 184. Mme de Montebello despised Victor Emmanuel and refused to be presented to him when she passed through Turin (Horace de Viel-Castel, *Mémoires sur le règne de Napoléon III, 1851–1864, publiés d'après le manuscrit original*, VI, 150–151).

[62] Rastoul, *Randon*, p. 259. See also Metternich to Rechberg, August 16, 1862, private, HHSA, IX/74, *varia*; also cited by Salomon, *L'Ambassade*, p. 64.

[63] Metternich to Rechberg, Paris, May 12, 1862, private, HHSA, IX/74.

[64] Metternich to Rechberg, Paris, June 9, 1862, HHSA, IX/72, No. 36 A–E; *ibid.*, private, August 16, 1862, IX/74, *varia*. See also Beyens, *Second Empire*, I, 200–204; Cowley to Russell, Paris, June 10, 1862, copy, PRO FO 519/230.

Emperor. While both agreed in principle on the desirability of evacuation from Rome, Napoleon was now the more propapal of the two. Thouvenel favored a simple bilateral agreement with Italy in which France would withdraw her troops after a period of time in return for an Italian promise to respect papal territorial integrity. The Emperor's plan envisioned papal reconciliation with Turin and a positive guarantee of the Catholic powers. By his plan the Pope would be protected from his enemies inside and outside of Rome.[65]

The Pope's brusque, disdainful refusal to consider the new French proposals nearly wrecked all Eugénie's hard work in bringing her husband to oppose Thouvenel's plans. If Garibaldi had not chosen that moment to reappear at the head of another filibustering expedition, she might have been unable to prevent the Emperor from turning once again to negotiation with Italy. But with Garibaldi on the loose, recruiting volunteers with the slogan "Rome or Death," any thought of French withdrawal from Rome was out of the question. The Empress and the clericals gleefully accepted this help from strange quarters. They saw in his march on Rome in August the long-anticipated event that would shatter Italian unity. Should the patriot establish a government of sorts in the Holy City the Emperor could declare the plebiscites null and void and revive plans for an Italian federation.[66] Garibaldi's rash march, if left unchecked by Italy, seemed like an answer to clerical prayers.

Victor Emmanuel understood his predicament perfectly and expressed his chagrin with characteristic directness and coarseness. Garibaldi was going crazy, he told the Prussian ambassador at Turin, and was letting himself be victimized by conspirators of the extreme Left and Right. The King was especially worried over the attitude of France. "The emperor is weakening visibly and the empress is our enemy and works with the priests. If I had her in my hands I would teach her well what women are good for and with what they should meddle."[67]

In August the King despatched the Marquis of Pepoli to Paris to seek permission for Italy to enter Rome, but the effort was in vain. Pepoli found himself totally unable to duplicate the fantastic success of Cialdini and Farini at Chambéry. The Emperor not only remained unshakeable in his

[65] In May the Emperor had shown to his Council a plan with even more concessions to the Pope. By it Pius IX would have received back nominal sovereignty over all his lost territories—even the Romagna. Thouvenel thought the plan "senseless" and "absurd" and, with all the Ministers except Walewski, prevailed on the Emperor to withdraw it (Case, *Franco-Italian Relations,* pp. 186–187. See also Cowley to Russell, Paris, May 23, 1862, copy, PRO FO 519/229; Beyens, *Second Empire,* I, 205).

[66] Beyens, *Second Empire,* I, 205–206; Metternich to Rechberg, Paris, September 1, 1862, secret, HHSA, IX/72, No. 50 A–C.

[67] Brassier de St. Simon to William II, Turin, July 31, 1862, *APP,* II, No. 481, p. 723.

determination not to abandon the Pope but also exposed the emissary to the heavy guns of the Empress. Metternich learned on excellent authority of her volley: "We do not know with whom we are dealing now. Is Garibaldi a decoy or not, that is the question. I prefer the undisguised enemy to the domino. If you say 'Rome or Death'—I declare that is my motto too, but I say it with far more candor than you."[68]

Seeing no other means of escape from his predicament, Victor Emmanuel stopped Garibaldi with his arms at Aspromonte on August 30. For a moment the Empress despaired. She had reckoned on the mad enterprise of "her friend" Garibaldi to generate a backlash that would destroy the Kingdom of Italy. But she was reprieved by the enemy itself. Foolishly, General Durando, Italian Foreign Minister, destroyed the good effect of the King's action at Aspromonte with a blustering diplomatic circular which demanded Rome for Italy rather than French evacuation. If she had dictated it herself, Eugénie declared, she would not have changed a word.[69] Almost simultaneously the British government lectured the Emperor on his unjustifiable defense of the temporal power which deprived the Romans of their liberty and alienated the Italian nation. The Emperor could not now withdraw his troops without giving the appearance of forsaking the Pope and submitting to the dictation of Britain and Italy. When Thouvenel continued to advocate French evacuation of Rome, the Emperor dismissed him from the Foreign Ministry and replaced him with Drouyn de Lhuys.

The implications of Thouvenel's retirement were not at first clear. The Empress and Walewski had hoped to evict the anticlerical Persigny from the Council along with the Foreign Minister. But the old Bonapartist protested furiously, and the other Ministers—especially Baroche, Fould, and Rouher—threatened to resign en masse. In the end Persigny and all the rest except Thouvenel stayed. Only Benedetti, Flahault, and La Valette, recalled from Turin, London, and Rome, exited with the Foreign Minister. The Emperor declared that the change was one of men, not of policy.[70] But a diplomatic circular issued by Drouyn de Lhuys, on the instruction of the Emperor, endorsed the principle of a collective guarantee by the Catholic powers of the remaining territory of the Pope. The despatch was a significant departure from Thouvenel's approach to the Roman question. Subsequent events showed that the Emperor had made perhaps the most critical single decision on foreign policy of his reign.

Thouvenel had been friendly to Italy and Russia and receptive to Prus-

[68] Metternich to Rechberg, Paris, circa Aug. 20, 1862, private, HHSA, IX/74.

[69] Thouvenel to Benedetti, October 11, 1862, Thouvenel, *Pages d'histoire*, p. 395.

[70] Cowley to Russell, Paris, October 14, 1862, copy, PRO FO 519/230; Case, *Franco-Italian Relations*, pp. 213–214.

sian feelers for support in Germany. Drouyn de Lhuys believed that the future of France lay in an alliance with Austria. To placate the Austrians he was prepared to destroy Italian unity. His entrance into the Quai d'Orsay meant the immediate discontinuation of efforts to negotiate a treaty with Turin for the evacuation of Rome, and, consequently, alienation of Prussia and Russia. The Emperor had arrived at the crossroads and had elected the high road to Vienna.

Why did the Emperor turn to a Foreign Minister known to advocate restorations in southern and central Italy? With his well-demonstrated sympathy for the Italian cause, why did he emphasize his decision to deny Victor Emmanuel "one more step"? To some extent the Italians had only themselves to blame. They had played their game roughly and had presented the Emperor with the equivalent of an ultimatum in the Durando circular. But Napoleon could easily have shelved the matter for a time, have allowed tempers to cool, and with the same Foreign Minister, have recommended negotiations a few months later. So he had done in 1860 and 1861.

Professor Lynn M. Case in his *French Opinion on War and Diplomacy during the Second Empire* has suggested that the Emperor's ministerial change was in large part dictated by considerations of public opinion— that he dismissed Thouvenel in order to "get right" with the clergy and the clericals in preparation for the elections of members of the Legislative Body scheduled for the end of May, 1863.[71] The Emperor knew, too, that the army was hostile to Italian unification. When he visited the military camp at Châlons in August he had been impressed by the force of the anti-Italian feeling.[72] The opinion of the army and of the public was no doubt sufficient to prevent him from abandoning the Pope, that is, from evacuating his troops from Rome in the face of Italian and British bombast. But it does not entirely explain the appointment of Drouyn de Lhuys. If his move were simply a pre-election maneuver, would it not have been more effective on an impressionable people if made closer to polling day? Public opinion, moreover, had sounded no clarion call to undo the revolutionary work of 1860 and 1861. It had been either favorable or simply indifferent to the creation of an Italian kingdom. While he would be complying with the desires of the clerical and Legitimist minority in France, the Emperor knew he would be running counter to the public at large if he restored Francis in Naples and the Pope in the Marches and Umbria.

More than impersonal factors swayed the Emperor. Before the minis-

[71] Case, *French Opinion on War*, p. 151.
[72] Metternich to Rechberg, Paris, August 24, 1862, HHSA, IX/73; Cowley to Hudson, Chantilly, September 2, 1862, copy, PRO FO 519/230; Beyens, *Second Empire*, I, 205–206.

terial change he wavered hesitantly between the warring factions in his entourage. Which persons could have influenced him? Prince Napoleon was in Switzerland during the crisis. But the majority of the Ministers supported Thouvenel. Listing his supporters, the Foreign Minister could name every member of the Council with the exception of Walewski, Randon, and Pierre Magne. Unfortunately for Thouvenel, he found the feebleness of his opponents' numbers offset by the presence on their side of a *"powerful auxiliary,"* the Empress.[73]

Much evidence affirms the sustained, daily activity of the Empress in the Roman question during the summer and autumn. In August, while the Emperor was at Châlons and while Garibaldi was rampant in Italy, she received a special emissary from Rome, Monseigneur Nardi, who informed her of the splendid impression on His Holiness made by her letters addressed to Mme de Montebello. Writing to the Emperor of her interview with Nardi, she obtained his consent to assure the Pope of French military protection in Rome until all trace of revolution in Italy had disappeared. Nardi was enchanted with the Empress and left much elated with the statement he had elicited.[74]

The Emperor's decision to dismiss Thouvenel occurred just after his return from Biarritz, where he had for a month been exposed to Eugénie's clique—the Walewskis, the Spaniards, and the Mexican *émigrés*. Diplomats often remarked on the frequency with which the Emperor's holiday in the Pyrenees immediately preceded some startling event. In 1861, for example, the commencement of the Mexican expedition had followed on the heels of his return. This year, noted Cowley, Biarritz certainly lived up to its reputation.[75]

The hostility between Eugénie and Thouvenel had flared openly just before she had left for the south. At the close of a meeting of the Council in which Thouvenel had pressed for evacuation from Rome, the Empress had dressed him down loudly. Undaunted, the Minister replied sarcastically: "Madame, if *the emperor* had said half of what Your Majesty has let me hear, my resignation would already be on its way."[76] The barb lay in the inference that the Empress' views had no weight.

In her contest with the Foreign Minister, she had recruited, in addition to Walewski, a new ally—none other than La Guéronnière, the author of *Le Pape et le congrès*. Either from conviction or venality, he became a most ardent supporter of the temporal power and opponent of Italian

[73] Thouvenel to Flahault, Paris, September 1, 1862, Thouvenel, *Secret*, II, 381–382.
[74] Metternich to Rechberg, Paris, August 16, 20, and 24, private, HHSA, IX/74; September 4, 1862, *ibid.*, IX/72.
[75] Cowley to Russell, Paris, October 17, 1862, copy, PRO FO 519/230.
[76] Lacour-Gayet, *Eugénie*, p. 61; Thouvenel, *Secret*, II, 382 n. 1.

unity. On her inspiration and with her protection, he founded a news-paper, *La France politique,* which openly opposed the pro-Italian tone of the official sheets. Despite the grumbling of Persigny, whose function was supervision of the press, the paper flourished unscathed and, a few weeks before Thouvenel's dismissal, aroused a furor in political circles with a pro-posal to replace the Kingdom of Italy with an Italian federation.[77]

The number of witnesses on the scene to testify to the predominant in-fluence of the Empress in the dismissal of Thouvenel is impressive, especially as they ranged in the political spectrum from Persigny to Count Mülinen, Austrian chargé d'affaires—from ardent Italianissime to devoted subject of Franz Joseph. Persigny was the most vehement, and he told the Em-peror: "You allow yourself to be ruled by your wife just as I do. But I only compromise my fortune, . . . whereas you sacrifice your own interests, and those of your son and the country at large."[78] The reprimand is prob-ably unique among pungent speeches addressed to reigning monarchs.

We do not know Prince Napoleon's judgment of the matter. But Ma-tilda's circle raged against the Empress and blamed her alone for the min-isterial change. "Marie Antoinette became unpopular under the name of 'The Austrian woman'; let the 'Spanish woman' take heed," threatened the Count of Viel Castel, reporter from her salon.[79] Less spiteful than Matilda's friends, Baroche, usually one of the Empress' admirers, re-gretted the appointment of Drouyn de Lhuys as revealing only too clearly the authoritative hand of the Empress.[80] Thouvenel himself regarded the Empress as a formidable adversary, although he did not hold her solely responsible for his disgrace. He told Cowley that he believed the Durando circular was the cause or at least the excuse for the Emperor's conduct. But the British ambassador, after exhausting all of his sources of information, was skeptical of the importance of impersonal factors. He reported: "For

[77] For information on La Guéronnière see Metternich to Rechberg, Paris, August 20, 1862, private, HHSA, IX/74; Metternich to Rechberg, August 24, 1862, *ibid.,* IX/73; Mülinen to Rechberg, October 18, 1862, secret, *ibid.,* No. 58; Gramont to Thouvenel, Vienna, September 15, 1862, Thouvenel, *Secret,* II, 390–391. See also Beyens, *Second Empire,* I, 205–206; Case, *French Opinion on War,* p. 150. La Guéron-nière continued to receive the Empress' protection until the very last days of the Em-pire. In the spring of 1870 she sought to have him replace Daru in the Foreign Minis-try. Failing that, she obtained his appointment to the embassy at Constantinople (see the correspondence between Lord Clarendon and Lord Lyons, May and June, 1870, Clarendon Deposit, Bodleian Library, Carton 474).

[78] Mérimée to Panizzi, Marseille, October 19, 1862, *Letters to Panizzi,* I, 295. There is no reason to doubt this testimony. The language ascribed to Persigny is so astonish-ingly bold as to virtually preclude the possibility of its fabrication. Mülinen also re-ported a violent altercation between the Emperor and Persigny and another between Persigny and the Empress (Mülinen to Rechberg, Paris, October 18, 1862, secret, HHSA, IX/73, No. 58 B).

[79] Viel-Castel, *Mémoires,* VI, 162–163.

[80] Baroche's notes, Maurain, *Politique ecclésiastique,* pp. 619–620.

my part, I believe that it is . . . weakness and duplicity mingled [on the Emperor's part] and that to paraphrase the former dictum of the Times 'The Empress has done it all'."[81]

Like that of other severe critics of the Empress, Cowley's testimony may be suspected of prejudice. He was fond of repeating gossip about her for the entertainment of Lord John Russell. Cowley himself had the reputation of being "soft" on Rome and had nearly lost his post when Russell replaced Malmesbury in the Foreign Office in 1859. One is tempted to see in his ridicule of the Empress' supposed fire-eating Catholicism a maneuver to ingratiate himself with his antipapal superior. But his testimony on the influence of the Empress in the Roman question in 1862 is corroborated at every turn by that of Metternich or Mülinen. The opinion of Mülinen, who was handling affairs while the ambassador was on vacation in the early fall, was as unequivocal as that of Cowley. His informants were Walewski, La Guéronnière, and Count Bourqueney, former French ambassador at Vienna. In a multi-paged despatch of florid prose he extolled the efforts of the "August Companion of the Sovereign" whose influence on the mind of "Her Husband" exceeded even that of Walewski and had brought to pass this fortunate event.[82]

Given from a different vantage point is the testimony of Prosper Mérimée. Admitted behind the scenes as a guest of the family at Biarritz and Saint-Cloud, and on intimate terms with the principals, he was appalled at the Empress' handiwork. France was being delivered into the clutches of the "Legitimist and Papist set," he moaned. "Our amiable *hostess* [Eugénie] is making a great mistake and is putting herself in the power of people who would betray her tomorrow or lead her to the brink of a precipice. The whole affair is positively stupid and lamentable."[83] Because Mérimée was outside of the political hurly-burly—his own career not at stake—and because he was genuinely devoted to the Empress, his testimony has the ring of truth to it.

Evidently the Empress' role was essential to the appointment of Drouyn de Lhuys and to the orientation of the Empire toward Austria. Luck was with her, of course, in evicting Thouvenel. Who could have anticipated Garibaldi's irresponsible enterprise, Durando's impudent circular, or Lord John Russell's irritating lecture? But it seems unlikely that the blunders of the Italians or of the British by themselves could have yielded more than a coolness between Paris and Turin and a temporary cessation of the negoti-

---

[81] Cowley to Russell, Paris, October 14, 1862, copy, PRO FO 519/230.

[82] Mülinen to Rechberg, Paris, October 18, 1862, secret, HHSA, No. 58.

[83] Mérimée to Panizzi, Paris, October 15, 1862, *Letters to Panizzi,* I, 293. See also Mérimée to Panizzi, October 28, 1862, *ibid.,* I, 297–298; Mérimée to an unidentified lady, Paris, Prosper Mérimée, *Lettres à une inconnue,* October 23, 1862, II, 204.

ations for evacuation from Rome. The Empress was the necessary agent to change the chemistry of the crisis.

THE POLISH REVOLT: A MARRIAGE OF INCLINATION?

The change in French foreign policy became evident early in 1863 when the Poles revolted against the Russians. Public opinion in France, horrified at the reports of ruthless Russian repression, sided unanimously with the insurgents and clamored for steps to ameliorate their lot. But before England, France, and Austria could despatch a joint note of protest to St. Petersburg, Bismarck threw a "firebrand" into the explosive situation by signing the Alvensleben Convention with Russia.[84] The agreement permitted Russian troops to pursue escaping Poles into Prussia and induced a *rapprochement* between the two powers. The French government believed the moment opportune to strike a bargain with Austria and to destroy by force the odious treaties of 1815.

The declamations of the Empress against Russia were among the loudest. The legendary bravery of the Poles in resistance to oppression had long excited her admiration. In 1861, influenced by the half-Polish Walewski, she inspired an anti-Russian article in the *Constitutionnel,* organ of the French Foreign Ministry.[85] In December, 1862, she annoyed the Austrian Foreign Minister by her intercessions in behalf of the Montenegrins. Slavs in general, except Russian Slavs, of course, were heroes in her eyes.[86] She disliked the ruler of Russia, although she had never met him, and had opposed Russian influence in the Balkans since the days of the Crimean War.[87]

But the Empress' advocacy of active intervention in behalf of the Poles, which was inconsistent with her antirevolutionary stand in the Italian question, was not entirely *politique de sentiment.* She had in mind the immense popularity of the Polish cause in France and the broad vistas of European diplomacy. For reasons of humanity or out of hatred for monarchy, republicans and Legitimists, freethinkers and clericals in France had united in condemnation of Russia. The Empress could brighten her image, tarnished by her association with the now unpopular Mexican expedition, by a show of sympathy for this democratic cause of the people.[88]

---

[84] The word of the Empress. Goltz to Bismarck, Paris, March 10, 1862, secret, *APP,* III, No. 324, p. 388.

[85] Lacour-Gayet, *Eugénie,* p. 63; Viel-Castel, *Mémoires,* VI, 112.

[86] Metternich to Rechberg, December 9, 1862, private, HHSA, IX/74; Rechberg to Metternich, December 2, 1862, *ibid.*

[87] Goltz to Bismarck, Paris, July 23, 1864. *APP,* V, No. 223, p. 321; *ibid.,* August 22, 1864, No. 257, p. 381; Marguerite Castillon du Perron, *La Princesse Mathilde, un règne féminin sous le Second Empire,* pp. 137–142.

[88] Cowley to Russell, Paris, February 29, 1863, copy, PRO FO 519/230.

Moreover she found the occasion propitious for the assertion of French leadership in Europe. Aware of the results of the recent analyses of the prefects' reports on public opinion, she told the Prussian ambassador that the Emperor would be obliged to intervene in behalf of the Poles lest the elections in May, 1863, go against him.[89] She may well have reasoned that should war result from the French action, the Emperor would have a united public behind him.

The Empress had in mind far more than the mere resurrection of an independent Poland. If France could ally with Austria she could tackle both Prussia and Russia and enter into the main arena of the conflict of the powers—the contest for central Europe on which her greatness depended. The moment had come for the demolition of the framework of 1815 and for the trial of strength on the Rhine. By-products of the far-ranging combat would include restorations in the Papal States and in Naples, the solution of the Venetian question, and the suppression of European Turkey. Thus, said the Empress, would the Emperor achieve the "consolidation of his dynasty and the happiness of the world."

The entire panorama of the new Europe to be revealed when the gunsmoke cleared is preserved for us in considerable detail by Metternich, who was the eager recipient of her confidences. Deciding that it was time that the Austrians realized the seriousness of the French desire to strike a bargain, the Empress declared she would tell all. "I know your emperor listens to you and loves you," she began. "Let him see the bottom of our sack. He will do what he wishes with it, but at least he will do justice to the frankness of a woman who is naturally more fantastic than men, but who has the interest of her adopted country, her husband and son too much at heart to risk lying when speaking of the future." Accordingly, she opened an atlas and conducted the ambassador, whose curiosity was by this time keen, on an imaginary but far-ranging peregrination of the states of Europe. For more than an hour, as the two bent over the map, she figuratively joined together, split asunder, resurrected, and destroyed. "What a *flight* and what a *bird*!" thought Metternich when it was all over.[90]

This blueprint which she drew for the Austrian ambassador has often been dismissed as romantic nonsense, a utopian phantasy far outside of the mainstream of French foreign policy. Such an assumption, however, is palpably false. Eugénie told Metternich that she intended only to "anticipate" (*devancer*) the Emperor. A few days later he made the Austrians a proposal of an offensive and defensive alliance. Basically it was a vari-

---

[89] Goltz to Bismarck, Paris, March 10, 1863, *APP*, III, No. 324, pp. 388–389.

[90] Metternich to Rechberg, Paris, February 22, 1863, HHSA, IX/76. This report, reproduced by Oncken (*Rheinpolitik*, I, No. 1, pp. 3–6), is well known to scholars; see Appendix.

ation on the already familiar theme of the three kingdoms in Italy with the addition of the Polish question. If, said the Emperor to Metternich, events in Poland forced Austria to evacuate her Polish province, Galicia, he offered her exclusive preponderance in the Balkans. Should the destruction of Italian unity and the division of the peninsula into three parts (Naples, Papacy, and Sardinia) require the cession of Venetia, the Emperor would support the Austrian bid for compensation in Germany.[91] Here was the flowering of the conservative plant—with a few revolutionary grafts—which had been growing since 1861. The Austrian government seriously considered the French proposals and called Metternich to Vienna for consultation.

What of the rest of the Empress' grand design? Was it merely a tale from the *Thousand and One Nights,* the fleeting invention of a febrile mind? Metternich feared not. He begged the Austrian Foreign Minister, Count Rechberg, not to consider her plan a joke. "I believe the empress and even the emperor well convinced of the possibility and of the *necessity* of realizing it some day." Rechberg needed no admonition. In alarm he expressed to the ambassador his "absolute repugnance" for parts of her plan, especially for her design of the future shape of the Germanies, which he found contrary to Austrian interests.[92] She had, he noted, divided Germany between Prussia and Austria. Prussia could annex Saxony, Hanover, and the Duchies north of the Main River; Austria would acquire Silesia from Prussia and take anything she pleased south of the Main. But in return for this booty they would concede the Rhineland to France and relinquish their Polish provinces to a resurrected Polish state.

Rechberg reminded Metternich that the idea of such a division of Germany had not originated with the Empress. Berlin had long pined to exclude Austrian influence from the north and to absorb the smaller states above the Main. France would stand to benefit from the consolidation of a relatively strong, but contained, Prussia as a counterweight to Austria in the south. French policy had traditionally favored Catholic Poland. Expansion to the Rhine, the acquisition of the "natural frontiers," moreover, had been a French ambition antedating the reign of Louis XIV. The idea was particularly in line with Bonaparte tradition. Foreign diplomats under the Second Empire were eternally on their guard against a Napoleonic breakout to the east.

Turning toward the East, for reasons of "public benefit and Christian morality," the Empress had dismembered the Turkish empire at one swoop. She destined Russia to receive Asia Minor in compensation for cession of

[91] Metternich to Rechberg, March 5, 1863, very secret, *ibid.,* No. 4, p. 11.
[92] Rechberg to Metternich, Vienna, February 27, 1863, private, HHSA, IX/76. This letter is not published by Oncken.

her Polish provinces and for other unspecified losses. She awarded the Sultan's possessions in the Balkans to Austria (along the Adriatic) and to a greater Greece which was to comprise even Constantinople. A native prince should rule over the Danubian provinces. The fate of the Levant as well as the future of the Sultan was apparently left unrevealed, or was at least left unreported by Metternich.

So facile yet sweeping a solution to the so-called Eastern question certainly seems to carry the mark of genuine Eugenian romanticism. Equally unrealistic was her suggestion that the European rulers dispossessed by her new arrangements betake themselves to the New World to "civilize and monarchize" the American republics in line with the example set by Mexico. Many of the other components of her composition, however, were familiar to diplomats. Thouvenel and Prince Napoleon had consistently supported revolution in the Balkans. For years the Quai d'Orsay had favored the union of Moldavia and Wallachia on the Danube under a native prince. The Empress' plan to compensate Austria along the Adriatic for the loss of Venetia at the expense of Turkey simply repeated what had for several years been pandered in diplomatic corridors. Napoleon and Thouvenel since 1861 had intermittently dangled such combinations before the Austrians. The British, especially Clarendon and Russell, were indefatigable promoters of such a combination. There was no more familiar pastime in the diplomatic world than the division of the possessions of the Turkish "sick man" in anticipation of his demise.

Unfortunately for the Empress, she was unable to integrate Mexico into her design as a compensation for Austria for the losses anticipated in Venetia and Galicia. Her allusion to the New World of necessity had to be brief. Just when the imperial couple most urgently needed some inducement to make the Austrians willing to part with Venetia, they found themselves unable to deliver the Mexican throne. The expeditionary forces had failed to take the City of Puebla the preceding summer and were bogged down in inglorious bushwhacking in the interior. The City of Mexico was still a distant goal. The Emperor was seriously reconsidering his plans for monarchy there. The candidacy of Ferdinand Maximilian had lain dormant for months.

In fact in 1863 the Empress found her Mexican venture an impediment rather than an asset to the realization of her dream of an Austro-French alliance. Many in the Emperor's government, especially Fould, now Minister of Finance, knew that Napoleon could not launch a major European war with nearly forty thousand men overseas, to say nothing of the contingent in Rome. Fould argued that the Emperor might parley with Juárez, Mexican President of the republic, once the honor of the army had been vindicated. Hidalgo and the other *émigrés* were in despair.[93] The over-extension of the French military forces gave the Austrians food for sober reflection. Suppose they consented to sacrifice Venetia and Galicia for the sake of the French alliance only to hear Napoleon confess: "I am in despair not to be able to come to your aid—my soldiers are in Mexico, my money is in Italy." What would the subjects of Franz Joseph say?[94] Prince Napoleon believed that in the event of a war French troops should immediately be brought back from Mexico.[95]

With the Mexican crown beyond his reach, Napoleon, and even Eugénie, had looked about for one nearer at hand for their protégé. They were at that very moment strongly backing him as ruler of either Greece or Poland.[96] Ferdinand Maximilian refused the Greek throne in February, 1863. Had he accepted, or had an offer of the Polish crown materialized, it seems probable that Napoleon would have abandoned entirely his pursuit of a monarchy in Mexico.

The Empress was not the only one to journey boldly over the map of Europe. On February 20 Prince Napoleon submitted to the Emperor an outline of his plans, which certainly equalled those of the Empress in grandiosity and excelled them in daring. He, too, looked forward to a war to resurrect Poland in which France would move to the Rhine, Austria would cede Venetia and Galicia, and Turkey would lose all her European possessions.[97] But the Prince planned to take on Russia and Prussia with only the help of Sweden and Italy. He hoped Austria would stay neutral

[93] Of many letters expressing uncertainty about the future of the Mexican expedition see Hidalgo to De Pont, Paris, February 21, HKM, Carton 3, No. 450; Rechberg to Ferdinand Maximilian, Vienna, March 7, 1863, *ibid.*, No. 449; Ferdinand Maximilian to Metternich, Miramar, June 13, 1863, *ibid.*, No. 431; Metternich to Ferdinand Maximilian, Paris, June 26, 1863, *ibid.*, No. 560. For Fould's opinion see Cowley to Russell, Paris, June 9, 1863, copy, PRO FO 519/230; October 3, 1863, *ibid.*, 519/231; Chantilly, November 12, 1863, *ibid.*, 519/231. See also Mérimée to Panizzi, Paris, June 1, 1863, *Letters to Panizzi*, I, 330; Cowley to Russell, Paris, May 24, 1863, copy, PRO FO 519/230.

[94] Metternich to Rechberg, Paris, March 5, 1863, very secret, HHSA; Oncken, *Rheinpolitik*, I, No. 4, p. 77.

[95] Note [by Prince Napoleon] for the consideration of the Emperor on Affairs in Poland, Paris, February 20, 1863, D'Hauterive, *Second Empire*, p. 267.

[96] Metternich to Rechberg, Paris, April 10, 1862, private, HHSA; February 15, 1863, *ibid.*, No. 15. Cowley to Russell, Paris, February 17, 1863, copy, PRO FO 519/230; Russell to Cowley, Foreign Office, February 16, 1863, *ibid.*, 519/200. In her conversation with Metternich on February 21 the Empress referred merely to "an archduke" or the King of Saxony for Poland. Subsequent remarks of Leopold to Charlotte make plain that Ferdinand Maximilian was in question ("Conversations avec cher Papa," Brussels, September 11–19, 1963, HKM, Carton 4, No. 918).

[97] Note [by Prince Napoleon] for the consideration of the Emperor on Affairs in Poland, Paris, February 20, 1863, D'Hauterive, *Second Empire*, pp. 261–268.

since her best interests, according to the Prince, lay in consenting to the double sacrifice asked of her. Italy would add Venetia to its unbroken union. The Emperor thanked his cousin courteously for these suggestions but urged him "not to dance faster than the violins."[98]

In reality, the Emperor was firmly committed to the idea of the Austrian alliance and rejected his cousin's alternative. When Arese, in March, journeyed northward in an effort to forge a Franco-Italian alliance on ideas similar to those of the Prince, he found himself put off by Emperor and Empress with honeyed circumlocutions. He left the French court empty-handed and much disheartened.[99] Prince Napoleon contributed to the defeat of his own plans and to the rejection of the Italian alliance. While Arese was still in Paris, the Prince erupted in another of those violent diatribes in the Senate which were becoming annual affairs. So unrestrained was his attack on imperial policy that the Emperor disavowed him in the *Moniteur*. To the joy of the Empress he left for Egypt in a huff.[100]

When the Empress so exuberantly bared to Metternich the French plans to rearrange the map of Europe did she, perhaps, simply act on the instructions of the Emperor? Had she been told to send up a sort of trial balloon to test the Austrian reactions? The conduct of the Emperor at the time precludes this possibility. While he was now persuaded that the road to the Rhine lay through Vienna, he attempted to conceal his ultimate goal from the Austrians. With Metternich he spoke only of the Polish and Italian questions. The ambassador, comprehending the delicacy of the situation, tactfully refrained from disclosing to him what he had heard about the Rhineland from the Empress. The Emperor had also cautioned Prince Napoleon to guard closely his dream of French expansion. In answer to the Prince's memorandum he agreed that his goal might one day be realized, but warned: "I have to deal with powers who are very touchy, and the moment they have any reason to see ambitious views on my part they will reject any kind of alliance."[101] It appears he was completely unaware that his wife was betraying the schemes he most wished to be kept secret.

Consequently, when Eugénie threw "her hat over the windmill," as she expressed it, she imperilled the success of the negotiation. With the "bit in

---

[98] Napoleon to Prince Napoleon, February 22, 1863, *ibid.*, pp. 186–187. The date given by D'Hauterive, January 22, is obviously a misprint.

[99] Grabinski, *Un Ami de Napoléon III*, p. 204; La Gorce, *Second Empire*, IV, 177–178; Pagani, "Napoleone III, Eugenia de Montijo e Francesco Arese," *Nuova antologia*, CCX (1921), 26; Case, *Franco-Italian Relations*, pp. 249–255.

[100] Ollivier, *L'Empire libéral*, VI, 176–181; D'Hauterive, *Second Empire*, pp. 187–194.

[101] February 22, 1863, D'Hauterive, *Second Empire*, pp. 186–187.

her teeth" (Metternich's unflattering metaphor), she monopolized the ambassador's time while Drouyn de Lhuys fumed at the Quai d'Orsay. Metternich was compelled to spend three days running from court to Foreign Ministry to appease the Minister and re-establish normal diplomatic intercourse.[102] Her "furia francesa" alarmed the cautious Austrians. The moment for an alliance was now, she pleaded. To delay would be to lose the occasion. Nothing would remain but chimeras and memories of futile pleasure excursions around the world. An alliance with Austria— that was the end of her desires. "*You* are the marriage of inclination, don't force us to make a marriage of *reason.*"[103]

The Polish revolt brought the Empress to the apogee of her influence and power and brought the foreign policy of the Empire to the uttermost of its incoherence. Many of her ideas she had borrowed from others; her originality—and her folly—lay in scrambling them into one indigestible potpourri of ingredients, some conservative, some revolutionary—support of revolution in Poland on the one hand and promotion of restoration in Italy on the other. Her Legitimist sympathies made her a ringleader in urging alliance with Austria and partial destruction of the *faits accomplis* south of the Alps. Hence the absurdity of offering Austria a "conservative" alliance by which Franz Joseph would lose straight away two of his provinces, Galicia and Venetia, to revolutionary states. Eugénie herself sensed but never entirely grasped the utter incongruity of her ideas. "Keep my letter for yourself," she directed Metternich during the negotiation. "It has a revolutionary aroma which would lower me in the eyes of Vienna while my *Sr. Benito Espagnol* puts me in bad here."[104] Her dilemma was that of the Empire itself after the fall of Thouvenel, as it strove in vain to harness under one yoke traditional, dynastic principles and the liberal ideal of national self-determination.

[102] Metternich to Rechberg, Paris, March 5, 1863, very secret; HHSA, Oncken, *Rheinpolitik*, I, No. 4, p. 10.

[103] Eugénie to Metternich, Paris, Tuileries, March 2, 1863, HHSA; Oncken, *Rheinpolitik*, No. 3, p. 9.

[104] *Ibid.*, p. 10.

CHAPTER 5

EMPIRE IN THE DOLDRUMS
The Loss of Hegemony, 1863–1866

A WOMAN SCORNED

The diplomatic union so ardently desired by the Empress was never to be consummated. From Vienna, whither Metternich had carried the French proposals, came a point-blank refusal to cede either Venetia or Galicia under the conditions posed. Rechberg assessed the value of the destruction of Italian unity as incommensurate with the risks entailed in a policy of action and with the sacrifices demanded. Austria would never admit the cession of Venetia to be favorable to her interests and would entertain it only *after* she had won compensation both in Germany and in the Balkans.

Although Austria rejected outright the proposed offensive and defensive alliance, she nevertheless worded her reply in a way to keep France dangling on her line. If the two countries might not be allies, they could at least be friends. Rechberg was not insensible to the advantage of French good will in the Eastern question. Perhaps the presence of a third party, Britain—who could be counted on to oppose a war in behalf of the Poles—would help cool the ardor of the French Emperor. Could not Austria, Britain, and France explore means of cooperating on the Polish question? Rechberg asked Napoleon. By a prolongation of the negotiation the Austrian government hoped to maintain some tie with France, however slack might be the line, and still retain its freedom of action.[1]

Hence the Crimean coalition ostensibly came to life and provoked a sterile exchange of notes between the three "allied" powers and Russia. The *démarche* advertised a diplomatic unity that did not exist and

[1] Rechberg to Metternich, Vienna, February 27, 1863, HHSA, IX/76, reserved. For accounts of these negotiations see Charles W. Hallberg, *Franz Joseph and Napoleon III, 1852–1864: A Study of Austro-French Relations,* pp. 320–341; Alan John Percivale Taylor, *The Struggle for Mastery in Europe, 1848–1918,* pp. 136–141; Friedrich Engel-Jánosi, *Graf Rechberg: Vier Kapitel zu seiner und Österreichs Geschichte,* pp. 92–98.

afforded the Russian Chancellor, Prince Gorchakov, the opportunity for a splendid diplomatic victory in the disdainful notes, verging on the insolent, with which he dismissed the collective protests against Russian policy. As Rechberg predicted, Britain, embroiled with the United States over privateers and rams built in British shipyards for the use of the Confederacy, was willing to admonish but not to act. Lord John Russell, British Foreign Secretary, stood in dread of an alliance between Washington and St. Petersburg and was casting about for "some mild, strong, conciliatory, threatening [note], saying more than it means and meaning more than it says" which he could send to Gorchakov to save the face of the British without outraging the Russians.[2] Austria was no less peaceable. Her abhorrence of the principle of nationalities and her reluctance to urge on the Russians the introduction of a government for the Poles more liberal than she herself provided for them in Galicia made her protests to Russia lacking in conviction. Of the ill-assorted troika, only France was willing to use force on Russia if she could but obtain a reliable ally.

Several times during the course of 1863 Napoleon made fresh overtures to Austria. In May he proposed a congress of the powers to settle the affairs of Poland and Italy. Late in August he had the Empress sound Metternich on a project to blockade Russian ports.[3] Since such a move implied war, the ambassador hastily objected. In the fall the Emperor apparently tried twice—once through the intermediary of Prince Czartoryski, a Polish nobleman close to the court, and once through Gramont in Vienna—to obtain Austrian consent to an active alliance.[4] But always the Austrian Ballhausplatz elected to play for time. Rechberg believed that if Napoleon persisted in his evident determination to use the Polish question to destroy the treaties of 1815 and provoked a war, Austria would eventually be obliged to ally with France. But until that evil day, Austria should avoid a definite commitment, string out the diplomatic exchanges as long as possible and prevent a rupture in her friendly relations with the French Emperor.[5]

By such dilatoriness Austria succeeded in holding her suitor at arm's

[2] Russell to Cowley, March 19, 1863, PRO FO 519/200.

[3] Metternich to Rechberg, Paris, May 7, 1863, HHSA, IX/75, No. 18 A–D; telegram, May 8, 1863, *ibid.*; August 4, 1863, private HHSA, Nachlass Rechberg.

[4] For the secret negotiation see Baron Napoléon Beyens, *Le Second Empire vu par un diplomate belge,* II, 22–23 and Engel-Jánosi, *Rechberg,* p. 114. Prince Ladislas Czartoryski was a Polish nobleman married to a daughter of Queen Christine of Spain and her morganatic husband, the Duke of Rianzarès. The Prince and especially the Princess were close to the court. The archives in Vienna and Paris contain no records of these negotiations of the fall of 1863. Metternich was on leave at the time. The chargé d'affaires was evidently not initiated into the secret exchanges.

[5] Engel-Jánosi, *Rechberg,* pp. 114–115; Hallberg, *Franz Joseph and Napoleon III,* pp. 333–334. Hallberg does not say that Rechberg's recommendations were in answer to renewed French proposals.

length for eight months. But while this diplomatic *pas de deux* between the Ballhausplatz and the Quai d'Orsay avoided an open breach it placed a heavy strain on Austro-French relations. Much of the good will engendered since the appointment of Drouyn de Lhuys was frittered away during its course. The alienation of affection became manifest after Napoleon's speech to a joint session of the legislative chambers on November 5. On that occasion, in a bold effort to recapture French initiative and without previous warning to Austria, he challenged the powers to meet in a congress to settle every question in dispute and bury forever the treaties of 1815. Austria, taken by surprise, was horrified at the prospect of discussing the Italian and Polish questions—the major issues of European diplomacy at the moment—around the green table of diplomacy. Inevitably she would be called to consider her own mutilation. Along with Britain, to the intense disappointment of Napoleon, the Austrian government politely but firmly declined the invitation. The Austro-French entente was at an end.

Napoleon was angry and chagrined over his failure to sweep the powers with him to the conference table, and he placed most of the blame on Austria; but with his habitual self-control he was able to discuss the fiasco calmly with Metternich. Such *sang-froid* was beyond the Empress, whose nerves had been jangling at the delays and sustained suspense of the months of abortive negotiations. Even before Napoleon appalled Vienna with his bid to a congress she had worked herself into a state of righteous indignation at what appeared to her evidence of Austrian weakness and even duplicity. Her heart set on the Austro-French alliance, she had been profoundly discouraged by the series of checks. The way ahead had seemed so clearly marked to the victorious summits, she wrote Metternich, yet Austrian obstinacy and distrust of France had brought them all to a standstill. The mountain had labored and brought forth only a dead mouse. "You know better than anyone that the emperor wanted to march loyally beside you," she scolded Metternich. "But after all, one must *march.*" Forgetting that she herself, acting for her husband, had placed before Metternich a plan which would have turned Europe upside down and brought France to the Rhine, she reproached Austrian newspapers for accusing the Emperor of warmongering. The Emperor had never wanted anything but peace, she grumbled to the ambassador; yet now everyone was saying he wished to destroy it.[6]

There is no reason to think that the Empress inspired Napoleon's call to the powers on November 5. Almost invariably in moments of crisis during his reign he suggested a European congress as a fitting denouement. But she

---

[6] Eugénie to Metternich, Compiègne, November 13, 1863, copy, HHSA, IX/77, *varia*.

grasped at it avidly as a last expedient to restore the Emperor's prestige and to salvage a part of her grand design. Eugénie was sensitive to the fact that Napoleon's diplomatic campaign had brought him neither profit nor honor. Russia had scarcely paid him the courtesy of listening to his protests in behalf of the Poles. At the very least a congress would move him again to the center of the European stage.

From the reports of Metternich and Cowley we can piece together a few of her preparatory maneuvers behind the scene.[7] Spain was cast in a strong supporting role. Napoleon again gratified the Empress' desire to elevate Spain to the ranks of the powers and included the Queen among the sovereigns invited to the congress. Isabella had been only too pleased to accept and, with a show of humility rare for her, even thanked the Emperor for thinking of Spain in so important a circumstance.[8] Now in the fall the Empress had gone from Biarritz to Portugal and to Spain and had seen the Queen during the last week of October. It is a fair supposition that she had sounded the ground at the time for the Queen's reaction to the invitation that was forthcoming. The Empress' plan called for the three Catholic powers, Austria, France, and Spain, to exert pressure at the congress for restorations in Italy. Spain was to raise the question of Naples, declare that the plebiscite of 1860 in southern Italy had been falsified, and demand the retirement of "Sardinian" troops. The collaboration of Austria was to be ensured beforehand. According to Cowley, the Empress spared no effort to induce the Pope to accept his invitation in order to bolster the conservative line. She confided to Metternich that even Gorchakov had been enlisted. He had secretly agreed to the congress if he could take shelter behind the Italian question and dodge discussion of Poland. Eugénie had high hopes that since the congress augured well for a conservative settlement in Italy, Austria would overcome its hesitations and accept her bid.

It is impossible to say if the congress would have lived up to her expectations. The Austrian refusal disposed of all her elaborate preparations and added insult to the injuries inflicted by the irritating delaying action of the preceding spring and summer. The collapse of the congress transformed Eugénie's petulance into the fury of a woman scorned. Her rage broke on Metternich—as it had once inundated Nigra—when he returned from a prolonged *congé* in November. "I congratulate you," she began briskly. "You have won the first two rounds, we shall see who shall win the third." No longer would she consider herself a friend of Austria, she declared. Austria's conduct had lifted from her conscience the burden of the unful-

---

[7] Cowley to Russell, Chantilly, November 17, 1863, PRO FO 519/231; Metternich to Rechberg, Paris, between November 13 and 27, private, HHSA, IX/77, *varia*.

[8] Barrot to Drouyn de Lhuys, telegram, Madrid, November 10, 1863, AMAE (Paris), Correspondance politique, Espagne, Vol. 864.

filled terms of Zurich and Villafranca.[9] "I know you to the tips of your fingers. You never really thought seriously of allying with us." Austria had found it very convenient, she added sarcastically, to tie the hands of France while playing for time. But she would rue the day that she had spurned the suit of France. The Emperor knew what was going on. In vain would Austria turn to Germany against France. The German people would be for the French, and dynasties had to follow their people. ". . . You ally with this one and that one, and you will end up at the tail end of the world."[10]

The wreck of the congress was not the only reason behind the Empress' tirade. During the course of 1863 a number of events and influences had combined to demonstrate to her the unfeasibility of much of her grand design and had gradually but inevitably revised her ideas. She meant every word when, in January, 1864, she wrote Metternich: "We no longer want to cooperate with you."[11]

In the preceding spring she had come to the parting of the ways with Walewski. The effect on the Empress was twofold. The alienation dampened her enthusiasm for the Poles, whom she began regarding as rebels against legitimate authority rather than as heroic defenders of freedom against tyranny, and drew her closer to Fould, Minister of Finance. In time Fould's prudent concern for economy helped curb the Empress' zeal for monarchy in Mexico.[12]

The cause of the rift between Eugénie and Walewski is obscure. Cowley reported that Walewski made too free use of Her Majesty's name in his support of the Polish cause. Possibly she disliked the Minister's desire to reform the government. A conservative in his foreign policy, he was a liberal at home. Walewski had re-entered the Cabinet as Minister of State in November, 1860, at the time of the decree permitting the publication of legislative debates and the vote on an address to the throne by the legislature each year. Since then he had pressed for additional constitutional reforms. The Empress' ideas about government had not yet crystallized into a clearcut opposition to a liberal empire; but she certainly failed to share the Minister's crusading spirit.[13] In any case, in March, when Fould and Walewski exchanged high words over a financial matter during a meeting

[9] Metternich to Rechberg, Paris, November 27, 1863, HHSA, IX/76, No. 54 A–F.

[10] Metternich to Rechberg, Compiègne, November 23, 1863, HHSA, reproduced by Robert Sencourt, "L'Impératrice Eugénie et la politique extérieure," *Revue de Paris,* XXXIX (May, 1932), 387–388.

[11] Eugénie to Metternich, January 19, 1864, *ibid.,* p. 389.

[12] Cowley to Russell, Paris, April 24, 1863, copy, PRO FO 519/230; Goltz to Bismarck, Paris, April 24, 1863, *APP,* III, No. 450, p. 509; Horace de Viel-Castel, May 10, 1863, *Mémoires sur le règne de Napoléon III, 1851–1864, publiés d'après le manuscrit original,* VI, 180.

[13] See for example, her remarks to Hübner in April, 1862 (Hübner to Rechberg, Paris, April 18, 1862, HHSA, IX/72, No. 2).

of the Council, Eugénie sided with the former. So spirited did the altercation become that Walewski, on the request of the Emperor, was obliged to
apologize to the Empress. But the rancor endured. In June, 1863, in the
reshuffle of Ministers after the elections he was forced out of the Cabinet—
mainly because of his incompatibility with Fould and Morny. The Empress apparently did not lift a finger to save him.[14]

The change in personnel was an omen of a shift in the trend of foreign
policy. Walewski had been a clerical and one of the loudest advocates of
war against Prussia and Russia on the behalf of Poland. In his place, with
the additional duty of representing the government in the legislative debates, was named Eugène Rouher, after Billault, the original designee, had
died. Rouher belonged to the Italianissimes and favored *rapprochement*
with Bismarck. He was one of those whom the Empress later contemp-
tuously labelled "our Prussians." Although Drouyn de Lhuys clung to his
post as Foreign Minister until 1866, the consensus of thinking on foreign
policy shifted perceptibly. From this time forward Drouyn de Lhuys was
powerless to direct policy. He came close to resigning in August, 1863. His
whole political philosophy was based on the Austrian alliance as the key to
alienation of the Emperor from Italy and the Ultra-Bonapartists.[15] The
fiascos of 1863 terminated the effectiveness of his ministry.

The results of the elections of May 30 and 31, 1863, of members of the
Legislative Body also forced the Empress to reappraise her policy. Although
the official candidates succeeded in winning a majority of seats, a surpris-
ing number of the opposition triumphed—especially in contests in the cities.
The results were interpreted as a defeat for the clerical, conservative candidates who were defenders of the Papacy, enemies of Italy, and advocates
of the Austrian alliance. Biggest gainers were among anticlerical republicans and liberal monarchists. The returns showed that no ground swell
had developed among the French people in favor of the destruction of
Italian unity.[16] The victories were thus a serious threat to the European
policies advocated by Eugénie.

The Mexican expedition was a major issue of the election campaign.
Although the city of Puebla fell to the French forces on May 19, word of the
victory did not reach Paris until June 1. It was plain hard luck that the
polls had closed only the day before. If only the news had arrived a few
days earlier, wailed the Empress, the results might have been altogether

[14] Françoise Chalamon de Bernardy "Un Fils de Napoléon: Le Comte Walewski,
1810–1868," MS, pp. 704, 714–716.

[15] Metternich to Rechberg, Paris, July 12, 1863, HHSA, IX/75.

[16] Lynn M. Case, *French Opinion on War and Diplomacy during the Second Empire*, pp. 155–159; Jean Maurain, *La Politique ecclésiastique du Second Empire de
1852 à 1869*, p. 665; Emile Ollivier, *L'Empire libéral: Etudes, récits, souvenirs*, VI,
260–261; Theodore Zeldin, *The Political System of Napoleon III*, pp. 111–119.

different.[17] Happier timing might have made some, but probably not much, difference. The French people were almost unanimously opposed to the financially burdensome and militarily embarrassing venture. Placards in the street blazoned the scorn of the opposition candidates for the imperial expedition. The election of many of these candidates to the Legislative Body must have demonstrated to the Empress that she had made a serious *gaffe* in becoming the patron of so unpopular an undertaking. Since her connection with it was only too well known, her popularity could be expected to suffer in consequence.

Rankling in the Empress' mind was the knowledge that while Austria rebuffed the advances of France, she listened receptively to Prussian proposals. Hoping to block the formation of an Austro-French alliance, Bismarck had in May, 1863, offered Austria a Prussian guarantee of Galicia in return for a guarantee of Posen, Prussia's Polish territory. In seeking an understanding with Austria, he explained with heavy humor, he was merely following the style set in Paris. "Why not?" he jested with Count de Launay, head of the Italian legation at Berlin. "Fashions are made in Paris. Especially the hoop skirts. . . ." He broke off suddenly, unwilling to voice his thought that the Empress exercised a commanding influence over French foreign policy.[18] His efforts in Vienna eventually culminated in the treaty of alliance of January, 1864, between Austria and Prussia and their combined attack on Denmark. She who introduced the crinolines in Paris was not amused by this concert of German powers, and she burned with resentment at Austria's fickleness.[19]

REACTION AND REPRISALS: ROME—

The rapid deterioration in Austro-French relations was not the only ugly outgrowth of the diplomatic muddle of 1863. The Polish crisis entailed a permanent breach between the French Empire and Russia. Since Gorchakov was willing to allow Prussia to expand in Germany at the expense of Austria, the loss of Russian friendship later became critically important. The year 1863 was the end, too, of the British alliance. Russell's denunci-

---

[17] Hidalgo to De Pont, Paris, June 4, 1863, HKM, c. 3, No. 521. Ollivier wrote in his diary on June 3: "L'Empereur reçoit à la fois, le 1er juin, deux avertissements solennels: le triomphe de l'opposition à Paris, la résistance courageuse de Puebla. L'un de ces événements signifie la liberté à l'intérieur, l'autre la paix à l'extérieur. Ecoutera-t-il et comprendra-t-il?" (Ollivier, *Journal, 1846–1869,* II, 76). See also Hidalgo to De Pont, Paris, May 30, 1863, HKM, c. 3, No. 515, and Hidalgo's reports of May 5 and June 4, *ibid.,* Nos. 487, 521; Gutiérrez to Cintrat, Paris, July 9, 1863, *ibid.,* No. 577–1.

[18] Launay to Visconti-Venosta, Berlin, April 7, 1863, *APP,* III, No. 393 A, p. 453.

[19] Drouyn de Lhuys apparently had quite good sources of information on the Austro-Prussian *rapprochement* (Metternich to Rechberg, Paris, May 20, 1863, private, HHSA, IX/77; *ibid.,* July 12, 1863, IX/75).

ation of the Emperor's projected congress cut the fragile bond which had endured since the Crimean War. So heavy were the blows dealt to French prospects and prestige that both Metternich and Cowley, noting Napoleon's morose taciturnity, worried lest he lash out in some unexpected fashion to recoup his losses.[20] In reality they had nothing to fear. While Austria and Prussia began their armed intervention in Denmark the Emperor allowed his government to drift and imposed on France a hazardous isolation.

The embarrassments and frustrations of his negotiations with Austria turned out to be the good fortune of the Italians. In September, 1864, after five months of negotiation, Napoleon signed a convention with Victor Emmanuel stipulating the withdrawal of imperial troops from Rome within a two-year period. Italy had to promise not to attack Rome, to assume part of the papal debt, and to move its capital to Florence—the last as a demonstration of good faith. Yet even though Rome was ostensibly protected, the September Convention was generally interpreted as another step toward Italian unification. It was, in fact, very similar to the proposals made by Thouvenel in 1862 which had cost him his portfolio and was a by-product of the Emperor's inability to marshal Austria into his plans to remake the map of Europe.[21]

The agreement restored cordial relations between France and Italy and wounded Austria in two ways: it gave additional sanction to the revolution in Italy and, by regularizing the Roman question, it directed all eyes toward Venetia.[22] The Convention demonstrated that Austria had lost her last real chance in 1863 to enlist French aid to break up the Kingdom of Italy. Napoleon had warned Metternich of this possibility as early as March, 1863, when he was trying to negotiate the Austrian alliance. On that occasion he had advised the Austrian government to say to Victor Emmanuel: "We give you Venetia on the condition that you return to the pope the provinces you have taken from him and to the King of Naples his kingdom." If Austria refused to bargain with Italy on such terms, the Emperor continued, he himself would be unwilling to "put so much value"

[20] See, for example, Cowley to Russell, copy, Compiègne, December 11, 13, 15, 20, 1863, PRO FO 519/231; Metternich to Rechberg, December 14, 1863, private, HHSA, IX/77.

[21] For an account of the negotiation of the Convention see Lynn M. Case, *Franco-Italian Relations, 1860–1865*, pp. 263–300; Maurain, *Politique ecclésiastique*, pp. 704–705; Beyens, *Second Empire*, I, 210–211; Taylor, *Mastery in Europe*, p. 155.

[22] For the Austrian reaction to the Convention see Rechberg to Mülinen, Vienna, September 21, October 12, 1864, Nos. 1, 2 (reserved), and 4, HHSA, IX/80; Mülinen to Rechberg, September 26, September 17, telegram, October 3, October 8, 1864, *ibid.*, IX/78; Hübner to Rechberg, Paris, October 2, 1864, *ibid.*, IX/78; Metternich to Rechberg, telegram, Johannisberg, October 2, 1864, *ibid.*, IX/78.

on the restorations.[23] When the ambassador asked for a clarification of Napoleon's attitude regarding Italy and Venetia in the fall of 1864 he received a confirmation of this dictum. Having failed to extract Venetia from Austria, Napoleon had abandoned the idea of partitioning the Italian peninsula. Hence the September Convention, which endorsed the *status quo*. France did not desire to bring back "former times" in Italy. The Emperor told Metternich: "I wish Italy to keep what she has, *neither more nor less.*"[24]

When the Convention was signed, Eugénie was taking the waters at Schwalbach, a small spa in central Germany. Her absence at that moment has caused some writers to infer, and many at least to imply, that she had strongly opposed the agreement and that the Emperor seized the chance to close his pact with Italy while his troublesome spouse was out of the way.[25] An examination of Eugénie's attitude and behavior in the summer and fall of 1864, however, disproves such an hypothesis. True, in July she had told Count Goltz, Prussian ambassador, that she anticipated spontaneous restoration in Naples and regarded the Papal States as an essential buffer between a northern and southern kingdom.[26] But the September Convention erected no barrier against "spontaneous" uprisings in southern Italy which, if successful, would probably entail not only the return of Francis but the restoration of the Pope in the Marches and Umbria. And the Empress was not likely to object to the Convention on the grounds that it displeased in Vienna. Her anger at Austria had not abated; rather it had swelled and even metamorphosed into dalliances with Italy and Prussia.

The "petites coquetteries" which she had once reserved for Metternich were now directed at Nigra, who was only too ready to forgive her for the scene in the drawing room over a year before. On a warm evening in June the court was treated to the spectacle of the handsome Italian propelling the Empress across the tiny lake at Fontainebleau in her gondola. To the ears of Metternich came the strains of a serenade in which the gondolier mingled praises of the beauty of his fair passenger with patriotic petitions for her aid in bringing the Queen of the Adriatic into the Italian union.[27]

[23] Metternich to Rechberg, Paris, March 29, 1863, HHSA, IX/75, No. 12 B.

[24] Metternich to Mensdorff, November 29, 1864, HHSA, IX/79, essential points of a confidential conversation.

[25] Henry Salomon, *L'Ambassade de Richard de Metternich à Paris*, pp. 36, 72; Maurain, *Politique ecclésiastique*, pp. 704–705; Anatole Claveau, *Souvenirs politiques et parlementaires d'un témoin*, I, 46.

[26] Goltz to Bismarck, Paris, July 11, 1864, *APP*, V, No. 201, p. 298.

[27] One such occasion was reported by Metternich to Rechberg, Paris, June 30, 1863, HHSA, IX/77. According to the Austrian, the Empress was displeased by the mention of Venetia and interrupted the serenade. By December 14 he wrote hopefully that her "petites coquetteries" with Nigra and the Italians had ceased (Metternich to Rechberg, Paris, December 13, 1863, *ibid.*, IX/77).

She was now seen in lengthy *tête-à-têtes* with the Prussian ambassador.[28] The Danish question with its attendant embarrassments for Austria frankly delighted her. She could not conceal her eagerness for further complications. She was only too happy, she declared, to watch from the balcony while others mixed it in the streets.[29] And although she approved of the French policy of neutrality during the Austrian and Prussian conquest of Schleswig and Holstein, she professed great admiration for the diplomatic finesse displayed by Bismarck.[30]

In her pique at the Austrians she read deliberate insult into their every act. Despite the denials of Metternich and Rechberg, she was convinced that they were working to foil her plan of a match between Anna Murat and Queen Isabella's brother-in-law.[31] And she took umbrage over Rechberg's refusal to release from an Austrian prison a Polish countess, accused of revolutionary intrigue, in whom she and Princess Czartoryski, daughter of Queen Christine of Spain, had interested themselves.[32] By the time of the September Convention between France and Italy, Austria had lost its best friend in the French court.

Her anger toward those whom she had formerly befriended extended in the summer of 1864 as far as Rome. She was already irked at the demands of the Church in Mexico for the return of all of the ecclesiastical property nationalized by the Republic—a claim which raised nearly unsurmountable obstacles to the establishment of a monarchy.[33] Some of her earlier enthusiasm for the cause of the Pope had dimmed in face of the inflexibility of the Roman curia. Goltz reported in July that she treated the Roman question with amazing impartiality. "It is foolish to call Her Majesty a bigot," he reported. "On the contrary she is tolerant and moderate."[34]

In August the Pope refused to allow the christening of the two sons of Prince Napoleon owing to the irregular positions of the godparents. Victor Emmanuel, godfather, was under the ban of excommunication, and the Queen of Holland, godmother, was a Lutheran. The Empress had been most eager for the ceremony to take place and had written personally to

---

[28] Goltz to Bismarck, Paris, July 11, August 22, 1864, *APP*, V, No. 201, p. 298, and No. 257, p. 381.

[29] Metternich to Rechberg, Paris, January 19, 1864, private, HHSA, IX/79.

[30] Metternich to Rechberg, Fontainebleau, July 3, 1864, private, HHSA, IX/78.

[31] Metternich to Rechberg, Paris, June 21, 1864, private, HHSA, IX/79; Rechberg to Metternich, Vienna, July 14, 1864, *ibid.*, IX/80.

[32] Metternich to Rechberg, Paris, April 19, 1864, HHSA, IX/79, No. 2; Rechberg to Metternich, Vienna, April 26, private, *ibid.*; Metternich to Rechberg, June 1, 1864, private, IX/79; Rechberg to Metternich, telegram, Vienna, June 7, *ibid.*, IX/80.

[33] Eugénie to Charlotte, March 16, 1864, HKM, reproduced by Egon Caesar Corti, *Maximilian and Charlotte of Mexico*, trans. C. A. Phillips, I, 397; Eugénie to Charlotte, September, 1864, *ibid.*, II, 849.

[34] Goltz to Bismarck, Paris, July 11, 1864, *APP*, V, No. 201, p. 298.

the Pope. But Pius replied that he could permit the christening only if the godfather re-entered the pale of the Church—which he could do by restoring to His Holiness the Marches, Umbria, and the Romagna. Irritated that the Pope should make the spiritual welfare of the children dependent on French foreign policy, the Empress expressed her displeasure to the papal nuncio and wired the Emperor at Châlons word of Pius' unsatisfactory answer. Diplomats at the French court believed that the incident clinched the Emperor's decision to sign the September Convention.[35] While its influence on the Emperor's Italian policy is conjectural, it is one more indication of the change in the Empress' outlook since 1863.

Family problems and personal sorrows in the summer of 1864 again crowded upon her and compounded the disappointment and disenchantment she had experienced in political affairs. By the early fall Eugénie was passing through another crisis in her private life and was again victim of a black depression. In August, during the elaborate entertainments in honor of the visit of Don Francisco de Asís, Isabella's husband, Eugénie's intimate friend Princess Czartoryski had died. The contrast between the brilliant festivities and the somber death chamber of the Spanish Princess revived the torturing memories of the death of the Duchess of Alba.[36]

At the same time the imperial ménage was once more in terrible disarray. The Emperor's affair with a lady from the demimonde, Marguerite Bellanger, was notorious. In her fury Eugénie went in person to Marguerite to demand her departure from Paris. As in 1860, when overpowered by an accumulation of troubles, she thought of flight. She chose for her refuge Schwalbach, a chilly, dreary little German spa—partly because of its seclusion, and partly, perhaps, because of its proximity to the ancestral home of the Duchess of Hamilton, who, now a widow, often stayed at Baden.[37]

The Empress' letters from Schwalbach breathed her unhappiness and her sense of injury at Napoleon's conduct. To Anna Murat, then away on a

[35] Both the Austrian and British chargés d'affaires reported this account, with minor variations, to their government. See Mülinen to Rechberg, reserved, Paris, October 3, 1864, HHSA, IX/78, No. 37 D; Grey to Russell, September 29, 1864, PRO FO, reproduced by Case, *Franco-Italian Relations*, pp. 297–298. Both reported that the Emperor was extremely angry over the Pope's stand, which played no small part in clinching his determination to sign the Convention.

[36] See Eugénie to the Countess of Montijo, August 21, 1864, Empress Eugénie, *Lettres familières de l'Impératrice Eugénie conservées dans les archives du Palais de Liria et publiées par les soins du Duc d'Albe avec le concours de F. de Llanos y Torriglia et Pierre Josserand*, I, 218; Hidalgo to Ferdinand Maximilian, Paris, August 27, 1864, HKM, c. 19, No. 10, pp. 438–439; Mérimée to Panizzi, Paris, August 22, 1864, Prosper Mérimée, *Letters to Panizzi*, II, 6–7.

[37] The fullest account of the Empress' residence at Schwalbach is given by Count Maurice Fleury (*Memoirs of the Empress Eugénie. Compiled from Statements, Private Documents, and Personal Letters*, I, 278–285).

Mediterranean cruise after the *non avenue* of her marriage prospects with the Infante, she mourned: "Unfortunately for me . . . once someone has entered [my heart], only by rending it asunder can he [*on*] leave it; I say unfortunately because it is rare in life not to experience deceptions, and it is always a cause of suffering to form attachments on this earth." In her melancholy she bade farewell to her youth, daydreamed of happier days in Spain, and wept over her "eternal" separation from her native land. "The tear which drops from the eye comes in truth from the depths of my soul," she wailed in romantic bathos.[38] To Charlotte she wrote that she was completely oblivious to affairs of state and thought only of living quietly and taking the waters faithfully.[39]

So it came about that the Empress, at Schwalbach, learned of the signing of the September Convention by reading the *Moniteur*.[40] Yet the evidence indicates that if the Emperor had deceived his wife in love, he had this time been foursquare with her in politics. She had long been aware of the negotiations on Rome even if she had not predicted the precise moment of their consummation. The Emperor, moreover, wrote to her immediately after he had signed the Convention of his determination to regard it as null and void if Victor Emmanuel did not live up to his side of the bargain and keep his hands off Rome.[41]

The Empress' subsequent attitude showed no trace of resentment against the Convention and gave small comfort to the clericals. When Cardinal Bonnechose, Cardinal of the Crown, called upon her to enlist her aid against the Convention, she countered with complaints about the rigidity of papal policy and added crisply that the terms of the Convention were favorable and advantageous to His Holiness.[42] Of course, she actually had little choice in the matter. Her own plans for Italy had foundered in 1863. Privately, she still hoped for the destruction of Italian unity. But, barring a spontaneous uprising in Naples, she saw faint prospect of changing the *status quo*. At least the Patrimony of St. Peter was safe; and Italian aspirations for a time would concentrate on Venetia. Partly from spite at Austria and Rome, partly from recognition of her own impotence, she acquiesced in the course which, two years before, she had so bitterly contested.

---

[38] Eugénie to Anna Murat, Schwalbach, September 11, 1864, Mouchy Papers, No. 25.

[39] Eugénie to Charlotte, Schwalbach, September 24, 1864, HKM, reproduced by Corti, *Maximilian and Charlotte*, II, 851.

[40] Besson, Mgr. Louis, *Vie du Cardinal de Bonnechose, archevêque de Rouen*, II, 49.

[41] Metternich to Rechberg, telegram, Johannisberg, October 2, 1864, HHSA, IX/78. Metternich was then on leave of absence. On the instructions of Rechberg he called on the Empress at Schwalbach.

[42] Besson, *Bonnechose*, II, 49.

—AND MEXICO

The same diplomatic contretemps of 1863 and 1864 that rescued Victor Emmanuel's kingdom from partition and advanced it toward its goal of unification gravely imperilled the successful consolidation of Ferdinand Maximilian's empire in Mexico. In the summer of 1863 Napoleon decided to continue his sponsorship of a monarchy overseas, but he now had entirely different reasons for wishing to hurry the Archduke into his new realm. Napoleon had conceived of the Mexican Empire within the framework of European diplomacy as a plum for Austria and as at least a partial compensation for her eventual loss of Venetia. In 1861 the French Emperor had been lavish in his promises of material aid and guarantees which would assure the successful life of the new empire.[43] But the unexpected resistance encountered in Mexico, the clamorous outcry in France against the expedition, and, above all, Austria's refusal to enter into an alliance with France had changed the Emperor's plum into a persimmon. He found himself backed into a tight corner, the honor of his flag at stake. In 1864 his desire was to liquidate the affair by foisting off on Ferdinand Maximilian the burdens of the crown which he had created. The Archduke, protégé of Napoleon, metamorphosed into the "archdupe."[44] Napoleon intended the arrival of Ferdinand Maximilian in Mexico to mark the termination of French expenditure of men and money. It would then be the turn of Mexico to repay France.[45]

The discordant relations between Austria and France had a catastrophic effect upon the Archduke's last negotiations with Napoleon prior to his departure. Not only the French Emperor was eager to wash his hands of the whole venture. Franz Joseph, fearful of French reprisals on Austria, painstakingly separated his government from the Mexican question and gave his brother not one iota of support in his bargaining with Napoleon.[46] Ferdinand Maximilian was caught between the sparring antagonists. Rechberg, at the height of the recriminations exchanged between Paris

[43] See, for example, Metternich to Rechberg, Paris, December 22, 1861, HKM, c. 1, No. 91–b.

[44] Philip W. Sergeant, *The Last Empress of the French, Being the Life of the Empress Eugénie, Wife of Napoleon III,* p. 310.

[45] See Napoleon's speech to the chambers on November 5. See also Stefan Herzfeld to De Pont, London, December 12, 1863, HKM, c. 6, No. 80s. The change in the Emperor's attitude is extensively worked out in Barker. "France, Austria, and the Mexican Venture, 1861–1864" (*French Historical Studies,* III [1963], 231–238).

[46] Rechberg to Ferdinand Maximilian, Frankfurt, September 2, 1863, HKM, No. 742; Rechberg to Ferdinand Maximilian, Vienna, September 24, 1863, HKM, Nos. 829, 833; Ferdinand Maximilian to Napoleon, Miramar, September 27, 1863, HKM, No. 853.

and Vienna in December, 1863, conscientiously advised the Archduke to get out of the affair and leave it with Napoleon.[47]

Still deluded as to his prospects in Mexico, Ferdinand Maximilian rejected this wise counsel and accepted the unfavorable terms laid down by France. Not only had he given up the guarantees from Spain and England that he had earlier required; he now relinquished even that of France. From Napoleon he extracted only the promise that France would withdraw her troops gradually over a three-year period so that by 1867 twenty thousand French soldiers would still remain in Mexico. The Emperor conceded this much "at swordpoint" because he was desperate to lay on the brow of the Archduke the thorny crown weighing down his hands. But even the secret articles of the convention did not pledge France to defend the new empire against its enemies. Considering the openly hostile attitude of the United States, now getting the upper hand over the Confederacy in the Civil War, the omission of a definitive French guarantee was ominous.[48]

The exigencies of European diplomacy gave the negotiation between Napoleon and the Archduke a last vicious twist which further embittered their relationship. After initialling the convention made with Napoleon and after receiving imperial honors in Paris, Ferdinand Maximilian returned to Vienna. There, confronted with Franz Joseph's family pact requiring him to renounce his rights to the Austrian throne, his appanage, and his rights as an archduke, Ferdinand Maximilian balked and suddenly retracted his candidacy. Knowing that the renunciation was essential to protect Austrian interests, Franz Joseph made it a prerequisite for his permission. The brothers had apparently reached an impasse. The Archduke would not take the Mexican crown if he must relinquish his rights to that of Austria; the Austrian Emperor would not permit him to accept the Mexican crown unless he gave up the rights forever.

Napoleon and Eugénie were absolutely furious. After all the difficulty in negotiating the convention and in inducing the Archduke to depart for his new realm, to be confounded by a family quarrel! The Empress saw in the dispute between the brothers a deliberate insult to France. She had Metternich summoned from his bed in the small hours of the morning to read her indignant protest. "In a most justifiable ill temper," she expostulated, "I say nothing of the appalling scandal which this will cause to the House of Austria, but, as regards ourselves, you must admit that there can be no excuse, whatever may be the obstacles which have arisen in various

[47] Rechberg to Ferdinand Maximilian, Vienna, December 7, 1863, HKM, c. 6, No. 56s.

[48] See Barker, "France, Austria, and the Mexican Venture," *French Historical Studies*, III, (1963), 237–238.

quarters." The brothers had had plenty of time to weigh and decide family questions. Now, when the arrangements for a loan had been concluded and the convention "signed," they could not permit private matters to throw the whole world into confusion. She asked the ambassador to notify his government that very night of the reaction of France. "Let us know your last word," she concluded sternly. "It is a most grave business."[49] The next morning, when Metternich hurried to the Tuileries, she and the Emperor emphasized the horrible embarrassment to which they would be subjected if Ferdinand Maximilian failed to depart and the "regrettable tension" between Austria and France which would inevitably ensue. "I must say," added the Emperor darkly, "I have no luck with Austria; it is as if I were abandoned on purpose at the last minute."[50]

These thinly veiled threats of reprisals had the desired effect on the brothers. Franz Joseph promised his brother his appanage and a suitable position in the event he returned to Austria; Ferdinand Maximilian promised for himself and for his descendants not to claim the throne while any other male representative of the house still lived. Within a few weeks, on April 14, 1864, the Archduke and his wife sailed down the Adriatic bound for Mexico.

But the episode left a bitter aftertaste. To the Empress, Franz Joseph's behavior had revealed the contempt in which he secretly held the parvenu French court. She told Metternich that should the Austrian ruler ever come himself to Paris she would do her best to entertain him; but, in view of his unfriendly and suspicious attitude toward her husband, she predicted that death would overtake her before that honor was hers.[51]

What part had the Empress played in the protracted negotiations which had preceded the Archduke's departure? Had she ever, like many in the French court, become despondent over the unexpected difficulties and advocated retreat? The evidence now known indicates her sustained although at times nervous faith in the future of the expedition. The fall of Puebla in the spring of 1863 had restored her confidence in the ultimate military victory of the French forces. She saw it as a "good omen" which would have a "moral effect" over the whole land, and she hastened to pick up the nearly broken threads of the negotiation.[52]

In September, 1863, while at Biarritz, she had conceived the idea of a

[49] March 27, 1864, HKM, quoted by Corti, *Maximilian and Charlotte,* I, 338–339.

[50] Metternich to Rechberg, Paris, March 28, 1864, private, HHSA, IX/79.

[51] Metternich to Rechberg, July 27, 1864, HHSA, reserved, IX/78, No. 28. For the Empress' views on the family contract signed by Franz Joseph and Ferdinand Maximilian see Metternich to Mensdorff, May 22, 1865, confidential, *ibid.,* IX/81.

[52] Fontainebleau, June 15, 1863, HKM, reproduced in Corti, *Maximilian and Charlotte,* I, 376–377. Corti has reproduced almost the entire correspondence between the Empresses and between Napoleon and Ferdinand Maximilian.

trip to Spain. She was motivated partly by sentiment, partly by desire to matchmake in behalf of Anna Murat, and perhaps by a plan to discuss Spain's participation in a European congress.[53] But her main purpose was the conversion of Isabella to a more favorable view of a Mexican empire under Ferdinand Maximilian and the extraction from the Queen of a Spanish guarantee of the new realm. In Madrid she reminded Isabella that the fate of Cuba depended on the success of monarchy in Mexico. With its consolidation other Latin American countries would be ripe for the re-creation of a vast Spanish empire. But the Empress' voyage, although it occasioned many brilliant galas and exchanges of florid compliments, yielded no positive results. The Queen pouted because one of her own daughters had not been chosen to rule in Mexico, and she declined to renew Spanish association with the venture.[54]

Despite her lack of success, once back in Paris in November, the Empress urged the Archduke to accept the crown and designated February, 1864, as a reasonable date for his departure.[55] At this time the fiasco of Napoleon's proposed congress and the acrimonious exchanges between London, Vienna, and Paris took place. With them was extinguished any final lingering hope of a British guarantee of Mexico.[56] Nonetheless, early in December, Eugénie received Ferdinand Maximilian's emissary, Kint von Roodenbeck, and told him that the Emperor would agree to all of the Archduke's requirements, including a guarantee of Mexico. The emissary returned to the Archduke's residence at Miramar with the most optimistic and, as it turned out, unrealistic ideas of the support to be expected of France. On the advice of Fould, who was eager to see the Archduke in Mexico and the expeditionary force back in France, she then wrote an insistent letter to Charlotte counselling Ferdinand Maximilian's prompt departure so that his "strong and energetic hand might regenerate the country."[57]

Was Eugénie guilty of a machiavellian design in pressing the Archduke to overcome his hesitations and assume his crown? Was she, like Napoleon,

[53] For accounts of the Empress' trip see Mérimée to Panizzi, Biarritz, October 1, 1863, Mérimée, *Letters to Panizzi,* I, 347–350; Anna Bicknell, *Life in the Tuileries under the Second Empire,* pp. 175–176; Mme Tascher de la Pagerie, *Mon séjour aux Tuileries,* II, 199–201.

[54] Gutiérrez to De Pont, Paris, November 5, 1863, HKM, c. 4, No. 979; Barrot to Drouyn de Lhuys, Madrid, October 19, October 21, 1863, Nos. 93, 95, AMAE (Paris), Correspondance politique, Espagne, Vol. 864; Corti, *Maximilian and Charlotte,* I, 276.

[55] Hidalgo to De Pont, Paris, November 4, 1863, HKM, c. 4, No. 977.

[56] Leopold to Charlotte, December 7, 1863, HKM, c. 6, No. 54s.

[57] Eugénie to Charlotte, Compiègne, December 9, 1863, HKM, reproduced in Corti, *Maximilian and Charlotte,* I, 291. Corti gives only a short excerpt from this lengthy letter.

Drouyn de Lhuys, and Fould, thinking only of France and seeking to shift the yoke of Mexico's burdens on the shoulders of another? She apparently took little direct part in the last wrangles over the terms of the convention; but what evidence we have of her views suggests that she too was thinking in terms of disengaging France from the new monarchy. When Ferdinand Maximilian came to Paris in February, 1864, she sided strongly with his demand that he be commander-in-chief of the army in Mexico. Just as vehemently, she opposed his requirement that the Foreign Legion, part of the material support offered by France, continue to fly the French flag.[58] Behind her position in both cases lay her conviction that Mexico could and should assume the burden of its own defense. Thus, she was later adamant on the withdrawal of French troops according to schedule and turned a deaf ear to pleas that they remain. When the young couple was at last in Mexico she urged the creation of a sizeable Mexican army of Indians and chided Charlotte when Emperor Maximilian disbanded the unruly Mexican militia.[59] She scoffed at the danger from Mexican guerrillas who roamed freely through the interior. They were just brigands, she wrote, without "political character." One of her friends had written her that really they were quite picturesque.[60] France could not be expected to pacify the whole country at once.

Eugénie had been chagrined to find that the Mexican campaign had hampered the realization of her grand design in 1863 and was impressed by the unmistakable hostility displayed by the French people to the project. She also was furious at Austria for having rejected an alliance with France. Notwithstanding this accumulation of grievances which would seem to suggest that she was prepared to vent her spleen on Ferdinand Maximilian, there is no real reason to conclude that she deliberately packed him off to an empire she thought foredoomed. On the contrary, she was still confident, even throughout most of 1864, of the ultimate successful consolidation of the new empire.

Her ignorance of the real conditions in Mexico was truly colossal. She had no idea of how tenuous was the hold of France on the country—that in fact it amounted to little more than control over a thin strip of land connecting the city of Mexico with the coast at Veracruz. Hidalgo was partially responsible for her unjustified optimism. Because of his close relationship with the Empress he had managed to have himself appointed

[58] Corti, *Maximilian and Charlotte*, I, 320.

[59] See Charlotte to Eugénie, Mexico, September 10, 1864, HKM, reproduced in Corti, *Maximilian and Charlotte*, II, 847; Eugénie to Charlotte, Compiègne, November 16, 1864, and undated, 1864, HKM, reproduced *ibid.*, pp. 855–856, 888–889.

[60] Eugénie to Charlotte, Tuileries, January 29, 1865, and undated, 1865, *ibid.*, pp. 876–877, 888.

Mexican minister at the French court. In this capacity he arranged with those in league with him in Mexico for the Empress to receive letters from overseas giving only favorable news on the prospects of the monarchy. This mail, along with the glowing accounts which Hidalgo extracted from his own correspondence to read to her, contradicted the depressing accounts emanating from Emperor Maximilian and Charlotte and persuaded her that either the new ruler was fretting over trifles or that he was avariciously bleeding France for as much as he could. From the accounts she read she was certain that the "poor Indians" gave the imperial couple a "delirious reception," and could be counted on, despite Charlotte's gloomy warnings, as loyal subjects.[61] So she could not understand and could not sympathize with Charlotte's alarms over the unrest in the country. Why worry about the guerrillas? Far more important, in her opinion, were some financial reforms in the Mexican government that could be reported to the hostile French Legislative Body.[62]

Eugénie never comprehended that the Mexicans were not a European people. The creoles among them were the small minority. Since the Mexicans spoke Spanish and worshipped in Catholic churches, in her book they were all Spaniards. From this premise it followed that the Empress, herself a Spaniard, was an authority on the proper governance of Mexico. She was liberal with unsolicited, pompous advice to Charlotte. "I can understand all the difficulty which Your Majesties must experience in finding men," she wrote in July, 1864, ". . . but the adage which says that what is needed is the iron hand in the velvet glove was never more applicable than in the case of peoples of Latin race, and especially Mexico."[63] Some months later she continued her lecture: "Every time a measure decreed is carried into effect, and people find themselves confronted with a *fait accompli*, I believe the resistance will grow less; I tell Your Majesties this because I know that race [Mexican], which at bottom is the same as the Spanish race."[64]

But the misplaced faith in the success of the Mexican monarchy disappeared not long after the arrival of the new sovereigns and with it all of her patience with her protégés. In 1865, in the midst of urgent European problems, she had no sympathy for the struggling couple overseas. Her

---

[61] Eugénie to Charlotte, July 30, 1864, *ibid.*, p. 843; Charlotte to Eugénie, Mexico, September 10, 1864, *ibid.*, p. 847. The voluminous reports of Hidalgo to Emperor Maximilian for the period 1864–1865 are in HKM, Carton 19. Over and over again he relates how, on the arrival of the mail, he would run immediately to the Empress to show her the most favorable parts of his private correspondence.

[62] Eugénie to Charlotte, December 15, 1864, HKM; Corti, *Maximilian and Charlotte*, II, 859.

[63] Eugénie to Charlotte, July 30, 1864, *ibid.*, p. 844.

[64] Eugénie to Charlotte, Tuileries, April 1, 1865, *ibid.*, p. 895.

letters became shorter, less cordial, frankly critical, and finally downright waspish.

The question of the property of the Church, which Juárez had confiscated and in part sold, was one of the earliest causes of friction. At first the Empress was censorious of the grasping demands of the Church for the restoration of its lands, and she approved of Emperor Maximilian's action in promulgating a decree confirming the nationalization of the ecclesiastical property. But Charlotte's vociferous denunciations of the clergy struck her as too violent. The nuncio in Paris had told Eugénie that the papal nuncio in Mexico had been instructed to be at first *"very black in order to get gradually whiter,"* and had counselled time and patience.[65] The French Empress came to believe that Charlotte and her husband had bungled the negotiation, and that Charlotte especially had been abrupt and undiplomatic. The new rulers, she thought, had opened before them an abyss where there should have been a strong union.[66]

As for the financial troubles of the new empire, she saw only that the proceeds from the loan were disappearing at an alarming rate, that heedless of lack of income, the Mexican Emperor was drawing draft upon draft. This, she reminded Charlotte, ruined Mexico's credit and caused herself and Napoleon personal grief. Since finance was the greatest guarantee for any country, she felt obliged to bring this matter to Charlotte's attention. On what could they be reckoning, she queried disagreeably, to get themselves out of this difficulty?[67]

The deterioration of the military situation in Mexico was another bone of contention. With the maddening assurance of the uninitiated, Eugénie continued to underestimate the force of the resistance of the population to the new regime and, from the security of the Tuileries, serenely predicted the inevitable pacification of the country. "One must make up one's mind to the guerrilla bands and not attach too much importance to them," she lectured. More important than the guerrillas was the attraction of capital to Mexico from Europe. The situation was just as it had been in Spain. "After the civil war [in Spain] there were guerrilla bands for more than ten years, and it is only since the introduction of the *gendarmerie* and the construction of railways that they have gradually disappeared."[68] She dismissed Charlotte's complaints about General Bazaine, commander of the French troops in Mexico, with rude haste. The General was France's

---

[65] Eugénie to Charlotte, Tuileries, January 29, 1865, *ibid.*, p. 876.

[66] Metternich to Mensdorff, Paris, February 16, HHSA, XI/81, No. 11 E; D'Hérillier to Charlotte, November 27, 1865, HKM, reproduced in Corti, *Maximilian and Charlotte*, II, 549–551.

[67] Eugénie to Charlotte, November 30, 1865, HKM, Corti, *Maximilian and Charlotte*, II, 923.

[68] Eugénie to Charlotte, Tuileries, April 1, 1865, *ibid.*, p. 895.

very best soldier, she admonished. Some "purely *formal* negligence" had probably given Charlotte a wrong opinion of him. If only Charlotte could read her correspondence, she would see how "right-minded" and "firm" were his judgments and, away from influences hostile to him, she would change her mind about him.[69] Eugénie also rejected, on the flimsiest grounds, the Mexican Empress' request for the removal of a certain General Boyer, who had made himself objectionable.[70]

By the time Eugénie became Regent for a second time, in the spring of 1865, she was thoroughly annoyed to be obliged to receive a special emissary from Mexico, Félix Eloin, who asked for an increase in the army of occupation. Why should Emperor Maximilian panic over the conclusion of the Civil War in the United States? Despite the strengthening and regrouping of the "Dissidents" in Mexico she saw no occasion for an increase in the number of French forces. Her letter of May 31 to Charlotte leaves little doubt of the unpleasant reception Eloin met with. Only grudgingly, and on the orders of Napoleon, did she assent to the replacement of men whose time of duty had expired. A homily followed on the excellent qualities of Bazaine and the inconsequentiality of Charlotte's desire to pacify the entire country at once.[71] She shuffled off to the absent Napoleon, who ignored it, Eloin's request of a guarantee of all the European powers. Privately, she told Metternich that Emperor Maximilian complained too much and asked for the impossible.[72]

Truth to tell, despite her brave words to Charlotte, the Empress had been badly scared by General Lee's surrender at Appomattox on April 9, 1865. When the minister from the United States, John Bigelow, told her of the great Northern victory, she asked anxiously, obviously embarrassed, what the Union army would do in the future.[73] Her concern over the attitude of the United States led her to adopt an ingratiating attitude toward its minister in the frequent conversations between them. By the end of 1865 she had swallowed her contempt for the revolutionary parvenu overseas and even professed to Bigelow a desire to travel in his country. On Christmas Eve, at a dinner party, she gave him the distinct impression that Napoleon was prepared to "close his account" with Mexico, and that he hoped the United States would do nothing to make this task more difficult.[74]

[69] Eugénie to Charlotte, Tuileries, July 15, 1865, *ibid.*, pp. 911–912.
[70] Eugénie to Charlotte, Tuileries, March 1, 1865, *ibid.*, pp. 889–890.
[71] Eugénie to Charlotte, Tuileries, May 31, 1865, *ibid.*, pp. 908–909.
[72] Metternich to Mensdorff, Paris, June 10, 1865, HHSA, IX/81, No. 30 B.
[73] Bigelow to Seward, Paris, April 28, 1865, John Bigelow, *Retrospection of an Active Life*, II, 511–512.
[74] Bigelow to Seward, Paris, December 26, 1865, *ibid.*, III, 300. See also Bigelow to Seward, Paris, June 6, 1865, *ibid.*, III, 61.

She was herself convinced of the necessity of evacuation. In November, General E. d'Hérillier, close friend of Charlotte and Maximilian, arrived in Paris and talked exhaustively with Eugénie of Mexican affairs. On every point, from ecclesiastical to military questions, she was free with reproaches of the Mexican Emperor's policies and revealed an unmistakable desire for the rapid organization of a Mexican national army and the disengagement of France. Cortés had been able to conquer Mexico with only a handful of followers, she remarked. Why were so many necessary *now*?[75]

By February, 1866, she was in the group urging the still reluctant Napoleon to make a clean break with Mexico. With the Marquis of La Valette, now beginning to move into the place at her side vacated by Walewski, and with Drouyn de Lhuys, Fould, and Randon, she clamored for the immediate evacuation of French troops. Hidalgo was completely out of favor and rarely seen in court. Emperor Maximilian had wakened to the fact that his minister at Paris was far more interested in feathering his nest at court than in defending the interests of his distant sovereign. In April, 1866, he removed him from his post as minister. As a private citizen, Hidalgo scurried about Paris in search of a rich bride and tried to prove to the Emperor and the Empress how satisfactory he had been. No longer hoodwinked by him, Eugénie let his notes and letters accumulate in her antechamber, where they languished unread by Napoleon.[76]

Biographers of the Empress have usually chosen to ignore her role in the last agonies of the Mexican Empire. It was certainly less than glorious. Some ignominy must attach to her, as it has to Napoleon, for her readiness to abandon her protégés. Yet many arguments in defense of her decision to disengage France may be mustered. Given the hopeless condition of Mexico in 1865 and 1866, both from financial and military points of view, the increasingly threatening attitude of the reunited powerful neighbor to the north, and the mounting violence of demands in France for the prompt termination of French participation, any other course would have been folly. A promise to stay with the sinking ship would have been so quixotic, so fatally hazardous to French interests as to have amounted virtually to treason. Moreover, although she suffered terribly over the knowledge that her impassioned advocacy of the Mexican Empire had driven her consort into a perilous venture[77] and led the Archduke and his wife to catastrophe,

---

[75] D'Hérillier to Charlotte, Douai, November 27, 1865, HKM; see Corti, *Maximilian and Charlotte*, II, 549–550.

[76] Note by F. Eloin, on board the Leider, February 8, 1866, HKM, Carton 15. Eloin based his information on a conversation with Baron Saillard, special emissary from Napoleon to Emperor Maximilian. Saillard had the confidence of the French Emperor and was well informed on the people and influences surrounding him.

[77] D'Hérillier to Charlotte, Douai, November 27, 1865, HKM; Corti, *Maximilian and Charlotte*, II, 551.

the Empress felt no guilty sense of breach of faith or betrayal. She wept over the fate of the Empire but did not blush for it. Lodged in her mind was the conviction that the young couple had brought much of their trouble on themselves. If they had displayed more diplomatic finesse with the clergy, if they had behaved more prudently in financial matters and had exerted themselves to get along with Bazaine, they could have overcome their difficulties. She made her *volte face* without shame. Finally, as the Mexican Empire numbered its last days, she was so absorbed in the contest between Austria and Prussia, that she of necessity pushed from her mind the hideous struggles of the Empire overseas.

PREWAR DIPLOMACY—PICKING A LOSER

The great issue of European diplomacy in 1865 and 1866 was the struggle for hegemony in Germany. By the Treaty of Vienna in October, 1864, Denmark had been forced to hand over Schleswig and Holstein to Austria and Prussia. From the quarrel between the two powers over the final disposition of the surrendered Duchies came the *casus belli* for the Seven Weeks' War of 1866. Austria inclined toward the formation of an independent state within the Germanic Confederation under the Duke of Augustenburg, both from the hope of gaining an additional ally in the German Diet and from a desire to frustrate Prussia's plans to acquire the Duchies for herself. The Prussian government, treading warily as it gauged the reactions of France and the smaller German states, maneuvered cautiously toward annexation of the conquered lands.

Napoleon and Eugénie greeted the prospect of a fight between the German powers with poorly concealed glee. Although the Empress expressed her concern lest the conflict turn into another Thirty Years' War,[78] just such a protracted struggle, draining the resources of Austria and Prussia, was her hope. The long contest which resulted in the Treaty of Westphalia in 1648 had dressed the stage for the brilliant reign of Louis XIV and French hegemony in Europe. Napoleon and Eugénie saw that a trial of strength between two relatively equal German combatants could elevate France in the balance of power and perhaps offer her an opportunity, as the arbiter of Europe in the peace settlement, to extend her own frontiers. As the Empress declared in a meeting of the Council of Ministers, territorial exchanges usually took place only after a war.[79] At the very least France could plan to shuffle off the Venetian question and at best to ex-

[78] Goltz to Bismarck, Paris, August 11, 1865, confidential, reproduced in Hermann Oncken, *Die Rheinpolitik Kaiser Napoleons III. von 1863 bis 1870 und der Ursprung des Krieges von 1870/71*, I, No. 21, p. 52.

[79] Protocol of a meeting of a Council of Ministers, Tuileries, May 18, 1866, Rouher's notes, Oncken, *Rheinpolitik*, I, No. 112 A, p. 210.

pand toward the Rhine. The peril to be avoided according to their calculations was an overwhelming victory of either one of the belligerents. The rivalry of Austria and Prussia for hegemony in Germany was a priceless asset of French foreign policy. Since everyone agreed that Prussia was the weaker of the two the Emperor encouraged her alliance with Italy. He intended to stand apart from the war shaping up, but would tincture his neutrality with benevolence with respect to Prussia.

Tension mounted in the spring of 1865 as Austria stirred up the German Diet to back Augustenburg in the Duchies. As the curtain seemed about to go up on the duel, Bismarck suddenly grew alarmed over the possibility of an Austro-French *rapprochement*. Napoleon was planning to take an extended trip to Algeria and to leave the Empress in Paris as Regent. Drouyn de Lhuys was still Foreign Minister. Goltz reported that Metternich seemed unusually busy at the Tuileries. Had the Empress reverted to her Austrophil phase? While the cat was away would the Austrian mice play?[80]

Bismarck's alarms were groundless. Indeed, Drouyn de Lhuys yearned for the humiliation of Prussia at the hands of an Austria allied with the small German states. He often disclosed his Austrian sympathies in conversation with Metternich. But he understood that Austrian retention of Venetia was the insuperable roadblock to cooperation with France. During the Emperor's absence he hewed obediently to his instructions and repeatedly affirmed the French position of neutrality. As for the Empress, she had abandoned the Austrian camp and let Goltz discern the benevolent attitude of the Emperor toward Prussia.

The Emperor must have had supreme confidence in the Empress' reliability or he would not have left her for so long at the helm in Paris. After his return from Algeria, after an absence of nearly six weeks, he stopped at his court only two weeks before jaunting off to Plombières and Châlons, excursions which lasted until late in August. Drouyn de Lhuys was away for long periods also—notably in the first two weeks of August at the height of the crisis in Austro-Prussian relations. Many of the other members of the diplomatic corps went on leave during the summer heat. Goltz and Metternich remained in the nearly deserted capital, circling each other warily and taking alarm at each rumor that the other had extracted some word of encouragement from the Empress.

Eugénie had genuine sympathy for the plight of Metternich, who was trying in desperation to penetrate Napoleonic enigmas while his country

---

[80] See Bismarck to Goltz, Berlin, April 20, 1865, *APP*, VI, No. 17, p. 59; Clarendon to Cowley, May, 1865, Frederick Arthur Wellesley (ed.), *Secrets of the Second Empire: Private Letters from the Paris Embassy; Selections from the Papers of Henry Richard Charles Wellesley, 1st Earl Cowley*, pp. 282–283.

was on the brink of a war on two fronts. She gave him her word that if Napoleon allied with Prussia she would herself "openly and quickly" warn him.[81] Otherwise she did not deviate from Napoleon's instructions. She showed the ambassador a letter from the Emperor promising that France would observe "the most strict neutrality" in a war between Austria and Prussia. If Italy attacked Austria in Venetia she would do so at her own risk and without expectation of help from France.[82]

Her line with Goltz was perceptibly more encouraging. She twice assured him that while the Emperor had no intention of interfering in Germany, he would be *benevolently* neutral toward Prussia. French policy, she said, was motivated by regard for the wishes of the people and the principle of nationalities. Therefore, France regarded Prussian annexation of the Duchies as the best solution. Prussia should be careful, she warned, not to do anything which might set European opinion against her. She believed the Prussian government must find some means of getting right with the representatives of the people and counselled Goltz to ask the advice of Rouher, the French Minister of State, who was so "inexhaustible" in such "expedients." As for Italy, Napoleon was willing to let her profit by the war to conquer Venetia. Victor Emmanuel must realize, however, that he acted at his own peril. Quite naturally, out of fear of finding himself alone against Austria, the King would not move until hostilities were already engaged between the two German powers. Goltz, who had heard that the old Austrophil sympathies of the Empress had revived, left her presence completely reassured.[83]

The report of these utterances, so strange on the tongue of the Empress, fell into the hands of the Austrian government, which had intercepted and deciphered a telegram from Goltz to Berlin. Count Mensdorff, Austrian Foreign Minister who had replaced Rechberg in the fall of 1864, saw it as evidence of warmongering on the part of Eugénie and sent it posthaste to Metternich. "This communication will let you see," he wrote, "that in Paris they [on] are far from discouraging Prussia."[84] Hastening to the Empress, Metternich found her able to carry water on both shoulders. She assured him that the French public and the army were quite generally

[81] Metternich to Mensdorff, letter of August 7, 1865, summary from protocol book, HHSA. The letter itself is missing. See Chester Wells Clark, *Franz Joseph and Bismarck: The Diplomacy of Austria before the War of 1866*, p. 285.

[82] Metternich to Mensdorff, telegram, Paris, August 5, 1865, HHSA, IX/81, quoted from Oncken, *Rheinpolitik*, I, 54 n.

[83] Goltz wrote that he was "doppelt befriedigt" with his reception by the Empress (Goltz to Bismarck, Paris, August 11, 1865, confidential, Oncken, *Rheinpolitik*, I, No. 21, p. 52). See also Goltz to Bismarck, Paris, May 14, 1865, *APP*, VI, No. 65, p. 121; Goltz to Foreign Office, telegram, Paris, August 10, *ibid.*, No. 241, p. 321.

[84] Mensdorff to Metternich, Vienna, August 11, 1865, private and confidential, HHSA, IX/80.

sympathetic to Austria. Prussia was intriguing in Florence for promises for which she had searched "in vain" in Paris. On the other hand, she knew it would be "*impossible*" to prevent Italy from taking advantage of the situation. France would not depart from "*strict* neutrality for less than serious events" (probably meaning an Austrian reconquest of Lombardy).[85]

Unable to elucidate French policy to its satisfaction and harassed by serious financial and other internal problems, the Austrian government suddenly flinched at the prospect of a war on two fronts. It yielded to Prussian demands and at Gastein on August 14 negotiated a compromise on the Duchies. With the differences between the German powers papered over, conditions suddenly returned to normal. Metternich set out on his overdue leave of absence. Napoleon, Eugénie, and their court departed for a holiday in Switzerland. To the intense disappointment of Eugénie, the war clouds evaporated.[86]

The Venetian question henceforth determined the shape of diplomacy. Despite his assurance to Metternich in 1864 that he wished Italy to keep what she had, "neither more nor less," Napoleon was still obsessed with the desire to fulfill his pledge of 1858. In the lull which followed Gastein, Austria rejected an Italian offer to buy Venetia for cash. In March, 1866, the Emperor suggested that she exchange it for the Danubian principalities whose prince, Nicholas Cuza, had just been overthrown. But because Napoleon had promised the Austrian ambassador never again to speak to him of Venetia, he used Eugénie as his spokesman.

Metternich reported that she brought the subject forward very deftly. Calling him to her study, she read aloud a letter from Baron Talleyrand, French ambassador at St. Petersburg. Talleyrand asserted that Russia was so "profoundly impotent" that her opposition to Austrian expansion in the Balkans could be discounted completely. Why then, the Empress asked Metternich, should Austria hesitate to cede Venetia to Italy and to take her compensation in Rumania? She warmed to her theme with an eloquence that reminded the uneasy ambassador of her "fougue politique" of 1863. Only this question, she asserted, kept the two powers apart. If Vienna would only be inspired to a "comprehensive and grandiose" policy, she would have France at her side. Italy, too, could be made to toe the line. What Eugénie had in mind for Italy is not clear. She probably still hoped

---

[85] Metternich to Mensdorff, telegram, August 12, 1865, HHSA, Oncken, *Rheinpolitik*, I, 54 n. 1.

[86] For the Empress' attitude see Goltz to William I, Paris, March 17, 1866, Oncken, *Rheinpolitik*, I, No. 49, p. 113. In a conversation with Metternich in April, 1866, she made it clear that she hoped nothing this time would prevent Austria from undertaking her long delayed conflict with Prussia (Metternich to Mensdorff, Paris, April 14, 1866, HHSA; Oncken, *Rheinpolitik*, I, No. 63, p. 135). See also Metternich to Mensdorff, telegram, Paris, May 1, 1866, *ibid.*, No. 74, p. 145.

that the destruction of unity on the peninsula might be a by-product of the Austrian cession of Venetia. But her proposal to Metternich specified only Rumania as compensation for Venetia and was nearly identical to those of Thouvenel in 1862.

This harping on the Venetian question angered the usually easygoing ambassador. He not only repudiated the proposal categorically but permitted himself some stringent observations on French foreign policy. He told the Empress that she and even the Emperor lacked that *"instinct for nuances,"* that feeling for the "correct moment," so necessary to the successful conduct of diplomacy. True, France found herself badly embarrassed in Italy. Was that reason for Austria to mutilate and disarm herself on the Adriatic? He went down a long list of errors which the French Emperor had committed in the Austrian book since the days of the Polish revolt. The Prince's vehemence did not appear to discomfit the Empress. Relaying his reproaches to the Emperor, she returned a few days later to concede, with a laugh, that neither she nor the Emperor understood anything about diplomacy.[87]

A grim irony lay behind the Empress' laughter. The Austrians had just sprung shut on themselves the trap which caught them in a war on two fronts. Rebuffed by the Ballhausplatz, Napoleon turned to Italy and Prussia for the solution of the Venetian question. On April 8, on Napoleon's advice, they signed a treaty of alliance. In the event of an Austro-Prussian war, Italy would join Prussia and receive Venetia as her reward.[88]

But the joke was not entirely on Austria. Napoleon and Eugénie were unwittingly preparing for their own downfall. Both completely underestimated Bismarck. The Emperor regarded him in a patronizing manner as an adventurer like Cavour but without the Italian's exquisite ability to turn events to his own profit. In Napoleon's opinion, Bismarck would never be able to accomplish "grandes choses."[89] Eugénie, although she admired the Prussian's diplomatic finesse, never doubted for a moment that in a contest with Austria he would come off second best. When Napoleon had met with Bismarck in Biarritz in the fall of 1865 he believed he had played his game adroitly in keeping France clear of commitments and in extracting the statement that Prussia refused to guarantee Venetia to Austria.

Even after Italy and Prussia had forged their chain, however, Austria might still have broken free. Learning of the terms of the treaty of April 8

[87] Metternich to Mensdorff, Paris, March 22, 1866, secret, HHSA, IX/82, No. 12 B; Oncken, *Rheinpolitik,* I, No. 50, pp. 115–117.

[88] Taylor, *Mastery of Europe,* pp. 160–161; Clark, *Franz Joseph and Bismarck,* p. 406. Prince Napoleon told Ollivier that he himself took a draft of the treaty to Victor Emmanuel on the orders of Napoleon and urged his father-in-law to sign it (Ollivier, *Journal,* II, 245).

[89] Metternich to Mensdorff, Paris, December 2, 1865, copy, HHSA, IX/81, No. 49 C.

through the indiscretion of two Italian diplomats,[90] the Austrian government shook off its immobility and offered to cede Venetia after she had won compensation in Germany (Silesia). The Italian government showed unmistakable eagerness to accept the offer and to avoid a war. Meanwhile, Napoleon again proposed a European congress. Preliminary negotiations on the topics to be discussed might easily be expended until the expiration of the treaty between Italy and Prussia on July 8.[91]

Unfortunately, Austria made the mistake of demanding the destruction of Italian unity in addition to Silesia. In a fatal attempt to revive Napoleon's offers of 1863, the Ballhausplatz stipulated the necessity of an Italian guarantee of the temporal power, a return of at least part of the Pope's lost territory, and some form of restoration in southern Italy.[92] Reluctantly, the Austrians had seen the need for parting with Venetia, but they refused to do so "for the purpose of facilitating the unification of Italy."[93] These conditions made the offer something less than palatable to the Italian government and caused it to hesitate uncertainly. Bargaining went on during most of May while Napoleon, rather at a loss as how to ride his "Venetian hobby,"[94] acted as an ineffective intermediary.

Eugénie contributed more than her share of confusion to the complex situation. Contrary to the supposition of some writers, she did not take up the cause of Austria.[95] In the thick of the arguments and parleys, she seized erratically on one idea after another and entangled herself in a maze of inconsistencies. Of only one thing was she really certain: the crisis between the two German powers must not be allowed to evaporate or dissipate into "another Gastein." Only in a war would the territorial exchanges take place from which France might benefit.[96] During the spring she frequently goaded the Austrians into action. "When I tell you to march," she exhorted Metternich, "it is not to make you fall into a trap. Muster more energy than you seem to have. . . . everything must tell you, as I do: advance,

[90] Ollivier, May 20, 1866, *Journal*, II, 245.

[91] See Barker, "Austria, France, and the Venetian Question, 1861–66," *The Journal of Modern History*, XXXVI (1964), 151–153.

[92] *Ibid.*, p. 151. Many of the records of this negotiation have disappeared, including the important despatch which left Vienna on May 1 bearing the terms of the Austrian offers. Its contents may be inferred from the counterproposals, the correspondence between Nigra and La Marmora, and other diplomats on the scene. See also Clark, *Franz Joseph and Bismarck*, pp. 411–412.

[93] Bloomfield to Clarendon, Vienna, June 5, 1866, most private and confidential, No. 327, PRO FO 356/22.

[94] Clarendon to Cowley, Foreign Office, May 29, 1866, private, PRO FO 519/180.

[95] See, for example, Elisabet Esslinger, *Der Einfluss der Kaiserin Eugenie auf dem ausser Politik des Zweiten Kaiserreichs*, p. 118; Beyens, *Second Empire*, II, 101.

[96] Protocol of a meeting of the Council of Ministers, Tuileries, May 18, 1866, Rouher's notes, Oncken, *Rheinpolitik*, I, No. 112 A, p. 210.

advance!"[97] The idea of a congress had small appeal for her. In the parleys France might be forced to join one or another block of powers and lose her freedom of action. Better for the Emperor to remain uncommitted—even to neutrality. If Prussia knew for certain that she could expect no aid from France, she might draw back from a contest with a stronger power, and the occasion for war would slip by.[98]

Since the Empress anticipated an Austrian victory, she believed the future of Europe would have to be arranged with Vienna. But France should make known its demands only after the war had begun. "A power which can mobilize 700,000 men always negotiates better after or during a war than before it," she told Metternich.[99] Her faith in Austrian invincibility suddenly caused her to leap to the defense of Persigny's design to divest Prussia of her Rhine provinces. His schema called for Prussia to annex the independent kingdoms in northern and eastern Germany (Hanover, Hesse, Saxony, etc.) on the condition that she divide among the dispossessed Princes the Prussian provinces on the left bank of the Rhine. Under the aegis of France a group of buffer states would be born. Austria would cede Venetia to Italy and receive Silesia from Prussia. France had only to promise Austria her neutrality and to keep Italy on its leash. "Austria will dictate the peace because she will beat Prussia," concluded Persigny. In other words, Austria would pull the French chestnuts out of the fire. Believing that of all the ideas suggested, that of Persigny was the most "honest," the Empress rallied to it gladly.[100]

The plan could operate only if Austria won a resounding military victory. Prussia could be expected to give up both Silesia and the Rhine provinces only if she were thoroughly whipped. But its realization depended on still another contingency: the consent of Austria to Prussian annexations north of the Main River and to the sacrifice of Venetia to a united Italy. In the past Austria had steadfastly withheld such consent and always rejected French offers of alliance on similar terms. Metternich groaned as he saw these ideas making headway with the Empress and other Ministers and foresaw what was coming: a French threat to take up arms with Prussia and Italy unless Austria agreed to the French terms.

---

[97] Metternich to Mensdorff, Paris, May 21, 1866, confidential, HHSA; Oncken, *Rheinpolitik*, I, No. 116, p. 221.

[98] Goltz to William I, Paris, May 11, 1866, reserved, Oncken, *Rheinpolitik*, I, No. 98, p. 192; Metternich to Mensdorff, telegram, Paris, May 8, 1866, HHSA, reproduced *ibid.*, No. 88, p. 178.

[99] Metternich to Mensdorff, Paris, May 16, 1866, HHSA, IX/82, No. 25; Oncken, *Rheinpolitik*, No. 109, p. 205.

[100] Metternich to Mensdorff, Paris, May 16, 1866, HHSA; Oncken, *Rheinpolitik*, I, No. 110, p. 206. See also Duke of Persigny, *Mémoires publiés avec des documents inédits*, p. 332, quoted in Oncken, *Rheinpolitik*, I, No. 112 B, pp. 211–212.

But secretly the Empress hoped to sweeten the pill for Austria. It came to the ears of Cowley that the Empress, "positively," and Drouyn de Lhuys, perhaps, were dusting off old plans to partition Italy into three kingdoms. This time the still unemployed Grand Duke of Tuscany, whose restoration Franz Joseph had always made such a point of honor, was designated for the throne in Naples.[101] Highly alarmed at this news, Lord Clarendon, British Foreign Secretary, instructed Cowley to warn the French Foreign Ministry of the unalterable opposition of Britain to any such scheme. Clarendon labelled it the worst kind of patchwork, one that could not last six months.[102] Without the French army, wrote the British Foreign Secretary, the Grand Duke would be unable to maintain himself at Naples. "It would be a second Rome, under ten times worse and more unjustifiable circumst[ances]." The Empress should be warned, he believed, that she was endangering the life of her husband since the plan would be sure to bring out "swarms of Mazzinians and other heroes *really ready* to die for their country."[103]

The plot died aborning and never emerged from the back eddies into the regular channels of diplomacy. Drouyn de Lhuys told Cowley, who voiced his government's objections, that "no foundation" existed for these plans, although he admitted that "they might have passed thro more than one brain."[104] The Emperor could not be won over. Ever since 1864 Napoleon had refused to force Italy to regurgitate either Naples or the Papal States. The Empress' "intrigues," as Cowley called them, served for nothing except to raise false hope in the Austrians and to clinch Italy's decision to reject Austria's terms for the cession of Venetia. Inadvertently, the Empress helped forge the iron ring around Austria.

But Italy's decision to fight left the future of Venetia still uncertain. Few thought she would win against Austria even with Prussian help. As Metternich had feared, Napoleon gave his screws on Austria another turn. Despite his past pledges that Venetia should never be a *casus belli* between the two countries, he threatened to join Prussia and Italy unless Austria would hand over Venetia even if victorious and promised to renounce a policy of restoration in Italy.[105] Stretched helplessly across the rack, Austria could but yield, and she purchased at this price French neutrality. On June 12 the two countries signed a treaty incorporating Napoleon's demands. Win or lose, Italy could not fail to receive Venetia.

[101] Cowley to Clarendon, Paris, May 17, 1866, copy, PRO FO 519/232; Paris, May 15, 1866, *ibid.*

[102] Clarendon to Cowley, Foreign Office, May 9, 1866, private, PRO FO 519/180.

[103] Clarendon to Cowley, Foreign Office, May 16, 1866, private, *ibid.*

[104] Cowley to Clarendon, Paris, May 19, 1866, copy, PRO FO 519/232.

[105] Metternich to Mensdorff, Paris, June 6, 1866, HHSA; Oncken, *Rheinpolitik,* I, No. 132, pp. 250–254.

The Empress was delighted with the bargain. She had been unable to revive the plan for the partition of Italy. But the treaty contained a loophole for the destruction of Italian unity in a French promise to respect spontaneous uprisings which might result from the campaign, and it saved the essence of Persigny's plan. Franz Joseph agreed that if Austria defeated Prussia he would not oppose the creation of a "new independent German state" on the Rhine.[106] The Empress rejoiced over what she called an Austro-French "rapprochement." Confident that Austria's victory would solve the problems of France, she predicted that all would now go well.[107]

In her estimate of the relative strength of Austria and Prussia, Eugénie was no more mistaken than anyone else in the French or even the British government. She can not be held primarily responsible for arranging the scenery for Sadowa. In fact, since 1863 she had but rarely exerted any real leadership in foreign policy. As the Empire had floundered after its humiliation in the Polish question, so had she. As she abandoned her Austrophil policy partly from pique, partly from the force of circumstances, she found no single life line to adhere to. Unfortunately, she contributed largely and unwisely to the diplomatic muddle. In prodding Austria to take the leap and in aiding and abetting Austria's unrealistic plans to destroy the revolution in Italy she helped clear the road for the Prussian steamroller. Italy preferred to fight rather than accept Venetia at the price of mutilation. The result was the ultimate victory of that national ideal which the Empress professed to detest—the triumph of a German nation over a heterogeneous union of nationalities.

[106] Gramont to Drouyn de Lhuys, Vienna, June 12, 1866, *OD*, X, No. 2661, p. 145; Clark, *Franz Joseph and Bismarck*, p. 437.

[107] Metternich to Mensdorff, telegram, Paris, June 18, 1866, Oncken, *Rheinpolitik*, I, No. 157, p. 280.

CHAPTER 6

AFTER SADOWA
"The Beginning of the End of the Dynasty"

THE IMPACT OF SADOWA

On the afternoon of July 3 the Prussians completely routed the Austrian forces at Sadowa in Bohemia. Vienna itself lay open to the invaders. The battle placed all of Germany at the mercy of Prussia and smashed beyond resurrection the European balance of 1815. The stunning Prussian victory affected all the powers, but none more than France. All the Emperor's calculations and preparations had been contingent upon the ultimate success of Austria. He had not thought it necessary to bargain with Bismarck on the future shape of Germany. His meeting with the Prussian Chancellor in October, 1865, had netted only the informal agreement that each would keep clear of an alliance with Austria. What should the Emperor do to prevent the eviction of Austria from the Germanic Confederation and the emergence of a military colossus on his eastern frontier? With little time for deliberation he was constrained to reappraise his policy and to hand down a decision on which the future of his Empire would depend.

". . . I have never been *italienne,* I will *never* be *prussienne,*" was the Empress' reaction to Sadowa.[1] The Austrian defeat obliterated all the coquetries in which she had indulged with Prussia and revived her strong conservative, Austrophil instinct, dormant since November, 1863. Forgotten were the grudges and petty animosities she had nurtured against Franz Joseph and Ferdinand Maximilian, regretted all the work in which she had participated in pushing Austria into a war on two fronts. In a flash she was transported back to 1863 when the Austrian alliance was the be-all and end-all of her policy.

---

[1] The Empress did not make this statement until April 11, 1867, in a replay of the events of the preceding July with Metternich. It epitomized, however, her reaction during the crisis (Metternich to Beust, Paris, April 11, 1867, HHSA, IX/86, No. 21, A–D; Hermann Oncken, *Die Rheinpolitik Kaiser Napoleons III. von 1863 bis 1870 und der Ursprung des Krieges von 1870/71,* II, No. 413, p. 310).

In the earliest hours of the crisis Eugénie, Drouyn de Lhuys, and the persuasive Metternich nearly succeeded in pushing the Emperor into a show of force against Prussia. Even before the Battle of Sadowa the Austrian government, foreseeing a military disaster in Bohemia, had begged Napoleon to take immediate possession of Venetia in order that its southern army might be rushed northward into service against the Prussians.[2] While the Emperor was reflecting on this proposal, he received the news of the Austrian defeat. Unaware for the first moment of the staggering extent of the Austrian losses that made further resistance virtually impossible,[3] Napoleon believed he saw an opportunity to curb the Prussians and to enforce a peace settlement on his own terms. He replied to Vienna that if Austria would accept as a basis for the peace the formula for Germany outlined in his open letter to Drouyn de Lhuys of June 11 (published in the *Moniteur* of July 12), he would accept the cession of Venetia and offer his mediation to Florence and Berlin.[4] The essence of his plan was the limited aggrandizement of Prussia north of the Main, the preservation of Austria's "great position" in Germany, and the organization of a third Germany (neither Austrian nor Prussian) into some form of union.[5] Since for Prussia it implied the defeat of her ambition to dominate the whole of Germany and for Austria it implied the preservation of her territorial integrity (except for Venetia) and her membership in the Germanic Confederation, the Austrian government was only too eager to accept. After the debacle at Sadowa, Austria could expect far worse from Bismarck.

On the evening of July 4 Metternich brought to the Tuileries the hastily wired message of acquiescence from Vienna and joined the Empress and Drouyn de Lhuys in a conference with the Emperor. At the end of four hours they had persuaded Napoleon to publish in the *Moniteur* his decision to intervene in the war as mediator. According to the Empress, a last spark of energy bazed up in the Emperor during the course of the evening. "The instinct of the magnificent role we [Eugénie, Drouyn de Lhuys, and Metternich] were preparing for him, the thought of the immense effects which

[2] Mensdorff to Metternich, telegram, Vienna, July 2, 1866, Oncken, *Rheinpolitik*, I, No. 168, p. 297.

[3] Metternich to Mensdorff, Paris, July 26, 1866, very secret, *ibid.*, No. 233, p. 380. Apparently Bismarck himself did not at first comprehend how great would be both the strategic and moral consequences of the battle which, in effect, rendered all of Germany helpless before Prussia (Benedetti to Drouyn de Lhuys, Berlin, August 6, confidential, No. 178, AMAE [Paris], Mémoires et documents, Autriche, vol. 6; *OD*, XI, No. 3308, p. 396).

[4] Metternich to Mensdorff, telegram, Paris, July 3, 1866, Oncken, *Rheinpolitik*, I, No. 171, pp. 298–299.

[5] Napoleon to Drouyn de Lhuys, Tuileries, June 11, 1866, *Moniteur*, June 12, 1866, Oncken, *Rheinpolitik*, I, No. 144, pp. 262–263.

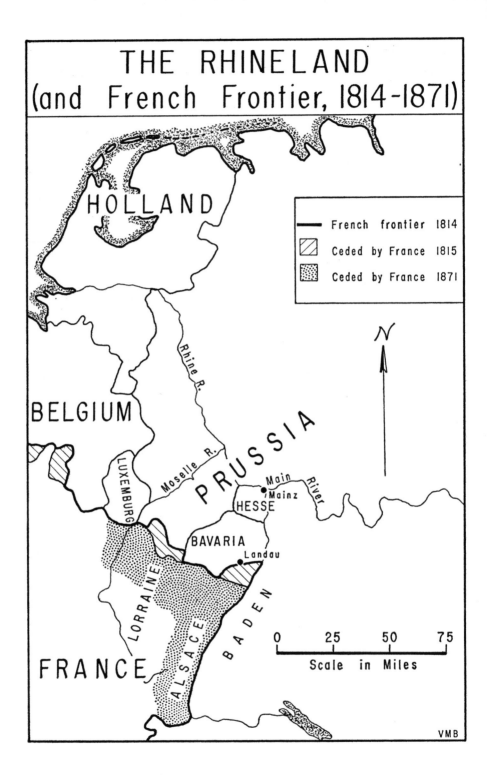

THE RHINELAND
(and French Frontier, 1814-1871)

HOLLAND

BELGIUM

PRUSSIA

LUXEMBURG

Rhine R.

Moselle R.

Main

Mainz

HESSE

BAVARIA

Landau

LORRAINE

ALSACE

BADEN

River

FRANCE

N

French frontier 1814
Ceded by France 1815
Ceded by France 1871

0   25   50   75
Scale in Miles

VMB

his note, which he had just readied for the *Moniteur* would produce on the world, all this had acted on him like alcohol."[6] Without consulting Prince Napoleon or his other Ministers he dictated his pronouncement to the Empress, who wrote it out carefully in her own hand. About midnight he gave it to La Valette, Minister of Interior, for publication on July 5. It proclaimed:

An important event has just taken place.

After having safeguarded the honor of his arms in Italy, the Emperor of Austria, accepting the ideas set forth by Emperor Napoleon in his letter of June 11 addressed to his minister of foreign affairs, cedes Venetia to the Emperor of the French and accepts his mediation to bring about peace between the belligerents.

The Emperor Napoleon has hastened to reply to this appeal and has immediately addressed himself to the kings of Prussia and Italy to effect an armistice.[7]

The pointed reference to the Italian defeat at Custozza was flattering to Austria and indicated unmistakably wherein now lay the sympathies of the French government. The very publicity given the Emperor's decision, moreover, implied that he would, if the need arose, implement it by coercion. So, in fact, did Metternich interpret the pronouncement, and he left the palace around midnight on the night of July 4–5 convinced that the Emperor would insist on his terms in Florence and Berlin "*with force.*"[8] So, too, did the French ambassador at Vienna diagnose the case, and he immediately spread it about that in the event of Prussian resistance, "France would not be long in throwing 100,000 men on the Rhine."[9]

Yet the Emperor had not made up his mind whether or not to show his sword. Within twenty-four hours, after learning the full extent of the Austrian disasters, he recoiled from his own boldness and shied at forceful intervention. The tergiversations and vacillations of the next ten days have been told too frequently to require repetition here. Many accounts exist,

[6] Metternich to Mensdorff, Paris, July 26, 1866, very secret, Oncken, *Rheinpolitik*, I, No. 233, p. 380.

[7] The draft, written in Eugénie's hand on paper bearing the imperial crest, is preserved in the Fonds La Valette, Archives Nationales, Paris, ABXIX/3038. On top is a note in La Valette's hand and signed by him: "Cette note écrite en la main de l'Impératrice Eugénie m'a été remise par l'Empereur le 4 juillet à minuit [word almost illegible] moins ¼. [signed] Lavalette."

[8] Metternich to Mensdorff, telegram, Paris, July 5, 12:15 A.M., Oncken, *Rheinpolitik*, I, No. 175, p. 302. The great value Metternich attached to the pronouncement is shown by his later remark to Cowley that if he had not obtained "on the moment the famous article of the *Moniteur*, the following morning would have been too late" (Cowley to Stanley, Paris, July 10, 1866, copy, PRO FO 519/233).

[9] Bloomfield to Clarendon, Vienna, July 6, 1866, most confidential, No. 414, PRO FO 356/22.

some in contradiction of each other on details. Very probably on July 5, pressed by Eugénie, Drouyn de Lhuys, and Randon, the Emperor came close to ordering a general mobilization of troops—the natural sequel to his statement in the *Moniteur*.[10] But the official newspaper appeared on July 6 without this significant order. The Emperor had decided to disavow the policy of July 4. Although both Prussia and Italy accepted *pro forma* Napoleon's offer of mediation, they continued the war and paid no attention to the terms which he had proclaimed his intention to uphold.

The magnitude of the Emperor's humiliation can hardly be overestimated. His premature display of lordliness was probably his worst mistake in the entire crisis. By his pronouncement he had gone on record before his own people and before the powers as intending to speak as the referee of Europe. The effect of his bravado, moreover, exceeded even his own expectations. The Parisians went wild with joy, ran up flags, illuminated buildings, and shouted in the streets. All the more cruel was his position, all the more painful was his mortification, when he did not make his voice heard. He had dressed the stage for the appearance of the masterful arbiter of Europe. Instead, out of the wings crept a paper tiger with neither teeth nor claws. Thus, he dramatized his own weakness and heightened French animosity toward Prussia, who had administered this snub. The episode helped render impossible graceful acceptance by the Second Empire of German unification. The natural aversion of France to the creation of a strong unified Germany acquired a dangerous fillip when compounded with questions of Napoleon's honor and French *amour propre*.

It may be debated whether the real blunder lay in the pronouncement itself or simply in its publication before a line of action had been determined. Perhaps a French show of force on the Rhine would have compelled Prussia to abandon her successes in Austria and retreat to cover Berlin. But an alliance with Austria negated the Emperor's prewar promises of benevolent neutrality and carried with it real risk of war.

---

[10] According to most accounts a decision was taken at a Council meeting on July 5 to convoke the chambers in order to obtain funds for a general mobilization. Sometime later that day or evening, however, the Emperor abandoned the war policy and decided to do nothing (Jacques Louis César Alexandre Randon, *Mémoires*, II, 145; Baron Napoléon Beyens, *Le Second Empire vu par un diplomate belge*, II, 144–145; George Maurice Paléologue, *The Tragic Empress: A Record of Intimate Talks with the Empress Eugénie, 1901–1919*, pp. 104–105; Emile Ollivier, *L'Empire libéral: Etudes, récits, souvenirs*, VIII, 415–421; Pierre de La Gorce, *Histoire du Second Empire*, V, 15–20; Jean Maurain, *Baroche, ministre de Napoléon III*, p. 311). All accounts agree that La Valette opposed a policy of action while the Empress championed it, although they disagree on details. The conflicts of opinion are well summarized and presented in a long footnote in *OD*, X, 329–331. For the Empress' desire for armed mediation see Eugénie to Metternich, July 9, 1866, Oncken, *Rheinpolitik*, I, No. 196, p. 327.

Moreover, Prussia was mobilized and France was not. A policy of action ran counter to the peaceful pressures of public opinion. Before being shouted from the housetop it ought to have been thoroughly thrashed out with the Ministers after the particulars on Austrian losses at Sadowa were known.

The Empress must share with the Emperor some responsibility for this imprudent misstep. It was a commonly held view in the diplomatic world that on the evening of July 4, affected by the Austrophil sympathies of his wife and by the distress of Metternich, Napoleon said more than he was later willing, on reflection, to uphold.[11] Could Metternich and Drouyn de Lhuys have prevailed on the Emperor without the support of the Empress? It seems unlikely. The Foreign Minister had been a nullity in the government since the fall of 1863. Metternich's mission had turned sour at the same time; but in its effective moments in the past, as Vienna was well aware, it owed much to Eugénie's remarkable patronage. Were it not for her the ambassador would not have been on that intimate footing with Napoleon which gave his arguments such sentimental force.

There was a last flurry of belligerency in France on July 9 and 10 in reaction to Bismarck's terms for peace: exclusion of Austria from German affairs, dissolution of the Germanic Confederation and Prussian annexations north of the Main. According to the Empress, they were *"far from pleasing here."*[12] The Emperor did not object to Prussian hegemony in the north. But the eviction of Austria from Germany was that which he had most desired to prevent. Meanwhile the Italians had crossed the Po and were promenading through Venetia. The Emperor ordered his fleet to depart from Venice, proposed to send Gramont to the Prussian military headquarters in order to head off a march on Vienna, and furnished Count Benedetti, French ambassador to Prussia, and Prince Napoleon with strong notes calling for an immediate armistice to present to the Prussian and Italian governments.[13]

But the Emperor's show of energy quickly faded before the threat of a war with Prussia. Goltz delivered a sharp warning to Napoleon and Eugénie of the dangerous consequences to be expected from a French departure from benevolent neutrality. He justified the vivacity of his lan-

[11] Stanley to Cowley, Foreign Office, July 23, 1866, private, PRO FO 519/182.

[12] Eugénie to Metternich, July 10, 1866, Oncken, *Rheinpolitik*, I, No. 199, p. 331.

[13] Metternich to Mensdorff, telegram, Paris, July 9, Oncken, *Rheinpolitik*, I, No. 195, p. 236; Drouyn de Lhuys to Benedetti, telegram, Paris, July 9, 1866, *OD*, X, No. 2923, p. 368; Drouyn de Lhuys to Malaret, Paris, July 9, 1866, *OD*, X, No. 2925, p. 369; instructions of the Emperor to Prince Napoleon, July 9, 1866, *OD*, X, No. 2928, pp. 371–372; Cowley to Stanley, Paris, July 10, 1866, copy, PRO FO 519/233; Bloomfield to Clarendon, Vienna, July 10, 1866, private and confidential, No. 429, PRO FO 356/22.

guage by the need to counter the force of the Empress' extreme Austrophil sympathies. A day or two later he was convinced that his lesson had taken effect, as both Empress and Emperor were far less belligerent.[14] The French squadron remained in Toulon; Prince Napoleon delayed his departure for Florence until July 16 and added a paragraph to his instructions which nullified the strong words before it.[15]

The policy of intervention was irrevocably abandoned on July 11 during a meeting of the Council. The Empress was present. The Emperor and Ministers decided that France would avoid war at all costs and should raise no objections to the terms of the allied belligerents. Apparently the Empress was not as cowed as Goltz thought, for she pointed out to the Ministers the evident disloyalty of this policy with regard to Austria. But she and Drouyn de Lhuys were easily overruled.[16] On July 14 Napoleon agreed with Goltz on the terms to be presented at Vienna. They were incorporated in the preliminary peace at Nikolsburg of July 26. Drouyn de Lhuys was obliged to counsel Vienna to accept her expulsion from Germany since the French Emperor could not enforce his terms of June 11.

Eugénie was profoundly downcast over the reversal of the policy of July 4 and confessed her impotence and frustration to Metternich: "My dear Prince, what do you want me to do, *everything humanly possible* I have done."[17] She, like the ambassador, felt that France betrayed Austria by accepting Venetia, offering mediation, and then permitting the Italians to parade through the territory which their own arms were unable to conquer for them. Out of sympathy for Franz Joseph in his misfortunes she had sent him a medal of the Holy Virgin to bring him good luck. Touched by the gesture, the Austrian Emperor thanked her not only for the token but for the noble service which she had rendered him in the recent crisis as the "friend of Austria." One sentence of his remarkable letter read: "For a long time I have known that you were the faithful auxiliary of causes which, if they are not always successful, preserve at least their justness in the sympathy of a noble heart."[18] What a declaration

---

[14] Goltz to Bismarck, Paris, July 11, 1866, very secret, Oncken, *Rheinpolitik*, I, No. 206, pp. 338–339.

[15] These instructions are in AMAE (Paris), Mémoires et documents, France, Vol. 2119. By the last paragraph, which nullifies the strength of the preceding statements, is a marginal note which reads: "Ce paragraphe a été ajouté en dernier lieu. Il est de la rédaction du prince Napoléon." In *OD*, X, No. 2928, pp. 371–372, these instructions are dated July 9. The editors maintain that the last paragraph was added by Drouyn de Lhuys (p. 372 n. 2).

[16] Metternich to Mensdorff, Paris, July 18, 1866, Oncken, *Rheinpolitik*, I, No. 219, p. 363.

[17] Eugénie to Metternich, Paris, July 11, 1863, Oncken, *Rheinpolitik*, I, No. 203, p. 333.

[18] Franz Joseph to Eugénie, July 12, 1866, copy, Oncken, *Rheinpolitik*, I, 334 n. 1. The original is in the Alba Archives.

to make to the wife of a sovereign who based his throne on the principle of nationality! Franz Joseph not only implied that in upholding principles of legitimate monarchy the Empress was acting in opposition to the Emperor of the French—which was certainly bad enough—but he also insinuated that her husband lacked both nobility of spirit and a sense of justice. Yet the Empress preserved the letter as a precious keepsake.

The Empress was arguing from a position of weakness. Only Drouyn de Lhuys, Walewski, Gramont, and Randon joined forces with her. Walewski, who pleaded for armed mediation in a letter to the Emperor, was in semiretirement, still out of favor.[19] Drouyn de Lhuys was on the point of resigning from office. Gramont, far off in Vienna, could not raise his voice in the Council of Ministers and could convey his arguments, well marshalled though they were, only through his written reports.[20] Eugénie's own judgment was impugned by her past patronage of the Mexican venture. Once before the Empress had counselled action, and look to what disasters it had led. Some thirty thousand troops in addition to the Foreign Legion were still in Mexico largely because of her work. The expedition had absorbed the best of French officers and regiments and to great extent was the reason for the military disorganization of France. For reasons of economy the arsenals, depleted in order to satisfy the needs of the forces overseas, had not been restocked. "My word has no longer any weight," she wrote Metternich. "I am almost alone in my opinion, they exaggerate today's danger the better to conceal that of tomorrow."[21] Marshal Randon spoke in favor of a military demonstration,[22] but neither he nor any of the generals could pretend that France was prepared for a major war.

Ranged on the other side were all of the other Ministers—notably Baroche, Rouher, and La Valette—avidly supported by Prince Napoleon. They could muster virtually unanswerable arguments: the folly of provoking Prussia when France was not prepared; the inconsistency in abandoning the principle of nationality; the absurdity in fighting Italy, the Emperor's own creation; the necessity of heeding French public opinion which unmistakably wanted peace.[23] Inaction, it was believed,

[19] Françoise Chalamon de Bernardy, "Un Fils de Napoléon: Le Comte Walewski, 1810–1868" MS, pp. 745–746.

[20] See, for example, Gramont to Drouyn de Lhuys, Vienna, July 17, 1866, *OD*, XI, No. 3036, pp. 89–94.

[21] Eugénie to Metternich, July 11, 1866, Oncken, *Rheinpolitik*, I, No. 203, p. 334.

[22] Randon, *Mémoires*, II, 145.

[23] Eugénie to Metternich, July 11, 1866, Oncken, *Rheinpolitik*, I, No. 203, pp. 333–334; for public opinion see Lynn M. Case, *French Opinion on War and Diplomacy during the Second Empire*, pp. 209–211; Paléologue, *Tragic Empress*, pp. 104–110; Alan John Percivale Taylor, *The Struggle for Mastery in Europe, 1848–1918*, pp. 167–168; La Gorce, *Second Empire*, V, 16–20.

would bring Venetia for Italy, the gratitude of King William and Victor Emmanuel, and the creation of a third Germany south of the Main.

The Empress was not yet ready to admit defeat and quit the field. After a five-day trip, from July 14 to July 19, to attend the centenary celebrations of Lorraine's union with France, she once again picked up the cudgels. "The influence of the empress is making itself felt," wired Metternich on July 21.[24] Several developments temporarily worked in her favor. The brilliant victory of the Austrian navy at Lissa on July 20 tended to discredit the Italians, whose demands for Tyrol as well as Venetia seemed greedy in the face of their military disasters. Eugénie regarded the Italians with a baleful eye. Taking cover behind the shield of their strong ally, they were making a laughingstock of the Emperor. From Vienna, Gramont was begging for a show of force. A demonstration on the Rhine, he argued, would transform the Emperor's mediation from a halting failure into a brilliant triumph. Without the slightest danger of war the Emperor could dictate the terms instead of submitting to them.[25] Moreover, Napoleon's supine behavior was having a detestable effect on public opinion—or at least Eugénie and the other Austrophils thought it was. She was convinced that the Emperor would soon see the necessity of energetic action.[26]

Eugénie was unable to rekindle in Napoleon that spark of July 4. On her return to Paris she found him "sick, irresolute, exhausted." He could scarcely walk, eat, or sleep, and was completely apathetic.[27] She had already been aghast at his docile acquiescence to the Prussian peace preliminaries, made and agreed upon during her absence. Then on July 22, without asking anything for France, the Emperor agreed to Bismarck's program of annexation of lands bringing four million new subjects to Prussia. Only at the inclusion of Saxony did he demur. Even the Prussian

---

[24] Metternich to Mensdorff, telegram, Paris, July 21, 1866, Oncken, *Rheinpolitik*, I, No. 224, p. 370.

[25] Gramont to Drouyn de Lhuys, Vienna, July 17, 1866, No. 90, *OD*, XI, No. 3036, pp. 92–93.

[26] Metternich to Mensdorff, telegram, Paris, July 22, 1866, Oncken, *Rheinpolitik*, I, No. 225, p. 371; Metternich to Mensdorff, July 26, 1866, very secret, *ibid.*, No. 233, p. 379. Cowley also wrote of the "discontent of the country" which might necessitate some satisfaction for "french amour propre" (Cowley to Stanley, Paris, August 7, 1866, copy, PRO FO 519/233).

[27] Metternich to Mensdorff, Paris, July 26, very secret, Oncken, *Rheinpolitik*, I, No. 233, p. 380. Some historians have suggested that the Empress and Metternich exaggerated Napoleon's illness (Taylor, *Mastery in Europe*, p. 168 n. 3; Thomas A. B. Corley, *Democratic Despot: A Life of Napoleon III*, p. 286). Perhaps they did. Although unquestionably he did become very sick late in the summer, in July he looked to Cowley to be merely "worse for wear" and lacking in energy (Cowley to Bloomfield, Deauville, July 31, 1866, PRO FO 519/233).

Chancellor had not believed such expansion possible without some compensation for France.[28]

The Empress regarded these concessions as proof of Napoleon's loss of judgment and his inability to reign. He was, she thought, "completely at the mercy" of his chief Minister, Rouher, who was to blame for the Empire's decline and who would have them dethroned if not checked. On July 23 she asked the Emperor to step aside, abdicate in favor of his son, and confer the regency on her. Unfortunately, she babbled the whole story to Metternich, who promptly reported it to his government. "We are marching to our ruin," she prophesied, "and it would be best if the emperor *suddenly disappeared,* at least for some time."[29]

She was incapable of concealing her alarm even from the Prussian ambassador. Although sparing him the account of her pass at the regency, she told him that the present state of affairs was "the beginning of the end of the dynasty." Goltz immediately gossiped to Cowley, so that London as well as Berlin and Vienna learned of the Emperor's pitiful weakness.[30] What fantastic imprudence to have thus advertised the physical and moral decline of the Emperor before Europe. This knowledge would not only convince Bismarck that he might act with impunity, but it would diminish Austria's faith in France as a potential ally. Unluckily for Eugénie, the matchless gift of reticence was never hers.

But if the Empress was indiscreet, she was not disloyal. She was no nineteenth-century Catherine the Great, capable of conspiring at the overthrow or perhaps even the death of her husband. Characteristically, she acted in a direct, foursquare manner. When the Emperor, with more vehemence than she had believed him capable of,[31] repulsed her move to supplant him, she desisted. She neither intrigued nor rebelled.

The explanation for her effrontery lay in her exaggeration of the Emperor's incapacity and of her own popularity. During the crisis, despite the black cloud of the Mexican expedition which hovered perpetually over her, she received some rare and genuine marks of affection from the French people, whose love she had usually solicited in vain. When she participated in that midnight conference of July 4 she had come that day fresh from a visit to the cholera-stricken town of Amiens. She had gone

[28] Goltz to Bismarck, Paris, July 23, 1866, Oncken, *Rheinpolitik*, I, No. 227, p. 373. See Taylor, *Mastery of Europe*, pp. 171–172.

[29] Metternich to Mensdorff, Paris, July 26, 1866, very secret, Oncken, *Rheinpolitik*, I, No. 233, p. 380.

[30] Cowley thought the Empress was exaggerating the seriousness of the situation, but agreed that the Emperor had lost prestige in the crisis (Cowley to Stanley, Paris, August 10, 1866, copy, PRO FO 519/233).

[31] Octave Aubry, *The Second Empire*, trans. A. Livingston, p. 393.

fearlessly to the bedsides of the victims in the fever wards, had contributed large sums of money to the hospitals, and had taken several orphan children under her protection. Probably only this once in her reign did she touch the heart of the people. Even Ollivier, who secretly believed that the Empress' charity sprang from an urge to impress rather than to serve, always saluted her bravery in going boldly among the sick.[32] Everyone was talking of her courage and of her impish humor when she bade farewell to the bishop at Amiens, who had not paid a single visit to the hospitals. "Good-by, Monseigneur," she admonished him wickedly, "above all take care of your health."[33] Ten days later she went with the Prince Imperial to Lorraine. At the military camp at Châlons and at every stop on the itinerary the Lorrainers acclaimed them with wild enthusiasm. Admiring crowds surrounded the carriage and chanted "Amiens! Amiens!" Eugénie was exhilarated not only by the reception but by the aptitude shown by the Prince in handling himself with the crowds. He was a natural campaigner, she boasted, capable of waving and smiling for hours during the parades and demonstrations. Thus, she had returned home with the thought that the two of them might well make a winning combination.[34]

After the summer of 1866 Eugénie frequently betrayed her loss of confidence in Napoleon. She was living only for the next generation. In her opinion her husband's timidity and bungling had cost him the respect of his subjects. Physically debilitated by his amorous excesses (her diagnosis of his illness) and broken in spirit by his mistakes, he could never again rally the country behind him. Since he would not abdicate, if they could just win one victory over the Prussians they would hang on until the Prince came of age. Her life was over, she would repeat. She would not cling to power, but would resign herself to be put out to pasture. If only the Prince were eighteen they would retire at once.[35]

THE FORAGE FOR COMPENSATIONS

On July 23, the very day on which Eugénie proposed to Napoleon that he

[32] Ollivier, December 29, 1865, *Journal*, II, 229; February 3, 1866, *ibid.*, p. 236.

[33] Robert Sencourt, *The Life of the Empress Eugénie*, pp. 217–218. For Eugénie's visit to Amiens see also Harold Kurtz, *The Empress Eugénie, 1826–1920*, p. 206.

[34] Eugénie to Anna Murat, Saint-Cloud, July 28, 1866, Mouchy Papers, No. 52. On September 1 Metternich reported ". . . She [Eugénie] thinks of the future of her son. She knows, and I am happy to verify it, that public opinion in France is more and more sympathetic to her. The army adores her since it has learned that she combatted with more energy than success the influence of Prince Napoleon. Her Majesty wants to strike while the iron is hot, and she will visit next month le Berry to rally the populations of the center. She told me that far from trying to paralyze the growth of her popularity, the emperor gives her a free rein and even lends her his support" (Metternich to Mensdorff, Paris, September 1, 1866, private, HHSA, IX/85 *varia*).

[35] Metternich to Beust, April 11, 1867, Oncken, *Rheinpolitik*, II, No. 413, pp. 309–310; Ollivier, July 8, 1867, *Journal*, II, 294.

abdicate, Drouyn de Lhuys launched his ill-fated diplomatic campaign for French compensations on the eastern border. He instructed Count Benedetti to present at Berlin the French claim to the frontiers of 1814, to Luxemburg, and to those parts of Bavaria and Hesse lying on the left bank of the Rhine.

The Empress favored this bold approach. Better ask for a whole loaf, including Mainz, or none at all, she thought.[36] While the Prussian army was still tied down in Bohemia she and Drouyn de Lhuys believed that French claims, if presented resolutely, must prevail. Such was also the appraisal of the British government. Cowley and Lord Stanley, the new British Foreign Secretary, could explain the Emperor's "incomprehensible" reversal of policy in July and his "betrayal" of Austria only by invoking the doctrine of compensations. Since the loss to Prussia would be negligible and the risk in refusal great, they had little doubt of Bismarck's acquiescence to French demands.[37]

The Emperor exerted little control over the quest for compensations. When Napoleon retreated to Vichy for a rest the Empress despatched Drouyn de Lhuys in pursuit.[38] While at the resort with his master the Foreign Minister renewed his instructions to Benedetti to persist in the demands for compensation. Napoleon had meanwhile suffered a painful and debilitating attack of bladder disease. Later in August, in a directive to La Valette, the Emperor attributed the idea of compensations to Drouyn de Lhuys alone and implied that the Foreign Minister had acted without authorization.[39] Outraged, the Foreign Minister protested that his despatches had been "read, corrected, and approved" by the Emperor.[40] However it may have been, the Emperor did not seem entirely familiar with the terms of the Foreign Minister's despatches. In his conversation with Goltz, just before leaving for Vichy, he spoke only of Landau and Luxemburg for France and omitted any mention of the left bank at Mainz.[41] When he returned from Vichy he at least simulated ignorance of Drouyn de Lhuys' claims, declared that Bismarck had misunderstood his intentions, and professed great alarm at arousing the ill will of all Germany for a few insignificant crumbs of territory. Faced with Bismarck's refusal, he begged that the *démarches* be considered "nulles et non avenues." On

[36] Aubry, *Second Empire*, p. 393; Sencourt, *Eugénie*, p. 194; La Gorce, *Second Empire*, V, 52; Beyens, *Second Empire*, II, 179.

[37] Stanley to Cowley, Foreign Office, August 8, 1866, private, PRO FO 519/182. Cowley was convinced that Napoleon would make Prussia pay for his neutrality (Cowley to Stanley, Paris, July 11, 1866, copy, *ibid.*, 519/233).

[38] Metternich to Mensdorff, Paris, July 26, 1866, very secret, Oncken, *Rheinpolitik*, I, No. 233, p. 380.

[39] Napoleon to La Valette, August 12, 1866, *OD*, XII, No. 3385, pp. 70–71.

[40] Drouyn de Lhuys to Napoleon, 1867 (see *OD*, XII, 71–72 n. 3).

[41] Goltz to Bismarck, Paris, July 27, 1866, confidential, Oncken, *Rheinpolitik*, II, No. 239, pp. 8–11.

July 12 he repudiated Drouyn de Lhuys and placed foreign policy in the hands of Rouher pending the nomination of a successor. It was freely rumored among the diplomats, startled by this incomprehensible *volte face,* that the Emperor's illness had affected his mind.[42]

The Empress burned with shame at this new humiliation at Bismarck's hands. She explained to Metternich that the idea of compensation had arisen from the need to offer the clamoring public some satisfaction from Prussia even if it was only a bone to gnaw on.[43] She now realized the futility of further demands unless accompanied by a show of force. By the second week in August the Prussian army was evacuating Bohemia and returning to the Rhine. France had let slip the moment to threaten without fear of immediate reprisal. With an instinctive shrewdness Eugénie sensed, better than many a sophisticated and experienced diplomat, that words alone would never yield a Prussian *pourboire.* By August 11, soon after Bismarck had made plain Prussia's inflexible opposition to French demands, she told Metternich that the episode had degenerated into a farce.[44] She had no part whatsoever in Rouher's clumsy pass at Belgium later in the summer. Probably she did not even know of it. With the disgrace of Drouyn de Lhuys, Eugénie was severed from active policy-making. No one told her of Drouyn de Lhuys' resignation until the Minister himself informed her, several weeks later, when he officially left office. She had not been aware of his purgatory in holding down his post at the Foreign Ministry while waiting for his successor to be named.[45]

Throughout the crisis Eugénie had been keenly aware of the alarmingly adverse reaction of public opinion to French policy. The moral she drew was that peace had been purchased at too great a price. Sadowa and its aftermath, she never tired of repeating, had reduced France to the rank of a third-class power.[46] Only a confrontation with Prussia from which France emerged victorious could restore her prestige. Even as early as August, 1866, it was plain to Cowley that she was becoming the leader of a group which would eventually, although not at the moment, go to war to re-establish French supremacy in Europe.[47] With awful prescience she

[42] Cowley to Stanley, Paris, August 16, 1866, copy, PRO FO 519/233; Beyens, *Second Empire,* II, 180–182; Goltz to Bismarck, Paris, August 12, 1866, confidential, Oncken, *Rheinpolitik,* II, No. 271, pp. 55–62.

[43] Eugénie to Metternich, August 13, 1866, Oncken, *Rheinpolitik,* II, No. 274, p. 65.

[44] Metternich to Mensdorff, telegram, Paris, August 11, 1866, HHSA, IV/83, No. 171.

[45] Metternich to Mensdorff, Paris, September 1, 1866, private, Oncken, *Rheinpolitik,* No. 300, p. 98.

[46] Report of Baron Beyens, April 3, 1867, Beyens, *Second Empire,* II, 224.

[47] Cowley to Stanley, Paris, August 14, 1866, copy, PRO FO 519/233.

half jestingly referred to a Prussian seizure of Alsace and Lorraine.[48] Only a few days after Sadowa she told Prince Reuss, Prussian envoy: "You have displayed such energy [that] . . . we run the risk of seeing you one fine day before Paris. . . . I shall go to bed French and wake up Prussian."[49] After 1866 war was merely a question of time for her. Have courage, she would admonish Metternich. "The moment will come. . . . If France once touches at the idea of the Rhine, she will follow through, believe me, just as surely as you will follow *another*."[50]

On the other hand, the diplomats of the appeasement party had convinced her of the woeful state of French military preparedness. In August she was so cowed that she estimated the strength of the Prussian army as twice that of France and she was desperately anxious to avoid an encounter with it. The answer then was to talk sweetly to Prussia, give no reason for offense, and meanwhile to arm as quickly as possible and mend diplomatic fences with Austria. The effort must have been supreme, as deceit came hard to Eugénie, but she managed an ingratiating attitude toward Goltz. She told him that Prussian supremacy was merely a "matter of time," and professed herself more sympathetic toward a power capable of such brilliant success than toward one (Austria) which everywhere demonstrated its "pitiable incapacity." She closed her audience with pleasant talk of the forthcoming Universal Exhibition in Paris and pious wishes for a lasting peace.[51] She hoped Austria would follow her example in dealing with Prussia. Let Bismarck alone, she preached to Metternich. "Imitate the conduct of Prussia who smiled at you until the day she struck you down."[52] As in 1863 she saw the germ of future greatness for France in an alliance with Austria. The next time the opportunity came knocking the two powers must be prepared.

Reform of the army and the development of new weapons became an obsession with her. The chassepot, a rapid-firing rifle being readied in the summer of 1866, especially engaged her attention. Having invited Marshal Canrobert and General Le Brun to dine at Saint-Cloud, she turned the table talk into a seminar on national defense. What was the range of the

---

[48] Goltz to Bismarck, August 20, 1866, Oncken, *Rheinpolitik,* II, No. 296, p. 93; Victor Wellesley and Robert Sencourt, *Conversations with Napoleon III. A Collection of Documents Mostly Unpublished and Almost Entirely Diplomatic, Selected and Arranged with Introductions,* p. 312.

[49] Reuss to William I, Paris, July 10, 1866, Oncken, *Rheinpolitik,* I, No. 198, p. 330.

[50] Eugénie to Metternich, August 13, 1866, Oncken, *Rheinpolitik,* II, No. 274, p. 65. See also Metternich to Mensdorff, telegram, August 17, 1866, *ibid.,* No. 282, p. 72.

[51] Goltz to Bismarck, Paris, August 20, 1866, Oncken, *Rheinpolitik,* II, No. 296, pp. 93–94; Wellesley and Sencourt, *Conversations with Napoleon III,* p. 312.

[52] Metternich to Mensdorff, Paris, October 24, 1866, confidential, Oncken, *Rheinpolitik,* II, No. 311, p. 118.

chassepot? How rapidly did it fire? "When the answer was favorable, she clapped her hands, bounding with pleasure like a child."[53] It followed naturally that she supported the strong-army bill, projected by the government in December, 1866, which would have raised an army of 800,000 by universal conscription. When Ollivier objected to some of its features, she leaped to its defense with "real eloquence."[54] She tried, although to no avail, to arouse the martial spirit of Frenchmen and to combat the very obvious aversion they displayed to delivering up their sons to the enlistment officers of the Empire. "They say enthusiasm is dying out. We must revive it," she wrote the Ministers of War and Interior. Her plan, never executed, was to elevate the status of the professional soldier by the erection of monuments or the dedication of public thoroughfares in honor of soldiers of rural France who had performed acts of heroism.[55]

If, in the days following Sadowa, Eugénie continued to formulate policies, she had little means of implementing them. The army bill, when finally passed, was a vitiation of the original draft and continued the system of 1832 with no important changes. The mobile national guard for which it provided was little more than a farce as an effective reinforcement of the army. In reality, active service had been reduced from seven to five years; the wealthy could still furnish substitutes for their sons. Just as the Empress had been unsuccessful in pushing Napoleon to act in July, so, discredited and isolated, she was powerless to reverse the alarming trend of events. She must have felt like a Cassandra, whose dire but accurate predictions fell on deaf ears.

During August, 1866, just as her influence was totally eclipsed by that of Rouher's, she had still another cross to bear. The Empress Charlotte, with tears and tirades, dropped on the French court "like a bolt out of the blue." "You can just imagine how pleasant it was for the emperor to see her, suffering as he is," Eugénie complained to Anna Murat.[56] For Eugénie her presence was an inopportune reminder of bygone greatness and of her own hazardous folly. Because of Napoleon's illness—he returned from Vichy suffering acutely—and because of protocol—Charlotte's journey technically was a visit to her sister ruler—the burden of their gruesome hospitality fell on her. Moreover, Napoleon was morbidly anxious to avoid a confrontation. Charlotte's arrival unluckily coincided with the moment

---

[53] Germain Bapst, *Le Maréchal Canrobert: Souvenirs d'un siècle,* IV, 50. She told Metternich that the army was "working night and day" on the rifle (Metternich to Mensdorff, telegram, Paris, August 17, 1866, Oncken, *Rheinpolitik,* II, No. 282, p. 72).

[54] Ollivier, January 11, 1867, *Journal,* II, 270.

[55] Identical and undated letters to Ministers of War and Interior; "July 12, 1867," is pencilled in above (AA c. 36–4, reproduced by Kurtz, *Empress Eugénie,* pp. 210–211).

[56] Saint-Cloud, August 10, 1866, Mouchy Papers, No. 53.

he had realized the futility of his quest for compensations and had learned of the irritation his demands had aroused in Berlin. The preceding April he had announced his decision in the *Moniteur* to evacuate his troops in stages from Mexico. It was unthinkable that now, when he was panicky at the risk of engaging a victorious and mobilized Prussia, he should consider further extension of his scattered forces. Quite naturally, he dreaded to tell her so. If Charlotte had been even slightly less strong-willed she would have been outmaneuvered by Eugénie's evasive tactics and would never have spoken with the ruler of France.

Contemporary accounts agree that Eugénie found her role agonizing.[57] Hers was not a callous nature. The sight of so much suffering brought involuntary tears. But what could be done? For over a year Eugénie had lost all faith in Maximilian and this government of his which could never establish itself. She had long been counselling evacuation. At this moment, with the looming menace of a united Germany across the Rhine, how much less likely that she would, out of sentiment, offer to engage France indefinitely in an unending war against Mexican guerillas and risk collision with the United States.[58] Although she put on a state banquet for Charlotte, turned out the Cent Gardes in her honor, and dressed the Prince Imperial in his chain of the Mexican Order of the Eagle, she spoke no word of encouragement. The Mexican Empress made her situation as difficult as possible. For fifteen days, refusing to take their silence and circumlocutions as dismissal, she haunted the court. At last, on August 22 she wrung a plain refusal from Napoleon and left Paris the next day.

With Charlotte's departure the Emperor's health began to improve. Eugénie, to escape the depressing sight of her debilitated and irresolute husband, prepared to go to Biarritz with the little Prince. The moment was the nadir of the imperial marriage. For many years the Emperor's marital infidelities had alienated the Empress' affections; but she had always retained some respect and awe for the ruler. For several years she had been alarmed at his lethargy and his absorption with his history of Julius Caesar. Eugénie admired boldness and action. She could easily excuse errors arising out of rashness; those from timidity, never. In the Sadowa crises she saw the Emperor lose his nerve, or so she interpreted it, just when he needed it the most. One of Metternich's private letters carried the account of the terrible quarrel between Emperor and Empress on the eve of her departure for Biarritz—or rather, of her recriminations and his sullen silence. After listing every error which in her opinion the Emperor

---

[57] Two good accounts, based on primary sources, of Charlotte's visit are Egon Caesar Corti, *Maximilian and Charlotte of Mexico,* II, 665–689 and Baron Camille Buffin, *La Tragédie mexicaine: Les Impératrices Charlotte et Eugénie,* pp. 222–226.
[58] Metternich to Mensdorff, Paris, August 25, 1866, HHSA, IX/83, No. 51.

had committed since the Crimean War, a procedure which required much time, she predicted the disaffection of his government and his people. His weakness, his half measures, his erratic course had by turns encouraged and then deceived both his natural friends and enemies. He had managed to set all Europe against France. What would come of it all? The result would be a mighty coalition of those whom he had at one time or another victimized—Austria, Prussia, Italy, and Russia. Perhaps then he would come to his senses and do something to save the dynasty and the country.[59]

Unable to elicit a response from her husband, the despairing Empress left for the south. Under the blue sky on the beaches of Biarritz she struggled to regain her self-control and to resign herself to the circumstances that she could not change. Her letter of October 7 to Anna Murat reflects the intensity of the conflict of the summer months and the completeness of her severance from affairs of state:

... I can tell you that these are the first good days that I have spent in two years. ... I believe that I shall no longer regret anything; far from the hurly burly of affairs I have begun to live thinking of nothing and taking a rest for a year; never have I felt as detached from all concern; I am conscious of having done everything I could, and if my life has small charm in general, and if it is impossible to do it over, I can at least forget and enjoy without thought of tomorrow the beautiful days of this privileged climate.[60]

POLITICAL LIMBO

Napoleon recovered from his severe illness of the summer and autumn of 1866; but although occasionally he displayed the sure and firm touch of former days, there was no doubt, after Sadowa, that he and his Empire were failing. Eugénie, no longer subject to the female disorders which had debilitated her in the early years of her marriage, was in robust health during the last years of the reign. Paradoxically, however, she participated less directly in foreign affairs and, with few exceptions, remained outside of the arena of policy-making.

For a time in the fall of 1866 the official position of the government toward the "independence of Germany" was antithetical to her own. The La Valette circular of September 17, 1866, intended to be a full-dress review of policy, preached the doctrine of nationalities and attempted to tranquilize French public opinion, apprehensive of the aggrandizement at Prussia. Germany was merely imitating France in her work of consolida-

---

[59] Metternich to Mensdorff, Paris, September 1, 1866, private, Oncken, *Rheinpolitik*, II, No. 300, pp. 98–100.

[60] Biarritz, October 7, 1866, Mouchy Papers, No. 56.

tion, ran the homily. Proud of her own unity, France should not deny it to another. A satisfied nation would be a peaceful nation, one more friendly than ever to France.[61] The reaction of the Empress, when she read the circular in the *Moniteur* while at Biarritz, can easily be imagined. It was the public repudiation of the ideas which she and Drouyn de Lhuys had advocated during the summer.

In the spring of 1867 came the futile French attempt, a sort of caboose on the train of the quest for compensations, to annex Luxemburg. The duchy was the nominal possession of the King of the Netherlands, who was himself the Grand Duke. But it had been a member of the old Germanic Confederation, had joined the Zollverein, and was garrisoned by Prussian troops. The negotiations involved a treaty of purchase from the Netherlands and the acquiescence of Prussia. They might have gone well if Bismarck had not belatedly expressed his disapproval of the arrangement and caused the Dutch King to refuse to sign the treaty. On the brink of another humiliating diplomatic catastrophe, France managed to salvage her honor only by the pressure of the other powers on Prussia at a conference in London late in April. By the agreement worked out Napoleon had to eschew annexation, but he obtained the neutralization of Luxemburg and the retirement of the Prussian garrison.

Although Eugénie told the Prussian ambassador that she was not initiated into the subject,[62] she frequently discussed the negotiation in detail with Metternich. But she was an observer only, and a disapproving one at that. Her view was still that of the preceding summer, that France should attempt nothing unless prepared to follow through with force. "We don't sulk," she bridled, "because a great nation must not sulk before being ready to *back up its grievances.*"[63] In her opinion La Valette and Rouher, directors of foreign policy, were a pair of incompetents, hopelessly "lost in the woods."[64]

In July, when the Prussian government reorganized the Zollverein and included in it not only the supposedly independent southern states but Luxemburg as well, Eugénie privately and personally protested to Goltz. The French public, she said, would see in the representation of Luxemburg in the customs' union an indirect annexation and would throw it in the face of Napoleon. She was sure, she added, that Prussia did not want

---

[61] *Moniteur*, September 17, 1866.

[62] Goltz to Bismarck, Paris, March 9, 1865, secret, Oncken, *Rheinpolitik*, II, No. 360, p. 233; *APP*, VIII, No. 282, p. 450.

[63] Metternich to Beust, Paris, March 16, 1867, Oncken, *Rheinpolitik*, II, No. 372, p. 251.

[64] Metternich to Beust, telegram, Paris, March 14, 1867, Oncken, *Rheinpolitik*, II, No. 369, p. 244.

war, but merely underestimated the difficulty of the Emperor's position and was asking too much of the French people. Yet she was careful to avoid any hint of a threat, took a very conciliatory tone, and never even mentioned the inclusion of the south German states in the Zollverein. Goltz, perhaps out of personal sympathy for the Empress, recommended some slight mitigating concessions to France, but he concluded that both Napoleon and Eugénie wanted to avoid giving offense to Prussia.[65] Once again Bismarck read the signs correctly. When he ignored the Empress' plea and proceeded with his plans for the incorporation of Luxemburg in the Zollverein, he heard no protest from the Quai d'Orsay.

The tragic denouement of the Mexican venture was one of the most important reasons for the Empress' political limbo after Sadowa. The news of Emperor Maximilian's death before a firing squad on June 19, 1867, fell heavily on the Empress. For once her self-confidence deserted her. Overwhelmed by this tragedy on top of the many diplomatic failures sustained by France in Europe, she confessed to her house chaplain, Abbé Bauer: "It is as if we are in a besieged fortress, one affair is scarcely finished than another begins. If only the Prince Imperial were eighteen, we would abdicate."[66] The disaster cancelled the gala state visit of Franz Joseph and the Empress Elizabeth to Paris, arranged for the latter part of July. Since Eugénie had long and in vain desired an introduction to the Austrian Empress and had hoped that this meeting of the sovereigns would warm the chilly temperature prevailing between the courts since Sadowa, she had spared no pains in readying the red carpet for them. Several times during the spring she had seconded the futile efforts of the French government to draw Austria into an alliance over the Luxemburg question.[67] The diplomatic side effects of Maximilian's death were thus an additional reason for remorse.

The following November, Persigny wrote a brutal indictment of the Empress. In a long memorandum to the Emperor he systematically unfolded the baleful results that he saw from her meddling in affairs of state. According to this old Bonapartist, the French public laid at her door all responsibility for the Emperor's difficulties with Rome, for the failure to help Poland, and for the Mexican debacle. The presence of the Empress at the meetings of the Council of Ministers created an undesirable division of authority in the Empire. He concluded that the popularity of the future

[65] Goltz to Bismarck, Paris, July 7, 1867, secret, *APP,* IX, No. 89, pp. 139–141.

[66] Ollivier, July 8, 1867, *Journal,* II, 294.

[67] Metternich to Beust, April 18, 1867, private, Oncken, *Rheinpolitik,* II, No. 432, p. 338; Metternich to Beust, April 27, 1867, *ibid.,* No. 451, p. 366.

Regent and the future interests of her government would be best served by her total withdrawal from politics at the present time.[68]

Unluckily, the Empress herself, opening the daily mail at the request of Napoleon, was the first to read the impudent document. She not only was furious but was also profoundly injured by the Minister's accusations. In her own defense she denied, in an eight-page reply to Persigny, any past intervention in foreign affairs and refused to admit the existence of any dualism in the government. Finally, she vowed never again to set foot in the Council of Ministers. Apparently she meant what she said. Word of her decision seems to have leaked out and probably prompted the letter from Admiral Jurien de la Gravière, Napoleon's naval equerry, which counterbalanced Persigny's blast. The Admiral advised the Empress not to despair over the memory of Mexico; the same illusions had been entertained by everyone at the time of the origin of the expedition. She had no right to efface herself. His thesis was the opposite of Persigny's. "She [the Empress] is one of our social forces. We are in peril, and it would be a sign of weakness to abandon us. All the political experience which She has acquired at the price of twelve years' training She must now use to our profit. . . . To work intermittently will give many people the appearance of capriciousness."[69]

The upshot of the squabble was a half triumph for Persigny. The Emperor wrote to his cantankerous old friend that decidedly he could not accept the Empress' sacrifice. Her abrupt disappearance from the Council would conjure up malicious rumors. In any case, the future Regent should be initiated into political affairs. Perhaps, then, suggested Persigny, the Empress could withdraw gradually. "And, in fact," he boasted, "that is what happened." After attending the sessions with some irregularity, she appeared less and less frequently and finally, in 1869, not at all. He concluded conceitedly: "I believe therefore to have rendered a true service to the emperor and to the empress herself."[70]

THE ROMAN QUESTION AGAIN

Persigny's bitter attack on the position of the Empress may have been triggered by her loud support of the temporal power in 1866 and 1867. In the autumn of 1866 when French troops withdrew from Rome in accordance with the terms of the September Convention, Eugénie caused a sen-

---

[68] The incident is related by Persigny in his *Mémoires publiés avec des documents inédits*, pp. 389–406. See also Aubry, *Eugénie*, p. 451.

[69] November 1867, AA, reproduced by Kurtz, *Empress Eugénie*, pp. 223–224.

[70] Persigny, *Mémoires*, pp. 405–406.

sation in the diplomatic world by her announced intention to pay a visit to the Pope. Although despondent and apathetic on her return from Biarritz, "knowing nothing of current foreign policy and wanting to know nothing,"[71] she roused herself to face the united opposition of the French Ministers and members of the diplomatic corps who, Metternich not excepted, advised against her pilgrimage. At any time the Roman question had the power to vibrate a chord in the Empress. Many assumed that her trip was to be a symbol of her protest against the imperial policy of evacuation—a flight similar to the one she had threatened in the tempestuous days of 1860. Lord Stanley, British Foreign Secretary, saw the project as "an act of insanity of her part," a declaration to Europe that "she has one policy, the Emperor another," and a pronouncement that if she became Regent (a contingency now frequently referred to by diplomats), "the priest party" would take over.[72]

But the extensive evidence exists—as usual, the Empress was very vocal on the question—that she was not opposed to the execution of the September Convention. If she lamented the evacuation, as she told Cowley, she nonetheless saw it as a "necessary political move." She would even admit that large temporal possessions were not essential to His Holiness.[73] When Cardinal Bonnechose implored her to stay the execution of the Convention, she repeated nearly verbatim the measured explanation of official policy employed on him by the Emperor.[74] Yet she wanted the Pope to be "perfectly independent," and intended her trip to emphasize those terms of the Convention, easily lost sight of by the public, which were favorable to the temporal power. She would demonstrate by her presence in Rome that evacuation was not desertion. If the Convention stipulated French withdrawal, it also required Victor Emmanuel's recognition of Florence, not Rome, as his capital. Thus, in hastening to the side of the Pope at this strategic moment, she believed she could reassure him that the imperial shield, although invisible, was still there, and guarded him from his enemies as before. As usual, concern for the dynasty was foremost in her mind. She saw her voyage as a means to rally Catholic opinion around her, heighten her own popularity, and avert a schism between clergy and Empire.[75]

---

[71] Her words to Goltz. Goltz to Bismarck, Paris, November 15, 1866, *APP*, VIII, No. 88, p. 145.

[72] Stanley to Cowley, Foreign Office, November 23, 1866, private, PRO FO 519/182. See also Cowley to Stanley, Paris, November 9, 1866, copy, *ibid.*, 519/233; *ibid.*, November 23; Maurain, *Baroche*, pp. 389–390.

[73] Cowley to Stanley, Compiègne, December 13, 1866, copy, PRO FO 519/233; Wellesley and Sencourt, *Conversations with Napoleon III*, p. 317.

[74] Mgr. Louis Besson, *Vie de Cardinal de Bonnechose, archevêque de Rouen*, II, 61.

[75] The Empress' arguments are taken from her many conversations with ministers

Few people except the Pope and a "few bigoted old ladies" (Cowley's ungallant gibe) appreciated her logic. Papal sympathizers pointed out that she might be walking into a trap. Her presence in Rome might be the signal for a Garibaldian uprising to which the Emperor, as he had done in the past, might give tacit consent. Anticlericals, horrified at this prospect of identification of France with the papal cause, dwelt on the false constructions which could be laid on her trip to the subsequent embarrassment of Napoleon. To parry her critics and lend a practical, political character to her journey, she tried to mediate between Italy and the Papacy. In a private negotiation conducted through Mme de Montebello in Rome and General Fleury, the Emperor's aide-de-camp, whom he obligingly despatched to Florence, she strove to elicit concessions from the Pope involving recruitment of soldiers for the Italian army and judicial reforms, and from King Victor Emmanuel a public statement that he renounced Rome as his capital.[76] Papal concessions would not only hush the foes of the Empress' voyage but would facilitate the Emperor's return to Rome later in the event of a revolutionary coup.

For nearly a month her trip hung in the balance as Eugénie held ministers and diplomats at bay. Napoleon, perhaps from lethargy, perhaps from his "horror of scenes,"[77] let her have her head. The King's speech from the throne on December 15 proved a disappointment, as it contained only a few vapid hopes for conciliation of papal and Italian aspirations and

---

and diplomats on the subject. George Peabody Gooch reproduces a conversation with Magne (*The Second Empire*, p. 170). See also Goltz to Bismarck, Compiègne, November 25, 1866, *APP*, VIII, No. 101, p. 160; Metternich to Beust, Paris, November 5, 1866, HHSA, IX/83, No. 63 B; Metternich to Beust, *ibid.*, No. 63 C, copy.

[76] Eugénie to Metternich, Compiègne, December 9, 1866, copy, HHSA, IX/84; Goltz to Bismarck, telegram, Paris, December 17, 1866, *APP*, VIII, No. 140, p. 215. This is one of the few times in which the Empress is frequently mentioned in the official correspondence published by the French Foreign Ministry (Fleury to Napoleon, Florence, November 26, 1866, *OD*, XIII, No. 3811, p. 159; Fleury to Eugénie, Florence, November 27, 1866, *ibid.*, No. 3822, p. 172; Eugénie to Fleury, Paris, no date, *ibid.*, No. 3823, p. 173; Fleury to Napoleon, November 29, 1866, *ibid.*, No. 3838, p. 190; Fleury to his wife, December 1, 1866, from his *Souvenirs*, II, 327–328, *ibid.*, pp. 210–211 n.; Napoleon to Fleury, Paris, December 6, 1866, *ibid.*, No. 3859, p. 212; Fleury to Napoleon, Florence, December 7, 1866, *ibid.*, No. 3867, p. 222; Fleury to Eugénie, Florence, December 7, 1866, *ibid.*, No. 3868, p. 223; Napoleon to Fleury, December 8, 1866, *ibid.*, No. 3876, p. 230; Napoleon to Moustier, Compiègne, December 10, 1866, *ibid.*, No. 3881, p. 233; Napoleon to Fleury, December 11, 1866, *ibid.*, No. 3888, p. 240). No one has as yet uncovered Eugénie's letter to Mme de Montebello. Its contents may be inferred from her note to Metternich and Fleury's correspondence. The Empress' trip was also the subject of much official correspondence between the Quai d'Orsay and the representatives in Florence and Rome (see *OD*, XIII, November and December, 1866).

[77] Mérimée to Panizzi, Cannes, November 29, 1866, Prosper Mérimée, *Letters to Panizzi*, II, 210.

nothing about a renunciation of Rome.[78] But it was the Pope himself who finally blew up the Empress' trip. With a martyrish air he rejected all but one of Eugénie's proposed concessions and made consideration of the exempted item contingent on the restoration of *all* his lost provinces.[79] Then, in a dolorous farewell address to the commander of the French garrison as the eagles were lowered, he astounded his audience and the French government with an ungracious allusion to the Emperor's failing health and vigor. By the last week in December, Eugénie, now comprehending that her presence in Rome would indeed amount to disloyalty, cancelled her plans.[80]

The *détente* in the Roman question occasioned by French withdrawal was destroyed the next year when Garibaldi reappeared at the head of an army marching on Rome. The patriot's impetuous actions were exceedingly embarrassing to Napoleon. Garibaldi had a knack of putting him to the test. If the Italians did not halt the revolutionary forces (and they would be unlikely to unless compelled by France), the Emperor would himself be obliged to intervene or allow Rome to fall. In 1860, when Naples was in question, Napoleon had looked the other way. But he was committed with Pius IX in a way that he had not been pledged to Francis. In 1867, after a few delays that evoked tremors of hope in revolutionary circles and howls of anguish among the clericals, he embarked his troops at Toulon. The French and papal troops crushed the Garibaldians at Mentana on November 3. Willy-nilly, Napoleon found himself back where he had been before the September Convention. His troops remained in Rome, or rather in nearby Civitavecchia, until the Franco-Prussian War.

During this crisis the Empress made it plain that she believed the duty and honor of France at stake. From all accounts, she was most articulate in urging intervention. Inwardly, she was gleeful at the discomfiture of the Italian government over the reappearance of the imperial eagles, and in speaking with the Marquis of Pepoli, envoy of Victor Emmanuel, "disguised with difficulty . . . the satisfaction of her soul."[81]

[78] Reproduced in part in a letter from Fleury to Napoleon, Florence, December 16, 1866, *OD*, XIII, No. 3925, p. 284. For Eugénie's reaction see Ollivier, *L'Empire libéral*, IX, 42.

[79] Armand to Moustier, Rome, December 13, 1866, *OD*, XIII, No. 3907, pp. 262–263.

[80] Sartiges to Moustier, Rome, December 29, 1867, *OD*, XIII, No. 3982, pp. 388–390; Mülinen to Beust, December 21, 1866, confidential, HHSA, IX/84; Cowley to Stanley, December 19, 1866, Wellesley and Sencourt, *Conversations with Napoleon III*, pp. 319–320; Mérimée to Panizzi, Cannes, December 21, Mérimée, *Letters to Panizzi*, II, 214; Maurain, *Politique ecclésiastique*, p. 743. The Pope later told the French representative that his words had been misinterpreted (Sartiges to Moustier, Rome, December 29, 1866, *OD*, XIII, No. 3982, p. 389).

[81] Pepoli to Victor Emmanuel, Paris, November 2, 1867, "Sulla via di Roma; da Aspromonte a Mentana documenti inediti," *Nuova antologia*, LXXXVII (June 16, 1900), 608.

When Garibaldi had escaped from the guarded island of Caprera and assumed the leadership of his band, Napoleon had been at Biarritz, where Eugénie's influence had exerted itself so effectively in the past. It seems unlikely, nevertheless, that her weight was necessary to swing the balance toward a policy of intervention. In reality, the decision had been made as far back as 1861 or 1862 when the Emperor cut his support of the Italian revolution short of Rome. It had been formalized in the September Convention. To have yielded before the parvenu Kingdom of Italy and Garibaldian bands, with the diplomatic humiliations of the past eighteen months still fresh, would have been unthinkable. This time the Italianissimes were only a forlorn and tiny minority—Prince Napoleon, La Valette, Persigny, and Baroche. Rouher, formerly of revolutionary hue, now was Minister of State and had elections on his mind. He crossed over to the support of the temporal power. The Marquis of Moustier, Foreign Minister since the fall of 1866, made the maintenance of the temporal power in Rome a question of his portfolio. From the records we have of the proceedings of the Council of Ministers it is apparent that the slight hesitation in embarking the troops at Toulon stemmed from uncertainty over Italy's willingness to check Garibaldi. At no time was abandonment of Rome seriously entertained. Everyone was well aware, from the reports of the procureurs general, that the bulk of the French nation expected Napoleon to vouchsafe for the safety of the Pope at Rome.[82] The Emperor could not escape his reluctantly assumed role of good Samaritan to an institution for which he had scant respect. Thus, although for entirely different reasons, both Emperor and Empress were disposed to accept the conditions imposed by the September Convention; she because she could do no more for the Pope, he because he could do no less.

Privately, the Empress still nourished her hatred for the Italians. To her they were always the bandits who robbed the legitimate ruler, ungrateful dependents who bit the hand that fed them. She told Pepoli that by their alliance with Prussia they were proving correct critics of the Empire like Adolphe Thiers, of the Orleanist opposition, who predicted ruin from the support of unitary movements in Italy and Germany. Of necessity, the Empress desisted in her efforts to undo Italian unity, but she had not become an Italianissime. She still hoped for the day of restorations even if she could not plan for them. Frank as usual, she disconcerted the Italian envoy of the King with upsetting reservations on the duration of a united Italian kingdom. *"Allons donc,"* she warned, "if war should come no one can predict what may be the consequence." Her concluding credo had

[82] La Gorce, *Second Empire*, V, 286–292; *Procès Verbal de séance du Conseil des Ministres* (Papiers de Cerçay), Saint-Cloud, October 16, October 17, *OD*, XIX, Nos. 5796, 5804, pp. 1–3, 8–9; Maurain, *Politique ecclésiastique*, p. 816; Case, *French Opinion on War*, p. 170.

anything but a tranquilizing effect. "I believe in the *independence* of Italy because it is the work of France, but not in its *unity,* which is the work of revolution."[83]

REALIGNMENTS AND REAPPRAISALS

By the time of Mentana the diplomatic fallout from the explosive impact of Sadowa had settled around Napoleon and presented him the rough shape of his problems for the remainder of his reign. Italy was a recognized political fact. The causes of the Duchess of Parma, now in her grave, or the Grand Duke of Tuscany, or Francis of Naples had transcended the boundaries of practical politics into a shadowy other world inhabited only by a few diehard Ultras or incurable romantics. Since Bismarck had now openly put on the mantle of Cavour, the question of German unification replaced the Italian question as the cynosure of all eyes. Before the prospect of a single, powerful German nation all other problems paled into relative insignificance. Internally, the issue of the late years of the Empire was "the liberal empire." In January, 1867, the government had introduced additional constitutional reforms that permitted the Emperor's Ministers to be interpellated in the Legislative Body and in the Senate. Further reforms were made in 1868 and 1869 until, by 1870, the government approximated a parliamentary form of monarchy. The step-by-step evolution of the Empire into a genuinely liberal regime provided the other major ingredient of the political ferment of the late sixties.

As the political kaleidoscope whirled in reaction to the new issues, it drastically rearranged factions in the court and government, especially in the Empress' circle. Found in juxtaposition around her were the advocates of drastic military reform in anticipation of a confrontation with Prussia and the old Bonapartists who were resisting further liberalization of the constitution. Part of the realignments of the factions of the later Empire was the unavoidable effect of the many deaths of Napoleon's relatives and Ministers. By the end of 1868 four Foreign Ministers were gone—Drouyn de Lhuys, Thouvenel, Walewski, and Moustier. Billault, Fould, Troplong, Morny, and Niel were either dead or fatally stricken. But, as far as the Empress was concerned, many of the changes stemmed from her deliberate reconciliation with former adversaries and formation of additional ties with the Right. It is not entirely an exaggeration to say that the Empress' "War Party" succeeded, or supplanted, her clerical coalition of the early 1860's.

---

[83] "Sulla via di Roma," pp. 608–609. See also Lyons to Stanley, Paris, November 11, 1866, Baron Thomas W. Legh Newton, *The Life of Lord Lyons: A Record of British Diplomacy,* I, 179–180.

From her post on the sidelines of the political arena she soon found the formerly despised "Prussians," La Valette and Rouher, to be her most valuable spokesmen. What influence she could exert was directed toward maintaining them in the Ministry. The truce between Eugénie and Rouher seems to have been called in 1867 and burgeoned into a solid partnership by 1868. In December, 1867, as Minister of State, Rouher had uttered his famous "Never" speech in the legislature. "Well, we declare it in the name of the French government," he orated. "Italy will never take Rome!"[84] Not even the Empress could ask for a more unequivocal statement. Moreover, Rouher had learned some bitter truths from his unrewarded attempts after Sadowa to pry compensations out of Prussia. In a message to the Emperor of September, 1867, discussing the best course for France in the face of the inclusion of the south German states in the Zollverein, he acknowledged French helplessness at the moment. Napoleon could not protest without provoking a war for which he was not prepared. Yet, in his opinion, the Empire could not continuously appease Prussia without endangering itself and feeding the attacks of its opponents. The remedy, then, was military reform and diplomatic alliances. From a position of strength the Emperor could in the future, depending on the situation, either through peace or war, resolutely claim his compensations.[85] Because this statement closely approximated Eugénie's credo since Sadowa, she revised her opinion of Rouher. Many observers believed her influence lay behind his continuation in the Ministry in the spring of 1868 when, having failed to prevent the introduction of a free press, he threatened resignation.[86] "M. Rouher is in a stronger position than ever," reported Metternich shortly after the Cabinet crisis. "He has made some concessions to the war party which have brought him together with the empress and the minister of war."[87] In the last years of the Empire and in her years of exile Eugénie had no more loyal and faithful supporter. As an old servitor of the Emperor, an accomplice of the *coup d'état* of December 2, he had his roots in the authoritarian Empire. Labelled the "valet" of the Emperor by Prince Napoleon, and the "vice emperor" by Ollivier, he was the despair of the liberals.[88]

Virtually the alter ego of Rouher was La Valette. Although not as unequivocal in his opposition to further constitutional reforms, he identi-

---

[84] *Moniteur,* December 6, 1867.

[85] Rouher to Napoleon III, Cerçay, September 27, 1867, *Papiers et correspondance de la famille impérial*, I, 371–378; Oncken, *Rheinpolitik*, II, No. 515a, pp. 468–469.

[86] Ollivier, February 11, 1868, *Journal*, II, 311; Alfred Darimon, *Histoire d'un parti: Les Irréconciliables sous l'Empire, 1867–1869*, p. 190.

[87] Metternich to Beust, Paris, May 30, 1868, confidential, HHSA, IX/90, No. 23 A–D; Oncken, *Rheinpolitik*, II, No. 601, p. 584.

[88] Ollivier, December 22, 1865, *Journal*, II, 227, and July 12, 1867, p. 297.

fied himself and his policies with the Minister of State to such a degree that when the one was forced out in the summer of 1869, the other had to follow. Like Rouher, he had trimmed his sails to the new breezes risen since Sadowa. In the past he had been one of those, as Mérimée quipped, who wished to persuade the Pope that his kingdom was not of this world. But after Mentana he acknowledged it the Empire's duty to prevent Italian entry into Rome. By 1869 Metternich believed he was firmer than Napoleon and Eugénie on the need for an Italian guarantee of the existing temporal power as a prerequisite to French evacuation. Foreign Minister in 1868 and in the first half of 1869, he worked industriously toward a triple alliance between Austria, France, and Italy. He established a close accord with the Empress, and, according to the British ambassador, he came to depend upon her representations to maintain himself in office.[89]

Other men with whom the Empress established connections were Arthur La Guéronnière and Jérôme David, both notorious opponents of the liberal empire and advocates of a tough policy with Prussia. La Guéronnière was a Legitimist, for a time director of the press, then successively minister in Belgium and ambassador at Constantinople. He earned Eugénie's gratitude by his able refutation in the press of attacks launched against Queen Isabella. Eugénie promoted him in vain for the post of Foreign Minister in the spring of 1870. But his debts and financial peccadilloes gave him so unsavory a reputation that even Metternich expressed qualms over his appointment, despite La Guéronnière's passionate Austrophil views.[90] Jérôme David was a personal friend of Rouher and an articulate spokesman for the Right. The Empress' influence was somehow instrumental in his nomination to the office of Vice President of the Legislative Body in the spring of 1867. After his installation he thanked the Empress for her intercession. "I am convinced that Your Majesty has contributed in great part to my nomination . . . . and I give to the empress a large part of the sentiments of profound gratitude which I experience." He was known to report to the

---

[89] Lyons to Clarendon, before July, 1869, Newton, *Lord Lyons*, I, 223; Metternich to Beust, Paris, June 3, 1869, secret, HHSA, IX/90 (not reproduced by Oncken). For other references to the Empress' close connections with La Valette see Ollivier, December 15 and December 16, 1865, *Journal*, II, 224–226; January 31, February 3, 1866, *ibid.*, pp. 233–236. When La Valette died, in 1881, Eugénie wrote in her note of sympathy to his widow: "I have shared your sorrow as for many years M. de La Valette was my friend. We went through much together and if sometimes we were not of the same opinion, agreement was soon reached for we knew that we each were convinced and *sincere in our ideas.* . . ." (May 22, 1881, Kingston on Thames, Fonds La Valette, Archives Nationales, ABXIX/3038).

[90] Metternich to Beust, Paris, December 30, 1869, private, Oncken, *Rheinpolitik*, III, No. 762, pp. 278–279. See also Ollivier, *Journal*, II, 444; private correspondence between Lyons and Clarendon, May and June, 1870, Clarendon Deposit, Bodleian Library, c. 474, for Eugénie's promotion of David for Foreign Minister.

Empress on debates in the chamber and, according to Ollivier, he spoke on the floor on her orders.[91]

Although outside the scope of foreign affairs, the Empress' views on the liberal empire can not be entirely ignored. They had too much bearing on her choice of political allies after 1866. Here the recent revisionist efforts of Harold Kurtz to portray the Empress as a liberal do not come off too successfully. Certainly she was not a reactionary advocate of divine-right monarchy like her Carlist relatives, just as she was not the religious bigot Prince Napoleon or Cowley made her out to be. She had accepted with little comment and in good grace the modest inauguration of constitutional reforms in November, 1860. But after 1866 the mounting discontent of the French public and growing opposition in the legislature caused her to doubt the wisdom of further relaxation of the reins. Early in 1867 she opposed the liberal measures, believing their passage would be construed as an evidence of weakness in the wake of the diplomatic humiliations after Sadowa.[92] From then on her antipathy toward a constitutional government kept pace with the mutiplication of the government's problems in seating official candidates in the legislature, in passing a genuine military reform bill, and in reassuring a public indignant at the successive annoyances caused France by Bismarck. At times she could almost be talked into grudging acceptance of the interpellation of the Ministers in the chamber or of freedom of meeting.[93] But she never retreated an inch from her stand on the need for press censorship. The press in fact became her special *bête noire*. Once unbridled in the spring of 1868 it vomited continuous discharges of noxious libel about the "Spanish woman." Her supposed frivolities, her wanton dissipations (*ses amants, ses orgies*), and her shrewish tyranny over her husband were raked over for public edification. "Marie Eugénie de Guzmán would sell the Vendôme column rather than give up her visit to the Sultan," slandered *L'Universel* at the time of her Mediterranean voyage to Constantinople and Cairo to celebrate the inauguration of the Suez Canal.[94]

Nor was the Empress ever reconciled with Ollivier and the concept of parliamentary monarchy. In 1873, from her exile, she reminisced on the

[91] Ollivier, *L'Empire libéral*, XIV, 351. See also Bapst, *Canrobert*, IV, 229–230. La Guéronnière's letter to the Empress, dated April 27, 1867, is in the Alba Archives, c. 38–59.

[92] Ollivier, January 11, 1867, *Journal*, II, 270.

[93] See, for example, January 30, 1867, *ibid.*, 281.

[94] Hoyos to Beust, Paris, September 29, 1869, HHSA, IX/90, No. 48. For Eugénie's views on the press see Eugénie to Duchess of Mouchy, Tuileries, January 25, 1868, Mouchy Papers, No 77; James Howard Harris, Earl of Malmesbury, *Memoirs of an Ex-Minister*, II, 414; Newton, *Lord Lyons*, I, 244; Beyens, *Second Empire*, II, 298; Ollivier, February 3, 1866, *Journal*, II, 235.

mistakes of earlier years: "What is certain is that parliamentarianism in France is the road to ruin. The emperor in 1814, Louis Philippe, and finally the emperor in 1870 are the proof of it."[95] This was not simply hindsight. She was nearly as explicit during the ministerial crisis of 1869. She told Metternich: "France is like an hysterical woman who has just had a fit. . . . the head of state must not yield on questions of material order and of his responsibility and his right of initiative."[96] Her record after 1865 showed consistent opposition to alienation of responsibility from the crown. Walewski, who had teamed up with Ollivier and talked himself back into favor with Napoleon to become President of the Legislative Body in January, 1867, never returned to her grace and died unlamented by her the following year.[97] With Ollivier she was never able to find any common area of agreement, although she tried. The recent publication of his diary brings to light a number of curious passages between the two in which the Empress, from the years 1865 to 1867, tried, by flattering attentions to the young idealist, to draw him away from the opposition and into the government before it had become fundamentally a liberal regime.[98] She and the Emperor apparently even stooped to bribery, and dangled before his eyes the editorship of a newspaper which they would subsidize. The diary not only documents the long history of Eugénie's efforts to block parliamentary reforms but bares the contempt, more or less successfully masked in his multi-volume history of the Empire, in which its author held his lady sovereign.

Finally, her actions as Regent during the Franco-Prussian War are proof of her authoritarian convictions. After the French defeats at Fröschwiller and Forbach the Legislative Body clamored for the scalps of the Ollivier Cabinet and for the appointment of new Ministers responsible to it. With "the courage of her lack of judgment,"[99] the Empress accepted the resignations of the discredited Cabinet members, but replaced them with

[95] Eugénie to Duchess of Mouchy, September 21, 1873, Mouchy papers, No. 175.

[96] Metternich to Beust, Paris, August 22, 1869, private, Oncken, *Rheinpolitik,* III, No. 722, p. 223.

[97] Chalamon de Bernardy, "Le Comte Walewski," pp. 761–762; Eugénie to Duchess of Mouchy, Biarritz, October 20, 1868, Mouchy Papers, No. 84.

[98] Ollivier, May 7, 1865, *Journal,* II, 191–194; June 27, 1865, pp. 196–198; July 14, 1865, pp. 201–202; September 10, 1865, p. 213; December 15, 1865, p. 224; December 29, 1865, p. 229; February 3, 1866, pp. 235–237; January 10, 1867, pp. 269–270; January 30, 1867, pp. 280–281. For other samples of Eugénie's views on parliamentary government see Hübner to Rechberg, Paris, April 18, 1862, HHSA, IX/72, No. 2; Eugénie to Charlotte, July 30, 1864, Corti, *Maximilian and Charlotte,* II, 844; Pierre M. A. Filon, *Recollections of the Empress Eugénie,* p. 81. Filon quotes the Empress directly. As he was in general very sympathetic toward her, his testimony is impressive. Darimon, *Histoire d'un parti,* pp. 4–5.

[99] Alfred Cobban, *A History of Modern France,* II, 200. See also Theodore Zeldin, *Emile Ollivier and the Liberal Empire of Napoleon III,* pp. 167, 180–183.

diehard Bonapartists of her own choosing, prominent among them Jérôme David and Clément Duvernois, an ardent Prussophobe. Ollivier was impotent before the coalition of the Empress and the Right. She halted the brief experiment of a parliamentary monarch with an even briefer reincarnation of the authoritarian Empire.

The transformation of the European scene in 1866 reduced the number of the Emperor's problems even if it did not facilitate the solution of the remainder. He was no longer troubled by indecision on the Roman and Italian questions. In the wake of his humiliation at the hands of Bismarck he could not afford to accept dictation on Rome from his client; neither would he move to break up the unity achieved under his aegis. But he was left facing two outsized dilemmas. Should France accept or resist the formation of a united Germany? Should the Empire continue its evolution into a parliamentary democracy or hark back to its authoritarian origin? The Empress never doubted of the proper and necessary answers if her son were to reign as Napoleon IV; yet she regarded the French passivity to Sadowa and the inauguration of the liberal reforms of 1867 as apparent omens of a policy of peace at any price and the alienation of the power of the crown. She as well as Drouyn de Lhuys had been repudiated. She again bucked the trend of the Empire and regrouped her forces. By joining with Rouher and La Valette to stave off the liberalization of the Empire and by working for the Austrian alliance, she strove to prepare for the redress of Sadowa.

CHAPTER 7

A TIME TO SPEAK
"Il Faut en Finir"

In Quest of Allies

The Luxemburg affair had demonstrated conclusively the futility of bargaining with Bismarck for compensation to offset the aggrandizement of Prussia. Consequently, the Emperor turned back to Austria for help in containing the unity movement in Germany and, should he be sufficiently persuasive in Vienna, in destroying the Treaty of Prague of 1866.

From the origin of the negotiation at Salzburg in August, 1867, down to her last desperate appeals to Franz Joseph during the Franco-Prussian War, Eugénie subscribed to the proposed alliance as the only means to restore French preponderance in Europe. Yet the diplomatic exchange apparently afforded her few opportunities for active participation. The Emperor, Rouher, and La Valette were as eager to strike a bargain as she. With the Venetian question interred in 1866, Napoleon had no need to call on his wife to prepare the ground for him with the Austrian ambassador. This time there was no repetition of the fireworks of 1863—no tempestuous scenes, no *fougue politique*. Only rarely, judging from the reports of Metternich and Count Vitzthum, Austrian envoy extraordinary at Paris, did the Empress appear on the scene. In the fall of 1868 she lent her voice to the Austrian plan, favored by Rouher, for general European disarmament. Needless to add, neither Empress nor Minister had the slightest intention of reducing French military potential. The *démarche* was planned as a ploy to embarrass Bismarck and to place on him the blame for the burdens and dangers of the large armies of the powers. The objections of Lord Clarendon and Napoleon suppressed the proposal.[1]

Eugénie was powerless to influence the negotiation. The Austro-French

---

[1] Metternich to Beust, Paris, September 14, 1868, private, Hermann Oncken, *Die Rheinpolitik, Kaiser Napoleons III. von 1863 bis 1870 und der Ursprung des Krieges von 1870/71*, III, No. 628, pp. 23–26; Metternich to Beust, October 28, 1868, *ibid.*, No. 642, pp. 53–56.

rapprochement foundered on obstructions emanating from Austria-Hungary's new orientation as the Dual Monarchy. The Ballhausplatz attached greatest importance to its position in the Balkans and would ally against Prussia only if France gave tangible evidence of good will in the east. Since 1866 Russia had displaced Prussia at the head of the black list of the Ballhausplatz. Napoleon's mind was fixed on his German problem. He offered Austria-Hungary an alliance against Prussia when the Austrians wanted French aid against Russia. The only result of the intermittent and unfruitful negotiations of 1868 and 1869 was a noncommittal exchange of letters betweeen the two Emperors that left Napoleon without Franz Joseph's support in 1870.

The Empire was no more successful with Italy. The snag there lay in the Roman question. The Italian government refused to march with France while imperial troops protected the Pope. In vain did Napoleon dust off the September Convention and proffer it to Victor Emmanuel. The King plainly had something else in mind. He would accept the Convention, but he would not guarantee it. "For," he later explained, "you understand, if the Italians were to enter Rome shouting *Vive Victor Emmanuel, Vive l'Italie*—what would you want me to do?!"[2]

The Empress' clericalism—her refusal to abandon Rome to Italy—has been blamed for the failure of the negotiation with Italy and the consequent isolation of France in the war of 1870. The accusation reads that during the critical moment of the bargaining in the summer of 1869 the Empress isolated the sick Emperor in his bedchamber and exercised exclusive surveillance over the terms offered to the Italians. She barred the door to all who might counter her arguments for prevention of the temporal power. La Valette, Foreign Minister, submitted to her dictation in order to curry favor with the future Regent. Afterward, she either carried away or burned the incriminating evidence of her disastrous Ultramontanism.[3]

The indictment is almost totally erroneous. True, the Empress seems never to have wavered in her resolution not to hand over Rome to Victor Emmanuel. In July, 1870, in typical Eugenian form, she "spouted fire and flames," when even Austria-Hungary supported the Italian claim to the last of the Pope's temporal power.[4] Yet there is nothing to distinguish her attitude, except the vivacity with which she expressed it, from that of the Emperor, La Valette, and Gramont, Foreign Minister, and even Ollivier

[2] Vitzthum to Beust, Florence, July 31, 1870, Oncken, *Rheinpolitik,* III, No. 939, p. 500. For Italy's demands in 1869 for a free hand in Rome see Metternich to Beust, Paris, July 14, 1869, private, *ibid.*, No. 717, p. 215.

[3] Henry Salomon, *L'Ambassade de Richard de Metternich à Paris*, pp. 221, 235–236.

[4] Metternich to Beust, Paris, July 27, 1870, private, Oncken, *Rheinpolitik,* III, No. 929, p. 482.

in the late spring of 1870. With the republican and socialist agitation in France, the government could not possibly reverse the policy of Mentana and risk alienation of clerical opinion. No shred of evidence attests to the Empress' opposition to the Italian alliance. She may well have reasoned that it was high time for Victor Emmanuel to work his way out of his great debt to France. Metternich believed that by the summer of 1869 the Empress was more flexible on the negotiations regarding Rome than even La Valette, a former Italianissime.[5]

The Empress did indeed closet herself almost day and night with the Emperor during his severe illness in August, 1869; but she did not pick up the threads of the negotiation broken by the resignation of La Valette and Rouher in an internal governmental crisis. On the rare occasions that she met Nigra she spoke only of her forthcoming state visit to Venetia, Constantinople, and Cairo.[6] The reports of Count Vitzthum, Austrian negotiator, indicate that he never discussed foreign policy with her. And when Eugénie and Victor Emmanuel met face to face in Venetia in October, 1869, on board her yacht, the King was unable to extract a word from her on the Roman question.[7] Her exclusion from the bargaining is easily understood. With her well-known record of hostility toward Italian unity she would have been an inappropriate choice as saleswoman for the alliance.

Finally, it was Metternich, by his own admission, and not Eugénie, who carried away from Saint-Cloud and burned all the records of the secret negotiations of 1869.[8] The papers burned by Eugénie before her flight from Paris in September, 1870, could have included only the last brief phase of the question in July, 1870. Admittedly, the evidence is and always

[5] Metternich to Beust, Paris, June 3, 1869, secret, HHSA, IX/90 (not reproduced by Oncken). La Valette's views are explained in the preceding chapter. For Gramont's position in 1870 see Metternich to Beust, telegram, Paris, July 27, 1870, Oncken, *Rheinpolitik,* III, No. 927, p. 480; Metternich to Beust, July 27, 1870, private, *ibid.,* No. 928, pp. 480–481. Gramont and Ollivier were indignant when Austria supported Italy's claim to Rome in 1870. Gramont said Beust was appeasing the Jews in Vienna. In 1869 Ollivier had seemed to favor immediate evacuation without any specific guarantees (Vitzthum to Beust, Paris, October 5, 1869, private, secret, *ibid.,* No. 739. pp. 248–249). But in 1870 he held to the September Convention as the limit of French concessions (see Metternich to Beust, Paris, July 27, 1870, private, *ibid.,* No. 929, p. 482).

[6] Vitzthum to Beust, Paris, September 11, 1869, private, Oncken, *Rheinpolitik,* III, No. 727, p. 230.

[7] According to General Menabrea, Victor Emmanuel remarked on emerging from Eugénie's salon on board her yacht: "L'Imperatrice non mi ha detto una sola di quelle paròla che io aspettavo; non abbiamo qua più nulla da fare; bisogna partire" (Claudio del Bene, La Triplice Italo-Franco-Austriaca del 1868–69 [Il Risorgimento Italiano, *Rivista Storica,* VII (1914), 239f.], Oncken, *Rheinpolitik,* III, 248 n.).

[8] Metternich to Beust, telegram, Tours, November 27, 1870, HHSA, IX/96, No. 552.

will be incomplete. Yet what exists indicates neither a division of opinion on the Roman question in the French court and government nor independent action on the part of the Empress.

THE FALL OF THE VICE EMPEROR

The reconciliation of the Empress with Rouher and La Valette in 1867 and 1868 had for a time slightly mitigated her loss of influence after Sadowa. Both Ministers had come to see the need to oppose German unity. At home Rouher especially personified resistance to parliamentary reform. But their forced departure from office in July, 1869, left her without spokesmen in the Cabinet and severed her ties with the Foreign Ministry. The results of the elections of 1869 which gave a reforming complexion to the Legislative Body and the able work of Ollivier in organizing behind him a union of the liberals with some of the less inflexible Bonapartists brought on the crisis in the government. But ironically the deputy who pulled the trigger on Rouher and La Valette for Ollivier was the Duke of Mouchy, husband of Anna Murat, who owed his seat in the chamber to Eugénie's influence. In a way the Empress could not possibly have foreseen, her own handiwork in behalf of the Murat Princess lowered the gate for the entrance of the Cabinet led by Ollivier in January, 1870. A private letter of Metternich, not reproduced in Hermann Oncken's *Die Rheinpolitik Kaiser Napoleons III*, and notes in Ollivier's recently published diary illuminate the background of the "incredible prank" that ushered in the liberal Empire.

When the Legislative Body convened in June, Ollivier drew up an interpellation asking for a Cabinet responsible to the chamber rather than to the Emperor. Napoleon, then in the midst of his secret negotiation with Italy, was desperately anxious to forestall parliamentary reform as it would inevitably entail his loss of Rouher and La Valette. He seemed safe at first, as the deputies discussed and deliberated harmlessly without affixing their signatures to the interpellation. But after two days, a sudden onslaught at the register brought the total number of names to 116. Many of the signers were official candidates of the government. These, in addition to the republicans, who had not signed lest they scare off the conservatives, were sufficiently numerous to require the Emperor to declare his intention to extend the powers of the Legislative Body and, as a sign of good faith, to accept the resignations of Rouher and La Valette.[9]

Those loyal to the authoritarian regime who had signed the interpella-

---

[9] Charles Seignobos, *Le Déclin de l'empire et l'établissement le la 3ᵉ république* (*Histoire de France contemporaine depuis la révolution jusqu'à la paix de 1919*, ed. Ernest Lavisse, VII), pp. 77–78.

tion had, in part, been swayed by Ollivier's moderating statement that it did not intend the total exclusion of the responsibility of the Emperor. But not until young Mouchy, elected to the Legislative Body in May, 1869, with the blessing of the Emperor, approached the register, pen in hand, did the others fall in line like sheep.[10] His connection with the imperial household was so intimate that his act was interpreted as a certain sign of Napoleon's approval. They hastened to follow his example. Eugénie was furious at these "ungrateful French" who forced the Emperor to sacrifice his Ministers. To be so inexplicably hoisted with her own petard!

Out of family loyalty, the Emperor had protected Anna and dowered her generously. But a profound affection had prompted the Empress' patronage of the Princess. Anna was her inseparable companion and probably the only truly intimate friend of her life.[11] For years in the early 1860's matchmaking for the pretty Princess was one of her most absorbing pleasures. Don Carlos, the Carlist pretender, the Grand Duke of Tuscany, the Count of Flanders, Prince Charles of Hohenzollern, Prince Nicolas of Nassau, and the brother of Isabella's husband had at one time or another figured on the Empress' active list of suitable candidates. Anna had herself inclined to Mouchy, of the cadet branch of the Noailles family, a brilliant figure in society, whom she met at court galas. Since the proposed political matches came to nothing, Eugénie hastened to abet the marriage to this distinguished descendant of the aristocracy of the Old Regime. Although the Noailles deplored the *mésalliance* with a *petite nièce* of a parvenu Corsican, the Empress supervised the wedding, which took place in the chapel of the Tuileries in December, 1865.[12] Under the aegis of the Emperor, Mouchy began a career in politics. What impelled this confused, well-intentioned young man to sign the interpellation is not explainable. Taken to task by the Emperor, he could only blurt: "Sire, I believe that in doing what I did I have perhaps saved the empire!" Eugénie poured out the history of the incident to Metternich. It really was, thought the ambassador, one of those cases of rotten luck which defy anticipation.[13]

The fall of Rouher and La Valette was followed by six months of confusion and disorder in France. Until the formation of the Ministry of January 2, 1870, a power vacuum existed in the government. Napoleon

[10] Emile Ollivier, July 6, 1869, *Journal, 1846–1869,* II, 372–373. The signature of another deputy, A. F. A. Mackau, thought to have Napoleon's confidence, also had its effect but did not produce the sensation of Mouchy's act.

[11] The present Duke of Mouchy has in his possession literally hundreds of letters of the Empress to Anna.

[12] Princess Caroline Murat, *My Memoirs,* pp. 172–173; Mme Jules Baroche, *Second Empire: Notes et souvenirs,* p. 289.

[13] Metternich to Beust, Paris, July 16, 1869, private letter, HHSA, IX/94 (not reproduced by Oncken).

was unable to form more than a caretaker government until after convocation of the chambers in the fall. The interim Cabinet, with no Minister of State, felt itself too weak to make serious commitments in foreign policy in the name of the Empire. The Emperor's severe illness in August and September caused rumors to mushroom that he had lost his mind, that he was about to abdicate, or that he was already, in fact, dead. Republican and socialist agitations became bolder. The government found itself forced to use soldiers to quell strikes and riots. The Communist International reorganized and, with the adherence of the French delegates, voted revolution and abolition of private property. The republicans, in the Legislative Body, aroused by the government's slowness to begin the session in the fall, demonstrated in the Place de la Concorde.[14] France was already "en pleine révolution" but not yet decided on the course to take.[15]

No one was more aware of the restive condition of the country than Eugénie. What illusions she might have preserved of her own popularity were shattered by her distinctly unpleasant trip to Corsica with the Prince Imperial in late August and early September to attend the celebration of the centenary of Napoleon I. The absence of the Emperor from this symbolic ceremony demonstrated the completeness of his physical decline and fed the gossip circulating about his death or abdication. The Empress' trip was an ominously stark contrast to her triumphant tour of Lorraine in 1866. The receptions she met ranged from the frankly hostile at Lyon, where the hisses of the revolutionary element nearly drowned out the hired claque, to the coolly indifferent at Ajaccio. There, in the birthplace of the dynasty, where she "had expected to walk on flowers," she received only the stiff formal bouquets of the city fathers.[16]

There is even good reason to think that her celebrated voyage to attend the inauguration of the Suez Canal in October and November was planned in part to remove her from the public eye in France during the domestic crisis, or at least that it was prolonged deliberately until after the dangerous moment of the convocation of the chamber had been safely passed. Malicious tongues could not then gossip of her alleged collusion with leaders of the Right to restore the authoritarian Empire by a *coup d'état*. From the accents of the Emperor in speaking of her itinerary, Metternich divined a deliberate design to delay her return until after the convening of the

---

[14] Seignobos, *Le Déclin de l'empire,* VII, 80–81.

[15] The opinion of Vitzthum, observer of the Parisian scene in the fall of 1869 (Vitzthum to Beust, Paris, December 9, 1869, private, Oncken, *Rheinpolitik,* III, No. 754, p. 268).

[16] Octave Aubry, *Eugénie: Empress of the French,* pp. 192–193. See also F. Dutacq, "Les Dessous d'un voyage officiel—visite de l'impératrice à Lyon en 1869, d'après les rapports de police," *Revue du Lyonnais,* XV (1924), 337–340.

Legislative Body.[17] If so planned, the maneuver was not very effective. Republican newspapers seized on her voyage as the newest evidence of her criminal extravagance. Nor did her absence allay suspicion of her supposed intrigue. Rouher and Baroche did not dare even to present their respects at court on her return, lest the purpose of their call should be perverted and add to the "odious calumnies" repeated by her enemies.[18]

While the Empress was away on her cruise, Napoleon initiated and advanced his negotiations with Ollivier to construct the Cabinet of January 2. Did Eugénie know of his decision? Evidence of her attitude toward the creation of the Cabinet is fragmentary. In August, before her departure for Corsica, she had received Ollivier at Toulon on board *L'Aigle*. It was their first meeting since he had publicly excoriated Rouher in 1867 and severed friendly relations with the Tuileries. Was it true as people were saying, he queried, that Her Majesty had become a reactionary and his enemy? The Empress replied emphatically that she had no ties with any party and was limiting herself to her "rôle de femme."[19]

The following December, after her return from Egypt, she wrote Baroche that she was remaining completely apart from political affairs.[20] Of necessity, she probably was. The experiences of the fall had demonstrated only too plainly that she had become a political liability to the Empire. Moreover, except for what personal influence she could exert on her husband, the situation in December, 1870, offered her few possibilities for action. Once Napoleon had made his decision to call on Ollivier, the complexion of the Cabinet depended on the Minister and the jockeying of factions within the turbulent chamber. The Empress' letters written from the Nile seem to indicate that she and Napoleon had talked over the feasibility of another *coup d'état* but had rejected the idea. "I am thoroughly convinced that true strength is found in consistency of ideas," she counselled. "I don't like counter *coups* [*àcoups*] and am persuaded that *coups d'Etat* can not be done twice in the same reign." Yet in the back of her mind lurked dread of some decisive moment toward which the Empire was rushing and for which heroic measures would be needed. "The more force necessary at a later period," she concluded ambiguously, "the more urgent is it to prove to the country that one has *ideas* and not *expedients*."[21]

[17] Metternich to Beust, Paris, November 25, 1869, HHSA, IX/90, No. 56. See also Philip W. Sergeant, *The Last Empress of the French, Being the Life of the Empress Eugénie, Wife of Napoleon III*, pp. 327–328.

[18] Baroche to Eugénie, Paris, December 18, 1869, Baroche, *Second Empire*, p. 559.

[19] Emile Ollivier, *L'Empire libéral: Etudes, récits, souvenirs*, XII, 51.

[20] Eugénie to Baroche, December 18, 1869, Baroche, *Second Empire*, p. 560.

[21] On the Nile, October 27, 1869, *Papiers et correspondance de la famille impériale*, I, 220–221.

The formation of the Cabinet of January 2 completed the political oblivion of the Empress. She neither attended meetings of the Council of Ministers nor sought to establish political or social ties with its members. Ollivier asserted with obvious satisfaction that she was quite without influence in his government. When addressed by a petitioner for a favor, she would reply: "Go talk to the ministers; I have not the slightest influence."[22]

Empress and Ministers were mutually antagonistic for both personal and political reasons. Ollivier detested what he called the "vulgar brouhaha" of Eugénie's entertainments. His bride, who made a fetish of plainness of dress, found the atmosphere of the court hostile. The wives of Ollivier's colleagues received chilly nods while those of their political enemies basked in the Empress' favor.[23] Politically, Eugénie feared the encroachment of the Ministers on the authority of the Emperor and distrusted their Orleanist connections. Her formal greeting on January 3, 1870, to the Cabinet contained a barbed reminder that it was still responsible, not to the Legislative Body, but to the ruler. "The ministers who have the *confidence of the emperor* are sure of my *good will*," she announced, emphasizing her words in a significant way. The Ministers retired with the conviction that they did not possess the *Empress'* confidence.[24] Nor did they. She knew Ollivier well enough not to doubt his loyalty even if she disliked his ideas. But he stood nearly alone in the Cabinet in his democratic and liberal idealism. Many of the rest had Orleanist backgrounds; Eugénie suspected them of being willing to present the Duke of Aumale with a ready-made Cabinet.[25]

In foreign policy Eugénie's opinions clashed head on with those of Ollivier. He professed to see no reason why Germany should not be permitted to complete her unification around Prussia and advocated a policy of "laisser faire" meaning, in this instance, "let Prussia go." It was his conviction that, next to the King of Prussia and Bismarck, the true authors of the war of 1870 and the downfall of the Empire were those like the Empress, who clamored that Sadowa had been a defeat for France which must be repaired.[26] Because of his soft attitude toward Prussia, Prince La Tour d'Auvergne, Foreign Minister in the caretaker government

[22] Ollivier, *L'Empire libéral*, XIII, 526. See also Seignobos, *Le Déclin de l'empire*, VII, 86, 95; Newton, *Lord Lyons*, I, 241, 244.

[23] Ollivier, *L'Empire libéral*, XIII, 525.

[24] *Ibid.*, XII, 347.

[25] Metternich to Beust, Paris, June 29, 1870, confidential, Oncken, *Rheinpolitik*, III, No. 776, p. 301.

[26] Ollivier to Napoleon, September 27, 1870, Ollivier, *Journal*, II, 448–449. For Ollivier's attitude toward German unification see also Lawrence D. Steefel, *Bismarck, the Hohenzollern Candidacy, and the Origins of the Franco-German War of 1870*, p. 225, and Theodore Zeldin, *Emile Ollivier and the Liberal Empire of Napoleon III*, pp. 168–174.

of the fall of 1869, refused to serve as his colleague in the Cabinet of January, 1870.[27] The Emperor denied Ollivier the portfolio of Foreign Affairs and gave it instead to Count Napoleon Daru, a member of the "center left." Daru, in his conversations with ambassadors and in his formal instructions consistently emphasized the respect for the *status quo* and the Treaty of Prague. But the effect of his admonitions was weakened by his willingness to undertake disarmament and by Ollivier's simultaneous assertions that French opposition to German union was unjust and ridiculous. Daru's short tenure of office, in fact, was entirely sterile. The Empress spoke of him in contemptuous terms—of his obstinacy, his cavilling, his defiance of his master.[28] He abraded Napoleon at every turn. Never admitted to the Emperor's confidence, he knew nothing of the secret negotiations with Italy and Austria-Hungary to forge a chain around Prussia. Under the guidance of Ollivier in the early spring of 1870, the Empire followed a course which the Empress believed fatally unwise.

REVOLUTION IN SPAIN

In September, 1868, an uprising in Spain forced Queen Isabella from her throne and into exile. Napoleon and Eugénie, then at Biarritz, greeted her courteously as she fled, offered her asylum in France, and placed the Chateau of Pau at her disposal.

Both recognized, although they instantly disclaimed any intention of interfering in the internal problems of Spain, that the Empire had suffered a heavy blow. Isabella had been cantankerous enough, but while she reigned, Napoleon could feel confident of Spanish benevolent neutrality should he become involved in a war on the Rhine. Just before the revolution the Queen had apparently agreed to shoulder the burden of protecting the Pope so that the Emperor could retire his troops from Rome for employment elsewhere.[29] A republic or a monarchy in Madrid hostile to the Emperor might join with Italy in opposing French occupation of Rome and cripple the Emperor's freedom of action against Prussia. Bismarck estimated that an unfriendly government in Spain could reduce French fighting effectiveness on the Rhine by as much as two army corps.[30]

---

[27] Vitzthum to Beust, Brussels, January 5, 1870, Oncken, *Rheinpolitik,* III, No. 764, pp. 284–285.

[28] Metternich to Beust, Paris, March 26, 1870, Oncken, *Rheinpolitik,* III, No. 798, p. 337.

[29] Oskar Meding, *De Sadowa à Sedan: Mémoires d'un ambassadeur secret aux Tuileries,* pp. 218–219; Steefel, *Bismarck, the Hohenzollern Candidacy,* pp. 239–240.

[30] Bismarck to William I, Berlin, March 9, 1870, Georges Bonnin (ed.), *Bismarck and the Hohenzollern Candidature for the Spanish Throne: The Documents in the German Diplomatic Archives,* No. 9, pp. 68–73.

The Empress had not the slightest intention of interpreting her banishment from affairs of state, gradually enforced on her since 1867, to apply to Spanish problems. By her birth, her upbringing in the swirl of Spanish politics, because of her many connections and voluminous correspondence with those in ruling circles, she felt herself peculiarly qualified to judge and act on Spanish questions. As she had once marked out Mexico as her special preserve, mistakenly supposing it to be a Latin nation like her native land, so she regarded Spain with its vacant throne as her legitimate sphere of influence. Even before the Queen fled, Eugénie had seen Spain as a likely breeding place for Prussian intrigue. The downfall of the Bourbons was such an obvious windfall for Bismarck that, like many others, she saw his hand in its preparation.[31]

The Empress' suspicions first fixed on Antoine of Orléans, Duke of Montpensier and husband of Isabella's sister, as a tool of the Prussian Chancellor. She was aware early in 1868 of Montpensier's aspirations to power and of the existence of a plot to supplant the Queen. One of her friends from girlhood days, Don Patricio de la Escosura, member of the Spanish Liberal Union Party, made a tactless attempt to win her support for the Duke. Escosura came to Paris in January, 1868, to inform her that the Queen was impossible and that a regency for her young son, the Prince of Asturias, would inevitably fail like all regencies, and would yield only civil war and disorder. Montpensier was the only solution. Eugénie, mindful of the twelve-year-old Prince Imperial and the weak health of the Emperor, took umbrage at his disdain of regencies and frostily dismissed him.[32]

In July, 1868, Isabella wrote the Empress that Prussia was subsidizing the Orleanist conspiracy. According to the Queen's informants, in the event of a Franco-Prussian war, Montpensier would permit Italy a free hand in the Patrimony of St. Peter in order to tie down French troops in Rome.[33] With the help of Metternich, Eugénie planted this story in an anti-Prussian Belgian newspaper. The result was a good deal of chatter in diplomatic circles and a vigorous denial in the official press at Berlin.[34] Thus, even before the revolution Eugénie underscored the importance of

[31] Ollivier, *L'Empire libéral*, XI, 67; Steefel, *Bismarck, the Hohenzollern Candidacy*, p. 12.

[32] Ildefonso Antonio Bermejo, *Historia de la interinidad y guerra civil de España desde 1868*, I, 57–61.

[33] Metternich to Beust, Paris, July 3, 1868, secret, Oncken, *Rheinpolitik*, III, No. 612, p. 10.

[34] Vitzthum to Beust, Paris, October 13, 1868, reserved, Oncken, *Rheinpolitik*, III, No. 636, p. 42; Willard A. Smith, "Napoleon III and the Spanish Revolution of 1868," *The Journal of Modern History*, XXV (1953), 221–233; Steefel, *Bismarck, the Hohenzollern Candidacy*, p. 12.

the Spanish throne in French relations with Prussia and anticipated the shape of the crisis of July, 1870.

Eugénie's suspicions of Prussian collusion with Montpensier in 1868 were perhaps groundless,[35] but they intensified in the spring of 1869 with the appearance in Madrid of a well-known Prussian *agent provocateur* and military man, Theodor von Bernhardi. Ostensibly on a military mission, he joined the Prussian legation, circulated in the political and diplomatic world, and often frequented the salon of the Countess of Montijo.[36] Although scholars have not confirmed a connection between his presence in Madrid and the candidacy of Montpensier,[37] the French imperial couple did not then doubt that it was real. Bernhardi had been in Italy at the time of Mentana and was reported to have incited Garibaldi to action in order to embarrass the Emperor.[38] The Empress' distrust reached such proportions that Goltz called on her during the summer to assure her in the name of Bismarck that his government did not at all favor "this Montpensier business."[39]

At the beginning of the interregnum in Spain, Eugénie, because of her Carlist connections and her fervent support in the past of the Bourbons in Parma, was thought to promote the candidacy of Don Carlos, husband of Margaret of Parma. Gossip had it that the apparent freedom with which Carlist bands moved across French borders indicated the Empress' protection. A correspondent of the *Augsburger Allgemeinen,* for example, wrote darkly of a high agent of the Carlist pretender who had once been one of the Empress' private secretaries.[40] But no reliable evidence exists to support

[35] Steefel, *Bismarck, the Hohenzollern Candidacy*, pp. 12–13.

[36] Theodor von Bernhardi, *Aus dem Leben Theodor von Bernhardis,* IX, 169, 171, 199, 218, 226, 229, 243.

[37] Steefel, *Bismarck, the Hohenzollern Candidacy*, pp. 16–18.

[38] Count Dubsky, counsellor of the Austrian legation in Madrid, wrote: "Parmi tous les noms mis d'abord en avant il n'y eut qu'un seul qui eût pu lui [Bismarck] convenir, c'était celui du duc de Montpensier. Je crois même que le chancelier de l'Allemagne du Nord l'eût préférà à son candidat actuel qui est le Prince Léopold de Hohenzollern" (Dubsky to Beust, Madrid, September 15, 1869, HHSA, XX/26, No. 56 C). Dubsky believed that Bismarck switched to the support of Leopold only because he realized the great unpopularity of Montpensier in Spain. This report was relayed by Beust to his chargé in Paris with instructions to give it to the French government. Hoyos, the chargé d'affaires, reported that he had fulfilled his instructions (Hoyos to Beust, Paris, October 14, 1869, HHSA, IX/94, No. 50 D).

[39] Undated memorandum by Napoleon, Count Maurice Fleury, *Memoirs of the Empress Eugénie. Compiled from Statements, Private Documents, and Personal Letters,* II, 195. From the context the conversation can be placed in the summer months of 1869.

[40] Don Carlos' father, Don Juan, renounced his claim to the throne in favor of his son in October, 1868. For the rumors of Eugénie's supposed support of Don Carlos see Richard Fester, *Neue Beiträge zur Geschichte der Hohenzollernschen Thronkandidatur in Spanien,* p. 92; Metternich to Beust, telegram, Paris, October 5, 1868, HHSA,

the contention that she ever deviated from a consistent and eager patronage of Alfonso, Prince of Asturias, Isabella's adolescent son, who was always Napoleon's preferred candidate. Quite to the contrary. In 1869 and 1870 observers in Paris were generally agreed that husband and wife were of like mind on the desirability of maintaining Isabella's dynasty. It would, in fact, have been quite difficult for Napoleon to have followed a line opposed by Eugénie in Spanish affairs, as he inevitably relied heavily on her contacts and private sources for his information.

A key figure in the promotion of Alfonso was none other than the Duke of Sexto, the Empress' girlhood swain, now married to the widow of Morny. Alas for those romantics who would have the Empress pine cruelly to the end of her days for the unrequited love of her youth. The Empress seems to have been able to recover completely from the chagrin of her girlhood. Throughout her reign and in exile she maintained with him a relationship of nonchalant camaraderie. Sexto had been a member of the Liberal Union Party in Spain but had remained loyal to the Queen. Even so, he was one of the few Isabellists to favor her abdication in favor of her son. Before the revolution, probably with the knowledge of Eugénie, he endeavored to convince her of the wisdom of stepping aside.[41] He was with the imperial couple at Biarritz when the Queen fled and, with their urging, took on himself the role of king-maker. As liaison man between the Tuileries and the court in exile at the Basilewsky Palace, Isabella's Parisian residence, he served as Eugénie's instrument in eventually prevailing on the Queen to abdicate.[42]

The Empress received the Queen frequently at her court and encouraged a friendship between Alfonso and her own son, who, it was reported, swore with youthful solemnity to help the older boy to mount his throne.[43] Marshal Prim, who became President of the Spanish Council of Ministers in the interregnum and who knew the Empress well, regarded her activities in behalf of Alfonso as a pernicious intrigue to force Bourbon restoration on Spain.[44] If he had the opportunity, he confided to the French ambassador at Madrid, Mercier de l'Ostende, he hoped to dissuade the Empress by revealing to her "the full truth" about her Spanish protégé—an allusion to the

---

IX/90, No. ?/324; Bernhardi, *Aus dem Leben,* IX, 18, 161, 173; Alfred Darimon, *Histoire d'un parti: Les Irréconciliables sous l'Empire, 1867–1869,* pp. 316–317; Baron Napoléon Beyens, *Le Second Empire vu par un diplomate belge,* II, 313.

[41] Bermejo, *Historia,* I, 69–71.

[42] Smith, "Napoleon III and the Spanish Revolution," *Journal of Modern History,* XXV (1953), 49.

[43] Meding, *De Sadowa à Sedan,* p. 222. See also Smith, "Napoleon III and the Spanish Revolution," *Journal of Modern History,* XXV (1953), 215; Fleury, *Memoirs,* I, 306–307.

[44] Howden to Lyons, Bayonne, June 7, 1870, copy, PRO FO 361/1.

Prince's rumored illegitimacy.[45] The British picked up the information from Salustiano de Olózaga, Spanish ambassador at Paris, that the Empress was looking ahead to a match between Alfonso and one of her nieces, daughter of the Duchess of Alba.[46] Such a plan would have been in harmony with her concept of the proper conduct of diplomacy in which matchmaking always played a large part. By June, 1870, the work of both Emperor and Empress had became so noticeable that the French ambassador at Madrid felt obliged to counsel cautious moderation lest Spanish sensitivities be offended.[47]

THE HOHENZOLLERN CANDIDACY FOR THE SPANISH THRONE

Unpalatable as was the candidacy of Montpensier to Napoleon and Eugénie, there was another far worse. Leopold of Hohenzollern-Sigmaringen, a distant relative of King William I, was an officer in the Prussian army. His father, ruler of a small enclave in southern Germany, had once been Minister-President of Prussia. Despite a connection with the Beauharnais on his mother's side, Leopold was a German and was subject to the authority of the King of Prussia. His election to the Spanish throne would have meant a serious disturbance in the European balance of power. The Orleanist candidacy was an insult to the Emperor's dynasty; that of the Hohenzollern was a provocation to France.

Scholars today are generally agreed in condemning Bismarck's secretive work outside regular diplomatic channels in the promotion of Leopold for the throne. In the selection of rulers for the vacant thrones of Belgium, Greece, Bulgaria, and Schleswig-Holstein (1852), the powers had established the custom of open consultation between them in order that the prince chosen should be acceptable to all. Napoleon had every right to express resentment in July, 1870, on learning that he was about to have a Hohenzollern ruler on his southern as well as his eastern border. Count Beust gave utterance to the view of the diplomatic world:

That France was not indifferent to this incident—nothing more just. That she saw in it at first unbecoming behaviour toward her and consequently an affront to her dignity—nothing more natural. That she declares her interests

---

[45] Mercier to Gramont, Madrid, June 25, 1870, very confidential, *OD*, XXVII, No. 8229, p. 423. See also Bernhardi, *Aus dem Leben*, IX, 414.

[46] Layard to Clarendon, Paris, November 21, 1869, private, Clarendon Deposit, Bodleian Library, c. 486.

[47] Mercier to Gramont, Madrid, June 10, 1870, *OD*, XXVII, No. 8202, pp. 365–366.

threatened by the accession of a Prussian prince to be the throne of Spain—again nothing to reproach.[48]

On the evening of July 2, 1870, Marshal Prim, his hand forced by the publicity that the negotiation with Leopold had acquired, acknowledged the Hohenzollern candidacy to the Spanish throne in an official conversation with the French ambassador. The Emperor learned the next day from Mercier's telegram that the affair was well advanced, perhaps already decided. Within two days the news that a relative of the King of Prussia had been invited to rule in Spain rampaged through France. Interpreted by the public as a fresh and intolerable provocation from Berlin, it prompted the Emperor to settle his score with Bismarck.

The existence of Leopold's candidacy was not news to Napoleon and Eugénie. They had both been aware within a few months of Isabella's dethronement of talk in Madrid of a Prussian prince for the vacant throne,[49] but, with the exception of one official inquiry at the Berlin Foreign Ministry in March, 1869,[50] they had not put on record with the Prussian government their objections to the consideration of a Hohenzollern as ruler in Spain. In the world of diplomacy there is a great difference between official and unofficial knowledge. A government must take cognizance of and react to the former; for its own convenience it may ignore the latter. The candidacy of Leopold was one of those open secrets in the corridors of diplomacy from which the Emperor, for reasons of his own, had chosen to avert his head.

Between the spring of 1869 and July, 1870, the imperial couple accumulated evidence in profusion to support their suspicion that Bismarck, having seen the futility of Montpensier's candidacy, had switched to the promotion of a Hohenzollern. Among the more important of the warnings were reports in the early fall from Austrian diplomats in Madrid, relayed as a courtesy to the French government by the Austrian Foreign Minister, which attributed the presence of Bernhardi to a delicate mission in behalf of a Prussian prince. The Spanish Foreign Minister had even admitted to the Austrian ambassador that Berlin had made "des démarches" in favor of Leopold.[51]

[48] Beust to Metternich, Vienna, July 11, 1870, very secret, Richard Fester, *Briefe, Aktenstücke und Regesten zur Geschichte der Hohenzollernschen Thronkandidatur in Spanien*, II, No. 430; Oncken, *Rheinpolitik*, II, No. 871, p. 424. British diplomats took a somewhat similar view. See Lyons to Granville, Paris, July 8, 1870, private, PRO FO, 30/29/85; Granville to Lyons, Foreign Office, July 6, 1870, copy, private, *ibid.*, 362/4; Granville to Loftus, London, July 6, 1870, *Bluebook*, Fester, *Briefe*, I, No. 299.

[49] Metternich to Beust, Paris, November 20, 1868, HHSA, IX/90, No. 46 A–D.

[50] Benedetti to La Valette, Berlin, March 31, 1869, despatch in cypher, *OD*, XXIV, No. 7363, pp. 118–120.

[51] Karnicki to Beust, Madrid, August 13, 1869, reserved, HHSA, XX/26, No. 52 B; Dubsky to Beust, Madrid, September 15, 1869, *ibid.*, No. 56 C. Beust sent these

That same fall, Charles of Rumania, brother of Leopold, told Napoleon in person of suggestions made to the family, although he believed his brother would be unlikely to accept the proffered throne.[52] In the spring of 1870 the French government even knew of the abortive project to put the youngest Hohenzollern brother, Prince Frederick, on the Spanish throne. The *Mémorial diplomatique,* joint organ of the French and Austrian Foriegn Ministries, announced: "The secret candidate held in reserve by Prim . . . is none other than P. Frederick Eugene, younger brother of Charles of Rumania."[53] Frederick's father became aware of Napoleon's knowledge of the negotiation and feared lest he voice his opposition to it. He hastened to make known his son's refusal of the crown to avoid the humiliation of bowing to the dictation of France.[54]

Meanwhile throughout the spring with insatiable vivacity the European press joined the guessing game on Spain's choice of a monarch. With more or less accuracy the journalists tattled of communications between Berlin and Madrid.[55] When Leopold's candidacy revived in earnest in June, de-

---

reports to the Austrian chargé d'affaires in Paris with instructions to show them to the French government. Both times the chargé d'affaires reported that he had fulfilled his orders (Hoyos to Beust, Paris, August 31, 1869, and October 14, 1869, HHSA, IX/94, Nos. 41, 50 D). Steefel is reluctant to admit that Bismarck was involved in Leopold's candidacy before 1870 (*Bismarck, the Hohenzollern Candidacy,* 20–22). Robert Howard Lord, who knew of the Austrian reports, was more ready to concede Prussian complicity (*The Origins of the War of 1870: New Documents from the German Archives,* p. 27).

[52] Memorandum of one of Napoleon's aides-de-camp, Fleury, *Memoirs,* II, 204. Leopold later said that the Emperor had raised no objection to his candidacy when he heard of it in the autumn of 1869 (Conversation of *Times* correspondent W. H. Russell with Leopold [*My Diary During the Last Great War* (London, 1874), pp. 97–98], Fester, *Briefe,* II, No. 594). Sybel asserted that Charles Anthony told Napoleon of the Spanish offer during this same visit to Paris: "Prince Anton [Charles Anthony], who, for the moment saw no occasion to report to Berlin, informed his old friend and near relative the Emperor Napoleon of the episode. The Emperor wrapped himself in profound silence, and from the absence of all dissuasion or warning the Prince drew the conclusion that Napoleon would not be unfavorable to his cousin's candidature. . . ." (Sybel, article in *Die Zukunft,* April 20, 1895, p. 103, quoted by Bonnin, *Bismarck,* p. 285).

[53] The article was reproduced in part by the *Frankfurter Zeitung* of May 13, 1870, cited by Fester, *Briefe,* I, No. 168. Fester was apparently unaware of the official nature of the *Mémorial.* It was established for the second time in the 1860's and was supported financially by both Austria and France (Metternich to Rechberg, Vienna, May 7, 1863, private, HHSA, IX/77).

[54] Charles Anthony's memorandum, April 22, 1870, Jochen Dittrich, *Bismarck, Frankreich und die Spanische Thronkandidatur der Hohenzollern: Die "Kriegschuld Frage" von 1870. Im Anhang Briefe und Aktenstücke aus des Fürstlich Hohenzollern- schen Hausarchiv,* Appendix, No. 40, p. 377.

[55] Fester cites at least fourteen articles that refer to a negotiation with a Prussian prince in the spring of 1870 in the French, Belgian, and German presses (*Briefe,* I, Nos. 145–152, 157, 166, 173, 208–210, 216).

spite stringent Prussian security measures, it was well known in diplomatic circles. Apparently realizing the futility of further concealment, Prim, harassed by intrigues in Madrid and his failure to extract an unequivocal statement from Leopold or his father, went before the Cortes to report on the state of his negotiations. After summarizing his unsuccessful overtures to Prince Ferdinand, titular King of Portugal, and to the Dukes of Aosta and Genoa, he spoke of a fourth candidate whose name he was unwilling to pronounce, but who had every needed qualification. He was Catholic, of a royal line, and of age. Although the Spaniard had been no more fortunate with this Prince, he implied that negotiations would be continued.[56] At this moment Mercier, seated in the audience, whispered to his neighbor: "It is Leopold of Hohenzollern in question."[57] Ollivier later admitted: ". . . Everybody could supply the name of the person anonymously designated."[58] Prim himself confirmed the accuracy of Mercier's supposition. After his speech he confessed to the ambassador, who reported the conversation to Paris, that the unnamed candidate was indeed Leopold. He hoped that when he went to Vichy in July he could explain to the Emperor the background of the negotiation.[59]

After Prim's speech the negotiation with Leopold became, in the words of the British Undersecretary of State in the House of Commons, "a matter of notoriety."[60] On June 17 the French Foreign Minister wrote Mercier that the government had information to the effect that the intrigue in behalf of a Prussian prince had been renewed.[61] On June 26 the counsellor of the Austrian legation learned that the affair was on the point of consummation. Several times in the last weeks of June and the first days of July he warned Mercier of the intelligence he was picking up.[62] The British representative at Madrid on June 25 reported that Prim would soon visit Paris and Vichy, and concluded: "I have no doubt, that he [Prim] will occupy himself during the week in '*buscando un rey*'—and I am told that his thoughts are now turned to the brother of Prince Charles of Rumania [Leopold of Hohenzollern]."[63]

We do not know all that Mercier reported to Paris in the last weeks be-

---

[56] Prim's speech summarized in Fester, *Briefe*, I, No. 203. Steefel gives an account of it (*Bismarck, the Hohenzollern Candidacy*, pp. 93–94).

[57] Ollivier, *L'Empire libéral*, XIII, 573.

[58] *Ibid.*

[59] Mercier to Gramont, June 12, 1870, *ibid.*; Fester, *Briefe*, I, No. 207. See also Mercier to Gramont, Madrid, June 25, 1870, very confidential, *OD*, XXVII, No. 8229, p. 423.

[60] *Hansard's Parliamentary Debates*, 3rd series, XXIII, House of Commons, p. 650.

[61] Gramont to Mercier, Paris, June 17, 1870, *OD*, XXVII, No. 8212, p. 389.

[62] Dubsky to Beust, Madrid, July 7, 1870, reserved, XX/27, No. 31 A–B.

[63] Layard to Clarendon, Madrid, June 25, 1870, private, PRO FO 361/1.

fore the candidacy of Leopold became public knowledge. Although the French Foreign Ministry has published three reports of the ambassador in late June, the rest of the correspondence has not yet come to light. The known reports reveal his uncertainties and perplexities. There had been a project to put Leopold on the throne, of that he was sure; but so far as he could see, it had now been abandoned. If the Prussian were really in question, the matter was a deep secret. Yet Prim was banking heavily on his trip to France, and hoped that this time he would be received by the Empress as well as the Emperor. In a letter carried by a trusted messenger he warned: ". . . there is a snake in the grass, for sure, and we can not be too much on our guard."[64]

We can tell from Mercier's account of his conversation of July 2 during which Prim officially acknowledged the candidacy of Leopold, that he had taken to heart the warnings he had received and was most suspicious of a Prussian *fait accompli*. As the Spanish marshal offered one excuse after another for turning to a Prussian prince, Mercier exclaimed: "Oh! I have been aware for a long time that M. de Bismarck was seeking to insinuate himself in your affairs, and you'll have to admit that, if he didn't think he had much to gain, he would not dare to play for such high stakes."

Prim demurred, denying that he had ever talked politics with the Prussian diplomats at Madrid.

Mercier pursued: "What about this Prussian squadron whose arrival has been announced to you?"

Prim: "I've never heard anything about it."[65]

Prussian warships indeed! Mercier had picked up the rumor that Leopold was to be smuggled into Spain on a Prussian vessel. Napoleon learned of it also, perhaps from Mercier, or at least from someone, and, by June 29 was making preparations to send his fleet out from Cherbourg in fighting trim.[66]

We still do not know precisely how the Emperor and Empress gathered their information, although we can easily perceive the numerous opportunities open to them. Probably many of these secrets went up in the smoke of the Empress' fire in the Tuileries the night before she fled Paris. The account of Fleury, son of Napoleon's aide-de-camp and confidant, is of special interest in this question. His discussion of the crisis over the

[64] Mercier to Gramont, Madrid, June 24, 1870, private, *OD*, XXVII, No. 8225, p. 415. The other two reports are dated June 23 and June 25, *OD*, Nos. 8223 and 8229, pp. 404–412, 423.

[65] Mercier to Gramont, Madrid, July 3, 1870, *OD*, XXVIII, No. 8243, p. 26.

[66] The Minister of the Navy wired the naval commander at Cherbourg: "What do you have available in: boots, stockings, gloves, undervests, hats for a northern campaign?" (Paris, June 29, 1870, *Correspondance de Berlin*, 1870, No. 132, November 14, Fester, *Briefe*, I, 119).

Spanish throne is based largely on private papers of the Empress, the Countess of Montijo, and memoranda of the Emperor. Although irritating in its partisanship, it is frequently borne out by recently published documents from the archives at Sigmaringen and the German Foreign Ministry. It never crossed Fleury's mind, although he was an apologist for the Second Empire in general and for the Empress in particular, that anyone could suppose Napoleon and Eugénie to be ignorant of Bismarck's negotiations with the Spaniards. He wrote of the information "pouring in" to the study of the Emperor on each successive development of the Hohenzollern candidacy and portrayed the Emperor as an alert and at times witty commentator on the parleys going on.[67]

Fleury often referred to the Empress' many connections with the political world in Madrid as sources of information. The Countess of Montijo had a keen nose for intrigue and maintained a salon which was a clearing house for the gossip of the capital. She had a way of being in the thick of things. The duel in June, 1870, between Montpensier, whom she detested, and the Infante Don Enrique, took place at her estate in the outskirts of Madrid.[68] Her salon was always crowded with politicians. Bernhardi was drawn to it like a moth to a candle for the people he met and the information he picked up. Eugénie would also have had at her disposal all the news gathered by Isabella and Sexto. Furthermore, she corresponded with ladies formerly in the Queen's court.[69] The lines crossed in another curious way. The house chaplain of the Empress, Abbé Bauer, a converted Jew, was the brother of the Rothschild agent in Madrid. The agent and his partner, Weiswiller, were the bankers of Bernhardi. Both were paid British informants.[70] A document recently published by Professor Joachim Dittrich in his *Bismarck, Frankreich und die Spanische Thronkandidatur* reveals that Weiswiller knew in April, 1870, that the Hohenzollern candidacy was again in question.[71] Here may have been one leak in Prussian security.

Napoleon and Eugénie had many other resources. The French em-

---

[67] Fleury, *Memoirs*, II, 191–218. The chapter is a loosely organized collection of excerpts from private papers, some of them obviously written after 1870, and some of them unidentified. The main difficulty in using the work stems from its internal structure, which sometimes makes it impossible to ascertain at what moment the Emperor learned of the events described. It becomes clear from his account that only a very few in the court were permitted to share the secret information. "Those who were in the secret" (II, 213) were Eugénie, the Duke of Gramont, and Fleury senior. Ollivier was almost certainly excluded.

[68] Bernhardi, *Aus dem Leben,* IX, 262.

[69] Fleury, *Memoirs*, II, 192.

[70] Bernhardi, *Aus dem Leben,* IX, 55–56.

[71] Bamberger to Charles Anthony, Paris, April 8, 1870, Dittrich, *Bismarck,* Appendix, No. 35, p. 373.

bassies were listening posts; French secret agents snooped on Bismarck's emissaries.[72] The Emperor could exert special leverage over Charles of Rumania, who owed his throne to him. Charles' agent in Paris, J. Strat, had the confidence of the Emperor and also knew something of the negotiation in March and April. Leopold's father suspected Strat as a source of Napoleon's intelligence.[73] Add to these possible sources, the unreliability of Spanish telegraphists, the frequency with which telegrams arrived in Madrid in garbled form, and the determined opposition of Baron von Canitz, North German ambassador at Madrid, to the project of the Hohenzollern candidacy.[74] Moreover, the cypher which Bismarck gave to Leopold's father to use in communication with Prim was lost in transmission and may have fallen into French hands.[75] Small wonder that Bismarck and his agent, Lothar Bucher, became convinced that the Emperor had gotten wind of the negotiation and tried desperately to bring off a *fait accompli*—the election of Leopold in the Spanish Cortes—before Napoleon broke his silence.

Napoleon and Eugénie had good reason to withhold their protest. They knew that Prim was coming to France in the second week of July to gain their consent to his candidate. There seemed to be little real danger of a Prussian king in Spain, especially after Prim dismissed the Cortes on June 23, and perhaps a great opportunity, in permitting the clandestine negotiation to continue unopposed. When the moment came to flush the negotiation into regular diplomatic channels the Emperor would have moral right on his side and could expect the support of the other powers in his protests against Leopold. Perhaps they could catch Bismarck *in fla-*

[72] See, for example, the many complaints made by Bismarck's agents of the work of French spies and agents in the diary of Max von Versen, Prussian general staff officer, published by Bonnin, *Bismarck,* pp. 261–282.

[73] Fleury, *Memoirs,* II, 208–209. In investigating the question of whether or not Charles warned the Emperor, the student is faced with a maze of contradictory statements. Baron Keudell, legation counsellor in the Prussian Foreign Ministry, later accused Charles of having informed the Emperor. Charles made no answer. The Prussian historian Hans Delbrück said that Leopold told him that his father had never given away the secret (Ollivier, *L'Empire libéral,* XIV, 22). Of course, Delbrück's assertion begs the question of whether or not Charles had warned Napoleon; nor does it cover Strat in any way. Ollivier said Franceschini Pietri told him that the Emperor had never received any communication from either the sons or their fathers—which, as already seen, was not strictly true (Ollivier, *L'Empire libéral,* p. 22).

[74] Bismarck to Bernstorff, telegram, March 17, 1870, Bonnin, *Bismarck,* No. 21; Bernstorff to Bismarck, London, March 18, 1870, *ibid.,* No. 31. There was no direct line from Madrid to Berlin or from Madrid to London. Telegrams from Berlin had to be relayed through Frankfurt on Main and Paris; those from London via Havre and Bordeaux. See also Salazar to Baron von Keudell, Madrid, March 25, 1870, *ibid.,* No. 52; Bismarck to Bernstorff, Berlin, March 27, 1870, *ibid.,* No. 56.

[75] Lord Augustus Loftus, *The Diplomatic Reminiscences of Lord Augustus Loftus, P.C., G.C.B., 1862–1879,* I, 273.

grante delicto and expose his evident *mauvais vouloir* toward France. The Prussian Chancellor would be required to choose between disagreeable alternatives: either to withdraw Leopold's candidacy, a humiliation when dictated by France, or to stand as the instigator of a quarrel with Napoleon. The Spanish throne was an ideal question for French confrontation with Prussia, since there was nothing in it to arouse the south German states. Their sympathies as well as those of the French public could be expected to lie with France.

There is much to indicate that in the spring of 1870 the Emperor and Empress were steeling themselves for an encounter of some kind with Prussia. Internally the country seemed stronger than in the previous year. The plebiscite of May 8 returned a vote of 7,358,786 for the new constitution with only 1,571,939 against and was apparently a triumphant vindication of the liberal empire. It was quickly followed by the resignation of Daru from the Foreign Ministry and the appointment of Gramont as his successor. The new Foreign Minister was a known Austrophil and an outspoken opponent of German unity. He was no sooner in office than he and the Empress proposed to move La Guéronnière to the key post in Madrid and to retire Mercier to the French Senate. But Prim would have none of the controversial journalist and diplomat, who was identified not only as a Prussophobe but also as an Isabellist. As a result of the representations of the Spanish ambassador at Paris, the Emperor let Mercier stay on in Madrid.[76]

During the course of the spring Napoleon began to work outside diplomatic channels to bring his negotiations with Austria to a successful conclusion. After the plebiscite he sent one of his aides-de-camp, General Lebrun, to Vienna for talks with Franz Joseph and Archduke Albert, head of the army. During most of June, Lebrun argued in vain for an Austro-French alliance and military cooperation of the two countries in the event of war with Prussia.[77] Meanwhile, on June 25, the Empress and Sexto at last persuaded Isabella to abdicate irrevocably to clear the path for Alfonso. Prim thought her conspiracy with the Spaniards not unlike that which had given birth to the Mexican expedition in 1861.[78]

The strain of waiting told on the Empress. The day after the Queen's abdication she gave an audience to the newly appointed minister to Washington, Prévost Paradol. After some perfunctory discussion of tariffs and

---

[76] Olózaga to the Spanish Foreign Minister, Paris, June 15, 1870, AMAE (Madrid), Correspondencia, Francia, XB, 1517, No. 259.

[77] Thomas A. B. Corley, *Democratic Despot: A Life of Napoleon III*, pp. 319–320; John Emerich Edward Acton, "The Causes of the Franco-Prussian War," *Historical Essays and Studies*, ed. John Neville Figgis and Reginald Vere Laurence, pp. 208–211.

[78] Howden to Lyons, Bayonne, June 7, 1870, copy, PRO FO 361/1.

postal rates, she suddenly shrugged off the subject of Franco-American relations and began to speak passionately of Prussia. "France has all but lost her rank in the world," she declared. "She must regain it or die." She must face up to Prussian insolence. "Il faut en finir." The Minister retired in wonderment at her unexplainable vehemence. A month later he committed suicide in the belief, according to his friend, Ludovic Halévy, that she and the Emperor had betrayed him in suppressing the knowledge of the war they knew to be approaching.[79]

Premature Exultation

When the news of Leopold's candidacy exploded like a bomb over Europe, Eugénie, Napoleon, and Gramont were jubilant. The season for silence was ended; now was the time to speak. On July 6 Metternich found the Empress looking ten years younger, radiant at the prospect of a political triumph or a war. She believed they had trapped their wiley opponent in a bad corner where the weight of European opinion would be against him. Should Bismarck attempt to deny his part in the intrigue with Prim, she asserted, the Spaniard, whom she knew well, would be just stubborn enough to publish the secret correspondence between them. But she thought it useless to speak of such an eventuality. "It will be very difficult for M. de Bismarck to get himself out of this affair without giving in all the way around or confessing the thing [his intrigue with Prim]. If he gives in, it will be only before our comminatory attitude, a humiliation which he will overcome with difficulty."[80] Napoleon, too, was in high spirits. "*Eh bien*, what do you say of our affair?" he greeted the ambassador gaily. He was "enchanted," even "thrilled" [*joyeusement monté*] at the prospect before him.[81]

Gramont endeavored to explain to Metternich why his government had not protested earlier against Leopold's candidacy. He confessed that they had some notion of the negotiations between Bismarck and Prim but for some reason which he did not explain they had paid them no attention. Prim had tricked Mercier into thinking the Duke of Aosta was the front runner. France had been watching the decoy rather than the real candidate.[82] Gramont's explanation was palpably false, and Metternich felt as if he were watching a bad comedy. Mercier's despatches for May and June published by the French Foreign Ministry mentioned the Duke of Aosta

[79] Ludovic Halévy, *Carnets, publiés avec une introduction et des notes, 1862–1870*, II, 158–159, 190.

[80] Metternich to Beust, Paris, July 8, 1870, Oncken, *Rheinpolitik*, III, No. 849, p. 402. The conversation took place on July 6.

[81] *Ibid.*, No. 848, p. 400.

[82] *Ibid.*, No. 847, p. 399.

twice, but each time stated that the Spanish government had failed to obtain his consent.[83] The Austrian ambassador saw to the heart of the affair. "You have jumped at the chance of either scoring a diplomatic success or of fighting a war on a subject where no German feeling can oppose you."

"You put it exactly," admitted the Foreign Minister.[84]

In the period between the announcement of Leopold's acceptance of the throne and the voluntary withdrawal on July 11, the Emperor and his Ministers, Ollivier not excluded, agreed that they must join the issue with Prussia and repel the candidacy at any cost, even by war. On the afternoon of July 6 in the Legislative Body Gramont voiced the government's resolution. French honor and national interests demanded Leopold's withdrawal. "If it should be otherwise, gentlemen, strong in your support and in that of the nation, we shall know how to discharge our duty without hesitation or weakness."[85]

Eugénie has been accused of inspiring Gramont's vigorous words.[86] But since she was not present when the speech was drafted or revised in the Council of Ministers, a good deal of imagination is required to establish her connection with it. Since she was excluded from the alien territory of the Ollivier Cabinet, she could play little or no part in the actions and decisions of the Ministers. Not until July 12, when the crisis entered a second phase, is there evidence of her personal participation in the formulation of policy. The meetings of the Ministers usually, though not always, took place at the Tuileries, whither the Emperor went daily. Eugénie remained at Saint-Cloud. Her chief contribution in the first days of the crisis seems to have been to bolster the flagging spirits of the Emperor on his return and remind him of the need for a bold stand to save the honor of the Empire and the dynasty.

There can be no doubt that Eugénie saw in the Hohenzollern candidacy

[83] June 12 and 23, 1870, *OD*, XXVII, Nos. 8206, 8223, pp. 377, 405.

[84] Metternich to Beust, Paris, July 8, 1870, Oncken, *Rheinpolitik*, III, No. 851, p. 405; Alan John Percivale Taylor, *Bismarck, the Man and the Statesman*, p. 119.

[85] Gramont's statement is reproduced in translation by Steefel (*Bismarck, the Hohenzollern Candidacy*, p. 114).

[86] The accusation is made by Achille Forbes, a vitriolic critic of the Empress, on information reportedly supplied by Joseph Ferrari, a close friend of Ollivier's brother ("The French Empress and the Franco-German War," *Nineteenth Century*, XXXII [August, 1892], 285–297). For the controversy over the drafting of Gramont's speech see Henri Welschinger, *La Guerre de 1870, causes et responsabilités*, I, 50–52; Ollivier, *L'Empire libéral*, XIV, 107–108, 568–573; Pierre de La Gorce, *Histoire du Second Empire*, VI, 226–227; France, *Enquête parlementaire sur les actes du gouvernement de la défense nationale (Annales de l'assemblée nationale)*, XXIII, depositions of Le Boeuf (p. 46) and Gramont (pp. 85–86). Recent scholarship by Zeldin demonstrates that it was Ollivier who added the belligerent passage to Gramont's declaration (Zeldin, *Ollivier*, p. 177).

a *casus belli*. Of the alternatives, a diplomatic victory or war, she frankly preferred war. Metternich reported on July 8: "I found the empress so worked up in favor of the war that I could not prevent myself from teasing her a little."[87] Mistakenly, along with many others, she thought France had an army that could whip Prussia. More accurately, she gauged the force of the spontaneous outburst of public indignation.[88] With the French people rampant and the army supposedly ready, she told Metternich that she hoped Prussia would not back down and withdraw the candidacy.[89] She had been waiting ever since Sadowa for just such an opportunity. The atmosphere of her court, swollen by generals and leaders of the Right, such as General Bourbaki, Marshal Le Boeuf, and Jérôme David, was loudly belligerent. One of the Empress' ladies, Mlle Garets, wrote during the crisis: ". . . everyone here, the empress foremost, is so desirous of war that it seems to me impossible that we shall not have it."[90] Eugénie and others of the Right seem even to have favored extending the quarrel beyond the question of the Spanish throne to Prussian infractions of the Treaty of Prague. By a demand for demolition of Prussian fortresses on the Rhine they would call Prussia to task and render war inescapable.[91]

Napoleon, despite his exultation at catching Bismarck red-handed, was far less bellicose than his Empress. A large body of evidence attests to his eagerness to see the candidacy disappear without war. In wretched health, he could not have looked forward to a campaign in the field with any pleasure. For the first time, about July 6, he made genuine efforts to block Leopold's election in Spain and instructed Mercier to express to Prim French objections to the choice of a Hohenzollern.[92] Although he refused to appeal openly to Charles Anthony, as beneath the dignity of France, he worked in back channels for Leopold's withdrawal. Charles Anthony,

[87] Metternich to Beust, Paris, July 8, 1870, Oncken, *Rheinpolitik*, III, No. 849, p. 401.

[88] For public opinion see Lynn M. Case, *French Opinion on War and Diplomacy during the Second Empire*, pp. 243–244.

[89] Metternich to Beust, telegram, Paris, July 6, 1870, Oncken, *Rheinpolitik*, III, No. 844, p. 396. See also Germain Bapst, *Le Maréchal Canrobert: Souvenirs d'un siècle*, IV, 194–195; Beyens, *Second Empire*, II, 469–471.

[90] Comtesse de Garets, *Souvenirs d'une demoiselle d'honneur auprès de l'impératrice Eugénie*, p. 187. Except for a few apologists like Fleury and Mme Carette, there is general agreement on the Empress' bellicosity which is thoroughly borne out by her attitude as the crisis developed.

[91] Steefel, *Bismarck, the Hohenzollern Candidacy*, p. 157. Metternich tells us that on July 11 even Ollivier was for a time one of this group. The ambassador wired: "Duc de Gramont est un peu en contradiction avec M. Ollivier qui voudrait [joindre] d'autres questions à celle de Hohenzollern pour rendre la guerre inévitable, tandis que Gramont veut la paix si le Roi de Prusse cède" (Metternich to Beust, Paris, July 11, 1870, HHSA, IX/95, No. 6615/802).

[92] Steefel, *Bismarck, the Hohenzollern Candidacy*, pp. 122–125.

father of the Hohenzollern Prince, wrote to King William: "Of Napoleon's PERSONAL desire to keep the peace I have today striking proof. Namely he has expressed it as his wish to King Leopold of the Belgians and requested him to press us for a withdrawal."[93] Napoleon sent the Rumanian agent, Strat, on a secret mission to Charles Anthony urging him to renounce the throne in the name of his son. When the Spanish ambassador asked him if war would be averted if the Prince withdrew, the Emperor replied that the question was hardly flattering to his intelligence. "It is clear," he asserted, "that if the Hohenzollern candidature were out of the way peace would be assured."[94]

Strat's mission was successful. On July 11 when Napoleon learned of the voluntary withdrawal of the candidacy he appeared relieved that the affair was terminated and that France had gotten out of it with a "certain *éclat*." The form of the renunciation, of course, was not all he had wished for. It came not from the King of Prussia, not even from the candidate himself, but merely from the candidate's father. The Prussian government had slithered out of any association with it. Yet the Emperor's mood, early on the afternoon of July 12, was one of resignation. "The country will be disappointed," he wrote Ollivier. "But what is there to do?" A few minutes later he received Nigra and told him plainly: "Yes, it is peace."[95]

The Demand for Guarantees

If the Emperor had continued in this resigned frame of mind, perhaps German unity and the confrontation of France and Prussia would have been deferred. But late in the afternoon of July 12 he authorized his Foreign Minister to ask King William for an assurance that he would not again authorize the candidacy of Leopold. About seven in the evening Gramont wired this instruction to Count Benedetti, French ambassador at Berlin. The demand for guarantees for the future reopened the question, led directly to Benedetti's unsatisfactory interview with the Prussian King, to the misleading account of their encounter in Bismarck's edition of the Ems telegram, and consequently to the French declaration of war.

Gramont and Ollivier both stated explicitly that the conference between Foreign Minister and Emperor from which emanated the demand for

---

[93] Charles Anthony to William I, Sigmaringen, July 12, 1870, Bonnin, *Bismarck,* No. 295. See also Charles Anthony to William I, July 13, 1870, *ibid.,* No. 300.

[94] Count von Arnim to Bismarck, Paris, January 14, 1873, A 147, pr. January 19, 1873, Bonnin, *Bismarck,* No. 307. The letter contains Olózaga's account of the origin of Strat's mission. Olózaga told essentially the same thing to a British diplomat (Howden to Meade, Paris, September 2, 1870, PRO FO 362/5).

[95] Nigra, "Ricordi diplomatici," *Nuova antologia* (March, 1894), p. 10, cited by La Gorce, *Second Empire,* VI, 265; Ollivier, *L'Empire libéral,* XIV, 241.

guarantees took place at Saint-Cloud. They placed it at approximately five o'clock in the afternoon. Ollivier related how the Emperor, who had left the Tuileries in a calm and pacific mood, was affected by the excited demonstrations he saw on the streets during the forty-five-minute drive to Saint-Cloud and, on his arrival, by the bellicose mood of the court. The Empress ran to meet and question him. On hearing that he was satisfied with Leopold's renunciation she cried hysterically: "It is a disgrace! The empire is turning into an old woman."[96]

Gramont arrived at the chateau soon after. Was the Empress present at the ensuing conference between Gramont and Napoleon? Ollivier did not know. He could only establish that none of the Ministers except Gramont was invited.[97] Gramont deliberately withheld particulars of the conference both in his memoirs and in his testimony before the republican commission of investigation of 1872.[98] The air of mystery which enveloped the conference led La Gorce to conclude that Gramont was shielding the Empress. "All appearances authorize the belief that the preponderant action [on the afternoon of July 12] was that of the empress."[99]

After the death of the Empress, Maurice Paléologue, diplomat of the Third Republic, published his record of the Empress' statements on foreign policy made to him during a series of meetings over the years of her exile. According to his account, she was not only present at the conference, in which only she, the Emperor, and Gramont participated, but threw the full weight of her support behind the demand for guarantees and with the Foreign Minister overcame Napoleon's hesitations. Paléologue quotes her: "This [the taking of the decision to ask for guarantees] happened at Saint-Cloud on July 12th, about five o'clock in the afternoon, at a council held by the Emperor, myself, and Gramont. The Emperor raised no objection."[100]

---

[96] Ollivier, *L'Empire libéral*, XIV, 253. According to Ollivier's wife, the young Prince Imperial became alarmed at the "attaque de nerfs" suffered by his mother when she learned of the Emperor's pacific inclination ("L'Epouse de l'empereur," *Revue de Genève* [February, 1921], p. 180, quoted by Steefel, *Bismarck, the Hohenzollern Candidacy*, p. 157).

[97] Ollivier, *L'Empire libéral*, XIV, 254.

[98] Antoine Agénor, Duc de Gramont, *La France et la Prusse avant la guerre*, pp. 130–132; deposition of Gramont, *Enquête parlementaire*, XXIII, 101.

[99] La Gorce, *Second Empire*, VI, 266.

[100] George Maurice Paléologue, *The Tragic Empress: A Record of Intimate Talks with the Empress Eugénie, 1901–1919*, pp. 133–134. Because of certain discrepancies between the accounts of Gramont and Ollivier and telegrams published by the French Foreign Ministry, the thorough and impartial scholar, Professor Steefel, has concluded that Gramont went not to Saint-Cloud, where the Empress was, but to the Tuileries for his conference with Napoleon (*Bismarck, the Hohenzollern Candidacy*, p. 155 n.). These telegrams prove that the Emperor did not arrive at the chateau until 6:15 (see *OD*, XXVIII, Nos. 8424, 8426, 8427, pp. 253–254). Since Gramont's telegram to Bene-

Other testimony in addition to that of Paléologue may be adduced to demonstrate Eugénie's eagerness for guarantees. Fleury relates that she warned the British ambassador, Lord Lyons, that he was going too fast when, on July 10, he wired his government that France would consider the crisis terminated should Leopold withdraw.[101] After Napoleon's death in 1873 the Spanish ambassador, Salustiano de Olózaga, told the German ambassador in Paris that the Emperor had never wanted the war. The decision to ask for guarantees had emanated from a conference with the Empress and Gramont.[102]

Once again the Empress had counselled action at a critical moment in the Empire's history. But on this account it is unfair to lay on her the

---

detti went off at 7:00, he could not, within that forty-five minutes, have debated the matter with Napoleon and Eugénie and have returned to the Quai d'Orsay in Paris to send his message. Yet to follow Steefel away from the conventional view is to reject the explicit statements of Gramont and Ollivier that the conference took place at Saint-Cloud. Moreover, if Eugénie were not present, a distinguished French diplomat of the Third Republic, ambassador to Russia and director-general of the French Foreign Ministry, must have fabricated his story out of whole cloth. The editors of *Origines diplomatiques de la guerre* have suggested that Gramont drew up and sent his telegram from Saint-Cloud (*OD*, XXVIII, 254 n. 2). Steefel rejected this hypothesis because at 7:55 the British ambassador wired to London an account of a conversation he had conducted with Gramont. If the Foreign Minister had sent the telegram from Saint-Cloud at 7:00 he could not have conversed with Lyons in Paris before 7:55. But is the existence of Lyons' telegram sufficient to overthrow the conventional view? Conceivably, Lyons too could have sent his telegram from Saint-Cloud. He was known to have visited the chateau at least twice between July 7 and July 12 for conversation with Napoleon and Eugénie (Fleury, *Memoirs*, pp. 226, 233). But another and more likely possibility is that Gramont talked with Lyons *before* he reported to the Emperor. Lyons' telegram contained no mention of a French demand for guarantees. He wired: "The renunciation of the Spanish Crown by the Prince of Hohenzollern in the name of his son has been received. The French Government hold that it puts an end to all dispute with Spain but they do not at present admit that in the form in which it had been given, it removes their complaint against Prussia. They are dissatisfied with the communication they have received from the King. They will determine at a Council tomorrow what course to take and announce it to the Chamber immediately afterwards . . ." (Lyons to Granville, July 12, PRO/FO 27/1805; unnumbered reporting telegram, in Werner Eugen Mosse, *The European Powers and the German Question 1848–1871, with Special Reference to England and Russia*, pp. 384–385). This report seems a more accurate reflection of the situation before rather than after Gramont's conference with the Emperor. Some interruption may have prevented Lyons from sending his telegram immediately upon leaving Gramont. He does not state the time of their conversation. Thus, it was possible for Gramont to have conferred with Napoleon and Eugénie at Saint-Cloud and still have gotten off his wire to Benedetti at 7:00. For these reasons, and in the face of the statements by Gramont and Ollivier, and the testimony of the Empress related by Paléologue, I have thought it necessary to adhere to the conventional view.

[101] Fleury, *Memoirs*, II, 233–234. Lyons' telegram actually said that the French government would be satisfied if Leopold withdrew "on the advice of the King of Prussia" (Lyons to Granville, Paris, July 10, 1870, Fester, *Briefe*, II, No. 409). See also Bapst, *Canrobert*, IV, 194–195.

[102] Arnim to Bismarck, Paris, January 13, 1873, Bonnin, *Bismarck*, No. 307.

responsibility for the outbreak of war. Gramont's views were nearly identical to hers. He alone might have persuaded the Emperor of the need for further satisfaction. In any case, there was considerable justification for the French demands. The fear that Leopold would disregard his father's renunciation of his candidacy and suddenly appear in Madrid to claim his throne was not unreasonable. In November, 1863, Prince Frederick of Augustenburg and in May, 1866, Prince Charles of Hohenzollern-Sigmaringen had done something quite similar in Schleswig-Holstein and Rumania, respectively.

THE DECLARATION OF WAR

Despite the decision taken on the evening of July 12, the next day was one of irresolution. A tug of war took place between the bellicose group of the Right, the Empress foremost, and the more pacific members of the Council of Ministers. Ollivier had been aghast at the important decision taken without his knowledge early in the evening of July 12 and wished to attenuate as much as possible the effect of Gramont's telegram. At a Council meeting at Saint-Cloud on the morning of July 13 the peace party temporarily prevailed. Although sharply divided, the Ministers voted that the demand should not be considered as an ultimatum. Should the Prussian King refuse, the French government would still regard the crisis as terminated.[103] Filing from the Council room to the dining room, the Ministers were greeted by a stony-faced Empress, who had just learned of the decision taken. During the disagreeable lunch Eugénie, seated next to Ollivier, broke her silence only with a few derisive gibes and finished by turning her back on him.[104]

In the Legislative Body that afternoon Gramont read the noncommittal statement of the Ministry prepared by the Council. It announced the "official" renunciation of Leopold (which was not precisely the truth, as there was nothing official about it) and the continuation of negotiations with Prussia (the purpose of which was not explained). Immediately, Jérôme David rose to heckle the Foreign Minister. Who had given the renunciation? Was it merely Charles Anthony? In a brutally worded interpellation he condemned the slowness of the negotiations which were injurious to business and to national dignity. Discussion was set for July 15.

David's interpellation may have been inspired by the Empress. It certainly had her approval. That evening Gramont, to his astonishment, encountered David emerging from Saint-Cloud after dinner. When he complained that David's presence at the Emperor's table, so soon after his

[103] Steefel, *Bismarck, the Hohenzollern Candidacy*, p. 162.
[104] Ollivier, *L'Empire libéral*, XIV, 293.

attack on the Ministry, would create a bad impression, Napoleon replied that the invitation had come from the Empress, and that he had felt unable to turn him away. "In truth," commented Ollivier, "one could have said that he had come to report on an assignment and to receive his felicitations."[105]

Despite the hostility of the Legislative Body and the Senate to the Cabinet, and despite the belligerence of the Right, Ollivier believed in the evening of July 13 that prospects for peace were promising. He professed to see the Prussian and Spanish acceptance of Leopold's renunciation as a sufficient guarantee of the future, and was persuaded that although the Emperor vacillated, he would come down on the side of peace when removed from the excited milieu of the Empress and her "camarilla."[106] The next day, he predicted the crisis would evaporate. Yet even as he was thus meditating Bismarck's abbreviated version of the Ems telegram, his "red rag to the Gallic bull" was beginning to appear on the streets of Berlin in an extra edition of the semiofficial *Norddeutsche Allgemeine Zeitung.*

The Ministers hesitated only a few hours after learning of the deliberate provocation emanating from Berlin. In a Council meeting presided over by Napoleon on the afternoon of July 14 they ordered the mobilization of the reserves, but, recoiling from the fatal significance of such an order, fell back on the tired device of an appeal to the powers for a European conference. The invitations were never issued. On his return to Saint-Cloud, the Emperor told his wife of the results of the meeting. Her reply is well known: "I doubt if that corresponds to the mood of the chambers and of the country." Le Boeuf, Minister of War, hurried in, perturbed at the discrepancy between the decision to mobilize the reserves and the idea of a congress. When the General at first hesitated to criticize the Council, she turned excitedly on this faithful servant of the Empire. "What! You too approve of this cowardice? If you will dishonor yourself, do not dishonor the emperor."[107]

Not the Empress' words but the utter inadequacy of the Council's decision in the face of the deliberate affront from Prussia quickly dissipated the chimera of a congress. Ollivier has described vividly his own realization that the congress was a useless expedient which, without saving the peace, would have forever discredited the Emperor. The Empress' revolt, he

---

[105] *Ibid.*, 350–351. The memoirs of Maxime du Camp assert that Eugénie sent a telegram to David which prompted his interpellation (*Souvenirs d'un demi-siècle: Au temps de Louis-Philippe et de Napoléon III, 1830–1870*, I, 280–281). The credibility of the account is greatly reduced by the author's confusion of dates and many inaccuracies.

[106] Ollivier, *L'Empire libéral*, XIV, 352.

[107] *Ibid.*, pp. 370–371.

admitted, was legitimate—"she felt, thought, and spoke justly."[108] Le Boeuf begged the Emperor to reconvene the Ministers. Meeting again that evening and again briefly on the morning of July 15 they maintained the order to call up the reserves, abandoned the appeal to the powers, and decided in favor of a declaration of war. The Empress, for the first time since the formation of the Cabinet of January 2, sat with the Council of Ministers on those two occasions, but she neither spoke nor voted on the grave matter before them.[109]

What then may be said of the Empress' responsibility for the outbreak of the Franco-Prussian War? La Gorce has labelled her the "principal author of the war," and many other historians have agreed with his interpretation.[110] La Gorce's term seems unjustifiably strong, certainly for the period after July 2. Proofs of the most positive nature would be necessary to demonstrate that the pressure of an excited public, the agitation of the Emperor's enemies of both the Left and Right in the Legislative Body, the strong anti-Prussian views of Gramont, and, most important of all after July 14, the work of Bismarck in editing the Ems telegram were of less

[108] *Ibid.*, p. 371.

[109] *Ibid.*, p. 393. Accounts of the Empress' demeanor at these two Council meetings flatly contradict themselves. I have followed that of Ollivier, mainly because it is the only firsthand testimony by an eyewitness. His testimony, so explicit and emphatic on the Empress' silence during the meetings, is especially convincing, as he in reality laid much blame for the war at the Empress' doorstep for her hue and cry over the French defeat at Sadowa. She and others of the Right, he believed, had laid the groundwork for war ever since 1866. Diametrically opposed to Ollivier's account of the two meetings is that of Welschinger, who based his account on information reportedly received from a former Minister, Grivart, who in turn took his facts from MacMahon and Pienne, chamberlain of the Empress. According to Welschinger, during the Council of July 14 the Emperor became ill and left the room. Profiting by his absence Eugénie took the floor and spoke passionately for war. Apparently swayed by her eloquence, the Ministers, on the return of the Emperor, voted to retain the order for mobilization (Welschinger, *La Guerre de 1870*, I, 153–155). Engelhaaf substantially agreed with this interpretation, although he placed her speech on the morning of July 15 (G. Engelhaaf, "Der Anteil der Kaiserin Eugenie am Krieg von 1870," *Die Grenzboten*, LXIII, 628). The memoirs of Malmesbury are often cited in support of this thesis. Malmesbury wrote that Gramont told him of an ardent speech by the Empress in favor of war, but he neither specified the date nor mentioned the Emperor's temporary absence from the meeting (Malmesbury, *Memoirs*, II, 416). La Gorce relied on Malmesbury (*Second Empire*, VI, 297). The Empress' own version of the declaration of war, if Paléologue recorded it accurately, contains nothing about a speech to the Council of Ministers (Paléologue, *Tragic Empress*, pp. 133–135). Depositions made later by Gramont and Le Boeuf before the republican commission of inquiry fail to enlighten us on her role. If one cares for muckraking, the study of the declaration of war offers splendid opportunities. See, for example, the spiteful account of Caroline Murat, older and unhappily married sister of the Duchess of Mouchy, which has the Empress bully Gramont into drawing up a declaration of war while the Emperor slept on a couch in his room. She then supposedly took the declaration to the Emperor, and before he was fully awake, forced him to put his signature to it (Murat, *My Memoirs*, p. 185).

[110] La Gorce, *Second Empire*, VI, 294.

importance than the warmongering of a single woman, highly placed though she was. After the news of the candidacy broke into public knowledge her role was essentially limited to what influence she could exert on her husband, both by words and by the creation of a belligerent milieu in the court. This may have been considerable. Yet the historian has no yardstick with which to measure it.

The Empress' enemies would have it that she gloated: "This is my war." The remark was probably the malicious invention of Prince Napoleon. But if she had said those words, there would have been a measure of truth in them. She had long seen the throne of her native land as a brand of discord between France and Prussia. For over a year and a half she and the Emperor had been aware of the possibility of the candidacy of a Prussian prince for the throne, but, after the beginning of 1870, had not lifted a finger to prevent it. A request for explanations in Berlin, a polite protest in Madrid, or an expression of the French viewpoint to the powers in a diplomatic circular would have forced Bismarck's game into the open. Well-established diplomatic custom gave France the right to exclude consideration of candidates dangerous to her national interests. In the spring of 1869, on the flimsiest of evidence, they had not hesitated to express their objections. Yet in June, 1870, when their ambassador at Madrid told them of Prim's negotiation with Leopold they maintained silence. Thus, they willfully permitted the development of a potentially explosive issue, set France on a collision course, and exposed her to the "accident" they knew might happen. Ultimate responsibility for foreign policy lay always with the Emperor. But Eugénie's special knowledge of Spanish politics and her many sources of intelligence lent her unusual leverage in this question. Her responsibility is the greater because she, unlike the Emperor, was resolved upon a war rather than a diplomatic triumph for the sake of French *amour propre*. When the threat of war was real, Napoleon flinched and made genuine efforts to induce Leopold to withdraw. The Empress' reaction was exactly the opposite. She saw that Bismarck had handed them the perfect *casus belli*, and she was determined not to let it slip from their grasp.

Indeed, partly through luck and partly through management, things did work out to the advantage of France in the first moments of the crisis. The British and Austrian governments felt the justness of French indignation, and they condemned Prussia and Spain for their failure to consult France. European opinion later turned against France largely because Bismarck denied his negotiation with the Spaniards and published Benedetti's memorandum of 1866 which led the British to think that France had immediate designs on Belgium.

Recognizing the Empress' general unpopularity in France, Bismarck took ungallant advantage of her Spanish birth and close connections with

Isabella. Immediately he launched a campaign in the press against her "dynastic views" which pushed France into war in behalf of a "corrupt dynasty." "She unquestionably arranged the farce of [Isabella's] abdication, and now, in her rage, she incites her consort and the Ministers." He directed his secretary: "Please see that this theme, a new war of [Spanish] succession in the nineteenth century is thoroughly thrashed out in the press."[111] How pitiless was the fate that appointed the Empress' beloved Spain the agent of her ignominious defeat.

[111] Excerpts from letters of Bucher to Busch containing Bismarck's instructions for the press (Moritz Busch, *Bismarck: Some Secret Pages of His History; Being a Diary Kept by Dr. Moritz Busch during Twenty-five Years' Official and Private Intercourse with the Great Chancellor*, I, 27–34).

CHAPTER 8

A HOUSE DIVIDED

A few days after the dethroned Empress landed in England in September, 1870, the British Foreign Secretary, Lord Granville, wrote: "I am glad the Queen thinks of writing to the Empress. Her misfortune is great, although it is much owing to herself—Mexico, Rome, war with Prussia."[1] Bismarck, Bernhardi, and the Prussian historian Heinrich von Treitschke soon attributed the fall of the Empire to the miscarriage of an Ultramontane plot, inspired by the Empress and the priests in the Tuileries, to save the temporal power.[2] Thiers went to London in the fall of 1870 and spread it about that Eugénie and the generals were responsible for the outbreak of the war.[3] Prince Napoleon and Matilda were soon in full cry after the Empress as the perpetrator of the ruin of the Empire.

Many of these charges have little bearing in fact. But why did so many of the Empress' contemporaries hold her responsible for foreign policy? With no official function in the government except when Regent, how did she acquire such notoriety? Very recently, in discussing the work of Eugénie in bringing down the Ollivier Cabinet during the war, a judicious scholar has observed that the "special evil of despotism" lies in "the backstairs influence of courtiers and women."[4] Yet no one has ever blamed the fall of the first Empire on Josephine or Marie Louise. What was the explanation for the Empress' special power in the Second Empire?

The personalities of husband and wife are one obvious answer. The sweet and gentle Josephine, all "gossamer and lace," bent to the will of the imperious Corsican. Eugénie, direct and outspoken, could strike *peur bleue* into the heart of the less resolute and more gentle nephew. Eugénie had certain decidedly masculine characteristics, although they did not destroy

[1] John Emerich Edward Acton, *Historical Essays and Studies*, ed. John Neville Figgis and Reginald Vere Laurence, p. 219.
[2] *Ibid.*, pp. 218–219; *Bismarck, the Man and the Statesman*, trans. A. J. Butler from Bismarck's *Gedanken und Erinnerungen*, II, 184.
[3] ———— to Lyons, September 13, 1870, PRO FO 362/4.
[4] Theodore Zeldin, *Emile Ollivier and the Liberal Empire of Napoleon III*, p. 183.

the femininity of her personality as a whole, just as the virile Emperor displayed certain qualities usually associated with women.

The relative ages of the couple and of their son bore significantly on the
Empress' position. When she married, the Empress was a self-willed, poised
woman within a few months of her twenty-seventh birthday—too old to be
malleable material. But if Eugénie was no child, her husband was well into
middle age. When the Prince Imperial was born the Emperor was approaching fifty and within ten years showed unmistakable signs of di-
minishing health and vigor. A regency was a probability if the dynasty was
to be preserved. The Empress did not shrink from the responsibility. In
1859, Regent for the first time, she thought that he, not she, had bungled
the negotiations for peace. In 1865 she was more than satisfied with her
administration. On the return of Napoleon she confided to Metternich:
"The ministers have not quarrelled, and I have kept them so well in hand
that I almost regret being obliged to relinquish the reins. I will say to the
emperor that I give him back a strong and united government, and I will
beg him to take care not to relax the bridle too much."[5] A year later she
requested the Emperor to abdicate and confer the Regency permanently
on her. Even in 1870, despite the vicious attacks of the press upon her and
despite the disappointing reception she had encountered on her trip to
Corsica, she did not fear to face the prospect of the Emperor's death.
Counting on the support of the right-wing Bonapartists who had been
thrust aside by the liberal empire, she planned a swift and forceful action
to rally a new government around herself and her son.[6] The general ex-
pectancy of a regency was not, in fact, foolish. When the Emperor died in
January, 1873, the Prince Imperial was only sixteen years of age. Throughout, as the future Regent, the Empress was thus a political force to be
reckoned with.

The Empress had no portfolio in the government and no constitutional
right to entertain affairs of state except when Regent. But she possessed
one matchless advantage over the Ministers. She could not be dismissed.
From the time of her marriage she was, with the exception of short inter-
vals, continuously by the side of the Emperor, where she could leave him
in no doubt of her opinions and wishes. Napoleon could not even break
temporarily with her and pack her off in disgrace on one of those long
excursions to distant points of the globe to which he occasionally sentenced
Prince Napoleon. Napoleon I had divorced Josephine. But Eugénie's
position as the mother of the heir to the throne was virtually unassailable.

[5] Metternich to Mensdorff, Paris, June 10, 1865, HHSA, IX/81, No. 30 B.

[6] Metternich to Beust, Paris, January 29, 1870, confidential, Hermann Oncken, *Die
Rheinpolitik Kaiser Napoleons III. von 1863 bis 1870 und der Ursprung des Krieges
von 1870/71*, III, No. 776, pp. 301–302.

Napoleon III had not made a prisoner of the Pope, and he lived in dread of the censure of clerical opinion. In Catholic France, for better or for worse, at least officially, he could cleave only unto her.

The hybrid nature of the Empire lent peculiar strength to the Empress' influence. The national unity of France was not of a monolithic, totalitarian kind. Unresolved were the social and political conflicts inherited from the French Revolution. In the person of the Emperor the so-called two Frances—the republican, anticlerical France of the Left, and the royalist, Ultramontane France of the Right—had come together in a temporary and discordant union. As a dynastic ruler with the trappings of royalty he could not be republican; he could never be a Legitimist. No one was more aware than the Emperor of the shape of his problem. "People reproach me for having two policies," he once complained. "It's true—I am obliged to have two, for I can not be a reactionary in view of my origin and I can not be a revolutionary because of the dangers that would bring me."[7]

Eugénie probably never understood the problem in abstract terms. In the early years she fluttered back and forth between such disparate heroes as the revolutionary Orsini and the Bourbon Duchess of Parma. Later she would readily abandon what seemed to be political principle because of an irritation of the moment. But usually she more or less identified herself with the conservatives. Realizing her influence with Napoleon they rallied eagerly to her. She and her "party" lent each other mutual strength. When Eugénie did not have behind her either the force of a large segment of public opinion or a strong faction of the Ministers she was usually powerless to accomplish much with the Emperor. With their aid she could remind him of the dual nature of his monarchy and draw him back from the revolutionary slopes whither he was inclined to wander. At first their efforts produced only minor but disconcerting deflections in the Emperor's course, as in 1860 and the spring of 1861; just as they seemed to have him secured, he would trickle through their fingers. Eventually they were able to effect a consequential reorientation of policy. From the security of her position as wife and Regent apparent, she could cross the master of France in a way no one else dared. Not even Prince Napoleon and the other members of the imperial family had the same immunity as she from public reprimand and humiliation. Thus, Ministers and diplomats could shelter behind her skirts and use her to press their views. Lack of synthesis was always the Emperor's greatest problem. Not only did the Empress not contribute to its solution, she was herself a major cause of his problem.

[7] Metternich to Rechberg, Paris, December 9, 1860, private letter, HHSA, IX/68, *varia*.

The perfunctory observer of the Second Empire, noting that its best days were before the Italian War, might erroneously see a causal relation between the entrance of the Empress into affairs of state and the beginning of the serious woes of Napoleon. She was Regent when he made what was probably the first really disastrous mistake of his reign—the premature withdrawal from the Italian War. After the war, because of his unfulfilled commitment, he was unable to begin with a clean slate. He was eternally apologetic to the Sardinians and permitted them unaccountable liberties. These in turn, together with the Venetian question, complicated his relations with Austria. Eugénie's record in the Italian War was lamentable. She had encouraged him to undertake it but then, by her alarms, contributed to his irresolute conduct of it. But hers was not the decisive voice which caused the Emperor to draw up short. About all she accomplished was a demonstration of her temper and lack of comprehension of political realities with her quixotic uproar over the Duchess of Parma.

In the years immediately following the war she applied increasing pressure on her husband and was able to influence policy more effectively than at any other time during the Empire. From a series of temporary triumphs, usually followed by a frustrating check, she progressed to the instigation of the Mexican expedition and finally to the capstone of her desires—the dismissal of Thouvenel. Mérimée was never more correct than when he predicted a dire future for his amiable hostess and for the Empire as a consequence of her handiwork in the ministerial crisis of 1862. Among other things, Thouvenel's disgrace meant that the Emperor had been persuaded to reverse his Italian policy of 1860 and 1861 and to participate in his wife's cult of the Bourbons. The decision was fatal. Austria, encouraged to believe she could at any time reckon on French support in wrecking the unity of the peninsula, deferred recognition of the Italian kingdom and refused to cede Venetia without concomitant restorations in central and southern Italy. Hence, in time, the Italian decision of 1866 to fight rather than to accept Venetia as a reward for her neutrality but at the price of her mutilation. Ironically, the secret French support of restoration redounded to the advantage of the Prussians, who caught the Austrians in a war on two fronts and were able to trounce them thoroughly.

The temporary ascendance of the Empress in foreign policy in 1863 brought incoherence rather than cohesion to foreign policy. She drove off recklessly in all directions. While offering the restorations in Italy as her *pièce de résistance* to Austria, she proposed to abet and exploit revolution in the Balkans and Poland. The Austrians were offered a conglomeration of terms so preposterously contradictory that they inevitably rejected them, despite their real desire to seize Silesia and contain Prussian aggrandizement in the north. In her conversations with Metternich on the proposed alliance she revealed her incapacity for diplomatic negotiation. Naïvely and spontaneously she babbled to the Austrian ambassador the details of the French design for the future of Germany, plans which above all else should have been withheld from him. The proposed division of Germany into two parts with Prussia ascendant in the north and the French advance to the Rhine were the very prospects which the Austrians had long combatted. These, combined with the other unpleasant (from the Austrian point of view) features of the schema, such as Austrian cession of Venetia and of her Polish provinces, aroused distrust and repugnance in the Austrian government. When Prince Napoleon had outlined a somewhat similar arrangement for French aggrandizement in a confidential memorandum, Napoleon had cautioned him "not to dance faster than the violins" lest the Austrians suspect his secret ambition. It is a pity that he was unable to keep his wife out of the ballroom.

If the French offer had been more prudently and reasonably stated, if it had not, as even the Empress vaguely sensed, enveloped principles of restoration in a cloud of "revolutionary perfume," Austria and France might have come together and largely changed the course of European history. During these negotiations, without realizing it, the Emperor approached the great divide between the successes of the past and the disasters of the future. The year 1863, not 1866, was the real watershed of the Empire from which subsequent troubles flowed. The Austrian rebuff of France and the consequent coldness amounting to hostility resulting from the abortive negotiations played into Bismarck's hands. Serene in the knowledge that the French Emperor would stand aside, he drew Austria into the Danish War and then turned against her to evict her from the Germanic Confederation and to form a Prussian colossus in the north.

Sadowa was only the inevitable, unavoidable consequence of the diplomatic muddle of 1863. It was nearly unthinkable then that France should break her promise of neutrality and bind herself to the "Austrian corpse" in its defeat. The French army, although capable of a show of force on the Rhine, was not prepared to sustain a major war. French forces were scattered in Algeria, Mexico, and Rome. The dilemma of the Empire was serious enough, yet still the Empress, hotheaded and impetuous, found a way to aggravate it. Before the Emperor knew the extent of Austrian losses at Sadowa and before he had thought the matter through, she talked him into a public pledge, boldly proclaimed on the front page of the *Moniteur,* to defend Austria's membership in the Germanic Confederation. When, upon reflection, the Emperor decided against a military demonstration and accepted the ejection of Austria from Germany, he had to humble himself and admit to the world his inability to carry through his purpose. The alteration in the balance of power by the creation of a great Prussia in northern Germany was in itself a heavy blow at France. But when it was coupled with the public humiliation of the ruler of France its effect was fatal. The public was as shocked at the Emperor's nonperformance as it had been jubilant at his earlier pronouncement of action. Perforce the Emperor was required to redeem himself before his people if his son was to succeed him on the throne. As Metternich later analyzed it, "Mexico was his Moscow, and Sadowa his Waterloo."[8]

After 1866 it was merely a question of time until Germany completed its unification and brought the French Empire to its final test. For Eugénie the four years were a period of chafing inactivity in which she impatiently bided her time to wipe out the diplomatic defeat by war and save the dynasty. But it is useless to reproach the Empress, as did Ollivier, for resistance to Prussian aggrandizement. What power has ever voluntarily renounced its great position when it thought it had a fighting chance to retain it? But unfortunately, she hastened the day of their Armageddon. Both Emperor and Empress saw in the Hohenzollern candidacy an opportunity for retaliation against Bismarck. The Emperor would have been content to rest with the voluntary withdrawal of Leopold. Eugénie, spoiling for war and mistakenly confident of the invincibility of the army, supported the demand for the fullest satisfaction of French honor. Thus, France fell into the war, which might have been deferred, before the diplomatic or military preparations were complete.

By 1870 the Empire had metamorphosed beyond recognition. The days of its successful wars were long past; the authority of the Emperor asserted in the *coup d'état* had dissipated. The Empress was virtually a ghostly reminder on the political scene of the blasted hopes of the reactionaries. Excluded from intercourse between the Ministers of the January Cabinet and the Emperor, she kept to her palace haunted with memories of bygone triumphs. From there she fanned the revival of right-wing Bonapartism and the old war spirit which, in July 1870, flared up more brightly than ever before only to be snuffed out by the rain of enemy fire.

When the Emperor was a prisoner of the Prussians, Eugénie, in one of her flashing changes of mood, compassionated his distress with tenderness and affection. On the anniversary of their marriage she wrote:

In happiness the bonds [of affection between us] relaxed. I thought them broken, but a day of storm has let me see their solidity and more than ever I am reminded of those words of the Gospel: a woman will follow her husband wherever he goes, in sickness and in health, for better and for worse, etc. You [*Toi*] and Louis are my life. . . . To be reunited at last is the end of my desires.

<hr>

[8] Metternich to Beust, Paris, January 21, 1870, Oncken, *Rheinpolitik*, III, No. 773, p. 294.

Poor dear friend, may my devotion let you forget for one instant the ordeals which your noble soul has endured.[9]

The letter is a moving one and does her great credit. With her generosity of spirit, her pluck, her perfect integrity, she was one of the most admirable women ever to grace a throne. In uprightness of character she was the undoubted equal of Victoria, whose lifelong friend she remained. Even Prince Napoleon, in mellower moments, would concede the Empress a goodness of heart, although he would add that she was both passionate and ignorant.[10] Certainly she was superior to the bewitching but irresponsible Josephine.

But her fine qualities did not add up to statesmanship. With regret, for her personality inspires respect and affection, it must be admitted that her influence very seriously undermined the foreign policy of the Empire. The record of her blunders is too long and involves questions of too great consequence for her role to be written off as one of minor nagging. On account of Mexico alone she must bear a large responsibility for the decline of the Empire in prestige and material force in its late years. In her attitudes toward Italy and Prussia she too often acted out of sentiment or out of the caprice of the moment and, many more times than the law of averages would ordain, tripped herself up with her own follies and repented of her own handiwork. Her reproaches shook the Emperor's confidence; her enthusiasms led him to commit some of his worst errors. He could neither depend upon her discretion nor rely upon her judgment. He could never expect her to be consistent. Chivalric and rash, she believed a noble aim and its realization were the same thing. Sober, objective reflection was beyond her. The harsh truth is that neither by temperament nor training was the Empress competent to make wise decisions on foreign policy.

[9] January 30, 1870, "Lettres à l'Impératrice Eugénie, 1870–1871," *Revue des deux mondes*, LIX (1930), 26.

[10] Emile Ollivier, *Journal 1846–1869*, II, 195; Cowley to Lord John Russell, Paris, April 11, 1862, copy, PRO FO 519/229.

APPENDIX

Metternich to Rechberg, Paris, February 22, 1863, Private (HHSA, IX/76)

J'ai eu hier une conversation de trois heures avec l'Impératrice au sujet de la Pologne et je me félicite d'avoir eu cette occasion de devancer en quelque sorte, ce qui forme l'objet de Votre télégramme de ce matin.

L'Impératrice m'a annoncé que vu la tournure que prenaient les choses, l'Empereur n'était plus préoccupé que de l'entente entre l'Autriche, la France et Angleterre, entente qui peut amener la solution de toutes les affaires, la consolidation de sa dynastie et le bonheur du monde. Il se réserve, me dit-Elle, de me parler franchement de tout cela lorsque le moment serait venu. Elle voulait, disait-Elle, jeter Son bonnet par-dessus les moulins et me dire tout ce qu'Elle pensait. Je la prendrais pour une folle si je voulais, mais comme elle était sûre que d'Elle à moi, cela ne porterait pas à conséquence, Elle voulait devancer l'Empereur et aller de suite beaucoup plus loin que Lui.—Je Lui dis que j'étais prêt à l'écouter puisque je n'étais destiné qu'à entendre des rêveries politiques sans conséquence comme toutes les pérégrinations auxquelles Elle m'avait déjà fait assister.

L'Impératrice me répondit: Je sais que Votre Empereur Vous écoute et Vous aime, faites Lui connaître le fond de notre sac. Il en fera ce qu'Il voudra, mais du moins Il rendra justice à la franchise d'une femme qui est naturellement plus fantasque que les hommes, mais qui a trop à coeur l'intérêt de Son pays adoptif, de Son époux et de Son fils pour se risquer de mentir en parlant de l'avenir.

Je me suis permis d'observer à Sa Majesté que je ne méritais pas les assurances flatteuses qu'Elle me donnait, mais que dans tous les cas je croyais pouvoir répéter tout ce qu'Elle me dirait sans crainte de mécontenter mon Souverain Maître. "Vous savez du reste, Madame" ajoutai-je, "que si réellement Vous trahissez tous Vos secrets, c'est là un fait d'une importance telle que Vos plans fussent-ils le renversement du monde, leur révélation aura un prix inestimable pour ceux auxquels Vous voudrez bien les confier, car au moins serons nous avertis."

L'Impératrice me dit en souriant: "Pour vous faire comprendre ce que je voudrais, l'idéal de ma politique, il faut que nous prenions la carte!"

J'avoue que ma curiosité fut piquée au plus haut degré de la perspective de voyager avec l'Impératrice à travers une carte bien souvent parcourue par le couple Impérial.

Sa Majesté prit l'atlas de Le Sage et m'expliqua pendant plus d'une heure le plan utopique, mais très curieux qui l'enthousiasme.

Je ne saurais suivre dans tous ses détails la pérégrination à vol d'oiseau (quel vol et quel oiseau!) de l'Impératrice et j'en arrive de suite à ce qui m'a paru être le but positif, l'arrangement décisif auquel on s'arrêterait une fois lancé dans les remaniements. *Je procède par la désignation des puissances.*

Russie

Refoulée en Orient et maigrement rétribuée de la perte de la Pologne et des provinces qui en faisaient partie par une compensation dans la Turquie d'Asie.

Pologne

Réconstituée avec un Archiduc comme Roi, si nous voulons, mais encore mieux avec le Roi de Saxe reprenant ses droits dynastiques en compensation de la cession de son royaume à la Prusse.

Prusse

Céderait la Posnanie à la Pologne, la Silésie à l'Autriche et la rive gauche du Rhin à la France, mais obtiendrait la Saxe, le Hanovre et les duchés au Nord du "Mein."

Autriche

Céderait la Vénétie au Piémont, une partie de la Galicie (Lemberg et Cracovie) à la Pologne, prendrait une longue ligne de nouvelles frontières à travers la Servie le long de l'Adriatique, la Silésie et tout ce qu'elle voudrait au Sud du "Mein."

France

ne céderait rein! mais prendrait la rive gauche du Rhin respectant la Belgique à cause de l'Angleterre à moins que cette puissance ne lui laisse Bruxelles et Ostende etc. etc. pour prendre Anvers.

Italie

Le Piémont aurait la Lombardie, la Vénétie, la Toscane, Parme, Plaisance, Bologne et Ferrare; mais restituerait les deux Siciles au Roi de Naples qui arrondirait le Pape.

Turquie

Supprimée pour cause d'utilité publique et de moralité chrétienne se laisserait partager en cédant ses possessions d'Asie à la Russie, la ligne de l'Adriatique à l'Autriche, la Thessalie, l'Albanie et Constantinople à la Grèce, *les Principautés comme une enclave indépendante à un Prince du pays. —Les Rois et les Princes dépossédés en Europe iraient civiliser et monarchiser les belles républiques américaines qui toutes suivraient l'exemple du Mexique.*

Voilà le plan de l'Impératrice et je Vous prie, Mr. le Comte, de vouloir bien ne pas le considérer comme une plaisanterie, je crois l'Impératrice et même l'Empereur très convaincus de la possibilité et de la nécessité de la réaliser une fois.

Mettons de côté ces phantasmagories napoléoniennes et permettez-moi d'examiner sérieusement la situation au point de vue de nos intérêts réels. Mon instinct me dit qu'en usant de la sagesse et de l'habilité qui a présidé depuis trois ans à notre politique nous pourrions profiter de nos avantages, ne fût-ce que pour amener l'Empereur à s'engager envers nous dans la question d'Orient. Pour y arriver il n'y aurait, je pense, qu'à laisser venir les événements et les avances que nous fera l'Empereur—là où nous pourrons faire cause commune, nous pouvons demander un engagement.

Je suis curieux de savoir si l'Angleterre entrera dans les idées de l'Empereur Napoléon?

Il est possible et désirable même que nous trouvions dans le Cabinet de Londres un auxiliaire précieux pour modérer la marche des manifestations diplomatiques à notre guise. Je suis charmé que nous ne soyons pas en tête-à-tête pour le moment, et j'encourage de tous mes efforts l'idée de l'entente à trois, parceque je prévois que la politique anglaise pourra nous être d'un grand secours.

Les dangers sont grands et les difficultés que nous aurons à surmonter sont immenses, mais je ne sais ce qui me dit que nous réussirons à mener au port notre barque si tourmentée par les orages depuis quelques années. La personnalité qui dirige la politique française aujourd'hui me paraît constituer une garantie réelle dans ces circonstances.

Mr. Drouyn de Lhuys est, en fait de principe, aussi correct que possible, son désir de s'allier avec nous ne date pas d'hier. La copie ci-jointe d'un rapport de M. Lightenvelt de l'année 1855 qui emprunte aux circonstances présentes un caractère d'actualité remarquable, en fait foi.

Si nous voulons commencer à obtenir dès aujourd'hui quelque avantage en Orient, il faudrait, je crois, tâcher dès-à-présent à demander, que l'influence française à Belgrade et à Bukareste se mette un peu à notre service, il faudrait que Mr. Drouyn de Lhuys fasse comprendre aux Princes Couze et Michel que nous sommes appelés à les prendre en tutelle, comme étant le voisin le plus intéressé et tâcher d'éloigner les éléments révolutionnaires.

Yesterday I had a three hour conversation with the Empress on the subject of Poland and I congratulate myself on having had that occasion to anticipate to some extent the subject of Your telegram of this morning.

The Empress announced to me that, in view of the turn things were taking, the Emperor thought of nothing but the entente between Austria, France and England, an entente which could lead to the solution of all affairs, to the consolidation of His dynasty and to the happiness of the world. He intends, She told me, to speak to me frankly about all that when the time is right. She wanted, She said, to throw Her bonnet over the windmill and tell me everything She was thinking. I could take Her for a fool if I wished, but as She was sure that coming from Her to me, it would be of no consequence, She wished to anticipate the Emperor and at once go much farther than He. —I told Her that I was ready to listen since I was only going to hear some political reveries without consequence like all the peregrinations which She had already had me watch.

The Empress answered: "I know Your Emperor listens to You and loves You, let Him see the bottom of our sack. He will do what He wishes with it, but at least He will do justice to the frankness of a woman who is naturally more fantastic than men, but who has the interest of Her adopted country, Her husband and Her son too much at heart to risk lying when speaking of the future."

I permitted myself to observe to Her Majesty that I did not deserve the flattering assurances She addressed to me, but that in any case I thought that I could repeat everything She told me without fear of displeasing my Sovereign Master. "As for the rest you know, Madame," I added, "that if truly You betray all Your secrets, that in itself is a fact of such importance, for were Your plans the overthrow of the world, their revelation would have an inestimable value for those to whom You are willing to confide them, as at least we shall be warned."

Smiling, the Empress said: "To make you understand what I would like, the ideal of my policy, we must have a map!"

I confess my curiosity was piqued to the highest degree at the prospect of travelling with the Empress across a map so frequently traversed by the Imperial couple.

Her Majesty took up Le Sage's atlas and explained to me for more than an hour the utopian but very curious plan which enthuses Her.

I could not possibly follow in all its details the peregrination of the Empress *as the crow flies* (what a *flight* and what a *bird*!) and I arrive immediately at what seemed to me the positive goal, the definitive arrangement at which They would call a halt once launched in the *doing over*. I proceed by designating the powers.

Russia

Driven back in the East and sparingly rewarded for the loss of Poland and the provinces which composed it by a compensation in Turkish Asia.

Poland

Reconstituted with an Archduke as King, if we wish, but better yet with the King of Saxony reasserting his dynastic rights in compensation for the cession of his kingdom to Prussia.

Prussia

Would cede Posen to Poland, Silesia to Austria and the left bank of the

Rhine to France, but would obtain Saxony, Hanover and the duchies North of the "Main."

Austria

Would cede Venetia to Piedmont, a part of Galicia (Lemberg and Cracow) to Poland, would take a long line of new frontiers across Serbia along the Adriatic, Silesia and all she would like South of the "Main."

France

would cede nothing! but would take the left bank of the Rhine sparing Belgium on account of England unless that power would leave her Brussels and Ostend etc. etc. in order to take Antwerp.

Italy

Piedmont would have Lombardy, Venetia, Tuscany, Parma, Piacenza, Bologna and Ferrara; but would restore the two Sicilies to the King of Naples who would round out the Pope.

Turkey

Abolished for reason of public benefit and Christian morality [it] would let itself be partitioned, ceding its Asiatic possessions to Russia, the shore of the Adriatic to Austria, Thessaly, Albania and Constantinople to *Greece,* the Principalities as an independent enclave to a native Prince. —The Kings and Princes dispossessed in Europe would go to civilize and monarchize the beautiful American republics which would follow the example of Mexico.

There is the plan of the Empress and I beg You, Mr. le Comte, please do not consider it a joke, I believe the Empress and even the Emperor are well convinced of the possibility and of the *necessity* of realizing it some day.

Let us put to one side the Napoleonic fantasies and permit me to examine the situation seriously from the point of view of our real interests. My instinct tells me that in making use of that wisdom and skill which for three years has presided over our policy we could profit from our advantages, were it only to lead the Emperor to pledge himself to us in the Eastern question. To attain that we would only have to, I think, let events and the advances that the Emperor will make to us come—there where we can make a common cause, we can ask for a promise.

I am curious to know if England will enter into the ideas of Emperor Napoleon?

It is possible and even desirable that we find in the London Cabinet a precious auxiliary to moderate the march of diplomatic manifestations to our way of thinking. I am pleased that we are not *tête à tête* [with France] for the moment, and I encourage with all my might the idea of a triple entente, because I foresee that English policy can be a great help to us.

The dangers are great and the difficulties that we will have to surmount are immense, but something tells me we shall succeed at last in bringing our ship, so tormented by storms for several years, to port. The person presently directing French policy appears to me a genuine guarantee in the circumstances.

Mr. Drouyn de Lhuys is, as a matter of principle, as correct as possible, his desire to ally with us does not date from yesterday. The enclosed copy of a report of Mr. Lightenvelt of 1855 which lends to present circumstances a remarkable quality of current interest is the proof.

If we want to begin to obtain some advantage as of today in the East we should, I think, henceforth request that French influence at Belgrade and Bucharest start to serve our need, Mr. Drouyn de Lhuys must make the Princes Couza and Michael understand that we are called to take them under our tutelage as their most interested neighbor and try to banish revolutionary elements.

BIBLIOGRAPHY

Unpublished Materials

Alba Archives (Montijo). Palacio de Liria, Madrid. (Cited as AA.)

A large collection of private papers of the Empress Eugénie in the possession of the Duke and Duchess of Alba, some of which have been published (*Lettres familières de l'Impératrice Eugénie*). In the collection are letters by and to the Empress and miscellaneous documents.

Archives de Ministère des Affaires Etrangères. Paris. (Cited as AMAE [Paris].)

Correspondance politique
  Espagne, Vols. 847–864
  Autriche, Vols. 474–476.
Mémoires et documents
  Autriche, Vols. 66–67
  Espagne, Vol. 366
  France, Vol. 2119
  Italie, Vol. 37.
Papiers Charles Robert.
  Robert was reporter to the Council of State during the Italian War and was attached to the Emperor's general headquarters. His sketches and papers were given to the Archives in 1934 by his daughter. Among them are telegrams of the Emperor and the Empress.
Papiers Thouvenel.
  A large collection of private correspondence, some of which has been published.

Archives Nationales. Paris.

ABXIX/3038, Fonds La Valette.
  Small collection of miscellaneous private papers.
F 90 365 980^B, File of telegrams.

Archivo del Ministerio de Asuntos Exteriores. Madrid. (Cited as AMAE [Madrid].)

Correspondencia. Embajadas y Legaciones. Francia. XB.
  Bundles 1506 (1854) to 1517 (1870).
Política. Francia. IIA.
  Bundles 2456 (1865–1869) and 2457 (1870–1874).
Sección Histórica. Candidaturas para el trono. II C. 2878.

Chalamon de Bernardy, Françoise. "Un Fils de Napoléon: Le Comte Walewski, 1810–1868." Unpublished doctoral dissertation, 1951. Bibliothèque de la Sorbonne (University of Paris). Paris.

Clarendon Deposit. Bodleian Library. Oxford.
    The papers were deposited by the sixth Earl of Clarendon. See the *Times* (January 21, 1950) for a brief description of the collection.

Haus–, Hof–, und Staatsarchiv. Vienna. (Cited as HHSA.)
    IX, Politisches Archiv, Frankreich, 1853–1870.
    XX, Politisches Archiv, Spanien, 1868–1870.

Hausarchiv Kaiser Maximilians von Mexico (cited as HKM), MSS in the Haus–, Hof–, und Staatsarchiv, Vienna. Photostatic copies in the Library of Congress, Washington.
    Ferdinand Maximilian's papers on the Mexican expedition and the Mexican Empire, 1861–1867.

Mouchy Papers. Paris.
    Hundreds of letters from Eugénie to Anna Murat, Duchess of Mouchy, in the possession of the present Duke of Mouchy. Many were written after 1870.

Public Record Office. London. (Cited as PRO.)

    FO 356, Bloomfield Papers.
    FO 361/1, Clarendon Papers.
    FO 519, Cowley Papers.
    A collection of papers accumulated by Henry Wellesley, first Baron Cowley, and his son, Henry Richard Charles Wellesley, first Earl and second Baron Cowley. They were presented to the Foreign Office in two batches in 1948 and 1953. A final batch was bequeathed to the state in 1954 under the terms of the will of Sir Victor Wellesley.
    FO 362/5 and PRO 30/29, Granville Papers.

Published Materials

Acton, Harold Mario Mitchell. *The Last Bourbons of Naples, 1825–1861.* New York: St Martin's Press, 1961.
Acton, John Emerich Edward Dalberg-Acton, first Baron. *Historical Essays and Studies.* Ed. by John Neville Figgis and Reginald Vere Laurence. London: Macmillan Company, 1908.
Alba, Duke of. *L'Impératrice Eugénie, conférence prononcée à l'Institut français de Madrid.* Madrid: Diana, 1952.
    A unique verbal portrait of the Empress by the grandson of her only sister. As a child and young man the late Duke was close to the Empress.
d'Ambès, Baron. *Intimate Memoirs of Napoleon III: Personal Reminiscences of the Man and the Emperor.* Trans. by A. R. Allinson. 2 vols. London: Stanley Paul and Company, 1912.
Aubry, Octave. *Eugénie: Empress of the French.* Trans. by F. M. Atkinson. Philadelphia: J. B. Lippincott Company, 1931.
———. *The Second Empire.* Trans. by A. Livingston. Philadelphia: J. B. Lippincott Company, 1940.

Auswärtige Politik Preussens, Die. See Reichsinstitut für Geschichte des neuen Deutschlands.

Bapst, Germain. *Le Maréchal Canrobert: Souvenirs d'un siècle*. 6 vols. Paris: Plon-Nourrit, 1904.

Barker, Nancy Nichols. "Austria, France, and the Venetian Question, 1861–66," *The Journal of Modern History*, XXXVI (1964), 145–154.

———. "Empress Eugénie and the Origin of the Mexican Venture," *The Historian*, XXII, No. 1, 9–23.

———. "France, Austria, and the Mexican Venture, 1861–1864," *French Historical Studies*, III (1963), 224–245.

———. "Napoleon III and the Hohenzollern Candidacy for the Spanish Throne, *The Historian*, XXIX (May, 1967), 431–450.

Baroche, Mme Jules. *Second Empire: Notes et souvenirs*. Paris: Crès, 1921.

Beaumont-Vassy, Viscount E. de. *Histoire intime du Second Empire*. Paris: Librairie Sartorius, 1874.

Benson, Arthur Christopher, and Viscount Esher (eds.). *The Letters of Queen Victoria from Her Majesty's Correspondence between the Years 1837 and 1861*. 3 vols. London: J. Murray, 1907.

Bermejo, Ildefonso Antonio. *Historia de la interinidad y guerra civil de España desde 1868*. Vol. I. Madrid: R. Labajos, 1876.

Bernhardi, Theodor von. *Aus dem Leben Theodor von Bernhardis*. Vol. IX: *In Spanien und Portugal, Tagebuchblätter aus den Jahren 1869–1871*. Leipzig: S. Hirzel, 1906.

Besson, Mgr. Louis. *Vie de Cardinal de Bonnechose, archevêque de Rouen*. 2 vols. Paris: Retaux-Bray, 1887.

Beyens, Baron Napoléon. *Le Second Empire vu par un diplomate belge*. 2 vols. Paris: Plon-Nourrit, 1925–1926.

Bicknell, Anna. *Life in the Tuileries under the Second Empire*. New York: The Century Company, 1895.

Bigelow, John. *Retrospections of an Active Life*. 5 vols. New York: The Baker and Taylor Company, 1909–1913.

Bismarck, the Man and the Statesman. Trans. from Bismarck's *Gedanken und Erinnerungen* by A. J. Butler. 2 vols. New York: Harper and Brothers, 1899.

Bismarck-Schönhausen, Otto Eduard Leopold von. *Die gesammelten Werke*. 15 vols. Berlin: O. Stollberg, 1924–1932.

Bonnin, Georges (ed.). *Bismarck and the Hohenzollern Candidature for the Spanish Throne: The Documents in the German Diplomatic Archives*. Trans. by Isabella M. Massey, with a Foreword by G. P. Gooch. London: Chatto and Windus, 1957.

Buffin, Baron Camille. *La Tragédie mexicaine: Les Impératrices Charlotte et Eugénie*. Brussels: A de Wit, 1915.

Busch, Moritz. *Bismarck: Some Secret Pages of His History; Being a Diary Kept by Dr. Moritz Busch during Twenty-five Years' Official and Private Intercourse with the Great Chancellor*. 2 vols. New York: The Macmillan Company, 1898.

du Camp, Maxime. *Souvenirs d'un demi-siècle: Au temps de Louis-Philippe et de Napoléon III, 1830–1870*. 2 vols. Paris: Hachette, 1949.

Carteggio Cavour-Nigra, Il. A cura della Reale Commissione Editrice. 3 vols. Bologna: Zanichelli, 1926–1929. A collection of Sardinian diplomatic documents.

Case, Lynn M. "Anticipating the Death of Pope Pius IX in 1861," *Catholic Historical Review*, XLIII (1957), 309–323.

————. *Franco-Italian Relations, 1860–1865*. Philadelphia: University of Pennsylvania Press, 1932.

————. *French Opinion on the United States and Mexico, 1860–1867: Extracts from the Reports of the Procureurs Généraux*. New York: D. Appleton-Century Company, 1936.

————. *French Opinion on War and Diplomacy during the Second Empire*. Philadelphia: University of Pennsylvania Press, 1954.

Castillon du Perron, Marguerite. *La Princesse Mathilde, un règne féminin sous le Second Empire*. Paris: Amiot-Dumont, 1953.

Chiala, Luigi (ed.). *Lettere edite ed inedite di Camillo Cavour*. 6 vols. Turin: Roux e Favele, 1883–1887.

Clark, Chester Wells. *Franz Joseph and Bismarck: The Diplomacy of Austria before the War of 1866*. (Harvard Historical Series, Vol. XXXVI.) Cambridge, Massachusetts: Harvard University Press, 1934.

Claveau, Anatole. *Souvenirs politiques et parlementaires d'un témoin*. 2 vols. Paris: Plon-Nourrit, 1913.

Cobban, Alfred. *A History of Modern France*. 2 vols. Baltimore: Penguin Books [c. 1961].

Comandini, Alfredo. *Il Principe Napoleone nel risorgimento italiano*. Milan: Fratelli Treves, 1922.

Corley, Thomas A. B. *Democratic Despot: A Life of Napoleon III*. London: Barrie and Rockliff, 1961.

Corti, Egon Caesar. *Maximilian and Charlotte of Mexico*. Trans. by C. A. Phillips. 2 vols. New York: Alfred A. Knopf, 1928.

Darimon, Alfred. *Histoire d'un parti: Les Irréconciliables sous l'Empire, 1867–1869*. Paris: E. Dentu, 1888.

————. *Notes pour servir à l'histoire de la guerre de 1870*. Paris: P. Ollendorff, 1880.

Daudet, Lucien. *Dans l'ombre de l'Impératrice Eugénie*. Paris: Gallimard, 1935.

Debidour, Antonin. *Histoire diplomatique de l'Europe*. 2 vols. Paris: F. Alcan, 1891.

Della Rocca, Enrico. See Morozzo della Rocca, Count Enrico.

Delord, Taxile. *Histoire du Second Empire*. 6 vols. Paris: G. Baillière, 1869–1875.

Desternes, Suzanne, and Henriette Chandet. *L'Impératrice Eugénie intime*. Paris: Hachette, 1964.

Dittrich, Jochen. *Bismarck, Frankreich und die Spanische Thronkandidatur der Hohenzollern: Die "Kriegschuld Frage" von 1870. Im Anhang Briefe und Aktenstücke aus des Fürstlich Hohenzollernschen Hausarchiv*. München: R. Oldenbourg, 1962.

Documenti diplomatici italiani, I. First series, 1867–1870. Vol. I. Rome: Libreria dello Stato, 1952. (Cited as *DDI*.)

Domenech, Emmanuel Henri Dieudonné. *Histoire du Mexique, Juarez et Maximilien*. 2 vols. Paris: Librairie internationale, 1868.

Du Barail, Général François Charles. *Mes souvenirs*. 3 vols. Paris: Plon-Nourrit, 1913.

Dutacq, F. "Les Dessous d'un voyage officiel—visite de l'Impératrice à Lyon en 1869, d'après les rapports de police," *Revue du Lyonnais*, XV (1924), 337–340.

Engelhaaf, G. "Der Anteil der Kaiserin Eugenie am Krieg von 1870," *Die Grenzboten*, LXIII, 628.

Engel-Jánosi, Friedrich. *Graf Rechberg: Vier Kapitel zu seiner und Österreichs Geschichte*. München: R. Oldenbourg, 1927.

Esslinger, Elisabet. *Der Einfluss der Kaiserin Eugenie auf dem ausser Politik des Zweiten Kaiserreichs*. Stuttgart: W. Kohlhammer, 1932.

Based entirely on published materials, especially Oncken and Paléologue.

Eugénie, Empress. *Lettres familières de l'Impératrice Eugénie conservées dans les archives du Palais de Liria et publiées par les soins du Duc d'Albe avec le concours de F. de Llanos y Torriglia et Pierre Josserand.* 2 vols. Paris: Le Divan, 1935. (Cited as *Lettres familières.*)
Private letters of the Empress from the Alba Archives, mostly nonpolitical in content.

Evans, Dr. Thomas W. *The Memoirs of Dr. Thomas Evans: Recollections of the Second Empire.* Ed. by E. A. Crane, M.D. 2 vols. New York: D. Appleton and Company, 1905.

Fester, Richard. *Briefe, Aktenstücke und Regesten zur Geschichte der Hohenzollernschen Thronkandidatur in Spanien.* 2 vols. Leipzig: B. G. Teubner, 1913.

———. *Neue Beiträge zur Geschichte der Hohenzollernschen Thronkandidatur in Spanien.* Leipzig: B. G. Teubner, 1913.

Filon, Pierre M. A. *Recollections of the Empress Eugénie.* London: Cassell and Company, 1920.

Fleury, Count Maurice. *Memoirs of the Empress Eugénie. Compiled from Statements, Private Documents, and Personal Letters.* 2 vols. London, New York: Appleton and Company, 1920.

Forbes, Achille. "The French Empress and the Franco-German War," *Nineteenth Century,* XXXII (August, 1892), 285–297.

France. *Annales de l'assemblée nationale.* Vols. XX–XXVI. *Enquête sur les actes du gouvernement de la défense nationale.*
An inquiry into the conduct of the government before and during the war of 1870. It is not without political overtones, but is valuable for the many sworn depositions made by imperial ministers and diplomats.

France. *Annales du sénat et du corps législatif.* For 1861–1870.

[France, Ministère des Affaires Etrangères]. *Les Origines diplomatiques de la guerre de 1870–1871: Recueil de documents publiés par le ministère des affaires étrangères.* 19 vols. Paris: G. Ficker, Imprimerie nationale, 1910–1932. (Cited as *OD.*)

Garets, Comtesse de (née Marie de Larminet). *Souvenirs d'une demoiselle d'honneur auprès de l'Impératrice Eugénie.* Paris: Calmann-Lévy, 1928.

Gaulot, Paul. *L'Expédition du Mexique, 1861–1867, d'après les documents et souvenirs de Ernest Louet.* 2 vols. Paris: Société d'éditions littéraires et artistiques, 1960.

Gooch, George Peabody. *The Second Empire.* London: Longmans, Green and Company, 1960.

Grabinski, Count Joseph. *Un Ami de Napoléon III: Le Comte Arese et la politique italienne sous le Second Empire.* Paris: L. Bahl, 1897.

Gramont, Antoine Agénor, Duc de. *La France et la Prusse avant la guerre.* Paris: E. Dentu, 1872.

Granier de Cassagnac, A. *Souvenirs du Second Empire.* 3 vols. Paris: E. Dentu, 1882.

Grew, Raymond, "How Success Spoiled the Risorgimento," *The Journal of Modern History,* XXXIV (September, 1962), 239–253.

Guérard, Albert. *Napoleon III: An Interpretation. (Makers of Modern Europe* series.) Cambridge, Massachusetts: Harvard University Press, 1943.

Halévy, Ludovic. *Carnets, publiés avec une introduction et des notes, 1862–1870.* 2 vols. Paris: Calmann-Lévy, 1935.

Hallberg, Charles W. *Franz Joseph and Napoleon III: 1852–1864: A Study of Austro-French Relations.* New York: Bookman Associates, 1955.

Hansard's Parliamentary Debates, 3rd series.

d'Hauterive, Ernest. *The Second Empire and Its Downfall: The Correspondence of the Emperor Napoleon III and His Cousin Prince Napoleon.* Trans. by H. Wilson, New York: George H. Doran, 1925.

Henrey, Robert (ed.). *Letters from Paris, 1870–1875.* London: J. M. Dent and Sons, 1942.

Hermant, Abel. *Eugénie, Impératrice des Français, 1826–1920.* Paris: Hachette, 1942.

Hübner, Joseph Alexander. *Neuf ans de souvenirs d'un ambassadeur d'Autriche à Paris sous le Second Empire, 1851–1859.* 5 vols. Paris: Plon-Nourrit, 1904.

Jerrold, Blanchard. *The Life of Napoleon III. Derived from State Records, from Unpublished Family Correspondence, and from Personal Testimony.* 4 vols. London: Longmans, Green and Company, 1874–1882.

Journal officiel.
    Official newspaper of the French imperial government after 1869.

Kurtz, Harold. *The Empress Eugénie, 1826–1920.* London: Hamish Hamilton, 1964.
    A lengthy biography with much detail on the Empress' private life. The author has set out to rehabilitate the Empress.

Lacour-Gayet, Georges. *L'Impératrice Eugénie: Documents et souvenirs.* Paris: A. Morancé, 1925.

La Gorce, Pierre de. *Histoire du Second Empire.* 7 vols. Paris: Plon-Nourrit, 1894–1905.

Legge, Edward. *The Comedy and Tragedy of the Second Empire: Paris Society in the Sixties, Including Letters of Napoleon III, M. Pietri, and Comte de La Chapelle and Portraits of the Period.* New York: Harper and Brothers, 1911.

Leonardon, H. "L'Espagne et la question du Mexique," *Annales des sciences politiques,* XVI (1901), 59–95.

"Lettres à l'Impératrice Eugénie, 1870–1871," *Revue des deux mondes,* Series 7, LIX (1930), 5–30.
    Letters exchanged between Napoleon and Eugénie during and after the war of 1870. Copyright by Prince Napoleon, 1930.

Lettres familières de l'Impératrice Eugénie. See Eugénie, Empress.

Llanos y Torriglia, F. de. *María Manuela Kirkpatrick, Condesa del Montijo, la gran dama.* Madrid: Espasa-Calpe, 1932.

Loftus, Lord Augustus. *The Diplomatic Reminiscences of Lord Augustus Loftus, P.C., G.C.B., 1862–1879.* 2nd series, 2 vols. London: Cassell and Company, 1894.

Loliée, Frédéric. *The Life of an Empress.* New York: Dodd, Mead and Company, 1909.

Lord, Robert Howard. *The Origins of the War of 1870: New Documents from the German Archives.* (Harvard Historical Studies, XXVIII.) Cambridge, Massachusetts: Harvard University Press, 1924.

Malmesbury, James Howard Harris, Earl of. *Memoirs of an Ex-Minister.* 2 vols. London: Longmans, Green and Company, 1884.

Martin, Theodore. *The Life of H. R. H., the Prince Consort.* 5 vols. London: Smith, Elder, and Company, 1875–1880.

Maurain, Jean. *Baroche, ministre de Napoléon III.* Paris: F. Alcan, 1936.

———. *La politique ecclésiastique du Second Empire de 1852 à 1869.* Paris: F. Alcan, 1930.

Meding, Oskar. *De Sadowa à Sedan: Mémoires d'un ambassadeur secret aux Tuileries.* 6th ed. Paris: E. Dentu, 1885.

Mérimée, Prosper. *Letters to Panizzi.* Ed. by Louis Fagan. 2 vols. London: Remington and Company, 1881.

————. *Lettres à une inconnue.* 2 vols. Paris: Michel Lévy frères, 1874.

Moniteur Universel.
Official newspaper of the French imperial government until 1869.

Monti de Rezé, Count René de. *Souvenirs sur le Comte de Chambord.* Paris: Emile Paul frères, 1930.

Monypenny, William Flavelle, and George Earle Buckle. *The Life of Benjamin Disraeli, Earl of Beaconsfield.* 6 vols. New York: Macmillan Company, 1916.

Morozzo della Rocca, Count Enrico. *Autobiografia di un veterano: Ricordi storici e aneddotici del Generale Enrico della Rocca.* 2 vols. Bologna: Ditta N. Zanichelli, 1898.

Mosse, Werner Eugen. *The European Powers and the German Question 1848–1871, with Special Reference to England and Russia.* Cambridge University Press, 1958.

Murat, Princess Caroline. *My Memoirs.* New York: G. P. Putnam's Sons, 1910.
A spiteful and unreliable account.

Napoleon, Prince. "Les Préliminaires de la paix, 11 Juillet 1859: Journal de ma mission à Vérone auprès de l'Empereur d'Autriche," *Revue des deux mondes,* Series 5, LII (1909), 481–503.

Newton, Thomas W. Legh, Baron. *The Life of Lord Lyons: A Record of British Diplomacy.* 2 vols. London: E. Arnold, 1913.

Ollivier, Emile. *L'Empire libéral: Etudes, récits, souvenirs.* 18 vols. Paris: Garnier Frères, 1895–1918.

————. *Journal, 1846–1869.* Ed. by Theodore Zeldin. 2 vols. Paris: René Julliard, 1961.

Oncken, Hermann. *Die Rheinpolitik Kaiser Napoleons III. von 1863 bis 1870 und der Ursprung des Krieges von 1870/71.* 3 vols. Stuttgart: Deutsche Verlags-Anstalt, 1926.

Pagani, Carlo. "Felice Orsini, Eugenia de Montijo et Napoleone III," *Nuova antologia,* Series 6, CCXXXIX (1925), 48–59.

————. "Napoleone III, Eugenia de Montijo e Francesco Arese in un carteggio inedito," *Nuova antologia,* Series 6, CCX (1921), 16–33.

Paléologue, George Maurice. *The Tragic Empress: A Record of Intimate Talks with the Empress Eugénie, 1901–1919.* Trans. by Hamish Miles. New York: Harper and Brothers, 1928.
Since Paléologue's record of the Empress' comments on the major crises of imperial foreign policy appeared after the Empress' death, no one can be sure whether she would have approved the manner in which she was quoted.

Papiers et correspondance de la famille impérial. 2 vols. Paris: Imprimerie nationale, 1871.
Miscellaneous papers found in the Tuileries Palace after the Empress fled.

Persigny, Duke of. *Mémoires publiés avec des documents inédits.* Paris: Plon-Nourrit, 1896.

Pflanze, Otto. *Bismarck and the Development of Germany: The Period of Unification, 1815–1871.* Princeton, New Jersey: Princeton University Press, 1963.

Raindre, G. "Les Papiers inédits du Cte Walewski," *Revue de France,* XI (1925), 82–96.

Randon, Jacques Louis César Alexandre. *Mémoires.* 2 vols. Paris: Typographie Lahure, 1875.

Rastoul, Alfred. *Le Maréchal Randon, 1795–1871, d'après ses mémoires et des documents inédits: Etude militaire et politique*. Paris: Firmin-Didot, 1890.

Reichsinstitut für Geschichte des neuen Deutschlands. *Die auswärtige Politik Preussens 1858–1871: Diplomatischen Aktenstücke*. 10 vols. Oldenburg: G. Stalling, 1933–1939. (Cited as *APP*.)

Rothan, Gustave. *Les Origines de la guerre de 1870: La Politique française en 1866*. Paris: C. Lévy, 1879.

Saint-Amand, Imbert de. *Napoleon III and His Court*. Trans. by E. G. Martin. New York: C. Scribner's Sons, 1898.

Salomon, Henry. *L'Ambassade de Richard de Metternich à Paris*. Paris: Firmin-Didot, 1931.

———. "Le Prince Richard de Metternich et sa correspondance pendant son ambassade à Paris, 1859–1871," *Revue de Paris*, XXXI (1924), 507–541, 762–804.

Seignobos, Charles. *Le Déclin de l'empire et l'établissement de la 3e république*. (*Histoire de France contemporaine depuis la révolution jusqu'à la paix de 1919*, ed. by Ernest Lavisse, Vol. VII.) Paris: Hachette, 1921.

Sencourt, Robert, pseud. [Robert Esmonde Gordon George]. "L'Impératrice Eugénie et la politique extérieure," *Revue de Paris*, XXXIX (1932), 382–397.

———. *The Life of the Empress Eugénie*. New York: C. Scribner's Sons, 1931.

Sergeant, Philip W. *The Last Empress of the French, Being the Life of the Empress Eugénie, Wife of Napoleon III*. London: T. W. Laurie [1907?].

Smith, Willard A. "Napoleon III and the Spanish Revolution of 1868," *The Journal of Modern History*, XXV (1953), 211–233.

Smyth, Dame Ethel. *Streaks of Life*. London: Longmans, Green and Company, 1920.

Steefel, Lawrence D. *Bismarck, the Hohenzollern Candidacy, and the Origins of the Franco-German War of 1870*. Cambridge, Massachusetts: Harvard University Press, 1962.

"Sulla via di Roma; da Aspromonte a Mentana, documenti inediti," *Nuova antologia*, Series 4, LXXXVII (Vol. CLXXI of collection, June, 1900), 593–610.

Tascher de la Pagerie, Mme. *Mon séjour aux Tuileries*. 2 vols. Paris: Ollendorff, 1893.

Taylor, Alan John Percivale. *Bismarck, the Man and the Statesman*. New York: Alfred A. Knopf, 1955.

———. *The Struggle for Mastery in Europe, 1848–1918*. Oxford: The Clarendon Press, 1954.

Thayer, William Roscoe. *The Life and Times of Cavour*. 2 vols. Boston: Houghton Mifflin, 1911.

Thouvenel, Louis (ed.). *Pages d'histoire du Second Empire d'après les papiers de M. Thouvenel, ancien ministre des affaires étrangères*. Paris: Plon-Nourrit, 1903.

———. *Le Secret de l'Empereur: Correspondance confidentielle et inédite échangée entre M. Thouvenel, le Duc de Gramont, et le général Comte de Flahault, 1860–1863*. 2 vols. Paris: Calmann Lévy, 1889.

Times (London).

Viel-Castel, Horace de. *Mémoires sur le règne de Napoléon III, 1851–1864, publiés d'après le manuscrit original*. 6 vols. Paris: Chez Tous les Librairies, 1883–1884.

Wellesley, Frederick Arthur (ed.). *Secrets of the Second Empire: Private Letters from the Paris Embassy; Selections from the Papers of Henry Richard Charles Wellesley, 1st Earl Cowley*. New York: Harper, 1929.

Wellesley, Victor, and Robert Sencourt. *Conversations with Napoleon III. A Col-*

lection of Documents Mostly Unpublished and Almost Entirely Diplomatic, Selected and Arranged with Introductions. London: E. Benn, Limited, 1934.

Welschinger, Henri. *La Guerre de 1870, causes et responsabilités.* 2 vols. Paris: Plon-Nourrit, 1911.

Wright, Constance. *Daughter to Napoleon: A Biography of Hortense, Queen of Holland.* New York: Holt, Rinehart and Winston, 1961.

Zeldin, Theodore. *Emile Ollivier and the Liberal Empire of Napoleon III.* Oxford: Clarendon Press, 1963.

———. *The Political System of Napoleon III.* London: Macmillan Company, 1958.

INDEX